Living On

Living On

**PSYCHIATRY AND THE FUTURE
OF DISASTER IN TURKEY**

Christopher Dole

STANFORD UNIVERSITY PRESS
Stanford, California

Stanford University Press
Stanford, California

© 2025 by Christopher Dole. All rights reserved.

No part of this book may be reproduced or transmitted in any form or by any means, electronic or mechanical, including photocopying and recording, or in any information storage or retrieval system, without the prior written permission of Stanford University Press.

Printed in the United States of America on acid-free, archival-quality paper

Library of Congress Cataloging-in-Publication Data
Names: Dole, Christopher, author.
Title: Living on : psychiatry and the future of disaster in Turkey / Christopher Dole.
Description: Stanford, California : Stanford University Press, 2025. | Includes bibliographical references and index.
Identifiers: LCCN 2024047772 (print) | LCCN 2024047773 (ebook) | ISBN 9781503641778 (cloth) | ISBN 9781503642515 (paperback) | ISBN 9781503642522 (epub)
Subjects: LCSH: İzmit Earthquake, Turkey, 1999—Psychological aspects. | Disaster victims—Mental health services—Turkey. | Disaster victims—Turkey—Psychology. | Earthquake relief—Turkey. | Psychiatry—Turkey.
Classification: LCC HV600 1999.T9 D65 2025 (print) | LCC HV600 1999.T9 (ebook) | DDC 362.2/5—dc23/eng/20241209
LC record available at https://lccn.loc.gov/2024047772
LC ebook record available at https://lccn.loc.gov/2024047773

Cover design: Jan Šabach

Contents

Introduction
Psychiatry in Ruins ... 1

PART I
Sensing the Conditions of Disaster

1 The End of the World ... 35
2 A Disaster in the Making ... 53

PART II
The Psychiatry of Disaster

3 Novice Humanitarians ... 71
4 Experiments in Scale ... 77
5 A Geo-Psychology of Disaster ... 96
6 Mediterranean Assemblages ... 115
7 Remains ... 134

PART III
Living On

8 "We Have Not Forgotten, We Will Not Forget" ... 141
9 Disaster's Minor Feelings ... 162
10 Loss and the Optimism of Catastrophe ... 186

11	Disability, Gender, Thriving	207
12	Urban Renewal and Psychiatric Protest	228
	Epilogue New Century, Different Disaster	247
	Acknowledgments	257
	Notes	261
	References	283
	Index	309

Living On

The remains of a light post marking a former shoreline. Gölcük, Turkey.

INTRODUCTION
Psychiatry in Ruins

Yüzyılın felaketi. The disaster of the century. At 3:02 a.m. on August 17, 1999, the western end of the North Anatolian Fault Zone ruptured along a 150-kilometer stretch when two enormous tectonic plates slid horizontally past each other, cutting through the most densely populated and industrialized region of Turkey. At this moment, the region's long and well-documented geological history of seismic activity converged with a history of national development that had prioritized economic growth over the enforcement of building regulations, to leave millions of lives vulnerable to the destruction unleashed by the earthquake. More than 20,000 people died and hundreds of thousands of residents were displaced. Entire neighborhoods were reduced to rubble. Large sections of the coastline, along with the buildings it supported, sank into the coastal waters. Chasms severed roads, bridges collapsed, and water and sewage lines ruptured. A massive chemical fire at Turkey's largest refinery complex would burn for five days, as one-third of the country's industrial infrastructure ground to a halt.

The state proved itself spectacularly unprepared for the disaster. Decades of neglect and entrenched corruption in the national agencies dedicated to emergency response were to become tragically apparent. Despite the region's seismic history—eleven major earthquakes had occurred along the same fault line in the preceding century—relief efforts were slow, uncoordinated, and inadequate. The state's "emergency relief fund" contained the equivalent of US$4.45 at the time of the earthquake. With little help from the government, residents scoured the ruins—with commandeered machinery, small tools, and their bare hands—searching for survivors. Surviving residents, exhausted and in shock, gathered in open fields and makeshift shelters. The putrid smell of decomposing flesh soon enveloped the region, as corpses of all kinds, trapped deep within the rubble, began rotting in the late-summer heat. As scenes of the destruction and suffering began circulating through the national media, government inaction was met with a massive outpouring of public compassion. Donations and volunteers began to flood the region. Schools organized food drives, tens of thousands of people emptied their closets, and trucks of donated food, clothing, and supplies clogged the ruined highways leading from nearby Istanbul to the earthquake region, as thousands of volunteers—by then part of an international response to the disaster—sought to contribute in some way to the relief efforts.

In this outpouring of public sentiment, the earthquake would generate an extraordinary mobilization of Turkish mental health professionals. Mobile teams of volunteer psychiatrists and psychologists, working outside of state and humanitarian institutions, fanned out across the region to assess and address the psychological and emotional aftermath of the earthquake. "Therapeutic tents" were set up in temporary housing settlements. Group therapy sessions were established. Art tents for children were erected. Foreign experts organized training workshops. Studies were designed, questionnaires created, and psychiatric checklists, scales, and inventories soon began to inundate the region. For the first time, tens of thousands of residents would receive psychiatric care. Meanwhile, beyond the disaster zone, psychiatrists and psychologists became regular expert guests on news programs and talk shows discussing the expected emotional effects of the earthquake, as a recently privatized media industry filled hours of coverage by providing firsthand accounts of the psychic toll of the earthquake. There was no precedent in Turkey for such a collective expression of concern for people's psychological well-being. Like no other disaster before it, the Marmara Earthquake had become a psychiatric event.

Two decades after the earthquake, I am visiting a town on the coast of the Gulf of İzmit whose name became synonymous with the epicenter of the earthquake. I'm here to attend the ceremonies marking the earthquake's twentieth anniversary. The town's seaside park, which holds one of the largest monuments commemorating the earthquake, is being transformed into a stage. As evening falls, portable outdoor lights bathe the park in a harsh glow. Search-and-rescue vehicles and the latest disaster response gear line the park's edge. Vendors wander the crowd selling balloons as a large screen streams promotional videos for the Disaster and Emergency Management Authority (Afet ve Acil Durum Yönetimi Başkanlığı, or AFAD). Staff from the Red Crescent are busy in a mobile kitchen. Tonight, they will be providing small pastries and hot tea to attendees. There's a sense of excitement and pride that is forming around the assembled equipment.

Few residents have been coming to these annual events for much of the past decade. Organizers hope that the twentieth anniversary will bring out a larger crowd. The ceremony—which will culminate at the precise time of the earthquake, 3:02 a.m.—begins late in the evening. By 9 p.m., the plaza is filling, and residents, many of whom came as families, stroll through the exhibits. Children laugh and play on the shiny new trucks. Parents look on somberly. The atmosphere is part fair, part memorial. The towering sound system beside the stage welcomes us to the Commemoration Program for the Martyrs of the August 17 Earthquake and announces that the evening's events will begin shortly. We make our way to seats. More than six hundred people have come; some later speculate that there were a thousand in attendance. While I don't see any of the psychiatrists or psychologists I had met over the previous decade, I do see many of their former patients scattered throughout the audience.

The emcee welcomes foreign and esteemed guests, the national anthem plays, and politicians and officials, local and national, begin offering speeches. No one on the program will be speaking as an "earthquake victim" (*depremzede*) tonight. They will only be spoken about. The head of the municipality talks about how he now lives in a beautiful city with new buildings: "Thanks to the government, we are a modern city." A representative from the Japanese consulate gives a speech (in Turkish) recalling his memory of the earthquake and how Japan helped Turkey in its time of need. The head of a local search-and-rescue club, which had recently expanded to include a summer youth camp, spoke about the importance of disaster preparedness.

This would be a popular theme for speakers. A local politician, imperious and didactic, warns the audience that they need to be prepared for the next disaster: "You can't rely on the state for everything. It's your responsibility." The message was clear. To be a good citizen, one must be prepared for the next disaster: "If you buy a house, you must inspect it closely. It's your responsibility." I find myself being overtaken by a familiar anger. How could he be saying these things, on this occasion, to an audience that had experienced such unimaginable loss in a disaster for which the state was in no small measure complicit? Is it really *their* responsibility alone to inspect their own homes? The speaker—the seeming embodiment of a callous and paternalistic state—continues to berate the audience. "You shouldn't be so dependent on the state." The audience looks on blankly, already knowing this all too well.

After the speeches, film crews gather around and focus their lights on a survivor tearfully recounting her experience of the earthquake. This isn't the first time she's told her story. Nor is this the first time that a news crew has recorded, edited, and aired such a story. She would later complain to me about how the ceremony did not include any survivors. Even in this moment—on the twentieth anniversary of the earthquake, in the state's performative commemoration of a "national tragedy"—they had been forgotten. Yet again. At 3:02 a.m., she joins other officials to drop flowers into the sea. We watch silently as they float off into the darkness. Just within the furthest reach of the light, the top section of an old light post sticks askew out of the water. In a former time, before the earthquake, it marked the edge of the shoreline. It's a strange, lonely sight. I still think of it as one of the most moving memorials of the Marmara Earthquake. Much more compelling than the enormous stone monument we were standing beneath.

Living On is an ethnographic and historical account of the psychiatrization of the Marmara Earthquake. Based on long-term research conducted throughout the earthquake region and in the networks of psychiatric expertise that assembled around the earthquake, it explores the intertwined legacy of the Marmara Earthquake within the communities and lives of its survivors, and among the Turkish psychiatrists and psychologists who intervened therapeutically in the earthquake's psychological and emotional aftermath. Moving across a period that stretches from the earthquake to its twentieth anniversary, I follow how a convergence of geological activity and psychiatric expertise charted thousands of lives over the ensuing decades, facilitated the entrance of novel psychiatric and psychological discourses into everyday lives in unprecedented ways, and, along the way, animated new visions of self, society, and technopolitical promise in what came to be regarded, briefly, as the "New Turkey."

The book weaves together two stories that span nearly twenty years. In the first, I explore the work of several groups of Turkish psychiatrists and psychologists as they struggle to intervene in the material, social, and psychological ruins of the earthquake. By tracking psychiatric forms of expertise as they move out of their familiar clinical spaces and extend across a devastated landscape, I consider the efforts of these psychiatrists and psychologists to fashion the earthquake's aftermath into both a site of intervention and an object of study—smoothing out the bumpy complexity of realities in upheaval, mobilizing and reworking assumptions about the psychological subject of disaster, reimagining the scalability of psychiatric expertise, and struggling to weave therapeutic techniques into the everyday social lives of communities. The second story, set outside of the urgency of disaster and in the temporality of what I call "living on," follows the legacy of this psychiatric response into the lives of people who lived through the earthquake—those who were, as my interlocutors frequently put it, "left behind" (*geride kalanlar*). At this meeting of geological volatility and psychiatric care, what forms of life would become possible? What kinds of lives were able to endure, even thrive, in the long, drawn-out aftermath of the earthquake? Working ethnographically in the ruins of psychiatry and the remains of disaster, I consider how the earthquake, and with it the psychiatric response it precipitated, would settle in complex, often obscure, yet formative ways into the everyday affective and social lives of those "left behind."

Although ethnographically and historically grounded in Turkey, this book engages broad questions about technical, social, and subjective world making in the wake of disaster. What, for instance, can the psychiatric response to the Marmara Earthquake tell us about the transnational fields of humanitarian knowledge and power circulating at the time, or, for that matter, the deeper historical role played by psychiatry in mediating Europe's relationship with the region's colonial peripheries? How might this account—of medical and technological fashioning at the (disastrous) margins of global medical and psychiatric hegemonies—challenge common assumptions about the "globalization of psychiatry," and perhaps even point to novel configurations of psychiatry and sovereignty in the process of forming? Alternately, how might the lives of those who lived through the Marmara Earthquake help us understand the legacy of disasters—or, for that matter, the past more generally—in ways that neither exaggerate the impact of large-scale events nor sentimentalize the ordinariness of the everyday? In turn, what might we find if we look beyond the dominant frameworks through which the psychological effects of disaster are commonly rendered—namely, psychological trauma and its psychiatric cognate post-traumatic stress disorder, or PTSD—to consider other possible ways that people manage overwhelming events? And how might a historically informed and ethnographically engaged approach be crucial not only for rethinking these inherited approaches but also for imagining other possible futures of disaster?

Living On explores these questions at a time when the specter of planetary destruction looms large. It tells its stories as news of large-scale disasters and impending catastrophes multiply day by day—news that heralds irreparable ecological devastation, the unbounded ravages of infectious disease, the geological and atmospheric precariousness of "nature," and the mounting toll of both state and nonstate forms of political violence. I thus write in a moment when the language of catastrophe and disaster has established itself as a defining idiom of life and survival in the contemporary world. Indeed, the catastrophic seems to command a monopoly over every imaginable future, such that the idea of a future catastrophe has become a real force in the ordering of lives and worlds in the present. With this in mind, this book joins a growing number of critical theorists, cultural historians, and scholars of science and technology studies who have argued for the necessity of forging new ways to tell stories about human flourishing in contexts of large-scale disaster and ecological transformation. In this regard, I am interested in exploring how people's struggle to "live on" in the long wake of disaster might show us the outlines of a model—tentative, improvisational, and unfinished—for human flourishing amid dramatic environmental transformation.[1]

Psychiatry in Ruins

The speed with which psychiatrists and psychologists in Turkey responded to the Marmara Earthquake was remarkable. Although they were able to quickly mobilize, nothing prepared them for the scale of loss and suffering they encountered as they began traveling to the earthquake region. This was especially the case for psychiatrists, whose professional lives had been forged in controlled clinical spaces built around the doctor-patient therapeutic dyad as the ideal form of psychological care. To make matters worse, the region's chronically underfunded mental health system was—like the broader medical system—in utter disarray.[2] And even if the psychiatrists and psychologists entering the region had been able to make mental health services widely available, it's unlikely that survivors would have been interested. Beyond a deeply entrenched distrust of psychiatry, those crowding the growing tent encampments were not accustomed to formulating their struggles in psychological terms. They regarded their problems as more basic; they needed shelter, food, and water, and to find family and friends.

In the face of these challenges, the psychiatrists and psychologists responding to the earthquake would labor—in the midst of overwhelming loss, and outside of formal medical and humanitarian institutions—to reinvent themselves. Accustomed to having to make do with limited resources, these "novice humanitarians" scoured university libraries, reached out to old acquaintances, and pored over self-help books looking for ideas about how they could help. They pieced together treatment protocols, designed research instruments, and built new institutional and professional networks. One of the most striking features of the psychiatric response to the Marmara Earthquake would be not only its scale but also the extent to which it was improvised. In what felt like the blink of an eye, psychiatry—as both a form of medical practice and set of ideas about human suffering—moved out of the shadows of popular conceptions of medical expertise (and institutional violence) to take center stage.

Unlike other studies of disaster and technology, *Living On* is not a story about technical systems collapsing or becoming dysfunctional in the context of crisis.[3] Rather, I am interested in how such a system was brought into existence in the immediate aftermath of a disastrous event. To characterize this makeshift and improvised psychiatric response to the earthquake as a "system" requires some explanation. Although the descriptions of the interventions that later filled studies and reports made them sound like carefully designed and systematically implemented sets of protocols and procedures, conversations with both those who developed the interventions and those who enrolled in them painted a far messier picture. As I interviewed psychiatrists and psychologists who responded to the earthquake, tracked down reports and publications detailing their work, visited sites of interventions, and interviewed their participants, it became clear that these interventions were not so much discrete collections of demarcated practices that formed an integrated "system." Rather, they were messy and highly unstable gatherings of people, ideas, practices, and values that cohered loosely around the imperative of easing the psychological and emotional suffering of earthquake survivors. In other words, as scholars of science and technology studies have taught us, these interventions were acting like technologies. That is, they both constituted and were constituted by a complex and historically contingent set of relations (involving human and nonhuman actors, categories and assumptions, instruments and institutions, and multiple nested systems) that were open-ended, translocally constituted, and—when the conditions were in their favor—held together across time.[4]

With this, I began thinking about the uncoordinated, decentralized, and makeshift psychiatric response to the Marmara Earthquake as representing an ad hoc sociotechnical infrastructure.[5] My research, in turn, became an exercise in mapping. I began tracing ethnographically how this post-disaster psychiatric infrastructure was assembled—the forms of expertise it attracted, the categories and techniques it mobilized, the sorts of professional collaborations it relied on, and the range of other sociotechnical systems on which it depended. Understanding the post-earthquake psychiatric response in this way proved critical to my efforts of making sense of how psychiatric techniques moved through the earthquake's aftermath—traveling through networks of global psychiatric expertise and across a devastated social and material landscape into the lives of those who had survived the disaster. It was here, in recognizing the ways this psychiatric infrastructure was able to constitute the realities it operated on, that I also began to conceive of the earthquake as a psychiatric event. That is, I began to think of this impromptu and improvised humanitarian response to the earthquake as a process of psychiatric world making.

But to whom did that world belong? As critical scholars of humanitarianism have long argued, humanitarian action represents a particularly insidious means through which European and North American forms of (medical) knowledge and expertise, as well as sovereignty, are extended into the Global South. Especially in their psychiatric forms, humanitarian interventions have been widely critiqued for privileging approaches that pathologize and individualize suffering, displace local idioms of suffering, obscure the structural conditions of people's distress, and further extend the reach of psychologically inflected notions of normality and governance. The humanitarian response to the Marmara Earthquake, if approached from a certain angle, seemed to confirm these critiques. In the immediate aftermath of the earthquake, with the state's response faltering, waves of humanitarian organizations—primarily from western Europe—quickly descended on the region to begin distributing water, food, shelter, and medical care. As the international humanitarian response grew, novel arrangements of professional and technical expertise proliferated in the ruins of the earthquake. The concerns of psychiatric experts quickly wove themselves into a humanitarian response, and PTSD emerged as the disaster's central psychological idiom—organizing the work of a vast array of experts and organizations, transforming the suffering of survivors into technical problems to be solved, and establishing new avenues and vocabularies for expressing suffering and seeking assistance. As such, the Marmara Earthquake appeared to be another instance of the inexorable spread of Western medical and scientific expertise to its peripheries in contexts of humanitarian crisis.

While indebted to how the critical literature on psychiatric humanitarianism draws attention to the role of psychiatry in mediating (imperial) relations of power and difference,[6] I found that my research told a less straightforward story. Foremost, I worried that these approaches unduly flattened and simplified the sociotechnical worlds they were intended to describe.[7] For instance, the psychiatric response to the earthquake was not a simple instance of a set of "local" or "indigenous" (read "non-Western") practices being by supplanted by the onslaught of "Western" psychiatric categories and practices in a moment of crisis, what Ethan Watters has characterized as the "globalization of the American psyche."[8] Not only had psychiatry in Turkey—and, before that, the Ottoman Empire—long been entangled in European forms and institutions of psychiatric expertise,[9] but the wide range of therapeutic options available at the time could not be easily slotted into categories such as "Western" and "non-Western."[10] Distinctions between "West" and "non-West" and "foreign" and "local," or, for that matter, "domestic" and "global," constantly blurred.[11] In other words, given these deep historical entanglements and the specific dynamics of the post-earthquake response, it didn't make sense to build an analysis around the extent to which a given technique or category "belonged" to one place or another.[12] Moreover, if my research was any indication, conventional critiques of humanitarian intervention ran the risk of exaggerating the actual influence of foreign expertise. Although relations between European experts and their counterparts in Turkey were certainly racialized and asymmetrical, my research suggested that the international psychiatric response was actually dwarfed by the domestic wave of psychiatrists and psychologists who responded to the earthquake. And even when experts were speaking the same language as local residents, those who enrolled in the interventions were not remade in any straightforward way by the categories and classifications being mobilized by this emergent psychiatric infrastructure.

With this in mind, this book explores the distinctive ways that psychiatry, disaster, and a set of shifting political and economic arrangements would come together in the wake of the Marmara Earthquake. In particular, I consider how the psychiatric response to the earthquake took shape at a series of overlapping junctures: at the encounter between long-standing national traditions of psychiatric practice and transforming global regimes of humanitarian intervention, in the tension between compassion for one's fellow citizen and the desire for the production of psychiatric knowledge and professional capital, and at the intersection of a widespread sense that the state had betrayed its promise to protect its citizens and a growing fascination with the promises of neoliberal reform. While I engage a moment in the history of psychiatry in Turkey that is more than two decades old, the approaches I examine—ranging from clinically oriented efforts to treat trauma and other "comorbid" conditions (e.g., depression, anxiety) to amorphous interventions aiming to empower participants and provide psychosocial support—remain largely conventional in the fields of humanitarian and disaster psychiatry.[13] In fact, the Marmara Earthquake stands as an early moment in a trend that soon became generalized, wherein large-scale disasters would elicit humanitarian interventions that placed special emphasis on technical responses to the psychological well-being of survivors. In Turkey, as we will see, this psychiatric response would play an important role in a wider normalization of psychiatry and, with it, the increasing psychiatrization of normality.

As this begins to indicate, when I speak of "psychiatry," I do not mean merely those clinical practices and theories of psychopathology dominant in the medical field of psychiatry. On the one hand, and following Nikolas Rose,

I approach psychiatry expansively, as a "heterogeneous complex of contested relations" among different professionals who claim theoretical and practical expertise over the "vicissitudes of the psyche."[14] As such, the field of psychiatry subsumes not only a wide variety of psychiatrists, but also a range of "psy" specialists variously dedicated to the psychological well-being of individuals: clinical psychologists, psychiatric social workers, psychotherapists, counselors, general practitioners who provide mental health advice, and so forth. On the other hand, by "psychiatry," I also mean to suggest what Elizabeth Lunbeck, in her study of psychiatry and gender in early twentieth-century United States, referred to as a certain "psychiatric perspective."[15] For Lunbeck, the cultural authority of psychiatry in the United States grew not because of psychiatry's institutional power or its claim to scientific expertise over insanity, but rather through its newfound claim to expertise over "normality."[16] Psychiatry's authority, in this regard, rests not primarily on its institutional power to identify and confine madness, but in its capacity to "leave the asylum" and come to bear on "every aspect of people's lives"—such that virtually all forms of deviation from social norms would gain a psychological meaning, which the psychiatrist was uniquely qualified to judge. Throughout this book, I thus use *psychiatry* broadly, to encompass the work not just of psychiatrists but also a wide range of psy experts who were drawn into the aftermath of the Marmara Earthquake. It is in this expanded conception of psychiatry that I've also come to think of this book as a contribution to the anthropological tradition of clinical ethnography, though one that follows clinical experts and forms of expertise as they move beyond the clinic and struggle to reconstitute themselves within a radically unstable social and material context.[17]

In this regard, *Living On* is quite literally a study of psychiatry in ruins. It is also a study of psychiatry as ruins. The psychiatric infrastructure born of the earthquake would, in time, disassemble and settle in complex ways into institutions, social relations, and collective lives. Like ruins that signal a former existence, this infrastructure would live on as a set of fragments and remains—technical, material, symbolic, affective—within which pasts were still obliquely discernible, even as they were being put to different uses in the present. While the recent upsurge in anthropological interest in ruins and ruination have been helpful in refining this approach,[18] my original inspiration actually emerged out of my reading of architectural and geological histories of the region. Like the Ottoman Empire's practice of repurposing material from Roman buildings (sometimes salvaged from buildings destroyed in earthquakes) to construct a new city's infrastructure, I came to think of these psychiatric remains of disaster both as indexing the past and as resources for fashioning individual and collective futures in the long wake of disaster. This book is positioned in the play between these two formations of ruin as a means of exploring the relationship between the psychiatric response to the Marmara Earthquake and how the psychiatric remains of the disaster would, in time, come to play an unexpected role in animating new rationales of governance, visions of self and society, and arrangements of subjectivity, politics, and expertise.

Living On

> Our history is the future.
> —NICK ESTES, 2019

Within days of the earthquake, survivors began appearing in the neighborhood where I was living—350 kilometers east of the earthquake's epicenter, on the outskirts of Turkey's capital city, Ankara. At the time, I was a graduate student struggling to complete fieldwork on my first research project. The visitors flowing into the neighborhood had abandoned what was left of their homes in the earthquake region and were stopping to visit relatives on the way to their family villages in central Turkey. One evening, I joined an extended family that had gathered to welcome visiting relatives. It was a familiar scene—large plates of food, with guests sitting around talking, singing, sharing stories, and drinking tea. During a pause in the conversation, I remember looking across the room to see a middle-aged woman sitting apart from the group, staring blankly off into the distance. The pain visible on her face was devastating. Her body spoke of utter exhaustion. I later learned that the apartment building where she and her family lived had collapsed in the earthquake. Her husband and three children had died, as had her parents, siblings, in-laws, and several cousins. She was the only survivor from the building. After our brief encounter, I would never see her again. She presumably continued on to her family's village—where, like thousands of others who made similar migrations, she no longer knew anyone particularly well. I would soon return to my research, but the encounter continued to haunt me.

Fourteen years later, in the summer of 2013, I traveled to a small town an hour's drive east of Istanbul, a town that was located near the earthquake's epicenter. It had been one of the most severely impacted towns in the region. Several thousand residents had died in the earthquake, and 80 percent of its buildings had been either damaged or destroyed. While there, I met a woman I will call Esra, who had become well known locally for her work advocating for disability rights following the earthquake. Although we would discuss this work, our conversations were overshadowed by her talk about the son she had lost in the earthquake. The force of her despair and continuing grief seemed unbearable. It was as if her feelings of loss, and the intensity of her attachment to her lost son, had not diminished in fourteen years. Over the course of our conversations—which would span six years—I found myself repeatedly returning to that evening in Ankara, more than a decade earlier, to the woman fleeing the earthquake zone. In time, I came to wonder how Esra's life might offer a glimpse into the future of the nameless woman I met in Ankara, as well as the psychiatric response to the earthquake that I had already begun piecing together.

I will return to Esra's story in Chapter 10, but I begin it here to expand the questions animating this book: What about those survivors who were the objects and subjects of the enormous, improvised psychiatric apparatus? What sorts of lives did this convergence of geological volatility and psychiatric expertise make possible? As much as I enjoyed mapping the emergence of the post-earthquake psychiatric infrastructure—tracking down sources, reconstructing interventions, charting networks—it also felt incomplete, if not problematic. I came to feel that a project focused exclusively on psychiatric expertise ran the same risk as the psychiatric infrastructure that assembled in the wake of the earthquake—of obscuring the lived reality of the earthquake among those who experienced it firsthand.[19]

With this in mind, *Living On* places the accounts of those who lived the earthquake at the center of analysis, and it does so for reasons both ethical and analytical. On the one hand, a sense of obligation would motivate me to stay with this project much longer than colleagues (and friends and family) thought I should. Although public attention quickly shifted away from the Marmara Earthquake, I knew that the feelings of loss and intense grief it precipitated continued to roil lives. As I gathered people's stories across the decades following the earthquake—and began to document the suffering caused not only by loss but also by the sense that they had been forgotten—I felt obligated to see this project through. On the other hand, I would, in time, come to appreciate how these stories also offered important lessons about the limits and possibilities of building livable futures in the wake of disaster.[20] In this regard, an important, if only aspirational, aim of this book is to shed ethnographic light on the possibilities of human flourishing in the aftermath of world-shattering destruction.

This shift of focus to consider experiences of loss and psychiatric care in the long wake of disaster would entail a shift in the temporalities of analysis. Intentionally set outside of the urgent temporality of disaster and crisis—with its characteristic fixation on the event itself—my research has followed the consequences of the earthquake over the ensuing decades, into the extended temporality of what I'm calling "living on."[21] I am attracted to this concept of living on for two reasons. First, I have found that it uniquely captures a common rendering of how my interlocutors characterized the insistence of life in the wake of disaster. In interviews with those who lived through the earthquake, questions about how one dealt with the loss of family and friends were time and again met with a shrug and the phrase *hayat devam ediyor*, "life goes on." Initially I regarded the phrase as formulaic and empty, a shrug of the world-weary and a resignation to fate, as if to say, "No matter what happened to me, no matter the sorrows of me and my family, no matter the home I lost, life continues." In time, I came to think of the phrase not as a resignation to fate but as a powerful commentary on the ontological status of life itself. Life, in this rendering, had a force of its own and a vitality that inexorably moved. As my interlocutors would suggest, life pushes and drags one with it, regardless of one's own wishes or desires. I thus use "living on" with the hope of conveying how many of the earthquake survivors I interviewed characterized the obstinacy of life in the wake of disaster.[22]

Second, I am interested in how this phrase resonates conceptually with the sorts of temporalities suggested by Lauren Berlant's notion of slow death and what Elizabeth Povinelli has characterized as the "cruddy" temporality of late liberalism.[23] Both Berlant and Povinelli are broadly concerned with the ways that life, death, and exhaustion are distributed within settings and situations indelibly ordered by contemporary regimes of capitalist accumulation. For both, making sense of the dynamics at play here entails attending not so much to the force of "big events" (e.g., financial crises, military conflicts, "natural" disasters) as to the slow, accumulating grind of the everyday, ordinary, and chronic. From this perspective, to focus exclusively on events or crises is to be distracted from that which is more decisive, for the injurious effects of contemporary political and economic arrangements are exacted in the extended, drawn-out temporalities of what Povinelli calls "quasi-events" and what Berlant refers to as "non-event-like events."[24] In my case, I am particularly interested in how these approaches offer us a way to think differently about disaster, and not merely in terms that modulate the velocity of disasters (e.g., "slow disaster"). Thinking in terms of "living on" will challenge us to conceptualize the Marmara Earthquake as simultaneously an acute event and a chronic condition, as both a sudden rupture and an enduring process in which the disaster's aftermath weaves into the quasi-eventfulness of the everyday. In this regard, living on is a temporality of both the catastrophic and the ordinary.[25] It belongs to the *longue durée*, as it also gathers together other temporalities (geological, national, genealogical, clinical) within which the event and the everyday inhabit one another—at times like a past that haunts the present,[26] at other times as a free-floating anxiety, and at still other times as an explosive rupture of the everyday.

To examine the everydayness of life in the long wake of the Marmara Earthquake thus insists on an approach capable of attending to both the earthquake as an exceptional (and exceptionally destructive) event and the varied ways that everyday forms of chronic insecurity, inequality, and violence have constituted people's experiences of the earthquake and its aftermath. In regard to the former, for instance, it will be critical to not lose sight of the distinctive qualities of the earthquake as a form of disaster in shaping people's experience of the event. Given its scale and collective impact, an entire generation of residents living in the region was transformed by the event. It established in people's lives a collective point of reference, a historical division that, from then on, would divide time into an era that preceded and an era that followed the morning of August 17, 1999. Likewise, the ways that the earthquake was framed as a "natural disaster" would play a decisive role in shaping how accountability was apportioned, and largely evaded, in the years that followed and, consequently, the trajectory of people's lives in the extended aftermath of the earthquake.[27] In other words, the earthquake, as an event, calls for fidelity.[28]

At the same time, focusing too narrowly on the eventfulness of the earthquake runs the risk of missing the slower, "cruddier" processes that prepared the way for disaster,[29] and, in so doing, reinscribing a set of normative assumptions about the presumed stability and security of the everyday as an ideal space of social belonging. While disasters may be exceptions to the everyday, they are also continuous with an everyday already filled with crisis, rupture, dispossession, and violence of many kinds—as scholars of indigenous dispossession and sovereignty have repeatedly observed.[30] Similarly, the long history of the study of environmental racism offers no shortage of examples of how everyday forms of dispossession and chronic insecurity render populations and bodies vulnerable to disaster.[31] In turn, it is not difficult to also discern in approaches privileging the exceptionality of disasters a set of implicit political assumptions that position the state as the securer of the everyday and thus exclusively capable of responding to disasters—thereby obscuring, if not obstructing, those endogenous ways of managing disasters that do not align with dominant political and economic rationales. While it is vital to appreciate the exceptionality of the earthquake as a disastrous event, my analysis begins from a set of assumptions within which "disaster" and "the everyday" stand not in opposition and in which events—even sudden and enormously destructive earthquakes—always exist within a longer history of loss, destruction, and insecurity that may not rise to the level of an event, but are nonetheless continuous with the disaster.[32] In short, my goal in this book is to develop an analysis that neither fetishizes the exceptionality of the event (as if it came from nowhere) nor romanticizes the ordinariness of the everyday (as if it were a terrain of uneventful calm and authentic social relating).

Thinking in terms of the temporality of living on proved decisive in my efforts to identify the specific ways that geological transformation, psychiatric expertise, and the shifting political-economic conditions of Turkey would converge to shape people's lives in the years following the Marmara Earthquake. As this project became more and more drawn out, and I worked to remain open to the range of possible futures set in motion by the earthquake, research would also push me outside of conventional approaches to the psychological effects of disaster. Reflecting wider trends in disaster studies, research concerned with the mental health consequences of disaster continues to be dominated by approaches focused almost exclusively on psychological trauma and PTSD. As Vanessa Pupavac presciently observed over twenty years ago, trauma has come to dominate "the West's conceptualization of the impact of wars and disasters in the South. Our attention is drawn to the psychological suffering of victims, their emotional scars, their sense of despair and helplessness."[33]

A focus on psychological trauma and PTSD in contexts of disaster is in some ways to be expected. After all, the psychological and emotional states captured by diagnostic categories such as PTSD are indeed common responses to large-scale disaster. Yet, conducting ethnographic research in the earthquake region for over a decade would bring into sharp relief the limits of the clinical, social-scientific, and literary approaches to psychic trauma that continue to monopolize North American and European studies of disaster. These approaches, as I explore in later chapters, are typically formulated around a temporality turned to, if not fixated on, the past. In turn, they generate analyses that tend to dwell in the stuckness and looping repetitions of traumatic experience, a pathological refusal to let go of the past, and a melancholic inability to move on. Here, we are again faced with those tenacious assumptions and distortions common to studies that focus narrowly on the eventfulness of disasters. "In critical theory and mass society generally," writes Lauren Berlant, "'trauma' has become the primary genre . . . for describing the historical present as the scene of an exception that has just shattered some ongoing, uneventful ordinary life that was supposed just to keep going on and with respect to which people felt solid and confident."[34]

Tracking the legacy of the Marmara Earthquake in people's lives over several decades would push me to think the psychological and affective remains of disaster otherwise than through the idioms of trauma and PTSD. Indeed, as we will see, the earthquake seemed to endure in people's lives less often as a precise and vivid (traumatic) memory than as an amorphous set of bodily traces and shifting atmospheres that would only rarely reveal their origins.[35] To be clear, to direct attention to the "otherwise than," or to move "beyond" trauma,[36] means not denying the existence of trauma, but recognizing that what we call "trauma" represents but one possible response to overwhelming events. In our case, especially as research extended into the temporality of living on, being open to this otherwise would bring into view a different sort of affective terrain born of the earthquake. This also suggested a form of living on that couldn't be reduced to mere "survival."[37] With this expanded sense of how disaster and the everyday can inhabit people's lives in the wake of disaster, research became increasingly attuned to how narratives of those who lived through the earthquake marked out a set of distinctive relationships between past loss and the building of livable futures in the long aftermath of catastrophe. Put differently, this project became preoccupied with the future of disaster, such that the passing of time carried us not further from the past but further into the disaster's ever-lengthening future.

Disaster in Context

Exploring the efforts of those who lived through the earthquake to fashion livable futures in the long wake of disaster required an approach that could account for not only the multiple ways that the earthquake was a long time in the making but also how the conditions for this fashioning were themselves shifting over time. As we will see, to live on in the wake of the Marmara Earthquake would entail enduring a series of momentous political and economic transformations (and crises), as well as escalating military conflicts, that had broad effects in society and particular consequences for those who lived through the earthquake. These transformations were not merely a backdrop to people's efforts to rebuild their lives. They were part and parcel of these efforts—providing the resources, constraints, and affordances for imagining and building livable futures. For some, these shifting conditions at times intensified their struggles, while at other times, and for different people, they provided new opportunities for dramatically reimagining lives. In short, to make sense of the ways lives were charted in the long aftermath of the earthquake, we have to understand how the convergence of disaster and psychiatry interwove, over time, with a series of structural transformations and transforming conditions that characterized the "New Turkey."

The Marmara Earthquake, together with a second large earthquake that occurred nearby three months later, would leave a calamitous mark on the end of a tumultuous decade.[38] The compassion, solidarity, and mutual aid ushered in by the earthquake was in sharp contrast to the everyday political life of the time. The 1990s had been a decade during which conflicts over ethnic, religious, and ideological difference had increasingly challenged the idea of national unity that had been so central to the state's version of the nation's founding. While the state had long been critiqued for its exclusionary authoritarian paternalism, the way it governed as if the nation were ethnically and religiously homogeneous, and its rigid control of religious expression in the public sphere, the 1990s was a period during which these critiques gained a critical mass and a much more audible public voice. There was much to complain about during this period: a series of damaging political scandals, widespread state corruption and the further entrenchment of an aging ruling political class, a zealously enforced secular public sphere, the rising influence of Islamist politics, the intensification of state violence against Kurds, Turkey's deepening integration into a global consumerist economy, and, with it, an increasing embrace of neoliberal principles of governance.[39]

The earthquake and its humanitarian response would occasion new political imaginations and possibilities, as it was also a quickening of political and economic transformations already underway.[40] Amid its catastrophic destruction, the earthquake gave rise to an unexpected sense of political hopefulness. In a moment when the state failed to live up to its (bio)political promises, citizens had risen up to support themselves. Communities spontaneously organized search-and-rescue teams, systems for distributing food and medications to the most vulnerable, networks of communication for relatives and friends to reach survivors, and informal security arrangements for guarding abandoned homes. These instances of mutual aid quickly became sites of political mobilization. Frustrated with government inaction, large groups of residents marched on the regional governor's offices to demand more assistance. New civil society organizations that were organized around the specific needs of earthquake survivors (rather than the priorities of political parties or religious foundations) soon emerged across the region and began coordinating in unprecedented ways. By the beginning of September—just weeks after the earthquake—a newly formed coalition of nongovernmental organizations (NGOs) had released a manifesto demanding that the state reform its disaster response efforts.[41]

Meanwhile, commentators discerned hopeful signs of a new politics to come in the ruins of the earthquake. Those longing nostalgically for political unity would see in this post-disaster solidarity the reanimation of a "national community" in which ethnic, religious, and ideological differences could be subsumed under a (fantasy of) collective political unity.[42] Others saw the post-earthquake period as a pluralist awakening—where people came together not despite but through their differences, to realize their common cause. "In the face of death and destruction, our mundane differences evaporated, and we all became one," wrote the Turkish novelist Elif Shafak, recounting a scene from the earthquake of a conservative shopkeeper in her neighborhood sitting amid the rubble to share a cigarette with a young transgender woman.[43] Others saw in the face of a state's failure to fulfill its role as guardian and protector of its citizens the awakening of a slumbering political consciousness. Commentators began to speak breathlessly about the birth Turkey's democracy out of the ruins of the earthquake. The playwright Behiç Ak would later capture this convergence of disaster and political awakening with exquisite satire in his play *Fault Line*: "If there are two or three more earthquakes, democracy will really take root in this country."[44]

This "romance of civil society" would be short lived.[45] As much as it felt like a decisive social and political transformation for those living the moment, this unity born of urgency would fade, and with particular speed among those who were not living in the earthquake region.[46] The future once again became a field of struggle. In the years to come, the massive display of public unity that emerged after the earthquake would be remembered wistfully as a moment of national solidarity, one in which everyday political, religious, and ethnic differences were seemingly overcome in the face of a national tragedy.

Whereas survivors of the earthquake saw in the ruins of the earthquake the signs of a broken state, the state seemed to find in the rubble a set of guiding principles for political and economic transformation. The mutual aid that emerged in response to the state's inability to provide basic support to those in need would be invoked repeatedly over the ensuing years to promote widespread neoliberal reforms in the state and economy. As Can Açıksöz has written, "Popular discontent over the state was shortly transformed into a neoliberal fascination about the potentialities of civil society, epitomized by NGOs. Indeed, in the post-earthquake context, NGOs filled in the gap created by the absence of a well-organized state response."[47] For those promoting neoliberal reforms, the earthquake, despite its tragedies, had revealed not so much the latent democratic spirit of society as the untapped productive potential of citizens, which had for too long been stifled by a paternalistic state.

The earthquake, as it gave rise to new political imaginations, also accelerated shifts already afoot, securing the legacy of the earthquake far into the future. Severe financial crises in 2000 and 2001 further accelerated these processes. The 2001 financial crisis in particular—which led to a massive currency devaluation, widespread unemployment, and a dramatic loss of personal savings—precipitated far-reaching governmental and societal transformations whose effects extended from banking regulations to new forms of consumer debt and transformed household economies.[48] Facilitated by a series of International Monetary Fund and World Bank programs and reforms associated with Turkey's European Union membership negotiations, the financial crisis proved a watershed moment for Turkey's integration into global finance networks, especially in terms of foreign capital investments.[49] The political and economic reforms of this period would set in motion a feverish growth in Turkey's economy and, with it, an unprecedented expansion of what commentators characterized as the "new middle class." Correspondingly, these reforms would also further hasten the state's neoliberal reform, especially in the state's withdrawal from a series of domains where it had previously been active (e.g., the privatization of significant aspects of the health care sector, social security services, and, among others, disaster management).

Building on widespread discontent over the state's handling of the earthquake and the ensuing financial crises, and following a series of weak coalition governments, a new political party, the Justice and Development Party (Adalet ve Kalkınma Partisi, or AKP), emerged from general elections in 2002 with a decisive majority. The AKP would become one of the most enduring and transformative political regimes in Turkey's history. Led by Recep Tayyip Erdoğan, the AKP initially distinguished itself as an Islamist-inspired, pro-Western, and pro-neoliberalization party that supported Turkey's entrance into the European Union and the democratizing reforms that this entailed. As the AKP moved into its second decade of rule, however, democratic reform gave way to increasingly illiberal and authoritarian politics that would dramatically transform the state. Among its many distinguishing characteristics, this was a period marked by a systemic reform of the state to undemocratically consolidate power, a repressive opposition to dissent (especially in the media), a neoconservative familism that animated an intensifying (and violent) policing of the public sphere, a vast purging of civil servants and the educational system, and—with a resumed war with Kurdish militias in eastern Turkey, Iraq, and northern Syria—a reinvigorated ethnoracial militarism.

While I don't want to exaggerate the role of the earthquake in these larger societal shifts—in some ways it was causative, and in other ways it was coincidental—the earthquake nevertheless came to be seen as a pivotal moment of a transformative era. Not surprisingly, the political and economic changes that took hold during this period would be refracted in distinctive ways through the lives of earthquake survivors. The story of Turkey's economic growth during this period is often told as the dramatic growth of Turkey's middle class and an expansion of middle-class patterns of consumption. "From 2000 to 2013," as the *New York Times* characterized this period, "average incomes more than tripled, poverty fell by half and Turkey entered the ranks of middle-income countries."[50] The majority of earthquake survivors—who were not able to enter the "new middle class"—experienced this period differently. The succession of economic crises and political reforms (among them a series of major reforms in the welfare system) would not propel them into the middle class but, rather, leave them in further debt and exposed in new ways to the effects of fluctuating markets as they struggled to rebuild their lives. In turn, across this period, the state would also become increasingly dependent on urban development schemes, state-led mass housing construction, and large-scale infrastructure projects (e.g., mega-project) to both demonstrate its sovereignty and keep its constituents employed. These changes in housing policy and markets—much of them justified, ironically, in the name of earthquake resilience—would exacerbate the struggle of those who survived the Marmara Earthquake, especially in their efforts to find and hold onto affordable housing.

Although I have underscored the culpability of the Turkish state in the devastation precipitated by the Marmara Earthquake—its policies and the corruption it fostered literally prepared the ground for an enormous loss of life, property, and livelihoods—I want to be clear that Turkey is not exceptional here. The processes I describe in this book—of profit-driven housing development, of the rationalization and politicization of disaster management, of nationalist ideologies that frame the state as the protector of dependent subjects, of government policy that prioritizes economic growth over the enforcement of building regulations—are all commonplace, as are the ways that the death and destruction of the Marmara Earthquake correlated with gradients of economic inclusion and exclusion. While the particular scenes and characters may vary from one setting to the next, the plot and resolution are tragically predictable. As such, the account I offer in this book is not intended as a commentary on Turkey's "progress" along some sort of Eurocentric "ladder of development" or path of "democratic development." Instead, my interests are in how people's struggle to fashion lives in the wake of the Marmara Earthquake might speak toward a more general configuration of conditions and forces that are increasingly shaping lives on a planetary scale .

Methods out of Ruins, Methods for Living On

The questions guiding the research for this book were born from the Marmara Earthquake. Although far from the epicenter at the time, the neighborhood where I was living in Ankara was close enough to the fault line to feel the earthquake and many of the subsequent aftershocks. Having never experienced an earthquake firsthand, I found the tremors profoundly unnerving. Already on edge from watching televised coverage of the unfolding scenes from the earthquake region, I distinctly recall the sense of panic that followed these tremors, as I and my neighbors rushed out of our apartments to gather in the street. Whereas the research I was conducting at the time—about religious and ritual forms of healing in contexts of urban poverty—was premised on a notion of the malleability of the world and people's bodily relationship with it, the earthquake would cast these ideas into a different light.[51] My thinking about the world-making potentialities of healing seemed to speak to something altogether different from the world I felt moving under my feet. For me, the earthquake would drive a wedge between what I thought of as the world and the planet, between the worldly time of social intimacies and the planetary time of geological transformation.

It would take time for these initial experiences and reflections to become a "project." Six years after the earthquake, I returned to Turkey to begin work on an exploratory study about emerging models of community-based mental health care. I was interested in how a series of political and economic transformations—especially Turkey's deepening integration into the global economy, the acceleration of neoliberal reforms, and the effects of the ongoing "EU harmonization" process—were playing out in the field of psychiatry. In dozens of interviews with psychiatrists and psychologists across the country, my questions would be repeatedly and unexpectedly directed to the earthquake. If I wanted to understand the development of community mental health care in Turkey, I was told, I needed to go back to the earthquake. In fact, if I was interested in psychiatric innovation in Turkey more broadly, I needed to study the earthquake—both in terms of its psychopathological effects on the population and as a transformative event within the field of psychiatry. In conversation after conversation, I was pulled back to the earthquake. In the decade that followed—during subsequent fieldwork trips that lasted between one and four months in 2012, 2013, 2017, 2018, and 2019—I began tracking the psychiatric response to and legacy of the Marmara Earthquake within the communities and lives of its survivors and among the Turkish mental health professionals who had responded to the disaster.

But how to go about studying the aftermath of an event as large, complex, and destructive as the Marmara Earthquake? Considering my interest in the psychiatrization of disaster, how to design a study attuned to both the scientific renderings of the event (the way psychiatric practices and technologies transformed the messy realities of lives into problems to be fixed and data to be analyzed) and the heterogeneous and shifting lives of people struggling to live on in the decades to follow—that is, the messy realities of actual lives? Despite a long-standing interest in themes of healing, recovery, and care,[52] I knew that extending these interests into a setting of such large-scale destruction and loss would be exceptionally challenging.

Ethnography—as a method of research, epistemic disposition, and genre of writing—proved well suited for this sort of project. Its empirical investment in being present in particular social worlds offered a sense of groundedness (if only illusory) in a context that was easily overwhelming, as its emphasis on charting relations across multiple scales and its openness to complexity, resonances, and the unexpected offered a methodological flexibility and mobility that was critical.[53] In turn, anthropology's ethnographic commitment to spending time with others (hanging out, shooting the shit, being curious about what's going on) and its cultivated attentiveness to the force of the unspoken in constituting worlds—its emphasis on, as Lisa Stevenson puts it, "listening differently"[54]—would also bring into view the often-invisible and unacknowledged ways that the earthquake lived on in people's lives. In short, what I learned about the legacy of the earthquake could not have been learned had I not spent extended periods of time in the earthquake region.

These ethnographic dispositions slowly evolved into a methodology, in step with my blurring sense of the earthquake as a bounded event. Although the idea of an ethnographic study grounded in one primary site—a neighborhood, a clinic, an organization—was appealing (and would have certainly revealed an important facet of the earthquake's legacy), the nature of the forms of expertise I was examining, to say nothing of the earthquake's broad effects, required a more peripatetic approach. The scale and complexity of the event also meant I was continually stumbling on unanticipated trajectories of research. Everywhere I went—from the earthquake region to my own campus in the United States—people had stories about the earthquake to share. Despite its seeming boundlessness as a topic of research, I came to think of the project as having two primary "field sites." These sites—sprawling, and at times intersecting—consisted of the translocal networks of psychiatric expertise that formed around the earthquake's aftermath and the communities that composed the cities, small towns, and villages of the earthquake region.

Tracing networks of expertise would entail research that was perpetually on the move. At times, I felt like a detective—methodically piecing together networks of people, institutions, and ideas. Even in Istanbul, where these networks were the densest, I was continually traveling back and forth across the city. Moving between documents, offices, websites, email and WhatsApp messages, and interviews, I hunted down clues and connected dots. At the outset of the project, I was fortunate to be affiliated with a group of psychiatrists and psychologists based at a major medical school in the United States who were tasked with making proposals to revise Turkey's national mental health policy. The relationships they had developed with mental health professionals and policymakers in Turkey, together with the many physicians and psychiatrists I had met in my previous research, would provide a remarkable vantage point from which to begin my research.

By the end of the project, I had conducted formal interviews with twenty-two psychiatrists and psychologists who had been involved in the humanitarian response to the earthquake. (Reflecting the broad profile of the psychiatric response to the earthquake, the majority of these interviews were conducted with experts who identified as psychiatrists.) I conducted additional research at a PTSD treatment and training center in the earthquake region, participated in conferences and training workshops for post-disaster psychological care, and read widely in the psychiatric literature that emerged out of studies conducted in the earthquake zone. Alongside this ethnographic and archival work, I interviewed a wide range of experts and professionals whose work touched, or was touched by, the earthquake—such as mid-level bureaucrats in provincial offices of the state's disaster management agency, urban planners in the earthquake region, members of outdoor clubs who provided disaster relief, bank officers who distributed loans to survivors, union leaders who coordinated relief efforts, staff at local branches of national humanitarian organizations, curators at museums dedicated to the earthquake, actors who performed in disaster preparedness trainings, and a number of novelists, filmmakers, journalists, and artists whose work sought to translate the disaster into words and images. (Unless otherwise noted, I use pseudonyms throughout this book.)

Again, although I enjoyed this detective work—accumulating clues and mapping relations in order to fill out a bigger picture—it also felt insufficient. If I wanted to understand the legacy of the earthquake, and the actual effects of the psychiatric response it inspired, I decided that I needed to stop moving (as much) and settle down somewhere. But this, too, was complicated. Simply living for stretches of time in one geographic location would not be enough. Understanding the living legacy of the disaster would also require a particular sort of listening. As anthropologists similarly interested in dwelling ethnographically in the affective, bodily, and structural dynamics of loss and vulnerability would recognize,[55] the efforts of survivors to live on in this context were, as with every life, necessarily complicated, ambiguous, and often difficult to distinguish from mundane responses to the practical demands of life. In my case, learning to listen for the legacy of the earthquake's psychiatric infrastructure entailed cultivating a capacity to listen for ruins—those shards and remains of a former time that lived on in the repurposing of psychiatric categories and former diagnoses within families, in the terms chosen to describe one's feelings and motivations, in fleeting recollections of advice offered by a psychologist.

The area most heavily affected by the earthquake was a series of cities and small towns that ringed the Gulf of İzmit. The destruction along the fault line had also extended eastward to the province of Sakarya (especially its capital, Adapazarı, fifty kilometers east of the İzmit) and westward to Istanbul's outer districts of Avcılar and Bağcılar. The second earthquake in November was centered in the provinces of Düzce and Bolu, approximately one hundred kilometers east of the epicenter of the Marmara Earthquake. Although research took me throughout the entire region—a reach made possible by the network of highways and public transportation that integrated the towns in the region, especially those ringing the Gulf of İzmit—I would spend extended periods of time in the provincial capital, İzmit, and in one of the small towns that had experienced severe damage in the earthquake. Although this was still a large area, these periods of place-based fieldwork were an essential component of my research. During repeated visits to these sites, I spent time in neighborhoods and apartment complexes where earthquake survivors had been resettled, in community health clinics that served these neighborhoods, in psychiatric units of regional hospitals, with community activists involved in organizing post-earthquake housing rights campaigns, in the offices of local disability rights associations and the regional public health directorate, and in local branches of humanitarian organizations and charitable foundations.

The in-depth ethnographic interviews conducted with earthquake survivors during this period—of which there were twenty-two—would sharpen a set of existing ethical considerations of this project that I want to note at the outset. Everyone I interviewed for this project willingly, and usually enthusiastically, consented to participate. Nevertheless, as people began talking about their experiences of the earthquake, the past would often come to life in unpredictable ways. This was not at all surprising, and I had to be prepared for moments when this became distressing. (As one of the psychologists who accompanied me on several interviews put it, "If we're going to let things out of the box, we have to be able to put them back in by the end.") While not nearly as straightforward as this might suggest, we had to be vigilant for signs that interviews were causing undue distress and ready to end conversations in ways that provided closure. This also meant we had to be attuned to how power differentials were shaping interview dynamics, with me as an American researcher and, at times, research assistants who were usually professionals from outside of the community.

At the same time—while vigilant to the pressures and power dynamics of these encounters—I also worked against a tendency to exaggerate the psychological fragility and vulnerability of my interlocutors (a tendency continually reinforced through ethical research review processes in the United States, which in turn reflect a wider national discourse on trauma and victimhood). In the context of negotiating interview dynamics, this meant that I remained open to trusting the feelings of my interviewees and followed their lead when it came to discussing potentially difficult topics. As my research would confirm, a defining feature of learning to live on in the wake of disaster was developing strategies for dealing with the innumerable reminders that suffused daily lives. The people I met over the course of the research for this book were remarkably (and tragically) experienced at being attuned to their moods and had developed ways to deal with incipient signs of personal distress—both within themselves and with others.

Research for this project would go on for much longer than I had expected at the outset. Professional and personal obligations made for research that could not follow the linear conventions of ethnographic ideals (a year or more in a faraway field site, followed by analysis and writing back at home). This was also emotionally taxing research. In hindsight, it is likely that the slow pace of this project can be partly explained by the fact that the more I heard stories about the earthquake—especially stories about the death of children—the harder I found it to leave my own children. In either case, the project was not only fundamentally (and exhaustingly) mobile and multisited, it also came together as a patchwork—of places, moments, stretches of time, technologies, and relations.[56] It consisted of long-term investment comprised of short-term and intermittent trips to "the field," a conceptualization of "the field" that could be accessed from "home" (via online databases and repositories, messaging apps, and social media accounts), and a nonlinear recursive movement of research, analysis, and writing.

This peripatetic, patchy, and mobile methodology would not have been feasible without my experience conducting research in Turkey over the previous two decades, as well as my professional position as a tenured professor at a well-resourced academic institution. On the basis of my earlier research, I had a grasp of the historical contexts within which I was working and the patterns of familial and social relating—especially the cultural patterning of loss, distress, and illness—were familiar, as were the varying ways my presence (as a white male professor from North America) shaped encounters in a range of settings. The extended period of research would also bring with it unexpected conceptual advantages. With the research unfolding over nearly two decades, I was able to trace the earthquake as it transformed from an event—an experience of sudden, overwhelming, and disorienting destruction—into an Event that continues to be recounted (along with other Events) in history textbooks, government ceremonies, public health campaigns, disaster preparedness drills, and urban planning proposals. The project would eventually come to an end, for no particular reason other than fatigue and a self-comforting illusion that the twentieth anniversary of the earthquake could be regarded as some sort of endpoint.

Writing the Disaster

Disasters are, by definition, exceptional events of such a magnitude that worlds and lives are dramatically overturned. Given the scale, complexity, and collective destructiveness of disasters such as the Marmara Earthquake, how does one convey to an audience the enormity of the destruction and loss it precipitated, and the innumerable ways—big and small—that it rippled through lives? How to describe a disaster in a way that captures both the contingent, open-endedness of its effects and the predictability of its destruction? Alternatively, how are we to square the idea of a disaster as an event that belongs to the historical coordinates of specific people and their social and singular lives, alongside an understanding of disaster that belongs to the temporal horizon of the planetary? Will counting the dead convey something of the earthquake's enormity? Enumerating its economic costs? Evoking what it felt like to experience the earthquake? I will try all these at different points in the following chapters. Each will prove inadequate. As the philosopher Maurice Blanchot long ago recognized, "The disaster . . . escapes the very possibility of experience—it is the limit of writing . . . the disaster de-scribes."[57]

Given these challenges, it should come as no surprise that the catastrophic has long been a theme through which thinkers, especially within European philosophical and clinical traditions, have explored (and imagined) the limits of meaning, reason, and rationality. From Immanuel Kant's reflections on the incomprehensibility of the mathematical sublime, to Blanchot's writings on the unrepresentability of disaster, to innumerable variations on a psychoanalytic conception of the unspeakability of trauma, the catastrophic has long functioned as a foil for conceptualizing the constitution of subjects, politics, and aesthetics.[58] As Janet Roitman has argued, "Crisis serves as a transcendental placeholder because it is a means for signifying contingency; it is a term that allegedly allows one to think the 'otherwise.'"[59] Anthropology, too, has long been animated by the catastrophic. The rush of anthropologists to rapidly colonizing spaces across the nineteenth and twentieth centuries in anticipation of the irretrievable loss of cultures, languages, and worlds at the joined hands of colonialism and capitalism could be read as an extended, complicitous anthropological reflection on the catastrophic. "Salvage anthropology" was, in this regard, already postapocalyptic.

This early entanglement of anthropology and the catastrophic prefaced the discipline's lasting interest in disaster as an empirical and conceptual problem. Here, one finds a rich body of social-scientific work providing models for how we might think about the social and moral dimensions of large-scale disaster.[60] More recently, anthropologists have extended this work by engaging disaster as a means of thinking about shifting configurations of crisis, technology, and governance.[61] Cutting across these varied interests in the anthropology of the catastrophic, one also finds a small collection of excellent studies concerned with the social, ethical, and technical implications of earthquakes as distinctive forms of disaster.[62] This body of work has been formative in my own thinking and writing about the legacy of the Marmara Earthquake, even as the arguments developed in this book at times look beyond modern European philosophical genealogies for theoretical inspiration.

Reflecting the fragmented and extended nature of my research, *Living On* moves through a series of scenes, encounters, and moments that date, roughly, from the time of the Marmara Earthquake through its twentieth anniversary. Part 1 begins the work of contextualizing the earthquake by situating a series of experiential accounts of the earthquake within the historical and material conditions that made them possible, especially those forces that conspired to render particular people and communities vulnerable to the earthquake's destructiveness. Part 2 focuses on the psychiatric infrastructure that took form within the earthquake's immediate aftermath. The chapters that constitute this section follow the work of several groups of volunteer psychiatrists and psychologists as they struggle, amid extraordinary loss and upheaval, to transform the earthquake's aftermath into a site of therapeutic care. I consider, in turn, their efforts to reimagine the scalability of their psychiatric expertise, rework their assumptions about the psychological subject of disaster, and weave therapeutic techniques into the everyday lives of suspicious communities. Exploring these emergent entanglements of disaster and psychiatry not only offers an account of how an improvised and decentralized post-disaster psychiatric infrastructure would, in time, touch thousands of lives, but also brings into view emergent arrangements of psychiatry, disaster, and security forming in the region over the same period.

Part 3 shifts into the temporality of "living on" to explore the ways this convergence of geological volatility and psychiatric expertise continue to shape lives decades into the earthquake's future. Grounded in long-term ethnographic research conducted throughout the region, the chapters in this part offer an account of the varied forms and formations of loss and possibility taking shape in the extended aftermath of disaster. Set against a recognition of the limits of trauma-focused approaches to disaster, I explore a set of pervasive moods, sensibilities, and affects that continue to unsettle inner and outer worlds—what I regard as disaster's "minor feelings"—and stories of enduring grief that articulate what I characterize as an "optimistic" relationship between past loss and livable futures. In writing against the grain of conventional accounts of disaster, this part also offers a series of ethnographic reflections on shifting arrangements of disability, citizenship, and expertise that the earthquake gave rise to, as well as the ways that the psychiatric response to the earthquake provided new idioms for political protest and occasions for people to be born anew out of experiences of catastrophic loss.

Just as I was completing this book, Turkey experienced another series of massive earthquakes, this time along its southern border with Syria. The scale of death and destruction was extraordinary. Although nearly twenty-five years had passed since the Marmara Earthquake, the scenes streaming from the region—of city blocks reduced to piles of concrete and rebar, of desperate residents digging through rubble in search of survivors, of tent settlements quickly filling cleared fields and emptied stadiums—were so familiar. While the similarities were impossible to ignore, much had also changed in the time between these two disasters. I return in the book's epilogue to a short reflection on how the legacy of the Marmara Earthquake, and especially the psychiatric response it inspired, would extend into this new disastrous present.

PART I

Sensing the Conditions of Disaster

ONE

The End of the World

kıyamet—tumult, chaos, doomsday, apocalypse, the end of the world
kopmak—to break, break off, snap, ache badly, rupture
kıyamet kopması—for the end of the world to come; for all hell to break loose

The challenges of representing disasters are well known. If disasters resist comprehension, how can one hope to ever convey their full, destructive complexity meaningfully? If they are radical temporal breaks—events that obliterate the very coordinates of normative time and history—how is one to write an account of a specific disaster that can capture both its history and its capacity to destroy history?[1] How to register, in other words, the historical continuity of disastrous events without losing sight of the specificity of their eventfulness? In short, if disasters exceed the capacity of language to describe, how to write the earthquake?[2]

What about the Marmara Earthquake in particular? Would it do to tally the number of dead (the government stopped counting after 17,000, but thousands more died) or the number of displaced residents (hundreds of thousands of survivors, suddenly rendered homeless, would fill tent settlements, while a massive internal migration would be set into motion as survivors returned to their home villages)? Should I recount the number of residents who lost a close relative (43 percent) or a neighbor, friend, or distant relative (also 43 percent)? Would it be more effective to calculate the damage to homes and property (20,000 buildings would collapse and 300,000 more were damaged) or the economic costs of the earthquake (upward of US$6.5 billion in wealth was lost in property damage, and with 35 percent of Turkey's industry based in the region, the national economy lost an estimated US$25 billion–$30 billion)? Would the geological reports that the earthquake occasioned offer an interesting perspective? While there's no official list of the dead to review (when the state stopped counting bodies, it stopped taking names), I could offer a tour of the nearby cemeteries to marvel at the number of tombstones bearing the same date: August 17, 1999. Then there's the internet. A quick search pulls up a rich visual archive largely made possible by the privatization of the media industry just prior to the earthquake—pictures of roads and bridges collapsed, bodies trapped in the rubble, desperate survivors pleading for bread and water, the nearby chemical plant sending a plume of black smoke over the Gulf of İzmit.[3]

None of these, individually or collectively, feels sufficient when it comes to capturing the scale and complexity of destruction precipitated by the Marmara Earthquake. Yet, we must start somewhere. With this in mind, my aim in this and the following chapter is to begin sketching out some of the more salient experiential and structural dimensions of the Marmara Earthquake. My discussion thus moves in two directions: one seeking to convey the lived experience of the earthquake by foregrounding the stories and voices of those who lived through it, and the other situating these experiences within the historical and material conditions that made them possible. This approach to introducing the earthquake will help us understand not only the earthquake's destructiveness from the point of view of those who lived it but also the forces that, first, conspired to render particular people vulnerable to the earthquake's destructiveness and, second, permitted public attention to shift quickly away from their persisting suffering and grief.

This chapter, which engages the earthquake as a particular type of experiential reality, gives special attention to the bodily and sensorial dimensions of disaster. This is significant for several reasons. On the one hand, and following a long anthropological tradition, I am convinced that we have much to learn about large-scale processes and events by attending to the voices and experiences of those caught up, often unwillingly, in their effects. On the other hand, and as an illustration of this point, I would come to appreciate over the course of this project how the experiences of the Marmara Earthquake—its characteristic sights, sounds, smells, feel, and feelings—would prove a vital aspect of its endurance over time. Those who lived through the earthquake repeatedly returned—decades later—to this sensorial register of disaster, for it was the bodily and affective remainders of the disaster that continued to reverberate through everyday lives. The disaster would literally remake people's relationships with their own bodies. At the same time, the ways that the earthquake made one feel were of primary importance to the psychiatric infrastructure that formed in the wake of the earthquake. Taken together, as this already suggests, the bodily and affective experience of the earthquake would prove, in the years to follow, an important site of future return.

3:02

There is a curious alchemy to stories recounting the moment of the earthquake—a distinctive admixture of the quotidian and the preternatural, scenes of unremarkable domesticity woven together with unexpected occurrences that would later be read as signs of a coming disaster.

"I remember that I was watching television."

"I had put the children to bed and I was sleeping."

"I was hanging out on the balcony with some friends."

Yet: "The night of the earthquake, I remember how there was a strange light in the sky, like nothing I had ever seen."

"I'll never forget how extraordinarily hot it was that day."

"The day before the earthquake, there was this thing in the sea, there were so many fish jumping out of the water!"

"I remember having this dream months earlier . . . a dream of me falling from a building."

"I remember this strange humming sound right before the earthquake. I've tried to explain it to people who didn't live the earthquake, but they never understand. It was like the ground began to speak."

Accounts of the events that followed were universally harrowing. While stories of the earthquake are necessarily singular in their convergence of life and event, they are also repetitive in their narrative arc. To give a general sense of this arc, and its singular manifestation, I rely heavily on the account of a woman I call Özlem. Özlem, at the time of the earthquake, was twenty-five years old and living with her husband and two small children in a small town near the earthquake's epicenter. The town would experience some of the most severe damage in the earthquake. Like many small towns in the region, the town center was a concentration of five-story, multiuse apartment buildings clustered around a central commercial area. As with the vast majority of apartment buildings in Turkey at the time, the buildings were constructed of reinforced concrete framing and infilled clay brick walls, with the ground floor left as an open space to accommodate the needs of the businesses and workshops that filled out the building's economy. At the time of the earthquake, Özlem was the neighborhood *muhtar*, a local elected official whose tasks included registering new residents to the neighborhood and issuing residency permits. Özlem's account not only captures recurrent experiences and conventions of stories of the earthquake, but it also provides, given her work as *muhtar*, insights into a series of post-earthquake dynamics that cut across the neighborhood, town, and region.

As with most stories of the earthquake, Özlem's begins on August 17, 1999, at precisely 3:02 a.m.:

> When the earthquake hit, I jumped out of bed. I remember the moment that the electricity went out. I had gone to bed at 2:45, so I had not yet fallen asleep. I got out of bed and went into the living room. When I entered the room, I could see the wall falling. My brother-in-law was yelling, "Where are you going? The coat rack is blocking the door." I told him that I'd climb over it. And then I fell into it. It's as if I lived my entire life in forty-five seconds. I went back in. I told my brother-in-law that I was going to go down the long hallway, to open the window to see what's happening. He told me to say a prayer, because we were going to die. It's the end of the world [*kıyamet kopuyor*]. The house was swaying so much. It seemed as if those forty-five seconds lasted forty-five minutes.

Because the earthquake happened in the middle of the night, many of the stories of the earthquake are stories of being suddenly awoken, and running—still groggy and disoriented—through a dark apartment as floors heaved and walls began to give way.

As did others, Özlem dwelled on the scene of a neighborhood collapsing. She scrambled down the hall and looked out the window to see nearby buildings tilt, then slide out of view. "I opened the window," recalled Özlem, "and

I could see the building next to us. I knew that my father was in the building, as well as my uncle's son. I watched as the seven-story building collapsed." Özlem, like others, was struck by the sound of the collapsing building. There was no sudden crash, as she expected, but rather a slow, grinding descent of concrete—followed, soon after, by an enormous, silent cloud of dust rising up from the ground.

Özlem and her brother-in-law, unable to open the building's front door, jumped off their balcony. Outside of a faint glow on the horizon—created by the burning oil refinery across the water—the area fell into darkness as electricity to the region was interrupted. The intensity of the darkness following the earthquake was a regular theme in interviews: "The darkness was like no darkness we knew. It was like being in a deep pit." People described the terror of trying to orient themselves in the darkness as the area became enveloped in a choking cloud of dust. Özlem knew that her arm was severely injured—she could feel the wetness of the blood running down her arm—but she could not see the extent of her injury. She would injure herself further as she stumbled in the darkness through the debris scattered across the road.

Once clear of the rubble, neighbors and relatives—many still wearing their night clothes—began gathering in the streets, trying to determine what had happened, who was accounted for, and who might still be trapped in their buildings:

> There were people running from the wreckage, and fifteen to twenty minutes later, my uncle came. And I kept waiting. Neither my mother nor my father came. Nobody from our family came. We gathered [on the street] together like a clutch of chicks. My aunt joined us, and I kept telling her that something had happened to my parents. My uncle, despite having been across from the building, wouldn't tell me anything. I told them that they were lying, that my mom had entered the top floor of the building.

Over the following two weeks, Özlem would learn about the death of thirteen close relatives in the earthquake, including her parents and younger sister.

The lack of light seemed to intensify other senses, as a distinctive sonic landscape emerged amid the darkness and destruction: "Thankfully, we made it down. And there was only the sound of screaming. Nothing else.

Screaming. We couldn't see anything in the darkness, in the cloud of dust. You couldn't tell who you were holding, whose hand you were grabbing, who you were helping." "When I came down, I couldn't see a thing. Cars were honking their horns. There was the sound of ambulance sirens. The sound of people screaming was rising from the wreckage." Stories from those trapped beneath the rubble describe a parallel, subterranean soundscape forming in the destruction—a coming to consciousness amid darkness and silence, soon broken by the sounds of others all around also trapped in the rubble. As one survivor who spent three days under the rubble later wrote: "I wasn't hearing anything. It was silent. Then the timid and feeble sounds of human moaning began to slowly increase. At first, it was the feeble moaning of the deepest pain, like the timidity of a person awaiting their executioner. The sounds affected one another and began to grow into screams. There were sounds coming from everywhere. It wasn't rubble, it was as if the building itself was wounded."[4] As the sounds grew, indistinct sounds of human pain became the screams and cries of familiar voices—of aunts, cousins, and neighbors also trapped in the rubble. The chorus of pain and desperation would gradually recede as the night wore on, as one voice after another fell silent.

The earthquake also produced its own moments of strange beauty, moments that appeared regularly in stories of survivors. As another woman—twenty-four years old, like Özlem, and living in the same town—described the earthquake:

> As the building shook, my child's head was being tossed back and forth. I was being thrown about, thrown up again the wall. I wrapped my child's head so that it wouldn't be struck, and then we ran out of the building. When we looked around, in every direction there was wreckage, dust, and the sound of screaming. And the stars were interesting. It was as if you could hold them in your hand. It was like they were close enough that you could catch them. And there was such a wonderful shooting star. This was after we had gotten out of the building, and we were trying to figure out what was going on. Everyone was in such a panic, nobody understood what had happened. At some point—who knows how much time had passed—we realized that there had been an earthquake.

Others would describe with similar awe extraordinary moments of unexpected beauty amid the ruins—stories of a wondrous sky, the profound darkness and silence of the city, the soothing sounds of the sea.

As the darkness gave way to morning light, a grim and disorienting scene came into view. The destruction was vast. Twenty-four thousand homes were estimated to have been destroyed in the town where Özlem lived. The destruction would continue to mount, as buildings that survived the initial earthquake gave way, days later, to the aftershocks. In towns along the coast, entire neighborhoods were flattened into fields of concrete. Özlem described an utterly transformed landscape and horizon:

> When it became light outside, I looked around. Where was this? My house was unrecognizable. My own street was unrecognizable. There was nothing. No apartment complexes remained, no large buildings remained. They all collapsed. Many fell into the sea. It wasn't so much that they collapsed, but it was like a knife sliced through them, and they slid into the sea. Wherever I went, there were piles, heaps of debris. There were the sounds of people screaming, yelling, wanting help. If you've never lived through an earthquake, you don't know what you'll do . . . you'll never know what sorts of capacities you have, or don't have.

Echoing Özlem, stories of the earthquake's immediate aftermath overflow with a profound sense of disorientation—buildings suddenly erased from the horizon, shorelines radically altered, streetscapes remade. That which anchored and oriented everyday existence had suddenly been undone.

This, together with the persistent aftershocks and tremors, gave rise to an intense and, for some, unbearable anxiety about the instability of the world. The ground one walked on could no longer be trusted. Yet, people walked, and walked. Stories from the earthquake recount days and days of walking. Walking the streets in a state of shock, looking for relatives and friends. Walking the city looking for water and food. Walking to a nearby village looking for a safe place to rest. Walking to a neighboring town to look for information. Relatives in Istanbul walking to the area in search of relatives. "I'll never forget," recalled a woman I met in the town of Gölcük, "how eight hours later, as I'm walking around, I notice that my feet are really hurting. 'Why are my feet hurting so much?' I asked myself. I look and see that the bottoms of my feet are all cut up. There are pieces of glass still in my foot."

INTERLUDE
Victim, Survivor, Remainder

Throughout this project, I have struggled with how to describe, collectively and anonymously, many of the people discussed in this book. How to describe them in a way that doesn't render their lives little more than effects of the earthquake? How to convey their agency as historical subjects whose lives were indelibly marked, but not fully determined, by the earthquake? In turn, how to portray their suffering without slipping into sentimentality or universalisms that obscure the historical specificity of experience?[5] With these questions in mind, the decision about what terms I'd use to generically characterize my interlocutors felt important, a decision that had tangible implications about how I understood pasts and futures to be arranged in their lives. A rich local vocabulary provided plenty of options. The most common term, *depremzede*, combines the Turkish term *deprem* (earthquake) with the suffix *zede* (struck, stricken) and is typically translated as "earthquake victim."[6] One also encounters similar constructions with *afet* (catastrophe), such as *afetzede*, and *felaket* (disaster), as in *felaketzede*. In public commemorations and memorials, an individual who died in the earthquake is also frequently characterized as a *şehit* (martyr), with all its sacrificial connotations. The majority of the people I interviewed for this project disliked both *depremzede* and *şehit*. They saw the first as connoting a helpless passivity that positioned them as objects of pity, and the second as carrying religious and nationalistic connotations that overshadowed the more mundane struggles that characterized the lives of those who survived. Instead, my interlocutors frequently spoke about *depremi yaşayanlar* (those who lived through the earthquake) or *geride kalanlar* (literally, those who were left behind). I agree that these latter phrases do a better job of capturing the dynamics at play here, and they have been instrumental in my framing of this book. Yet, I decided that referring in each instance to "those who were left behind" was unwieldy and distracting. I therefore move between different concepts throughout the book, although I most commonly use the term *survivor* as an imperfect translation of *geride kalan*.

Aftermath: Duration

Narratives chronicling the night of August 17 typically offered precise, detailed descriptions of the moment of the earthquake and its immediate aftermath. Accounts of the ensuing days and weeks—especially the period between the earthquake and the establishment of tent cities over the ensuing weeks—were, in contrast, narrated as a blur of days, dates, and happenings. They are narratives of seemingly undifferentiated time, or eventless duration, that lack firm temporal coordinates. Days and weeks flow into one another. The timing of particular developments is difficult to pin down. "It wasn't clear when it was night or when it was daytime. I didn't sit around idle at all. News would come that the sound of a person was heard. It didn't matter if it was three in the morning, five in the morning, you go. You'd work, you'd direct people, you'd provide whatever support was needed."

Like Özlem, many described life becoming organized by and around the rubble. Those able to would spend every waking hour amid the rubble: digging through the debris, sometimes with bare hands, in search of survivors; helping neighbors and relatives clear their belongings from their destroyed homes; searching the rubble for material to build shelter for themselves and neighbors; looking for fuel for the construction equipment being used for search-and-rescue; keeping guard over destroyed homes to protect against robbers; keeping track of elderly neighbors; assisting people who came to the region looking for missing relatives; distributing gloves and masks, and food and water, to volunteers. Afraid to pause, let alone sleep, many residents recount this period as one of continuous work, interrupted only by an occasional nap in a field before they returned again to the rubble.

These were busy, urgent days. Özlem, like many others, found refuge in this work. "When I entered the rubble, I forgot that I myself was a victim of the earthquake." Yet, the intensity of this work exacted a price on survivors. Accounts of these sorts of rescue efforts map a range of reactions familiar to scholars of disaster—alternating and overlapping feelings of numbness, despair, confusion, hopelessness, and impotence in the face of the destruction. Residents searching for survivors would soon need their own assistance, as they began to collapse from exhaustion and dehydration.

Where some found refuge in searching for survivors, others wandered. Mustafa, a retired navy officer whose home was destroyed in the earthquake, and whose wife was seven months pregnant when the earthquake struck, described the period after the earthquake as a prolonged state of shock, during which he wandered the ruins of the city:

> It's like we weren't really there. We were in shock. . . . We were in such a state of shock that we were just wandering around, from one area to another, seeing destruction here, and destruction here, and destruction here. There wasn't really any possibility for us to help, because there wasn't any activity, there wasn't anything. . . . We were in shock. For the next day or two, we slept in a car, we slept outside. After that, we went to Istanbul. I have a brother-in-law there and we thought that we could perhaps rest there. It was bad there too. He also didn't have any space.

Mustafa's wife would travel with his brother-in-law back to the family's home in Malatya, a large city more than a thousand kilometers to the east. Mustafa returned to the earthquake zone to guard their destroyed home.

Days passed and naps in open fields and empty lots turned into something more permanent, as those left behind carved domestic scenes out of public spaces: "You're eating and drinking in the street, you're meeting all of your needs amid the dust and debris. There's not even a bathroom. After a few days, we dug a hole for a toilet and made three walls around it with stakes and sheets." Tarps were strung between trees and makeshift beds fashioned, as supplies of clean water and cooking fuel started arriving. Meanwhile, large fields began to be cleared to make room for the truckloads of tents on their way to the earthquake zone. The tents would soon arrive, but many, especially those provided by the state, would be of such poor quality that they provided little shelter from the heavy rains that soon passed through the region. And with the rains came rumors—of thieves descending on the area and of an "organ mafia" harvesting organs from orphaned children and those trapped alive in the rubble.

As with others, Mustafa was afraid to leave his house unattended. He was also afraid to enter it: "You were afraid to enter your house. You go into your house, but you run out, because you're afraid. You're afraid of your own house, you're afraid of your own neighborhood. There could be an earthquake any minute while you're inside. There were so many aftershocks. That is, when you'd sit down, you would feel one hit you from below, and you'd think it was another earthquake." Geological events, it turns out, have blurry boundaries. That is, the Marmara Earthquake didn't end on August 17, 1999, after forty-five seconds. According to reports, there were more than two thousand aftershocks in the months that followed—an average of twelve per day. Yet, as Mustafa hints, the difference between an earthquake and an aftershock isn't always clear—especially when some of the tremors that followed the Marmara Earthquake measured 5.8 on the Richter scale.[7] For those who had recently lived and survived the Marmara Earthquake, how to know, in the moment, if the trembling one was feeling would end momentarily, or if it was the beginning of something bigger? When another large earthquake struck a few months later in a nearby city (approximately a hundred kilometers east of the first), many of the reported deaths—which, in the end, would total more than a thousand—were attributed to panic, as people jumped from their balconies for fear that the building would collapse.

Nechronology

The flow of time in stories of the earthquake is recurrently structured not so much by the temporality of calendars—the passage of days, weeks, months—than by the rhythm of death, a *nechronology* that was at once corporeal and olfactory. This temporality of death, which also became a tempo of living, was marked by the number of days after the earthquake that a family member's body was pulled from the rubble, the time it took for the stench of rotting flesh to envelop and then clear the city, the day of the makeshift funeral for a parent, sibling, or friend. For Özlem, this period would stretch on for nearly two months. "We had been working for the previous fifty-two days. We were working with a bulldozer up until the fifty-second day. On the fifty-second day, we pulled out our last body. After that, they ended their work. We weren't going to find any bodies after that." For the family and friends of the many bodies that were never found, this nechronology would remain open, like a wound in time.

Before even a semblance of stable housing could be established, survivors struggled not only in their efforts to find the living but also to deal with death. With the last weeks of summer ahead, the bodies trapped in the rubble quickly began to decompose. The putrid odor—of both human and nonhuman bodies—consumed the entire area: "It smelled bad, everywhere you went. You couldn't escape it." The smell was not merely nauseating and inescapable. It was also a sign of a bad death. In accords with Muslim conventions, the burial of the deceased should occur as soon as possible after death.[8] It was common, before the earthquake, for the deceased to be washed, prepared for burial, and buried within twenty-four hours of death. The challenge of accessing the dead trapped under the rubble, and the sheer scale of death, rendered this unfeasible. Further complicating the desire for a good death was the disrupted regional transportation and, with it, the shortage of supplies reaching the area. "I saw so much," recounted a middle-aged woman who grew up in Gölcük, "I saw so many dead bodies pulled from the rubble. Because of the heat and constriction, they were swollen and black and blue. And there was no water to wash the bodies for the funerals. Naturally, because they were trapped under the rubble, and their bodies had swollen, the clothing on the bodies was in tatters at the funerals. There was nothing to wrap the bodies in. As you know, because of our beliefs, we clean and enshroud bodies for funerals. This is something that needs to be done. But it couldn't be done."

The scale of death, and thus corpses, overwhelmed local capacity. As officials struggled to secure sufficient water to wash bodies and perform ablutions, acquire fabric to shroud the dead, and coffins for their burial, bodies began to accumulate. A local ice-skating rink—which had been built just before the earthquake, with the hope of making the provincial capital into an international center for ice hockey in Turkey—was transformed into a makeshift morgue for unidentified bodies. Residents describe (and newspaper images relay) a macabre scene of dead bodies—covered in an assortment of sheets, blankets, and plastic (there was also a shortage of body bags)—lined up in rows along the ice. Visiting the rink in search of missing relatives was one of those scenes that punctuated nearly all interviews.

Meanwhile, religious personnel struggled to keep up with the demand for burial services. The Ministry of Religious Affairs would release a set of revised guidelines to accommodate the death toll—notifying religious personnel that it was permissible to perform ablutions with dry earth if no water was available, that a single sheet was sufficient for shrouding bodies, and that mass graves could be mixed gender, so long as there was at least a small amount of soil between bodies. For religious personnel working in the region, the pace of preparing bodies for burial, leading prayers, burying the deceased, and consoling families—as they themselves struggled with the loss of family and friends in the earthquake—was overwhelming. Indeed, they would become regular visitors to the psychiatrists and psychologists entering the region at the time.[9]

The Smell of a Rotting State

As hundreds of thousands of people like Özlem struggled in the earthquake's aftermath—digging through the rubble, struggling to get food and water, burying friends and relatives, passing nights outdoors unable to sleep because of nightmares—the prime minister, Bülent Ecevit, downplayed the scope of the disaster. He announced to a worried and anxious public that the situation was under control and that the state was responding to the disaster. Firsthand accounts from the earthquake region painted a starkly different picture. Initial relief efforts were—if present at all—slow, uncoordinated, and wildly inadequate. The state seemed to have no concrete plans for such a situation, despite the region's well-documented history of earthquakes. Although there is much to be said about the state's response to the earthquake—which I return to in the following chapters—I want to acknowledge here how the experience of living through the earthquake was in part also an experience of feeling betrayed by a state that had failed to fulfill its promises in a time of desperate need.

The smells emerging from the ruins of the earthquake provided new idioms for narrating such experiences. A column published four days after the earthquake, in the conservative newspaper *Yeni Şafak*, is typical of the commentaries appearing in the wake of the earthquake. Under the title "We Were Victims of the State," the author writes:

> İzmit smells of corpses. In Adapazarı, 5,000 people lie under the rubble. Değirmendere has been erased from the map. Yalova was broken in half. In Gölcük, no stone remains unturned. We are unable to get any information from a number of areas. . . . And we learn that they are unable to transfer to the region those with the capacities [to help with the rescue operations]—they are not able to send cranes, or bread, or water. The state is not there. The part of the state that is there is doing nothing more than making the work more difficult. . . . Yes, İzmit smells. But, everywhere in this country, the state smells. This earthquake has destroyed the foundation of the state.[10]

As this suggests, the failures of the state were not only a matter of inadequate services and equipment but also the failure of a particular idea of the state. The significance of this cannot be overstated. Since the founding of Turkey in 1923, the state had cultivated a model of citizenship that idealized itself as the ultimate protector and guardian of its dependent subjects. Although cracks were becoming visible in this nationalist contract during the 1990s (they had, of course, always been there, especially for those who did not fit into the vision of an ethnically and religiously homogeneous national body), the idea of a paternalistic state continued to be a site of intense political investment. The experience of the earthquake for many was the breaking of this contract. The state was rotten.

In contrast to the state's response, international disaster relief agencies began arriving almost immediately. Search-and-rescue teams poured into the earthquake zone—from Hungary, Russia, Israel, France, South Korea, Iceland, Egypt, Switzerland, and the United States. The sounds of heavy machinery quickly replaced the silence. The International Federation of Red Cross and Red Crescent Societies joined the Turkish Red Crescent Society to begin distributing food, water, tents, and supplies. Waves of humanitarian organizations, primarily, though not exclusively, from western Europe, followed to provide clean water, medical care, food, and shelter—a relief effort that would grow exponentially as days passed. Mobile health units and open-air clinics—with beds and IVs filling empty lots—gave way to large medical tents. With the local medical infrastructure in ruins (and much of the region's stock of medications and medical equipment literally under rubble), many of the injured would be transferred to other medical facilities—the most urgent to Istanbul, and others back to hospitals in their home provinces.

The condition of regional roads and rail lines made movement difficult. The earthquake had cut a long chasm, at places more than five meters wide, through many of the major roads. Leaving the region by vehicle was further complicated by the shortage of fuel, as well as the disruption of the banking system. Although the prime minister would blame the conditions of the roads for the state's absence, it was not lost on those watching the disaster unfold on television that news crews seemed to have little problem getting to the area. Indeed, the contrast between the media's presence and the government's absence was jarring. Among the many milestones marked by the earthquake, it proved an important moment in the history of corporate media in Turkey, as the recently privatized media industry—and rapidly multiplying television stations—offered uninterrupted, firsthand coverage from the region. The Marmara Earthquake would thus become the first major disaster of a mass-mediated era in Turkey, and the public it called forth was angry.[11] As the journalist Stephen Kinzer described in a series of articles written from the region, "Millions were glued to their screens, watching scenes of heartrending devastation and suffering along with streams of interviews with enraged survivors, the intensity of whose anger was shocking in a country where exaggerated respect for the state has always been part of the national psychology."

Comings and Goings

For residents who remained in the region, an everyday gradually took shape amid the ruins. Routines formed as large fields transformed into sprawling tent settlements. Systems for distributing food and water and for handling waste were established. Settlements began to receive regular electricity. Gendered divisions of familial labor adapted to new conditions—as able-bodied men spent the day searching the rubble and assisting rescue teams as women worked to create a makeshift domestic space in vacant lots and open fields. NGOs began setting up schools for children living in the tent cities—schools that were as much to establish a sense of normalcy for children as to create a sense of purpose for teachers also living in the tent settlements.

Tent cities multiplied, and as hundreds of thousands of people displaced by the earthquake sought shelter, a massive reconfiguration of the regional population was set in motion. Nearby villages swelled:

> In the village, there were forty or fifty people at the table eating. It was crowded. People were spending the night in houses, and others were staying in tents. Everywhere was filled with tents. Homes were filled. People would get up and go [in the morning] to search their destroyed homes, to pull their belongings from their homes. They would go to search for those who had died and help pull them from the rubble. Whenever I stayed the night in the village, there would be funerals. Those days, there wasn't any washing, there wasn't anything. And the putrid smell of people. For this reason, I cannot forget the earthquake.

For those without relatives nearby, the earthquake sent survivors farther afield. The post-earthquake displacement brought back into the open vast networks of migration that had led people, decades earlier, from the countryside to Istanbul and other towns and cities in western Turkey. Ties and routes that had been maintained since those early waves of migration—through regular returns for seasonal harvests and the commemoration of births, marriages, and deaths—grew again with those displaced by the earthquake. In that many of these routes passed through the neighborhood in Ankara where I was living at the time, I experienced this post-earthquake migration as a disorienting oscillation between watching news coverage of rescue efforts on television and welcoming those fleeing the earthquake region into the homes of friends and neighbors. Importantly, the enormous movement of populations triggered by the earthquake was not merely a dispersal of bodies but also a dispersal of wounds—physical and psychic—across the country, into settings where people had a limited understanding of what these new arrivals had recently experienced. With this, the disaster would become, very tangibly, a national disaster.

For those who remained in the region, the passing of time brought with it a series of slow transitions in living conditions. By the end of the year, as a long summer gave way to winter, 150,000 people were living in tent settlements scattered across the area.[12] In the year to follow, emergency shelters became temporary housing, which gradually transformed into something more permanent.[13] Against the wishes of a majority of residents—who wanted financial support to rebuild their homes—the state invested enormous sums into contracts with construction firms to build thousands of prefabricated homes. A year after the earthquake, more than 130,000 people were living in approximately 40,000 prefabricated buildings spread across eighty sites in the region.[14]

Although these settlements were a source of great profit for local construction firms (many of which were implicated in the destruction caused by the earthquake), they proved particularly ill suited for the forms of community life that had been disrupted by the earthquake. These settlements were defined less by the needs of residents than by the constraints of economic efficiency and abstract geometry. With precisely proportioned homes divided by narrow gaps and aligned in perfect rows, the new settlements created a range of obstacles to reestablishing familial and communal sociability. From seemingly simple oversights—such as not placing a window on the front of buildings, so that residents could see who was visiting—to foreseeable problems concerning the lack of privacy within and between buildings, as well as a lack of social spaces for gathering,[15] decisions about the design and arrangement of homes would actively work against people's efforts to begin rebuilding their lives. In the end, the cost of constructing prefabricated homes was roughly half the cost of building new permanent homes for everyone. Within a decade, they would be little more than fields of cement foundations dotting the region.

This post-earthquake period of development would remake the material and social topography of the region. With a death toll well above 20,000 people, a noticeable proportion of the population was simply gone. In Gölcük alone, more than 5 percent of the population died in the earthquake.[16] In turn, many more survivors fled the region, never to come back. The area was, if only temporarily, far less crowded than it had been on August 16, 1999. In time, however, the population would begin to grow. The earthquake and ensuing exodus of residents had created a precipitous drop in property values, which, together with the rebuilding and expansion of factories, would attract a countermovement of migration back into the region. By 2007, when I began visiting the region regularly, the provincial population had already surpassed its pre-earthquake level, and little visibly remained of the earthquake.

The aim of this chapter has been to begin introducing some of the prominent experiential dimensions of the Marmara Earthquake, as an initial effort to convey its world-transforming effects. Privileging the experiential as a starting point was intended not only to orient the reader but also to signal that the bodily and affective experience of the earthquake would prove, in the years to follow, a defining legacy of the earthquake, as well as a vital site of return. Earthquake survivors—decades later—repeatedly returned to this sensorial register of disaster, for it was the bodily and affective remainders of the disaster that continued to reverberate in everyday lives. It was also the defining terrain over which the psychiatrists and psychologists entering the region would stake their expert claims. With that said, beginning an account of the Marmara Earthquake through stories of those who lived it carries its own risks. Focusing too closely on what it was like to live the earthquake, for instance, runs the risk of obscuring those broader structural forces and historical conditions through which these experiences took shape, and which rendered particular people vulnerable to disaster. At the same time, privileging an experiential account of disaster also risks missing the countless ways that the disaster, as an exceptional event, was both indebted to and an extension of those everyday if uneventful forces that profoundly shaped people's experiences of the earthquake. Building an analysis situated at this intersection of the exceptional and the everyday, the experiential and the structural, is a central preoccupation of this book, which I begin exploring in more detail in the next chapter.

TWO

A Disaster in the Making

As has been long recognized, "natural disasters" are anything but natural.[1] The Marmara Earthquake was no different. The destruction of lives and property was neither indiscriminate nor solely a result of the earthquake's seismic activity. An entrenched logic preceded the earthquake, one that cleared the way for the disaster's movement through the region. There was, in other words, a cruel yet predictable history being revealed by the spatial distribution of injury and death, and in the trajectories of lives in the years to follow. In this chapter, I step back from the scene of the earthquake's devastation to sketch out some of the larger forces and histories that came together with the earthquake's seismic activity to occasion its distinctive distribution of mortality and destruction. Drawing inspiration from studies of environmental racism and disaster vulnerability—which explore, broadly speaking, how communities and populations are unequally exposed to risk, injury, and death[2]—I offer a broad overview of the sorts of political, economic, and geological forces that charted the lives and deaths of thousands of people before and after the earthquake. Put differently, I am interested in considering how Özlem's experiences of the earthquake—which organized much of the preceding chapter's discussion—were at once idiosyncratic and all too common.

As I began to read deeply into the history of the region, and situate lives such as Özlem's in this history, it became increasingly difficult to think of the Marmara Earthquake in the singular. Indeed, to speak of the earthquake in terms of an "it" (that "did" something to someone) came to feel both insufficient and excessive, as granting too much coherence and agency to the lived enormity of the earthquake. Here, "the earthquake" came into view less as a distinct event with clear (geographic or temporal) boundaries than as a complex and open-ended convergence of multiple processes that long preceded and extended far beyond the earthquake. With this in mind, my discussion of the earthquake in this chapter pushes against a set of defining assumptions that underlie conventional approaches to disaster and crisis, whose analytic frames are built around an understanding of events such as the Marmara Earthquake as being exceptional, bounded, and set apart from the everyday. In this chapter, I approach the Marmara Earthquake not so much as a coherent object of analysis than as an amorphous and deadly gathering of multiple intersecting and interactive forces, each and all a long time in the making.

Whereas the previous chapter sought to convey the experiential specificity of the earthquake, I now want to consider how it also belongs to history. But what history or histories does this event belong to? What histories do we need to grasp in order to understand the patterns of loss, life, and destruction that the earthquake occasioned? This chapter ranges widely, and in many places superficially, in an effort to provide a broad introduction to the multiple histories at play here. I limit the discussion at this point to three: the region's interconnected history of geological activity and human mobility; the historical interweaving of construction technologies, building regulation, and national economic development; and a national and regional history of disaster management.

Geology, Geography, Industry

That which makes for many of Turkey's scenic vistas—mountains dropping precipitously into glimmering seas, enormous ecological diversity along verdant coastlines, the arid beauty of eastern Turkey's rugged mountains—are all signs of its geological plasticity. Wedged at the convergence of what geologists refer to as the Eurasian, African, and Arabian Plates, Turkey covers a small but volatile tectonic plate that makes the country one of the most seismically active regions of the world. More than 90 percent of the country faces the threat of earthquakes. Not surprisingly, the Marmara Earthquake was not the first earthquake in the area. Almost three centuries before, in 1719, an earthquake along the eastern edge of the Gulf of İzmit destroyed virtually every structure along the coast. The earthquake left 80 percent of the city of İzmit in ruins, including its major shipyard. In 1939, on the eastern end of the North Anatolian fault, a 7.8 magnitude earthquake struck in the city of Erzincan, killing more than 30,000 residents. Subsequently, between 1942 and 1967, the region would experience periodic earthquakes along the same fault—moving, erratically, closer to the Gulf of İzmit.[3] In the context of the region's long history of seismic activity,[4] these are all recent events. Stories of enormously destructive earthquakes reach far back into antiquity. As with the region's ecological beauty, the striking ruins of past empires that one finds in Turkey are not merely evidence of a history of conquest and empire building, but also a history of enormous geological volatility.

Along with this geological account of the region moves an interwoven history of human settlement and economic activity. To understand the scale and pattern of the Marmara Earthquake's destruction, as well as the humanitarian attention that the earthquake attracted, it is critical to understand how, over the course of the twentieth century, the area became the most densely populated and heavily industrialized region of the country. İzmit, the regional capital at the time of the earthquake, has long been a center of commerce. Formerly known by its Greek name, Nicomedia, İzmit's history—which extends back to at least the third century BCE—can be narrated as a succession of empires and disasters. The city's early growth as the eastern capital of the Roman Empire would be interrupted by a massive earthquake and subsequent fire that reduced it to ruins in 358. With its rebuilding, the city remained under Byzantine rule until the eleventh century. Over the ensuing eight centuries, the city would fall under the control of successive empires, shifting between Seljuk, Byzantine, and Ottoman rule, before being briefly occupied by the United Kingdom after World War I. The Turkish military took control of the region during the War of Independence (1919–1923), a transfer of control that was marked by yet another catastrophe, namely the massacre of 12,000 local Greek and Armenian residents.

The history that leads up to the region's contemporary status as a national industrial center begins in earnest in the early twentieth century, with the near-total deforestation of the area to meet the growing market for cheap charcoal. This would set the course, in the decades to come, for a fossil-fuel intensive investment in regional economic development, one that later centered on chemical production. By the time of the Marmara Earthquake, the area was regarded as the nation's industrial heartland. The wetlands in the region had long been drained, expanding the city of İzmit and its industry onto fertile (and unstable) land. Anchoring this industrial expansion, İzmit became home to the largest chemical refinery in the country, the Tüpraş Petroleum Refinery, which produces a third of the nation's petroleum and petrochemical products. In addition to dozens of other chemical production facilities, İzmit and the surrounding towns also became centers for a range of national and transnational corporate production facilities. Today, the region is home to factories for Ford, Toyota, Siemens, Goodyear, Pirelli Tires, Unilever, and scores of smaller factories fabricating products that feed into global supply chains. By some estimates, the province, at the time of the earthquake, contained approximately 75 percent of Turkey's industrial facilities and was responsible for nearly 30 percent of the country's gross domestic product.[5]

This history of settlement and industrial development would leave behind, by the time of the earthquake (and into the present), a large provincial capital and series of small towns ringing the Gulf of İzmit. By 1999, the provincial capital, İzmit, had a population of approximately 285,000 people, with a provincial population of 1.2 million people. The smaller towns along the coast—interconnected with İzmit by a system of municipal buses, private minibuses, and ferries—had populations ranging from 20,000 to 50,000. The earthquake region as a whole—stretching from Istanbul (one hundred kilometers west of İzmit) to Adapazarı (fifty kilometers east of İzmit)—was similarly interconnected by a vast network of minibuses and intercity buses.

Reflecting its economic development, the region experienced divergent patterns of human mobility. Moving in one direction—typically from the eastern provinces to the urban centers of the west—the industrialization and urbanization of the region that began accelerating in the mid-twentieth century drew a substantial number of migrants from central and eastern Turkey seeking relatively stable and well-paying factory jobs. Although Istanbul was a primary destination for many migrants, İzmit also exerted a strong pull. A corollary wave of labor migration followed, to provide the range of services needed to support the living and consumer habits of a growing regional population—staffing department stores and boutiques, markets and grocery stores, cafés and restaurants, office and home-cleaning services, and private security firms. At the time of the earthquake, the majority of the workers not employed in the nearby factories earned livings as small enterprise workers, local tradesmen, domestic workers, and public workers and civil servants.[6]

Alongside these patterns of labor migration—emerging from interconnected economic conditions and reflecting the explosive growth of Istanbul across the second half of the twentieth century—was a movement of people in the opposite direction, typically from the wealthy suburbs of Istanbul eastward. During the 1990s, as Turkey's economy was opened to the global economy, capital became increasingly urbanized and the fortunes of the wealthy and upper-middle-class residents of Istanbul improved markedly. This coincided with an overall expansion of the middle class and, with it, changing class tastes and consumption habits. A growing desire for seasonal and weekend leisure migrations—to escape the bustle and stresses of city life—spurred a small construction boom in coastal towns near Istanbul. Towns such as Yalova, a short ferry ride from Istanbul, became a popular site for weekend and summer vacation homes. This seasonal vacation migration and the timing of the earthquake—in August, the most popular month for vacationing—thus account for one of the curiosities of the earthquake's impact, namely, the way that the aggregate class profile of earthquake victims was pulled toward the higher end of the socioeconomic scale by the relative wealth of these itinerant residents of the region—even if, overall, poor and working-class residents accounted for the vast majority of deaths.

This history of industry and human mobility rendered the region and its residents vulnerable in particular ways to the Marmara Earthquake. The investment in industrial production as a means of regional development, for instance, would give the disaster one of its distinctive features. What had already been a long, slow ecological catastrophe—with the waste output from the local factories and refineries making the Gulf of Izmit into one of the most polluted sites in the region[7]—the earthquake set off a massive chemical fire at the Tüpraş plant. By the time the fire was put out, it had burned for four days and consumed six chemical storage tanks.[8] In turn, the rapid population growth in the region, together with lax state regulation and entrenched corruption in the construction industry, had led to the proliferation of poorly built apartment blocks that extended the city onto unstable soil created by drained swamps. In turn, the history of human transience and economic development in the region left residents with limited social memory of the region's history of earthquakes and the more recent filling in of wetlands. Taken together, this combination of migration, settlement, and economic development that the region experienced across the twentieth century would play a determining role in the earthquake's destructive and deadly impact.

This geography of national development also helps explain the scale of the humanitarian response to the earthquake. The infrastructure of roads, highways, and ports that carried goods out of the region into global supply chains would greatly facilitate the movement of foreign humanitarian organizations in the opposite direction. Beyond this infrastructural accessibility, the pull of humanitarian compassion to the region was also enabled by interlocking visions of racialized deservedness. On the one hand, especially for residents of nearby Istanbul, the proximity and familiarity of earthquake survivors certainly contributed to the outpouring of assistance. Had the earthquake occurred in a remote Kurdish town in eastern Turkey—as has happened numerous times over the past century—the intensity of public concern would surely not have been as significant, nor the humanitarian response as robust. On the other hand, for European humanitarian organizations working outside these local frameworks of racialized deservedness, Turkey fit easily into the imaginative horizons of humanitarian action. As a nation of nonwhite Muslims, the suffering of earthquake survivors was sufficiently distant and the victims sufficiently different to transform compassion to humanitarian action.[9]

To Drown in an Earthquake

Stories of the earthquake describe the terror not only of the violent shaking of the ground but also of long stretches of the coastline breaking off and sinking into the sea. "Entire buildings slid into the sea," one resident recalled, "and there are dead bodies they have yet to remove. They are still there." More than five hundred people are estimated to have drowned in the earthquake. To understand this sort of gruesome fate—and how it was that entire blocks of towns were seemingly untouched by the earthquake while others were reduced to piles of shattered glass, brick, and rebar—I want to turn briefly to how histories of construction technology, building regulation, and national economic development converged to set the stage for the Marmara Earthquake's destruction.

For even the casual observer, the pattern of devastation after the earthquake was not random. While the destruction tracked along the fault line, other patterns were also discernible amid the ruins. Perhaps the most prominent pattern emerged out of the interaction between regional home construction techniques and long-standing corruption among local developers and contractors. Unlike older regional styles of construction—such as timber and masonry, much of which survived the earthquake—the most severely impacted areas consisted of multistory residential buildings made of reinforced concrete frames.[10] The structural integrity of these buildings, which were typically five to seven stories, depended significantly on unreinforced walls made of hollow clay bricks that filled in the reinforced cement framing. Maximizing their profitability, and contributing to their vulnerability, contractors typically reserved the ground floor of multistory buildings for commercial purposes—which tended to be taller spaces that lacked infill walls, so as to increase their flexibility (e.g., retail stores, small-scale production workshops, parking garages). These methods of construction would explain one of the characteristic visual features of the earthquake's destruction, where multistory buildings experienced a succession of floor failures, resulting in entire blocks of multistory buildings flattened into what looked like stacks of pancakes (i.e., "pancake failure").

Despite the vulnerabilities created by these techniques, many of the buildings—and their residents—would have survived had it not been for endemic fraud in the construction industry. Investigations conducted after the earthquake revealed that it was common practice for contractors to mix insufficient cement into their concrete or use salt water drawn from the sea to mix the concrete, both of which significantly weakened the resulting structures. Contractors, seeking to increase profits, and largely unhindered by regulators, further cut corners by hiring poorly trained and underpaid laborers. Not surprisingly, given the scope and pervasiveness of corruption revealed by the earthquake, the contractor—or *müteahhit*—would emerge as one of the great villains of the earthquake.

This corruption was abetted by lax code enforcement and entrenched clientelism between the state, the construction industry, and several professional organizations.[11] While the modern history of disaster in the Ottoman Empire and, subsequently, the Republic of Turkey may have left in its wake a detailed system of building regulations, particularly building codes for high-risk areas,[12] these codes were selectively enforced. The bribing of government regulators by contractors was the proximate cause of selective enforcement, although this also operated within a broader political calculus that worked to incentivize limited regulation. More construction projects meant fewer people unemployed, as well as a steady supply of affordable housing—both of which eased pressure on the state. More transactionally, developers and contractors also regularly mobilized their resources (and workers) to support political parties. In such a context, those charged with the responsibility of inspecting the construction of new buildings—which were local agencies with limited staff and little backing from the national government—were easy targets for wealthy developers and contractors.[13] Meanwhile, local officials and communities were systematically excluded from city and regional planning initiatives.[14] The drive for profits, together with limited government regulation and the exclusion of local communities from planning, would have a predictable result: permission would be regularly granted to developers and contractors to construct buildings on unsuitable sites or with techniques inadequate for the conditions. Vast stretches of recently filled wetlands (with soil that was prone to liquefaction in seismic events, of which there was a long history) would be developed, as large sections of notoriously unstable "reclaimed land" along the shoreline were allowed to be developed for residential purposes.

There was also a larger political economy at work here. The earthquake came on the heels of a decades-long housing boom, one that had been spurred by national policymakers who dreamed of unleashing the productive forces of the population in the name of developing Turkey's economy and society. The prime minister widely regarded as the architect of Turkey's neoliberal reform, Turgut Özal (prime minister from 1983 to 1989), famously sought to free these productive energies by systematically targeting what he regarded as restrictive rules and regulations. Many who sought to capitalize on this new economic order, facing limited options (in terms of both existing industrial infrastructures and levels of workforce education), would turn to the construction industry as a means of entry. Hundreds of new construction companies would appear during this period. The state—driven by the spirit of deregulation and a desire to keep low-income workers employed—allowed, in turn, for the construction industry to flourish with limited restraint. This, together with the rapid urbanization of the country (by 1997, 60 percent of Turkey's population was living in cities, as compared to 18.3 percent in 1945 and 16.4 percent in 1927), created the conditions for the extraordinary growth in new construction throughout the 1990s. These conditions would conspire to create a large housing stock constructed of substandard concrete on top of shallow foundations on unstable soil in communities with very limited authority. This combination of greed, corruption, economic policy, and criminal failure on the part of the state would set a stage for the massive loss of life and property when the ground began to shake on August 17, 1999. Simply put, as Penny Green has aptly observed, the Marmara Earthquake was a "disaster by design."[15]

Devlet Baba: Administrating Disaster

"The Image of 'Father State' Has Collapsed" (*"Devlet Baba" İmajı Çöktü*), announced the newspaper columnist Nur İncioğlu in the wake of the Marmara Earthquake, conjuring a scene of a paternalistic state left in ruins. Like no other event in Turkey's modern history, the Marmara Earthquake posed a decisive challenge to the idea of the state as a protective guardian of its dependent subjects—a political fantasy that had been carefully and diligently cultivated since the founding of the republic in 1923.[16] With this in mind, I turn in this section to consider how the state's response to the Marmara Earthquake belongs to a long national history of disaster management. I want to begin, however, not with the state's (many) failures but with a more fundamental question: Why did people expect so much from the state? Where did these desires and demands for protection and intervention come from? To begin to answer these questions, and thus sketch out another critical aspect of the historical conditions of disaster in Turkey, we need to situate the Marmara Earthquake not merely within the ideological history of Turkish nationalism but also within a wider political history of the modernization of disaster.

Marie-Hélène Huet has argued that the history of the "modernization" of disaster is a story of its increasing rationalization. For Huet, coincident with the advent of the Age of Reason—itself inaugurated by disaster, namely the Lisbon earthquake of 1755—disasters began to lose their mythic and tragic dimension to become objects of science and reason. "The history of disasters is thus also the history of humans wresting from the heavens the source and reason of their misfortunes."[17] With this shifting conceptualization of disasters—from signs of divine wonder or vengeance (a sign of God's wrath, a test, a lesson, an opportunity to become closer to God) to "natural events"—they simultaneously became problems of political administration. While I am leery of such sweeping historical accounts of societal transformation—for disasters are still seen by many as sources and signs of wonder, as well as divine vengeance—I want to follow Huet by drawing particular attention to the political administration of disaster as the critical characteristic of modern disasters. As Huet describes, the emergence of disasters as administrative problems is a transformation that unfolds across the European continent throughout the eighteenth and nineteenth centuries, as the containment of disasters—earthquakes, floods, epidemics—was more and more approached as a threat to the stability of political orders and thus was folded into the administrative responsibilities of the state. The more the desire to control "nature" deepened, the more volatile and capricious it seemed to become—a looping of desire and anxiety within which political orders staked their claims as the protector and mitigator of disaster.

In the history of disasters in the Ottoman Empire, the nineteenth century proved a decisive period for establishing the framework through which contemporary disasters in Turkey are conceptualized politically. The European political history of disaster management becomes particularly relevant for our story in the context of a massive earthquake that struck Istanbul in 1894. If we are to understand the history of the state's desire to monopolize the management of the Marmara Earthquake, as well as survivors' desires for the same, we need to understand the sorts of political, economic, and scientific transformations that became manifest in the Ottoman Empire during this period. The earthquake of 1894 would mark the end of a period of significant reform in the empire, a period that saw the establishment of many of the state institutions that the Turkish Republic would later inherit. Known as the Tanzimat—the era of ordering and centralization—the Ottoman state, heavily in debt to European lenders, introduced a series of broad reforms to centralize and codify the state and economy, which aimed to more fully integrate the empire into European political and economic institutions, and thus guarantee the repayment of loans.[18] The Tanzimat reforms are broadly regarded as marking a significant era of modernization within the Empire that presaged the modernization campaigns of the Turkish Republic—in terms of state institutions, scope of religious law, minority rights, education, and so forth.

These changes to the Ottoman state, and with them changing ideas about the role of the state in relation to its subjects, played out in parallel ways in the context of disaster management.[19] Prior to these reforms, as Yaron Ayalon describes in his account of the history of natural disasters in the Ottoman Empire, the Ottoman state had, through the eighteenth century, largely left responses to disasters and epidemics to provincial and local officials. While the techniques of disaster management—especially the control of epidemics—drew on European conceptions of public health and hygiene, the Ottoman state did not position itself as bearing the responsibility of systematically managing disaster.[20] The priority of the Ottoman state during this period, as Ayalon describes, was less about the suffering of its citizens than about managing taxation, controlling threats to political order, and ensuring that disasters did not interrupt the shipment of food within the empire.[21] By the time of the Istanbul earthquake of 1894 (which followed well-documented earthquakes in 1489, 1509, 1557, 1597, 1648, 1659, 1690, 1719, and more), the political nature of disaster in the empire had shifted. From the mid-nineteenth century onward, the state would take on the responsibility of offering immediate government assistance to disaster survivors—initially providing lodging and food, and subsequently state funding and aid to rebuild homes.

The 1894 earthquake, while modest in its effects (1,300 residents of the region are estimated to have died, and 300 in Istanbul), set off a substantial social, political, and scientific shift.[22] In the Ottoman state's response to the earthquake, and in the reactions and expectations of residents, we see the consolidation of a set of trends that would set the basic course for disaster management in the region for the foreseeable future. Accounts of the 1894 earthquake sketch a familiar landscape of destruction—wide swaths of destroyed buildings, residents trapped in the rubble, panicked survivors abandoning their damaged homes, searching for survivors, gathering in open fields, and passing nights in makeshift tents. Meanwhile, the humanitarian public that was coming into existence during this period would respond in recognizable ways. Neighborhoods collected donations and fund drives were launched, which fed into a large-scale outpouring of aid from others in region. Support from foreign governments, municipalities, chambers of commerce, civil society organizations, and other charitable groups from around the world arrived to Istanbul, as did the foreign press. The state, in turn, assumed a central role in managing the disaster by establishing a commission to coordinate the collection and distribution of local and foreign aid to earthquake survivors. Reflecting changing rationales of governance, the state charged another committee with the task of not only finding solutions to the needs of citizens but also collecting information about the effects and cost of the earthquake.[23] In turn, as the historian Amit Bein writes, "[The Ottoman intelligentsia] seized upon the earthquake of 1894 to disseminate knowledge of modern earth sciences and implement new methods of scientific study of seismic events in the Ottoman lands . . . believing these to be essential requirements for the modernization of the Ottoman Empire."[24] The 1894 Istanbul earthquake would ultimately receive its own scientific report detailing the economic effects of the earthquake, the aid distributed to residents, and plans for rebuilding the city.

The response to the 1894 Istanbul earthquake established a template for the political rationales and rationalities of future disasters. It would take another earthquake, however, for the further legal codification of these new relationships between the state and disaster. In 1944, in response to a devastating earthquake that struck Erzincan five years earlier, the government passed its first disaster law dedicated specifically to earthquakes. The law placed special emphasis on disaster planning and preparedness, as it also set up frameworks for compensating survivors for lost property and the funding of provincial rescue and emergency aid committees.[25] In 1959, the law was expanded to cover additional forms of disaster (e.g., floods, landslides, fires). As with the initial law, provincial rescue and aid committees were charged with developing detailed disaster response plans, and subsequent additions to disaster law would work to further coordinate and consolidate the state's role in disaster management (which systematically excluded communities and nonstate organizations). Legislation also established a national disaster fund to be used to support the state's response to disasters.

As the foregoing indicates, the expectation that the government would take responsibility for managing the effects of the Marmara Earthquake emerged out of a particular political history in which the state, beginning during the Ottoman period and intensifying with the establishment of the Republic of Turkey in the early twentieth century, positioned itself as the (bio)political guardian and protector of its dependent, vulnerable subjects. Indeed, throughout this period, disaster management was a vital venue for the ideological cultivation of such an understanding of and affective attachment to the state. In tandem with building this political, legal, and affective infrastructure of disaster management—itself part of a wider social contract developed over the twentieth century—the state also worked to monopolize the field by eliminating or absorbing the efforts of nonstate organizations and actors who had previously played prominent roles in responding to disasters. By the time of the Marmara Earthquake, turning to the state for assistance in times of crisis had become not only common sense but also pragmatic. There were few other options.

$4.45: Responding to Disaster

If one focuses on disaster law and institutional planning, one could say that the state was reasonably well prepared for the Marmara Earthquake. Formal legal frameworks for managing disasters existed, as did codified zoning regulations for high-risk regions and dedicated funds for disaster relief. Disaster planning maps had been drawn up, flow charts created, and institutional plans drafted in preparation for the possibility of a large-scale disaster.

Then there was an actual disaster.

On August 17, 1999, the national disaster fund—which was the total amount of money dedicated to disaster preparedness and disaster response in the country—had a balance of US$4.45. On the ground, in terms of helping actual survivors in the immediate aftermath of the earthquake, the state was virtually absent. Despite repeated previous earthquakes, the specialized search-and-rescue teams that existed in various planning documents did not seem to exist in reality. Meanwhile, the highly respected volunteer search-and-rescue association, AKUT (Arama Kurtarma Derneği), along with other organizations trying to assist survivors, would experience active obstruction by the state.[26] Sensitive to the growing political influence of Islamist-inspired political parties, the state also blocked several Islamic charitable organizations—both domestic and international—from joining the relief efforts.[27] In its attempt to monopolize the relief efforts, the state worked to regulate the flow of emergency relief to the region and urged people not to donate to religious or private organizations and instead direct all donations to either an official fund that had been established at a government-owned bank or to Kızılay, Turkey's Red Crescent Society.

Governmental officials charged with leading the relief efforts proved unable to meet the challenge. In a much-publicized encounter, the minister of health and member of the far-right nationalist party, Osman Durmuş, publicly rejected offers of assistance from other countries. When he later relented in the face of intense public criticism, he was reported as saying, "Even if aid was accepted, none should come from Armenia; that earthquake victims should be especially careful to refuse any blood sent from Greece; and that there was no need for portable toilets in the devastated region because many mosques had sanitary facilities, and anyway the Sea of Marmara was close by."[28] Critics began referring to Durmuş as the "minister of ill health." As Durmuş was rejecting foreign aid, the country's president, Suleyman Demirel, publicly berated residents of the earthquake region for questioning the state. When Demirel decided to visit the region after a long delay, he and his staff would shut down vital roads carrying emergency responders and relief, only to castigate audiences of survivors for being critical of the government's response. The earthquake, he explained, was the will of God. Audiences booed. Demirel returned to Ankara.

Turkey's Red Crescent Society, Kızılay, which works in conjunction with the state to provide support after emergencies, was revealed to be similarly unprepared for the disaster. Although it had a strong public reputation for its humanitarian work, the earthquake cast a stark light on its weak institutional capacity. It came to light that the effectiveness of Kızılay had long been undermined by nepotism and clientelism. Kızılay, as the journalist Stephen Kinzer reported from the earthquake region at the time, "had become a dumping ground for incompetent and greedy hacks who spent their budget mainly on lavish trips and stays in luxury hotels. The few tattered old tents it scrounged up when the quake struck quickly become symbols of the government's incompetence and apparent callousness."[29] In the face of government inaction and Kızılay's lack of preparedness, the Turkish military positioned itself as the principal coordinator of emergency aid distribution.

Residents of the area, desperate for help, welcomed the blurring of humanitarian and military action. Although the military would later be praised for the speed of its post-earthquake relief work, the picture on the ground, at the time of the earthquake, was less celebratory. Residents of the region report significant frustration with the military's response, pointing out that its arrival was much slower and its actual work far more limited than reported. Some residents of Gölcük recalled with particular anger how the military prioritized the rescue of naval officers—buried in collapsed buildings on Gölcük's naval base—over nearby citizens. In this respect, the earthquake would deal a blow to the reputation of not only the state but also the military. This is particularly significant in that the military was widely regarded at the time as the guardian and guarantor of Turkey's secular democratic political traditions, an institution that operated above the infighting and corruption that characterized the government.

The shortcomings of the state were made all the more apparent when juxtaposed to the foreign humanitarian operations that entered the region. For many in Turkey, the material and logistic assistance from western European humanitarian and nongovernmental organizations would again confirm their sense that Europe saw Turkey as yet another impoverished country in need of Western humanitarian assistance.[30] In turn, the government's inability to handle the international aid entering the country was seen by many as reinforcing Turkey's servility to European economic and political power. The state, for these critics, couldn't even organize that which was being given "freely." Although the military, together with Kızılay, would slowly expand operations, and eventually gain some sense of control over the disaster relief efforts, the state's response to the earthquake nonetheless proved its own kind of disaster, a response that would dramatically (and negatively) affect the life and death trajectories of thousands of the region's residents, as we will see in the chapters to follow.

Despite the terms upon which this humanitarian response was based—both domestically (with regard to the state and military response) and internationally (with regard to the humanitarian organizations flooding the region)—residents largely refused the role of helpless disaster victim. In the face of the state's faltering response, survivors throughout the region quickly formed networks of mutual aid.[31] Food preparation and distribution centers were established, as radio stations were repurposed to connect survivors and distribute aid. Within weeks of the earthquake, more than thirty local and domestic NGOs established an umbrella group to coordinate activities. Out of these combined efforts would soon emerge a series of new civil society organizations, and with them a sense of new political possibility. "On September 1 [two weeks after the earthquake]," wrote the political scientist Paul Kubicek, "over one hundred NGOs published a manifesto in all the major newspapers, calling on the state not to centralize relief efforts and to extend gratitude to NGOs instead of belittling and threatening them. It heralded 17 August as the beginning of a 'new era,' one in which national and moral values would be preserved thanks to grassroots initiatives and NGOs."[32] These developments would later be celebrated as the "birth of civil society" in Turkey, and thus a milestone of Turkey's democratic development. If this was in fact the birth of Turkey's civil society, it was a messy birth—as dozens of NGOs, representing a dizzying assortment of issues and agendas, formed tenuous relationships with amorphous groups of earthquake survivors and forged a wide array of ad hoc agreements (with one another, with local businesses and transnational corporations, with politicians and bureaucrats at a range of levels in the government) to facilitate the distribution of aid and assistance to survivors (who were often one another).

To the extent that disaster represents the "limits of writing," this and the previous chapters have sought to offer a provisional point of entry into the scenes and conditions of disaster that characterized the Marmara Earthquake. Whereas the previous chapter introduced the ways that the earthquake was experienced as a sudden, world-shattering event, this chapter has focused on the earthquake as a complex convergence of structural forces and historical conditions within which these experiences took form: a history of economic development that transformed an entire region into a densely populated and heavily industrialized landscape ready-made for human and ecological disaster; a history of housing construction techniques, widespread corruption in the building industry, and criminally lax oversight by the state that created a reservoir of cheaply constructed buildings located on dangerously unstable land; and a history of disaster management in which the state both monopolized and chronically underfunded the institutions designed to uphold its biopolitical obligation of caring for its vulnerable and dependent subjects. Appreciating how these registers of disaster constituted one another—such that the earthquake can be understood as both a sudden rupture and the realization of a long history, as both an acute event and set of chronic conditions—is vital as we turn our attention to the psychiatric infrastructure that assembled within the ruins of the Marmara Earthquake.

PART II

The Psychiatry of Disaster

THREE

Novice Humanitarians

The Marmara Earthquake generated an enormous outpouring of public compassion, and with it, an unprecedented mobilization of Turkish mental health professionals. Within days of the earthquake, hundreds of psychiatrists—in a country that had, at the time, little more than a thousand practicing psychiatrists[1]—would drop everything to join the growing relief efforts. Despite their passion, very few had any professional experience treating people outside of clinical settings, especially within the settings and for the forms of emotional distress created by the earthquake. Their training, their understanding of mental illness, the techniques they commonly relied on, and the working conditions to which they were accustomed were all ill suited for the scenes of devastation they were entering. Drawn to the region by a desire to use their therapeutic skills to help those in need, they found themselves having to literally reinvent themselves within the ruins of the earthquake.

Working in a context of dramatic upheaval, and outside of formal state and humanitarian institutions, the psychiatrists and psychologists I introduce in this part would struggle to overcome the limits of their own expertise and improvise a means of extending their psychiatric care across an entire population of earthquake survivors. The responses they developed—though improvisational, uncoordinated, and decentralized—would, in short course, touch the lives of tens of thousands of local residents and thereby play a decisive role in transforming the earthquake into an extraordinary "natural" experiment in psychological care.[2] With this chapter, we begin exploring the emergence of this makeshift post-disaster psychiatric infrastructure by following the initial efforts of a team of psychiatrists and psychologists as they entered the region and struggled to respond to the disaster. The short vignette at the center of this chapter begins introducing the sorts of conditions these novice humanitarians were working in at the time, the therapeutic desires that motivated their action, the institutional and therapeutic limits they confronted, and the professional arrangements and networks that came together in the wake of the earthquake.

Like the majority of Turkey's psychiatrists, Dr. Kaya was living in Istanbul at the time of the earthquake. Although her neighborhood would experience no visible damage, the magnitude of destruction unfolding just east of the city was impossible to ignore. As volunteers across the country mobilized to provide aid to earthquake survivors, Dr. Kaya—a young psychiatrist who had recently completed her psychiatric training—felt an intense desire to join the relief effort.[3] The available options, however, were discouraging. She had little interest in joining the state's disaster response efforts. The government's inability to manage the disaster had been made clear, and joining the state's efforts promised to be frustratingly ineffective. Meanwhile, she had little faith in the foreign humanitarian organizations accumulating around the earthquake. She welcomed their assistance, but knew from experience that their presence would be transient.

Dr. Yavuz, a more senior psychiatrist who had become an important mentor for Dr. Kaya during her training, felt a similar compulsion to care. With a larger professional network and access to more resources, he quickly gathered a group of like-minded colleagues and, within two weeks of the first earthquake, set out on a two-day tour of the earthquake region to distribute aid and find a potential place to realize their therapeutic desires. The scenes of destruction they toured, as Dr. Yavuz recalled, were overwhelming—entire city blocks leveled, residents digging through the rubble with their bare hands searching for relatives and neighbors, traumatized survivors crowded into tents struggling to secure food and water. The group eventually settled its attention on one of the dozens of large tent cities that had been quickly established in the region following the earthquake, which would collectively house hundreds of thousands of displaced residents for the months and, for some, years to come. With a sense of the scope of the destruction and a site to begin their work, Dr. Yavuz and his colleagues returned to Istanbul to begin developing an intervention.

The scale of loss and suffering was of such a magnitude that the initial hopefulness of the group soon gave way to despair, as Dr. Yavuz and his team struggled along several fronts to develop an intervention. Though close to Istanbul, they found themselves working in a region with an already chronically underfunded mental health care system in utter disarray. As with other countries, Turkey's mental health system focused almost exclusively on institutional forms of care, which were especially ill equipped to meet the needs of the moment. At the time of the earthquake, Turkey's formal mental health infrastructure was largely concentrated in urban areas and consisted of inpatient and outpatient mental health services offered through state-run psychiatric hospitals, along with a modest network of private psychiatrists (who typically maintained affiliations and saw patients in university hospitals).[4] Based on a report released by the Ministry of Health following the earthquake,[5] there was, on average, one licensed psychiatrist per 100,000 residents in Turkey at the time (as compared to sixteen in the United States and ten in the European Union). In the earthquake region, there were only two psychiatric experts living and working full-time when the earthquake occurred.[6]

Further complicating their work, Dr. Yavuz's group shared a broad psychiatric vocabulary that proved poorly suited for the situation. Despite a widespread embrace of psychodynamic approaches and efforts to develop community-based mental health services,[7] psychiatric practice in Turkey was dominated by a psychiatric orientation that conceptualized mental disorders as discrete entities with biological underpinnings.[8] As Dr. Kaya recalled: "I was working with neuropsychology, on ADHD, when the earthquake struck. That was where my training was. The earthquake was a major shift for all of us, in our careers." This biological psychiatric orientation, which was heavily dependent on the widespread use of psychopharmaceuticals, meant that Dr. Yavuz and his colleagues had limited practical experience working outside of controlled clinical spaces. Moreover, a history of mental health care reform and psychiatric training that had invested heavily in hospital-based inpatient forms of care also meant that there was no community-based mental health network to draw on. Meanwhile, clinical psychologists and other mental health professionals were legally barred from providing mental health care outside of the supervision of a psychiatrist. Beyond these epistemic and structural obstacles within psychiatry, Dr. Yavuz's group was entering a setting where "mental illness" (which was typically equated with "madness") was heavily stigmatized and psychiatry was widely associated with the institutional neglect and violence of large psychiatric hospitals.[9]

Given these challenges, how were they going to help? With no mental health system to rely on and an entire region of "patients" who had recently experienced unimaginable loss, and who were now living with thousands of other survivors in open fields and tents, what was to be done? Dr. Yavuz and his colleagues began to improvise. In the weeks and months to follow, they labored—in the midst of massive loss and social and professional upheaval—to reinvent themselves and build a makeshift psychiatric infrastructure in the tent city where they were working. Several of the psychiatrists I interviewed would refer to their work during this period as "spontaneous." They scoured university libraries. They pored over journals. They searched bookstores for self-help books. All the while, they continued traveling back and forth from Istanbul to the earthquake region—frequently a two-hour drive—multiple times a week, trying to simultaneously learn new approaches, design an intervention, and help survivors cope with their loss in the meantime. "Amidst all of the chaos," recounted Dr. Yavuz, "we developed several scales [and] validated them while we proceeded. We did all of our preparations while in the field. I have ten, twelve revisions, modifications of [protocols and measures]. And we were revising it every week."

Dr. Yavuz and his colleagues were novice humanitarians in a field that was just coming into existence, and they embodied its ethos.[10] "The first steps in humanitarian psychiatry," write Didier Fassin and Richard Rechtman in their account of the history of humanitarian psychiatry, "involved much improvisation and experimentation, do-it-yourself methods combined with inventiveness."[11] Although they had few resources, they were—as with other experts working at the peripheries of European and North American economic, scientific, and medical hegemonies—accustomed to making do with limited financial support.[12] This would afford them flexibility to tinker with ideas and techniques in ways that professional humanitarians entering the region were not able. While a handful of professional organizations would offer Dr. Yavuz and his team help with coordination (such as the Turkish Medical Association and the Psychiatric Association of Turkey), they ended up having limited capacity, and as with other organizations at the time, their staff was overwhelmed by the scope of the destruction.

Dr. Yavuz's group wouldn't find much support from the foreign experts entering the region. Although there were instances of collaboration between Turkish psychiatrists and European organizations and the World Bank in the wider response to the earthquake,[13] they were repeatedly undermined by a sense that foreign experts saw Turkey as yet another impoverished country in need of their humanitarian assistance and that they did not regard local psychiatrists and psychologists as professional peers (despite their deep, intertwined professional histories). As one psychiatrist would later describe the dynamic: "They wouldn't listen to our suggestions or requests. They acted as if the West was 'all-powerful.' It can be said that they developed this attitude from years of experience working in poor countries in Africa, Asia, and Latin America. After [the earthquake], they approached us with the same attitude. They expected that we were like these others countries. They looked down at us." They also seemed to exaggerate their contributions to the relief efforts. Indeed, many of the European humanitarian workers I interviewed suggested that the psychiatric response to the earthquake came primarily from foreign psychiatrists and psychologists entering the region. For my interlocutors in Turkey, however, the efforts of these foreign experts were seen as at once limited, uncoordinated, and largely ineffective.

Recognizing the limits of their training, and especially the inefficiency of treating individual patients on a one-on-one basis, Dr. Yavuz began seeking advice not from the foreign experts entering the country after the earthquake but from fellow psychiatrists in the United States, western Europe, and Israel—colleagues who were part of a global professional network he had built over a long career of international fellowships, conferences, and training workshops.[14] Within weeks, a team of Israeli mental health professionals would arrive to Istanbul to assist them in developing an intervention. It was during this period that Dr. Kaya was drawn into the group and began making the 150-kilometer drive from Istanbul to the earthquake zone. Over the coming weeks, Dr. Kaya, along with Dr. Yavuz and other colleagues, continued to shuttle back and forth between the earthquake region and Istanbul several times a week. This would be a period of frantic work and long, sleepless nights. They read everything they could get their hands on. They talked with colleagues scattered across time zones. They spent time in the tent encampment developing relationships with local union leaders, school administrators, teachers, and other community members. Within months of the earthquake, they had developed a training program for teachers and were implementing a school-based trauma prevention intervention for students—an intervention I discuss in detail in the following chapters.

Drs. Yavuz and Kaya were among hundreds of mental health professionals who, in the face of immense destruction and suffering, joined a widely expressed public ethics of care to help mitigate the damage wrought by the earthquake. With no functioning institutions to organize their therapeutic desires and a psychiatric training in biological psychiatry that offered few tools for intervening on such a scene, they struggled to develop ways to comprehend, measure, and intervene on the psychological aftermath of the earthquake. If considered in isolation, their intervention, like the many post-earthquake psychiatric interventions that came into existence in the earthquake's aftermath, might seem inconsequential. A few psychiatrists spend a few weeks visiting a tent settlement. A few dozen survivors attend a public meeting that turns into a group therapy session. A "therapeutic tent" staffed by volunteer psychiatrists gets erected amid a sea of thousands of other tents, to only see a handful of patients before it is unceremoniously replaced by tents for more survivors. When taken together, however, this dispersed, patchwork, and improvisational work of hundreds of psychiatrists—some working alongside one another, others working in opposition to one another—formed into an unprecedented albeit heterogeneous post-disaster psychiatric infrastructure within which thousands upon thousands of survivors would have their first experience receiving professional psychiatric care. With this in mind, I turn in the next chapter to the work of three teams of Turkish psychiatrists and psychologists as they struggled, in different ways, to overcome the limits of their own expertise and scale up their psychiatric desires.

FOUR

Experiments in Scale

Over the past two decades—beginning, coincidentally, around the time of the Marmara Earthquake—scholars have become increasingly interested in the relationship between psychiatry and humanitarianism. This work has examined the ways that humanitarian action addressing the psychological effects of large-scale crises—especially that range of effects commonly characterized in terms of psychological trauma—facilitate the globalization of Western conceptions of psychological distress, ignore or undermine local meanings and means of addressing such problems, and, by framing crises in terms of individual psychopathologies, draw attention away from the structural or political conditions of people's suffering.[1] Here, scholars have been particularly interested in the distinctive political and moral entanglements of trauma-focused humanitarian action.[2] This body of work, together with the wider anthropological literature on humanitarianism and humanitarian action,[3] has been remarkably effective in highlighting the historical and lived realities of humanitarian intervention and the sorts of unacknowledged politics and ethics embedded within humanitarian claims of apolitical compassion and care.

While informed by these works, this book explores the intersection of humanitarianism and psychiatry on different terms. For the psychiatrists and psychologists responding to the Marmara Earthquake, the defining problem they confronted was less ethical than technical: How to develop a therapeutic response to the earthquake capable of addressing the enormity of suffering they were confronting? With no functioning institutions to organize their therapeutic desires and a psychiatric training in biological psychiatry that offered few tools for intervening on such a scene, how were they to "scale up" their expertise? Rather than regard practices of psychiatric scaling and scale making as simply neutral technical means to larger therapeutic ends, I am interested in how these scalar practices oriented therapeutic action and organized an ethics of care in the urgent and indeterminate complexity of the post-earthquake context. In other words, building on João Biehl's call to attend to the "ethnographic ambiguities and the complexities of how [global health] projects are actually conceptualized, implemented, and worked out,"[4] I examine in this chapter the specific ways that Turkish psychiatrists and psychologists struggled within the earthquake's aftermath to imagine and enact their expertise across new scales of therapeutic possibility.

Although it is rarely acknowledged, humanitarian and global health interventions are inescapably scalar projects. From concerns about how to distribute medications or administer vaccines within a community to conceptual questions about the biopolitical rationale of public health, from concerns about supranational sovereignties to discussions of how humanitarianism's language of moral transcendence becomes immanent within the lives of recipients, questions about scale and scale making cut through humanitarian and global health interventions, as well as the critical literatures they have inspired. In thinking through these scalar qualities of humanitarian intervention, I follow, on the one hand, the work of human geographers who have interrogated the sorts of contested social and material labor involved in making spatial scale appear natural or ontological, and the concurrent ways that scales reproduce hierarchies that in turn reflect dominant political and ideological orders.[5] On the other hand, I join scholars in anthropology and science and technology studies who have sought to critically interrogate both their discipline's own conventions of scaling and the scale-making practices of social and material actors in a range of settings.[6]

In extending the critical questions of scale and scale making raised by these scholars to the field of (psychiatric) humanitarian intervention, I have found Anna Tsing's conceptualization of scalability particularly helpful. For Tsing, scalability is the capacity or feature of a "small" project or system to be transformed into a "large" one without transforming the basic operation or output of the original.[7] Although the scalability of a system may seem transparent or implicit within the system itself, Tsing underscores the labor involved in producing scalability. "Scalability," she writes, "is not an ordinary feature of nature. Making projects scalable takes a lot of work."[8] I am concerned in this chapter precisely with this labor, what I characterize as the *work of therapeutic scalability*—the ways that the psychiatrists and psychologists who responded to the Marmara Earthquake struggled to arrange assumptions about psychological subjectivity and modify features of interventions such that thresholds could be diminished, the bumpy complexity of realities could be smoothed, and scales made to slide. Tracking these practices of scalability will not only capture the improvisational and experimental qualities of their work but also raise a series of questions about the psychological subject of disaster, the transnational mobility of technoscientific expertise, and the politics of both life and scale at play in psychiatric humanitarian intervention.

In what follows, I explore three interventions developed by three teams of Turkish psychiatrists and psychologists in the immediate aftermath of the Marmara Earthquake. These interventions not only reflect some of the heterogeneity within the psychiatric humanitarian response elicited by the earthquake; they also represent three prominent, and in some cases controversial, approaches within the fields of humanitarian psychiatry and disaster psychiatry: cognitive behavioral therapy (CBT), eye movement desensitization and reprocessing (EMDR), and community-based psychosocial intervention. Rather than regarding these approaches as coherent and ready-made frameworks of expertise—which could move effortlessly between different settings—I consider how they were actively reworked and negotiated as they were adapted to the specific conditions of the earthquake's aftermath. Because I am interested in building an analysis through the juxtaposition of three divergent interventions, my discussion of each is necessarily partial. I focus on a narrow window of time (roughly the first six months after the earthquake) and consider how each group struggled to identify and isolate the feature of scalability in their respective interventions, before turning to a broader set of reflections on the politics of life, scale, and value animating humanitarian psychiatry.

Self-Administration

With a distinguished career in the study of mass trauma, Dr. Baykal was one of the few psychiatrists in Turkey prepared, in a psychiatric sense, for the psychological toll of the earthquake.[9] Before being drawn into the humanitarian response, Dr. Baykal had worked in the former Yugoslavia studying and treating war-related PTSD and was involved with a major trauma research institute in the United Kingdom. I met Dr. Baykal, and later one of his colleagues, Dr. Eser, in 2012 at the offices of a research center they had established in Istanbul to continue their work on trauma treatment and mass violence. Reflecting how the earthquake had dramatically altered the course of both of their careers, their research and therapy had come to focus on refugees who had resettled in Turkey. Sitting in newly renovated offices of an aging Ottoman-era building, Dr. Baykal recalled how, in the immediate wake of the earthquake, he reached out to colleagues he thought might be interested in joining him in his efforts to help earthquake survivors. He quickly gathered a group—which included Dr. Eser, then a graduate student in psychology—and began surveying the psychological effects of the earthquake.

As our conversations revealed, and as a review of documents detailing the development of their intervention confirmed, they quickly came up against the same therapeutic limits that frustrated other psychiatrists working in the aftermath of the earthquake. Given the magnitude of suffering, it was immediately apparent that building an intervention around the intimate, one-on-one therapeutic dyad of conventional treatment models would be inadequate. Moreover, given the disarray in the earthquake region, it was unlikely that their intervention would be able to keep track of individuals over the period required for typical treatment protocols. Drawing a connection between his past work in settings of large-scale political violence and his observations in the earthquake zone, Dr. Baykal had a sense of the sorts of challenges they'd be confronting.

Dr. Baykal seized the opportunity provided by the earthquake. With his clinical background in cognitive behavioral therapy, his familiarity with the region, and a feeling of obligation to respond to the suffering of fellow citizens, Dr. Baykal and his team set to adapting existing CBT trauma treatment models. The aim of their work was, from the start, twinned: to address the immediate and long-term traumatic effects of the earthquake and to assess the rates of PTSD and co-occurring mental disorders among earthquake survivors. Within weeks of the first earthquake, they developed a screening instrument and launched an epidemiological study in several tent settlements in the region. Drawing on the results of these initial studies, as well as the clinical work they were doing in the region, they began refining—through a recursive process of testing and revising—a treatment protocol that condensed the standard eight- to ten-session treatment to four weeks or, if necessary, a single sixty-minute session. In their efforts to redesign existing treatment models, Dr. Baykal and his team sought both to minimize the role of the therapist and to enable what they conceptualized as patients' latent capacities as agents of therapeutic change. Dr. Baykal would later reflect on this moment as a "major milestone for our work in providing not only an opportunity to test [the intervention] more extensively but also valuable insights into natural processes of recovery from trauma."

The therapeutic approach they developed was not, in its broad outline, novel. The intervention consisted of three steps: the identification of presenting problems (e.g., fear, avoidance, hyperarousal), the explanation of the treatment and its rationale to the patient, and the setting of treatment goals and providing instructions for "self-exposure." As with common behavioral approaches, the intervention emphasized the procedure of exposing individuals to distressing reminders of a traumatic event as a means of gaining control or mastery over the event. Novel to the intervention, however, were the procedures it created for exposing patients to such traumatic cues. Rather than an extended, therapist-mediated protocol, the intervention was envisioned as a form of self-treatment—such that, with the initial aid of a trained therapist, and later the assistance of a manual, patients could administer the protocol to themselves. Importantly, unlike longer treatment models, Dr. Baykal's intervention was not envisioned as entailing a systematic cognitive restructuring of patients. Rather, he and his collaborators argued that gaining control and self-mastery over fear and distressing reminders of the traumatic event would forestall the "cascading negative effects" of the behavioral symptoms.

For Dr. Baykal, this capacity for self-administration was critical to the intervention's scalability. Without requiring the presence of a psychological expert—they were few and far between—a self-administered intervention would be able to reach far more survivors far more quickly. Dr. Baykal and his colleagues also envisioned a fully self-administrable version of the intervention in the form of a self-help manual that required no expertise other than what was embedded in the text (a technique referred to in the literature as a "manualized intervention"). Dr. Baykal would later see this development as offering the promise of nearly limitless scalability, with the manual (in print, audio, or visual formats) reaching millions of mass trauma survivors spread across the world.[10] Within nine months of the earthquake, Dr. Baykal and his team were testing the effectiveness of the compressed, self-administered intervention in temporary settlements throughout the region. Over the following years, thousands of survivors (more than ten thousand, according to his estimate) would participate in the interventions they designed.

At this point, I want to briefly draw attention to some of the defining assumptions about the participants being recruited into these interventions. From its inception through its latest iteration, Dr. Baykal's intervention was built on a model of trauma treatment focused on correcting habituated behavioral and emotional disturbances through a regulated process of exposing participants to stressful reminders of traumatic events. As with conventional CBT approaches, symptoms were conceived as learned reactions to stressful situations, and that treatment entails replacing "maladaptive" habits with "adaptive" responses to such situations. The psychological subject of disaster that comes into focus here is thus a fragile play of habituation, conditioning, and adaptation that can, through technical intervention and structured self-action, be rendered malleable. In other words, this is not a psychoanalytic or psychodynamic subject of disaster (with unconscious desires, repressed memories, compulsions to repeat) but the behavioral subject of cognitive structures and maladaptive behaviors. It is also worth noting at this point that the subject (as well as the object and objective) presumed by this intervention is entangled within a set of broader cultural and ideological assumptions about self and subjectivity. That is, the subject of disaster at the center of this intervention, as with the other interventions, bears a striking resemblance to the autonomous, self-knowing and self-mastering liberal subject of the modern psy disciplines.[11] This is by no means surprising. The model of trauma treatment underlying this intervention is conventional, both within global and disaster psychiatry, as well as within mainstream psychiatric discourse in Turkey.

As such, the novelty and innovation that interests me in this intervention is not so much the model of the psychological subject that it presumes, but instead, the efforts—improvisational, iterative, and experimental—that Dr. Baykal and his colleagues undertook to overcome the perceived limit of their expertise. In this particular case, animated by a therapeutic desire for efficiency and scalability, the response of Dr. Baykal's group to the problem of scale took practical form as a strategy of compression and self-administration. By minimizing the role of the expert and activating the latent capacities of the patient, the mobility of the technique could be enhanced and their psychiatric care could be extended, quickly and cheaply, across an entire population of disaster survivors.

Iteration: Lateral Movement

Dr. Şahin, a prominent psychologist based in Istanbul, spent much of the spring before the earthquake organizing a series of training sessions to introduce eye movement desensitization and reprocessing into Turkey. Dr. Şahin had learned about EMDR—a therapeutic technique designed to treat symptoms of PTSD through a multistep procedure that entails patients recalling distressing images as they experience bilateral sensory input, such as side-to-side eye movements or rhythmic tapping on alternate sides of one's body— several years earlier, while receiving training in family therapy at a research institute in northern California. Although it was beginning to gain limited credibility (as well as significant criticism) in the United States and Europe at the time, EMDR was virtually nonexistent in Turkey, according to Dr. Şahin. The earthquake, happening months before the scheduled workshops, would accelerate his plans. Within two days of the earthquake, he submitted a proposal to the EMDR Institute in California, and by October, sixteen trainers and facilitators were on the ground, training 110 Turkish psychiatrists and psychologists to administer EMDR to earthquake survivors.

When we met ten years later, in the offices of the private research and treatment center he was directing, Dr. Şahin described how EMDR was ideal for the post-earthquake conditions in Turkey, in that the technique did not require patients to either discuss their traumatic experiences or complete "homework" between sessions, as was common with other treatment protocols. At the same time, Dr. Şahin and his colleagues, like Dr. Baykal, quickly realized the challenges posed by the scale of the disaster. The slow labor of EMDR, which usually takes a minimum of four to seven sessions, was ill suited for the scope of destruction caused by the earthquake. Moreover, as with Dr. Baykal, he realized that the nature of the disaster meant that the social networks and everyday forms of sociability needed to support the individual during treatment were also in disarray. Yet Dr. Şahin and his colleagues were still convinced that the technique could make a difference. Over the following months, a daily minibus organized by Dr. Şahin would take shifting teams of EMDR practitioners to the earthquake region, leaving early in the morning and returning back to Istanbul late the same night. Dr. Şahin recalled this period as a sleepless blur of despair and perpetual movement. As they moved back and forth between two jarringly opposed realities—the disarray and desperation of the earthquake zone and their own middle-class lives in the city—Dr. Şahin and his colleagues would develop a twofold response to the scale of the disaster.

They first targeted the problem of access. To make EMDR available to more people, they focused on the training of EMDR practitioners, and especially the training of trainers. They worked to pare down the protocols for trainers, and within weeks, newly trained EMDR practitioners, and newly trained trainers, fanned out across the region. Interviews with scores of earthquake survivors, relief workers, physicians, and other therapists confirm the speed with which EMDR traveled. As one psychiatrist working in the region explained, "You would open almost any door, and there you would find someone doing EMDR, moving their hands back and forth." In the months and years to come, according to Dr. Şahin, this wave of EMDR-trained practitioners would treat thousands of survivors.

Dr. Şahin and his team felt that increasing the number of EMDR practitioners was still insufficient given the magnitude of the problem. Like others working in the region following the earthquake, EMDR specialists struggled against the limits imposed by the therapist-patient relationship, which served as the backbone of many of the interventions. This therapeutic intimacy seemed to be an insurmountable obstacle to the problem of scale. With this in mind, Dr. Şahin turned to a second strategy to expand the effects of EMDR. In our interview, he described in detail the moment when he realized that the very nature of the disaster meant that EMDR's effects could be multiplied. "Normally with EMDR," he explained, "everyone's story is different, so you have to work with them individually. But with earthquakes—or bombings, or other mass traumas—everyone experiences the same scene, which means you can work with them together."

With this realization—which was itself a novel conceptualization of shared trauma—his team set to redesigning protocols for a scaled-up EMDR intervention. Soon after, they began gathering larger groups of survivors from the surrounding tent cities to be collectively stepped through a group-oriented EMDR intervention. These sessions consisted of a lead therapist instructing groups of survivors gathered together in a large tent or common outdoor space to recall distressing images from the earthquake as they experienced the bilateral sensory input that characterizes EMDR. When asked how they produced the bilateral sensory input within such a large crowd, he explained—with a sense of thrill that echoed across other interviews, when describing moments of insight or breakthrough—how they had "figured out" that the input could be self-generated: "We had hundreds of people facing us, as they recalled disturbing scenes, tapping themselves on their chests or legs, left right, left right, left right."

While EMDR is distinctive in terms of how it conceptualizes the relationship between (bilateral) sensory input and the processing of traumatic memories, the psychological subject of disaster presumed in this intervention was closely aligned with that of CBT. As with Dr. Baykal's approach, Dr. Şahin's intervention was built on a conception of the psychological subject as a dynamic play of habituation, conditioning, and adaptation. As a treatment modality, however, conventional EMDR distinguishes itself by both its emphasis on sensory input and the role of the therapist in facilitating therapeutic change. That is, the therapist's role is conceived primarily as one of facilitation—of guiding the patient through a set of structured imaginative and sensory exercises—and in this, there is not an expectation that the patient must experience an intense reliving of trauma as a prerequisite for recovery. For Dr. Şahin and his colleagues, these differences opened up alternative ways of imagining the scalability of therapeutic care. In the face of the same sorts of limits encountered by Dr. Baykal and others—the limits of the therapeutic dyad and the widespread (social) upheaval of the earthquake's aftermath—Dr. Şahin's team sought to scale up their intervention through a strategy of multiplication. Initially, this took the form of multiplying the sites of psychiatric contact by accelerating the processes through which experts were produced. This would in turn open up new psychiatric imaginations, wherein Dr. Şahin and his colleagues came to envision a commonality of traumatic cues and thus the possibility of collective healing.

Relatedness: Activating Community

I return in this section to the work of Drs. Yavuz and Kaya. I first met Dr. Kaya in 2004, while she was a psychiatric fellow at a major US medical school. She and another colleague were there to continue to develop the work they had begun following the earthquake. I would interview Dr. Kaya and her colleague subsequently in 2007 and 2012, as well as Dr. Yavuz in 2007. These interviews, along with interviews with other members of the group, a review of the publications and reports that came out of the project, and a visit to the site of their intervention would reveal a familiar starting point: an intense desire to help those who experienced the earthquake and a clinical background that offered few useful skills for addressing the forms of emotional distress they encountered. Their response to the latter, however, would take a substantially different form from that of other groups.

As with many young psychiatrists in Turkey—who have extensive transnational professional ties, especially in western Europe and North America—Dr. Yavuz and his colleagues were aware of the current interest in "community-based mental health care" among global mental health policymakers, an approach they imagined would be well suited for the conditions within which they were working. Yet, as they recalled in interviews, the "community" dimension of "community-based mental health care" proved challenging. As one of the psychiatrists reflected: "We had so many ideas about helping, but how to find a community? The houses were demolished and everything was in total chaos." Uncertain about how to proceed, Dr. Yavuz reached out to an Israeli psychiatrist he had met several years earlier while completing a psychiatric fellowship in the United States. The Israeli colleague, he recalled, had been involved with a team that had developed a post-disaster community-based mental health intervention in Tel Aviv. Given this background, Dr. Yavuz saw his Israeli counterpart as offering the technical expertise to conceptualize the social aspect of the psychology of disaster.

Within months, seven Israeli psychiatrists, psychologists, and social workers would join Dr. Yavuz's team. Amid the disarray of the immediate post-earthquake period—as Dr. Yavuz's team traveled back and forth between Istanbul and the earthquake zone, and as teams of mental health experts traveled back and forth to Israel—an intervention took shape. The resulting intervention was an assemblage of protocols that brought together techniques offered by the visiting Israeli experts, recommendations emerging from the Turkish psychiatrists' own expertise and knowledge of the target population, and an assortment of techniques drawn from searches of available journals, textbooks, and self-help books. (I discuss this intervention, and especially the transnational collaborations that comprised it, in greater detail in Chapter 7.) The post-earthquake intervention would ultimately take the form of a school-based, teacher-mediated disaster relief intervention consisting of "group debriefings" for "processing traumatic experiences" and a combination of psychoeducational modules, cognitive behavioral techniques, and play activities.

For the group working with Drs. Kaya and Yavuz, the problem of scale presented itself differently. While they recognized the limit posed by the therapeutic dyad as the model of care, they were also aware of the deep antagonism to psychiatry among many earthquake survivors. In fact, they would be one of the only groups to discuss the local forms of resistance that met the psychiatric care entering the region after the earthquake. Accordingly, they quickly realized that simply providing more psychiatrists or greater access to psychiatric techniques was not going to solve the problem. With the help of their Israeli collaborators, they began working on an explicitly "social" technique for scaling up their intervention. They focused not on multiplying discrete therapeutic encounters, but on the "community" as a site of therapeutic action. As one of the lead psychiatrists explained:

> We came to recognize that it was hard to get people to come to us for therapy, or for group therapy sessions to help many people. We started to think about ways to integrate our work into everyday social gatherings. We began organizing areas for children to play, or women to gather, that would also create opportunities to treat people—where we could provide individual counseling, psychotherapy, art therapy, and so forth. This took away from the stigma of survivors having to come to the "therapy tents" [which had been set up to provide counseling services to earthquake survivors]. Instead, they'd be coming to sew with other women, or to have their children play. And then we could help them.

Animated by this social conception of care, they worked to embed psychiatric forms of expertise into the community itself, as they began training prominent individuals in the community (teachers, police officers, and, later, imams) to become "lay experts" in providing "psychological first aid" to disaster survivors.

Their intervention—which they would later learn to characterize as reflecting a "psychosocial" approach—represented a significant departure from the forms of mental health expertise circulating in the earthquake zone at the time. While relying on the same basic psychiatric vocabulary as CBT and EMDR specialists, they approached the problem of scale differently. Mobilizing their transnational networks of professional and psychological expertise, Dr. Yavuz and his team came to formulate the social as a site of intervention. The challenge of scaling thus became a problem of conceptualizing and intervening on the social, framed in terms of "community." Rather than privileging the therapeutic dyad as the foundational setting for treatment and the basis of scalability, their approach sought to work through the social relationships that constituted community. That is, their efforts of scaling were aimed neither at accelerating the movement of experts in the region nor at multiplying the points of psychiatric contact between experts and sites of psychic damage. Rather, their approach privileged an understanding of the damaged survivor as existing within a network of social relations. Accordingly, they sought to constitute, or "activate," the social as a therapeutic community.

The Work of Scalability: Administration, Iteration, Relation

The Marmara Earthquake generated a remarkable domestic mobilization of psychiatrists and psychologists. In this unprecedented outpouring of concern for the psychological well-being of earthquake survivors, groups of psychiatrists and psychologists would quickly form—some reflecting old professional divisions, others suggesting new possibilities for collaboration, but most reproducing familiar gendered professional hierarchies (with senior male psychiatrists taking the lead—and the credit). In the face of extraordinary upheaval and human suffering, these novice humanitarian psychiatrists and psychologists set to improvising a post-disaster mental health infrastructure at what I've come to think of as the disastrous margins of global psychiatry.

In this section, I want to draw close to the particular ways that these psychiatrists and psychologists, working in the disarray of the earthquake's aftermath, sought to identify and enact the scalability of their psychiatric expertise—the divergent ways that they arranged assumptions about the psychological subject and struggled to modify specific aspects of an intervention such that complexities could be smoothed, limits overcome, and scales made to slide. Here, I return to what Anna Tsing would characterize as the "scalability" of their therapeutic labor. For Tsing, again, scalability indexes the desire to transform a "small project" into a "large project" without changing the nature of the project itself: "To scale well is to develop the quality called scalability, that is, the ability to expand—and expand, and expand—without rethinking basic elements."[12] "By its design," she continues, "scalability allows us to see only uniform blocks, ready for further expansion."[13] In this section, I focus on the way that these psychiatrists and psychologists sought to identify and isolate the feature of scalability in their interventions and how, in the process, they fabricated out of the social and material chaos of the setting such "uniform blocks" ready for expansion.

Although I have emphasized divergent responses to the problem of scale, it is important to acknowledge the extent to which the different groups nonetheless relied on overlapping psychological and therapeutic assumptions about the traumatized psychological subject. Indeed, across these interventions, a shared conceptualization of the psychological subject of disaster—as a behavioral subject of habituation, conditioning, and adaptation with the capacity for self-directed action—seemed to be a prerequisite, if not condition, for imagining the scalability of therapeutic expertise across the different interventions. The psychological subject of disaster was, in Tsing's terms, a "uniform block" awaiting expansion. This shared psychiatric imagination would play a vital role in facilitating relationships within and between groups, with humanitarian psychiatrists and psychologists coming from outside of Turkey, and along transnational routes of psychiatric expertise.[14]

It is worth noting here the extent to which cultural difference was *not* conceived as a challenge to this uniformity and the sliding of scales. That the limit to the problem of scaling was not conceived in cultural terms shouldn't be surprising. On the one hand, the psychiatrists and psychologists I interviewed did not understand their relationship with injured survivors of the earthquake in terms of cultural difference. Rather, they understood themselves as being bound (indeed, obligated) to their patients by a shared (national) culture—which was not the case for the foreign humanitarian experts entering the region. (Importantly, this sense of a shared "national culture" masked the extent to which their humanitarian compassion was founded on a tacit sense of shared ethnic identity, a sense that would become explicit—and complicated—in an earthquake that struck Turkey's eastern and largely Kurdish province of Van twelve years later.) On the other hand, their interventions were predicated on a conceptualization of a universal psychological subject in which cultural processes are rendered secondary or epiphenomenal to cognitive processes. "Culture," in this formulation, enters as a "problem" in so much as it accounts for people's resistance to psychiatric care (e.g., fatalism, ignorance). There's a complex history at play here, which, for now, I can only gesture toward. That is, in the ways that class differences between Turkish psychiatrists and working-class earthquake survivors were frequently framed in religious terms (especially through the idiom of fatalism), we can see how the history of psychiatry in Turkey entailed the authorization not only of European forms of medical expertise but also, together with them, a set of Orientalist discourses ready-made to explain instances of psychiatric refusal.

Despite their shared assumptions, the different interventions nonetheless developed distinctive responses to the challenge of therapeutic scalability. The behavioralism of Drs. Baykal and Eser's intervention, for instance, responded to the inefficiencies of the therapeutic dyad by seeking to dramatically compress conventional CBT approaches to trauma treatment through the mobilization of what they regarded as the intrinsic therapeutic capacities of survivors to treat themselves. Their approach to psychiatric self-administration—which was imagined, at its extreme, as replacing the psychiatrist with a textual proxy, disarticulating expertise from expert—would free the intervention from the constraints of therapist-mediated protocols, and thus allow therapeutic scales to slide. The work of scalability with Dr. Baykal's team was thus focused on mobilizing what they conceptualized as a core capacity of the psychological subject and, by isolating it, achieving scalability by tinkering with both the temporality of care (the compression of conventional protocols) and the displacement of expertise into a manual. This, in turn, would operationalize a scalability that envisioned expansion in both quantitative and spatial terms: the ability of the intervention to reach more people as it spread effortlessly (and cheaply) through a social and material landscape dramatically remade by disaster.

The EMDR-based intervention relied on a kindred conception of the post-disaster psychological subject, yet imagined differently the scalability of psychiatric expertise. Rather than diminishing the role of the expert, they worked to slide scales by multiplying, distributing, and amplifying points of therapeutic contact. Unlike the other groups, Dr. Şahin did not envision the therapeutic dyad as an impossible obstacle to the problem of scale. Instead, his group isolated the combined effects of bilateral sensory stimuli, therapist-mediated imaginative guidance, and the distinctive "trainability" of EMDR as the scalable features of the intervention. With this, their response to the problem of scale would be twofold. The first response sought to scale up the intervention by multiplying the points of psychiatric contact between expert and survivor. This focused foremost on the process of training, which was itself facilitated by an understanding of the "trainability" of EMDR as a therapeutic technique. This process of scaling through multiplication also carried with it a set of spatial deliberations, as they worked to distribute experts (and trainers) throughout the earthquake region. From these efforts to multiply and distribute points of therapeutic contact emerged an understanding of the commonness, and thus commensurability, of traumatic events. Such a conceptualization of a "common trauma" would dramatically smooth the psychological and social terrain of the intervention—freeing psychiatric imaginations and allowing scales to slide even further. Whereas the first iteration allowed for the intervention to scale up spatially through the movement of practitioners and trainers through the earthquake region, the second development allowed them to imagine the distribution of therapeutic points as nodes, capable of exposing entire groups of survivors simultaneously to the intervention. Here, multiplication came to be seen in exponential terms, as points of psychiatric contact transformed from dyadic relations to therapeutic assemblies.

Whereas the previous two groups held on to the necessity of the therapeutic dyad, if even relegated to a textual proxy, the group developing a community-based psychosocial approach would look elsewhere in its work of scalability. Rather than envisioning the expansion of an intervention as the multiplication of points of contact with psychiatric expertise, the group with Drs. Yavuz and Kaya focused their attention on the interpersonal relationships that were conceived as constituting the social environment in which the psychological subject was sustained. They would thus overcome the limits of their expertise by intervening on networks of social relatedness, as a means of "activating" community. In this respect, their approach sought to remake the community through psychiatric means and, from this, would issue the reordering of cognitive, emotional, and behavioral disturbances in individuals. The problem of expanding care across a population was similarly envisioned in social terms. Rather than approaching the challenge of distributing care as a problem of geographic space, they focused on how the intervention might propagate itself within communal relations. In other words, they came to conceive of the problem of scaling as a problem of relatedness, such that a successful intervention would weave psychiatric power into the very fabric of community life—transforming, simultaneously, interpersonal and cognitive processes.

Out of the interplay of therapeutic desires, humanitarian compassion, the forms of expertise they brought with them to the disaster, and the transnational professional ties they were able to mobilize, the psychiatrists and psychologists who responded to the Marmara Earthquake engaged in a set of iterative and experimental efforts to overcome the limits of their training and forge a meaningful therapeutic response to the disaster. Reflecting the complexity and tumult of the contexts in which they were working, these efforts to imagine and enact the scalability of psychiatric expertise would take multiple forms.[15] In our case, we have explored three divergent projects through which psychiatrists and psychologists, working in settings of profound disarray, struggled to isolate "uniform blocks"—whether they be assumptions about the psychological subject, technical features of the intervention itself, or understandings of collective social life—that could be manipulated so that their psychiatric expertise could be enacted across new scales of therapeutic possibility.

The Value of Scales

Much scholarly attention has been dedicated to denaturalizing the psychiatric categories and techniques described above, especially those organized around the category "PTSD."[16] While I am indebted to this work, my interests in this chapter have been elsewhere, namely with the ways that psychiatric experts, working within the urgent constraints of an enormously destructive event, confronted and struggled to overcome the limits of their own expertise. In exploring their therapeutic responses to the disaster, I don't want us to lose sight of the immensity of the challenges they confronted—

the magnitude of the destruction, the intensity of their desire to help others, the extent to which they were grossly unprepared to do so, and how their response was cobbled together, on the fly, out of bits and pieces of what they could find at hand, at the moment. In this chapter, I have been particularly interested in tracking ethnographically their work of therapeutic scalability—their iterative and improvisational efforts to smooth the bumpy complexity of realities and expand their psychiatric care across an unstable material and social terrain. This work of therapeutic scalability, I argue, played a decisive role in both expanding the reach of their psychiatric imagination and, in the process, transforming the earthquake into a psychiatric event. Before turning in the next chapter to how this unfolded in tandem with a set of parallel, interwoven efforts to measure the psychological effects of the earthquake, I want to briefly consider a set of questions that this focus on therapeutic scalability raises with regard to the politics of life, scale, and value at play in psychiatric humanitarian intervention.

Humanitarian action, as Didier Fassin has argued, articulates a politics that is irreducibly about the valuation of life. "Humanitarian action . . . constitutes one of the paradigmatic forms of a politics of life," writes Fassin, "in that it takes as its object the saving of individuals, which presupposes not only risking others but also making a selection of which existences it is possible or legitimate to save."[17] While the psychiatric humanitarian responses I have been discussing were necessarily constituent parts of a larger politics of life at work in the earthquake's aftermath (instantiated in such questions as, Where should search-and-rescue teams be sent, or where should clean water and food be directed?), it is also important to note that the deliberations among the psychiatric humanitarians with whom I worked were not so much about sustaining biological life as they were about fostering emotional or psychological well-being. That is, their attention was not on the biological subject of humanitarianism (although they were, of course, concerned about lives being saved), but on the psychological subject of disaster (again, the vulnerable behavioral subject of habituation, conditioning, and adaptation with the capacity for self-directed action). In this regard, we can understand the forms of valuation at play in these interventions as articulating themselves not through deliberations about risking or saving (biological) lives, but instead through the sort of (psychological) subject of disaster that organized psychiatric improvisation.

It is here, I want to argue, where a politics of life intersects in particular ways with the politics of scale. As critical geographers of scale have repeatedly underscored, scales are not neutral. Scales necessarily privilege some positions and perspectives over others, and scale making is fundamentally about deciding what counts, and thus what is of value.[18] As the geographer Erik Swyngedouw has argued, scales are "the embodiment of social relations of empowerment and disempowerment and the arena through and in which they operate."[19] Scales and scale making, as these arguments suggest, obscure realities as they reproduce social hierarchies. They are not, again, merely neutral technical means to, in our case, larger therapeutic ends. If we put these observations in conversation with the critical literature on psychiatric and psychosocial humanitarian intervention—especially those critiques that highlight how the technical and pathologizing frameworks of conventional humanitarian intervention obscure the structural origins of people's distress—we can begin to appreciate some of the distinctive implications of scaling for humanitarian action. That is, not only does scaling presume an expert hierarchy—with the expert being the one able to rise above the complexity of the moment to envision new scales of therapeutic possibility—but to scale, as an act of rising above, is to also move even further away from the messiness of actual lives. Indeed, to paraphrase Anna Tsing, the specificity, diversity, and complexity of social lives stand in direct opposition to scaling and scalability. To scale, as such, is therefore to abstract lives from social realities as a pretext of expanding over these realities. In so doing, these practices of therapeutic scaling contribute in particular ways to concealing the ways that the death and destruction of the earthquake was in fact the predictable realization of a long political and economic history.

Out of the dispersed and improvisational efforts of these novice humanitarian psychiatrists and psychologists to meaningfully respond to the enormity of suffering precipitated by the Marmara Earthquake, a vast, if makeshift, post-disaster psychiatric infrastructure would quickly come into being. Within this, the work of therapeutic scalability proved critical to the broader psychiatrization of the Marmara Earthquake and the specific ways that psychiatry began to enter into communities and lives. In an unprecedented collective expression of concern for people's psychological well-being, tens of thousands of earthquake survivors would, for the first time, receive some form of psychiatric care. With that said, our discussion has thus far considered only one facet of the psychiatric response to the earthquake. It would take more than this to fashion the disaster into a psychiatric event.

FIVE

A Geo-Psychology of Disaster

> At present, sporadic efforts, provoked mostly by the advent of major disasters, appear to constitute the main literature of psychological trauma work in Turkey.
> —TAMER AKER, PINAR ÖNEN, and HANDE KARAKILIÇ, *International Journal of Mental Health*, 2007

> Disasters create unrivaled opportunities for scientific and technological advancement, both basic (e.g. in setting conditions for "natural experiments") and applied (e.g. investigative teams organized to identify causes of specific system failures). This, in turn, can fundamentally alter the organization and substantive content of existing scientific fields.
> —KIM FORTUN and SCOTT FRICKEL, "Making a Case for Disaster Science and Technology Studies," 2012

Dr. Sibel Mercan, writing for the website *Populer Medikal*—a site that launched the same year as the earthquake—described the implications of the earthquake in the following terms:

> As a society, we came face-to-face with the REALITY OF EARTHQUAKES after the August 17th earthquake. Some of us have witnessed, either firsthand or on television, what has happened to the survivors who experienced the earthquake directly. . . . After such major natural disasters, it is natural that some psychological problems occur in people who are directly exposed to trauma or witness it. However, over time, these problems ought to diminish and daily life continue. When the response is expected to be severe or prolonged, it is necessary to evaluate it from the perspective of a disease.[1]

For Dr. Mercan, the reality of the earthquake was irreducibly psychological. Natural disasters produce natural psychological reactions; disasters of the natural world precipitate disasters of inner worlds.

Dr. Mercan's commentary on the psychic reality of the earthquake was not exceptional. Within a recently privatized and rapidly expanding media landscape, the uninterrupted news coverage coming from the earthquake region would regularly turn to mental health professionals to help explain the expected psychological effects of the earthquake. In the early days of a new era of mass-mediated expertise, psychiatrists and psychologists (along with geologists) appeared as frequent guests on daytime talk shows and evening news roundtables, as they also became featured contributors to newspapers and news websites. Beyond television screens, teams of psychiatrists and psychologists traveled to schools throughout the region to give presentations to students and lead training workshops for teachers and school staff. To an extent formerly unimaginable, mental illness and psychiatry became an unremarkable topic of everyday conversation in the wake of the Marmara Earthquake.

This new public face of psychiatry spoke in a voice that was at once clinical and pedagogical. Experts appearing on television and in newspapers both described in detail the psychological effects of natural disasters and established a set of expectations of what counted as a "normal" or "natural" reaction. Brochures and flyers from psychiatric, psychological, and medical organizations circulated widely to alert people to feelings of anxiety, guilt, panic, and hopelessness that typically accompany traumatic events. The Turkish Psychological Association distributed 200,000 informational booklets describing the psychological effects of trauma in the earthquake region.[2] Psychoeducational programming became a regular component of public health and "collective education" (*toplu eğitim*) campaigns in communities of displaced earthquake survivors. Across these different public-awareness campaigns, the setting of expectations typically took the form of a list of diagnostic categories. "In a society following an earthquake," wrote Dr. Mercan, "various psychiatric disorders can appear. Among these mental disorders, one commonly sees post-traumatic stress disorder, depression, anxiety, atypical grief response or prolonged grief response. . . . The most common complaint is sleep disturbance. Sleep disturbance alone is rare, however, and is usually accompanied by a variety of mental illnesses (such as depression and anxiety, which can be accompanied by physical illnesses such as asthma and heart failure)." Dr. Mercan continues on—as do most examples from this genre—with a lengthy description of the causes, symptom profiles, and effects of the psychic reality of disaster.

Just behind this newly vocal public psychiatric discourse was an enormous clinical and epidemiological apparatus that was mobilized in the immediate aftermath of the earthquake. As described in the preceding chapters, waves of psychiatrists and psychologists rushed to the region to address the psychological and emotional aftermath of the earthquake. Like nothing seen before, the Marmara Earthquake unleashed public and expert concern for people's psychological and emotional well-being. By the time this psychiatric wave receded from the region, tens of thousands of survivors had participated in studies examining some facet of the psychological consequences of disaster. These studies would, in turn, generate a minor literature—with hundreds of peer-reviewed articles, appearing in prominent English- and Turkish-language psychiatric journals, published over the months and years to come. Although few outside of the region were aware of the extent of this research, this massive mobilization of psychiatric research proved important. In addition to providing a rich evidentiary foundation for the emerging public psychiatric discourse, it also played a decisive role in setting the course for the long-term trajectories of survivors and the professional lives of their psychiatrists and psychologists. In short, this work was instrumental in transforming the Marmara Earthquake into a psychiatric event.

How precisely did the Marmara Earthquake become the "natural" psychological event that Dr. Mercan describes? Whereas the previous chapters traced the emergence of the earthquake as a therapeutic challenge, this chapter turns to how the earthquake was simultaneously made into a research problem. For many of the psychiatrists responding to the earthquake, these were, in fact, two sides of the same coin. The psychiatry of disaster that formed after the earthquake was constituted from the outset by a twinned set of desires: the desire to heal and the desire to measure. With this in mind, this chapter explores how the earthquake generated a set of novel research questions for psychiatrists and psychologists coming to the region and how these questions, in turn, laid the groundwork for a series of studies that aimed to measure the psychological and psychopathological effects of disaster. In tracing how the earthquake was made scientifically knowable, I consider the ways that a set of psychiatric techniques and categories—part and parcel of global flows of technoscientific expertise and technologies of psychological subject making—were formulated and administered within a radically unstable set of conditions. In so doing, I ask how the conditions of vulnerability (for survivors) were transformed into the conditions of professional opportunity for the novice humanitarian psychiatrists entering the region.

This chapter is primarily concerned with what I'm characterizing as psychiatric world making—the work of expert categories, techniques, and modes of psychiatric apprehension to render a (socially, experientially, and geologically) precarious set of conditions into a reality open to comprehension, measurement, and intervention. With this, I want to return to my argument that the uncoordinated, improvised, and decentralized psychiatric response to the Marmara Earthquake was, in effect, a makeshift sociotechnical infrastructure. In this chapter, I extend these ideas by highlighting the ways that this infrastructure was itself a networked assemblage.[3] This is useful for two reasons. First, it pushes us to recognize how these researchers and their knowledge production practices existed within and were dependent on complex, heterogeneous, and widely dispersed networks of social and material relations. In this regard, I am interested in this body of research not so much for what it tells us about universal psychological processes, but for the light it sheds on the constellations of people, ideas, practices, objects, and even geological processes that came and held together in the earthquake's aftermath. Second, and relatedly, this approach helps us understand the role this research played in creating the very realities it was intended to measure. In his essay "Seeing Like a Survey," the sociologist and science studies scholar John Law writes: "Knowledge practices, and the forms of knowledge that these carry, become sustainable only if they are successfully able to manage two simultaneous tasks. First, they need to be able to create knowledge (theories, data, whatever) that *work*, that somehow or other hold together, that are convincing and (crucially) do whatever job is set for them. But then, second and counterintuitively, they have to be able to *generate realities* that are fit for that knowledge."[4]

Building on these insights, this chapter puts my ethnographic research in conversation with the psychiatric literature on the earthquake to track the ways that extraordinarily unstable experiential realities (clogged with the dust of a devastated landscape, undone by loss and death) were transformed into thousands of data points, to be ordered and gleaned for a psychological future for the region's residents. Tracking this will entail an account of the ways that a scientific and clinical infrastructure was (quickly) brought into existence, the sorts of citational practices that constituted this world, and how this research—from the design of instruments, to the collection of data, through the publication of results—would give the earthquake psychological depth and texture. This collective labor would contribute not only to the ontological reality of the disease categories being used,[5] but also to the earthquake itself.

Charting the emergence of this reality, in these terms, requires an attention to technical specificities that can be exhausting—for both writer and reader. Reflecting the world that I'm trying to depict, much of the following overflows with the technical terms that this reality relies on for its own reproduction. Similarly, in the way that these categories and studies relentlessly reified and rose above the reality of people's lives in search of numerical clarity, the actual experiences of earthquake survivors will remain distant for the time being. As such, while some may find this discussion tedious, it is vital to consider in detail the scientific labor that was involved in constituting the earthquake psychiatrically. As will become especially clear in this chapter, the psychiatric world taking shape in the ruins of the earthquake formed in the tension between compassion for one's fellow citizen and the desire for the production of psychiatric knowledge and professional capital, as well as between long-standing national traditions of psychiatric practice and emergent global regimes of psychiatric knowledge production. As I argue, to understand how the earthquake became a psychiatric event, we have to understand not only how it was made therapeutically available, but also how it was made legible as an object of knowledge.

Establishing a Baseline, Creating a Canon

An overriding priority for clinicians working in the earthquake region was the desire to understand the nature and scope of the problems they were seeking to treat. Efforts of comprehension were regarded as a pretext, if not prerequisite, for intervention. Reflecting a clinical professionalism that was constituted through transnational psychiatric ties, this was the new common sense of an emerging "evidence-based medicine": in order to develop an intervention, one needed data that would confirm whether or not the intervention was working. At the same time, psychiatrists and psychologists argued that it would be scientifically irresponsible to pass up this opportunity to gather data about the prevalence of psychopathology after natural disasters. With their ethics oriented toward a hypothetical future horizon—"imagine," recalled one psychiatrist, "how this will help future survivors of earthquakes"—they understood their work as both addressing the immediate suffering of actual earthquake survivors and contributing more generally to the medical and psychiatric sciences.

The psychiatry of disaster that formed after the earthquake was conceived along two defining axes: that of the symptom and that of prevalence. In other words, the clinical attention of psychiatrists and psychologists working in the earthquake region was directed both at the individual (as the bearer of symptoms, in need of clinical attention) and the population (as an aggregate of symptoms measured by prevalence, in need of epidemiological attention). Dr. Kaya would recall the twinned nature of their humanitarian imperative: "We didn't realize what we did actually while we were doing it. We did it because something had to be done. That was our belief. But probably our advantage was having a *scientific eye*. We were trying to really document what we did. To keep a critical eye on what we were doing in order to improve it." This double vision of a scientific eye structured post-earthquake interventions, as treatment protocols were coupled together with a set of epidemiological instruments that would be used to generate data to make claims about the prevalence of pathology across the population.[6]

For Dr. Baykal—the psychiatrist with extensive experience in the study of mass trauma who we met in Chapter 4—designing a set of instruments for measuring rates of PTSD and other conditions common to disasters was inseparable from the work of developing a post-earthquake therapeutic intervention. Out of this recognition would emerge the most extensively published and widely cited research into the psychological toll of the Marmara Earthquake.[7] Dr. Baykal and his colleagues began their research—into the prevalence of psychopathologies among earthquake survivors (especially PTSD, major depression, and a range of symptoms of comorbid psychological disorders, such as anxiety)—within weeks of the earthquake. Initially conducted in open fields and tent settlements, it would later be extended into prefabricated housing settlements and rebuilt apartment complexes spread across the earthquake region—reaching from small towns along the eastern end of the Gulf of İzmit to outlying districts of Istanbul. Within a year, the studies had enrolled thousands of residents, administering to them a broad array of psychiatric examinations and psychological checklists to determine the psychopathology of disaster. By the final study, conducted three years after the earthquake, more than 6,000 residents of the region had taken part in field surveys and epidemiological studies completed by Dr. Baykal's group, with observational data from 12,000 survivors.

Reflecting the importance of epidemiological concerns in the post-earthquake psychiatric humanitarian response, the earliest publications to emerge from these studies were methodological. The first article (appearing in the international *Journal of Traumatic Stress*) describes their efforts to develop and validate a screening instrument in the immediate post-earthquake period.[8] The instrument, which would become known as the Screening Instrument for Traumatic Stress in Earthquake Survivors (SITSES), was based on diagnostic categories from the American Psychiatric Association's *Diagnostic and Statistical Manual of Mental Disorders-IV* (DSM-IV) and relied heavily on existing PTSD and depression checklists and screening instruments, which had already been translated and validated in Turkish.[9] The bulk of the SITSES was a twenty-three-question section that included a seventeen-question Traumatic Stress Symptom Checklist (TSSC) and a six-question measure of depression symptoms. The TSSC section would be validated with 130 earthquake survivors—completed during the first weeks after the earthquake—using the Clinician-Administered PTSD Scale (CAPS) and the Major Depressive Episode (MDE) module of the Structured Interview for DSM-IV (SCID).

For readers not familiar with this psychiatric world—as I was when this project began—the novelty of this instrument may be difficult to discern. Why all the acronyms, and why does this instrument deserve its own? Importantly, as I will return to later, the novelty of the SITSES was decidedly not in the way it engaged the specificity of the context within which it was operating. Questions concerning cultural difference, for instance, were largely reduced to a matter of translation.[10] Rather, its novelty resided primarily in the way that it assembled other existing instruments into a new whole. With a nod to the work of Gilles Deleuze and Felix Guattari,[11] I've come to think of the SITSES (and the psychiatric epidemiological response to the earthquake more generally) in machinic terms—as part of an assemblage of techniques, knowledges, people, institutions, and materials that generated data as they also produced new psychiatric desires and social worlds, and more instrument-machines for generating yet more data and more desires. These psychiatric machines—which were neither centralized nor unified, but strikingly consistent and productive in terms of their output—would play a defining role in constituting the psychiatric reality that took shape amid the earthquake's ruins. Taken together, they would give the earthquake quantitative complexity, epidemiological texture, and psychological substance.

To give a sense of the speed with which the SITSES, as a machine, was compiled and operationalized, the number of people it enrolled, and what it apprehended, take the following examples. In a study that started the month after the earthquake, Dr. Baykal and his colleagues found that, among 1,000 survivors living in temporary housing settlements near Gölcük, 43 percent of the respondents could be diagnosed with PTSD and 31 percent with major depression.[12] In another study that administered the SITSES to 1,027 earthquake survivors in a nearby town, the findings indicated rates of PTSD at 63 percent and major depression at 42 percent.[13] As time passed, and studies multiplied, the SITSES became the basis for a longitudinal picture of post-disaster psychopathology. In a study conducted fourteen months after the earthquake and run concurrently near Gölcük and in Avcılar (a suburb of Istanbul that experienced substantial damage in the earthquake), Dr. Baykal's team administered the SITSES to 950 randomly selected residents and found that rates of PTSD and major depression were significantly higher at the site closer to the epicenter.[14] Additional studies conducted at twenty months and thirty-six months after the earthquake, spread over twelve sites and administering the SITSES to 586 and 769 area residents, respectively, found persistently high rates of PTSD and major depression.[15] A series of treatment studies, based on the SITSES, shadowed these prevalence studies.[16] The results would lead to a string of publications in almost exclusively English-language journals (e.g., *Journal of Traumatic Stress*, *Journal of Nervous and Mental Disorders*, and *Disasters*). Taken together, the studies—and the SITSES in particular—proved instrumental in codifying the psychological profile of the Marmara Earthquake.

The SITSES instrument turned out to be enormously productive. Its use expanded with the multiplication of the group's own projects, and it was also incorporated into other studies being conducted in the region. A series of important studies conducted across sites throughout the earthquake region (for both the August 17 and November 12 earthquakes) administered the SITSES to nearly 3,000 more residents.[17] In turn, as the work of Dr. Baykal's group expanded beyond the earthquake in the years to come, the SITSES was adapted for different audiences, each getting its own acronym (e.g., SITSE-C for children, SITSOW for survivors of war), and developed into structured interviews for survivors of torture (SIST), survivors of war (SISOW), and survivors of earthquakes (SISE). Meanwhile, a new set of treatment protocols would also develop in conjunction with the SITSES's growing popularity (see Chapter 4). By the tenth anniversary of the earthquake, the SITSES, in original or modified form, had been administered to tens of thousands of participants, generated dozens of research articles and commentaries, and served as the basis for a textbook dedicated to the SITSES and the accompanying treatment protocols created by the team.[18]

The SITSES was not the only psychiatric machine at work in the earthquake zone. In addition to dozens of small-scale studies, another group of psychiatrists and psychologists would conduct a parallel set of influential studies of the psychological consequences of the earthquake within tent settlements near İzmit. Working in the upheaval of the earthquake zone and drawing together existing translated instruments, such as the PTSD Self-Test (PTSD-S), also based on DSM-IV categories, the group quickly pieced together their own instrument—a one-hour, self-report questionnaire referred to as the "earthquake inquiry form." The initial study enrolled 910 residents and findings indicated that 25.4 percent of respondents met DSM-IV criteria for PTSD.[19] In another study of seventy-six camp residents, a team made up of many of the same researchers again found high rates of both PTSD and major depressive disorder.[20] As with Dr. Baykal's team, these early studies would establish a baseline for a series of psychiatric futures. The same group conducted another large study thirty-six months after the earthquake, enrolling 683 more participants. On the basis of face-to-face interviews using a modified version of the Composite International Diagnostic Interview (CIDI), Traumatic Stress Symptom Scale, General Health Questionnaire, and Beck Depression Inventory, they once again found, three years out, persistently elevated rates of PTSD and major depression.[21]

As this partial picture begins to suggest, the Marmara Earthquake generated an extraordinary number of psychiatric and psychological studies—an outpouring of concern, and data, that was new in the history of both psychiatry and disaster in Turkey. Meanwhile, across these projects, the twinned imperatives—of care and measurement—left little room to question the categories of the research itself. While researchers might, as many did, question the necessity or even utility of using diagnostic categories for therapeutic purposes—that is, perhaps diagnosis need not be the priority in treatment—the validity of the categories themselves were largely unchallenged. At a basic level, then, this body of research contributed in fundamental ways to the reification of the psychological and emotional suffering of survivors (fashioning their experiences into "things" and "disorders" to be measured), which, in turn, further authorized symptom-based diagnostic approaches to psychological and emotional distress (especially as represented in the *DSM*).[22] Regardless, as a key operator in the earthquake's psychiatric machine, the research chugged along, smoothing out complex and messy realities to generate data that could be analyzed, compared, and published.

Out of this constellation of technology, affect, and desire—at the meeting of compassion for one's fellow citizen and the desire for the production of psychiatric knowledge and professional capital—issued not only publications but also a flood of new instruments, techniques, and acronyms. Taken together, this body of research and writing offered new ways to think and speak about disaster. It provided a psychiatric idiom that had been, until the Marmara Earthquake, marginal and technical. At the same time, this enormous body of research would also introduce psychiatrists and psychologists into people's lives in new ways. As we will read in later chapters, this psychiatric discourse of disaster entered a setting where very few people had direct contact with psychiatrists and resistance to psychiatric care was deeply entrenched. In the wake of the earthquake, however, thousands of residents, distributed across dozens of sites in the region, would be recruited into some sort of psychiatric study, as word of this type of "psychological first aid" became part of everyday conversations to a formerly unimaginable extent.

INTERLUDE
Local Canons, International Genres

As I began to read widely and deeply into this body of research, I found myself relating to the collective psychiatric representation of the earthquake that it offered less as a scholarly "literature" to review than as a historical "archive" to explore. Approaching these publications as an archive—dispersed across multiple journals, publishers, libraries, the headquarters and regional branches of professional associations, online repositories, conference proceedings, and even individual offices (in that much would take the form of self-published reports)—was a novel experience for me, one that invited a different sort of reading.[23] Rather than simply comparing data, methodologies, and findings across studies, I was drawn to the discursive patterns that formed and linked texts, the constellations of actors, concepts, and citations that congealed into a cast of recurrent characters. I became particularly interested in the introductory sections of these scientific articles, where authors described the larger significance of their research and situated their work within the existing literature on a given topic. For the experts for whom these articles were written, these were the sections one skimmed over, so as to get to the real purpose of the article—its data and findings. As I read these introductions with increasing interest, I became fascinated by the stories they told about the psychiatric world being fashioned in the earthquake's ruins, and the distinctive way it was taking shape at the encounter between long-standing national traditions of psychiatric practice and global regimes of psychiatric knowledge production. In this section, I want to briefly consider how this archive rendered the interconnected histories of disaster psychiatry and trauma research within the professional psy sciences in Turkey—which long predates the earthquake—and how that history would preface the dramatic expansion of global psychiatric discourses on trauma and disaster in the immediate aftermath of the earthquake.

Despite the unprecedented and improvisational quality of their efforts, the Turkish psychiatrists and psychologists who worked to measure the psychological effects of the earthquake were by no means inventing a genre. As the Turkish psychiatrists and psychologists I interviewed combed through the available literature to design their studies and interventions, they would discover a domestic history of disaster psychiatry that had formed, tentatively, in response to previous earthquakes over the previous decade—especially the earthquakes in Erzincan in 1992, Dinar in 1995, and Adana in 1998. These disasters and their psychiatric responses would generate the earliest publications in an incipient national literature of disaster psychiatry.[24] They stood as the domestic precedent for psychiatric research on earthquakes, and as a common set of citations across this archive, the authors of the Marmara studies actively wove themselves into this history.

The intertextual references of this literature would, in turn, enact a global and globalized geography of psychic disaster. An important aspect of the construction of the Marmara Earthquake as a psychiatric event was the way researchers positioned it within a global history of (disaster) psychiatry. As these researchers wove themselves into this history, they would in turn weave Turkey into an emerging international literature and geography of global disaster and trauma. The Marmara Earthquake—later to be joined by the Indian Ocean tsunami (2004) and the Sichuan earthquake in China (2008)—would soon count among a limited set of go-to examples in global, systematic reviews of the mental health effects of large-scale disaster.[25] As these different disasters were made psychiatrically commensurable, new sorts of comparisons and global hierarchies would emerge: "This rate for PTSD," observed a psychiatrist working in the Marmara region, "was higher than found among earthquake survivors in the United States but lower than that found in an Armenian study. The rate of PTSD in the present study is concordant with those found after an earthquake in China."[26] In short order, the Marmara Earthquake would assume its place in a global geography of trauma and disaster.

Alongside, but rarely overlapping, with this literature on disaster psychiatry was a parallel domestic history of research on trauma and PTSD. The psychiatric study of trauma and PTSD in Turkey was, of course, not new. The study of "war neuroses," for instance, had a well-established history in Turkey, reaching back to Ottoman period.[27] Yet as the psychiatrist Tamer Aker notes, this work "was followed by a lengthy period of silence on the topic of trauma until there appeared a sharply renewed interest about the effects of traumatic experience in the last 20 years."[28] Until, that is, the Marmara Earthquake, when trauma and PTSD would become the psychological idioms of the earthquake. Leading up to the earthquake, interest in trauma and PTSD was located on the margins of mainstream, prestige-generating psychiatry in Turkey—which was dominated by research agendas and pharmaceuticalized interventions in line with dominant biological psychiatric approaches. The small group of psychiatrists and psychologists interested in trauma and PTSD were in two principal camps: one that conducted a series of influential studies examining the prevalence rates of PTSD among political detainees who experienced police torture, and another that conducted a cluster of studies focusing on gender-based violence and PTSD in cases of sexual assault and rape. Although this research was well regarded within the field, it was not considered by mainstream psychiatrists as making an important scientific contribution to the study of psychopathology. The research was seen as being politically rather than scientifically significant.[29]

With the Marmara Earthquake, interest in trauma and PTSD exploded. As the psychiatrist Cemal Dindar describes, "Those who were engaged in a nosological and even ideological debate on the existence of post-traumatic stress disorder became 'fast traumatists' after the earthquake."[30] The annual number of studies focused on psychological trauma in Turkey would double annually in the years following the Marmara Earthquake.[31] This explosion of interest (and publications) was driven by two factors. On the one hand, as described in the previous chapters, a large number of psychiatrists and psychologists were swept up in the public outpouring of humanitarian compassion following the earthquake. Given the skills they had to offer, together with the distinctive psychological and emotional effects of the earthquake, their attention was predictably drawn to trauma and PTSD. At the same time, this drawing of one's psychiatric attention cannot be understood outside of a globally ascendant trend in medical humanitarianism that regards the psychological effects of disaster as a critical domain of post-disaster intervention.[32] These two factors would feed each other and set in motion the dramatic growth of interest in trauma and PTSD following the Marmara Earthquake.

The idiom of trauma and the category of PTSD would become an important point of linkage and transfer between local compassion and global psychiatric expertise, which was not in fact "global" but, rather, dominated by European and North American experts, institutions, instruments, and journals. The director of a prominent trauma center in the earthquake region would characterize trauma as the earthquake's "traumatic bridge." Trauma was fundamental to the shared psychiatric imagination among the Turkish psychiatrists and psychologists responding to the earthquake and, as described in Chapter 4, it played a vital role in facilitating relationships within and between groups, with humanitarian psychiatrists and psychologists coming from outside of Turkey, and along transnational routes of psychiatric expertise. Again, the shared vocabulary of the traumatized psychological subject of disaster was a basic condition for both international collaboration and imagining the scalability of therapeutic expertise in the aftermath of the earthquake. As this "traumatic bridge" aided the movement of data, people, and interventions through region, it also facilitated the movement of global networks of trauma research—and funding—into Turkey. As trauma moved into the psychiatric mainstream, so did its experts. Previously marginalized psychiatrists would find themselves coordinating teams of mental health professionals, brokering between foreign experts and their Turkish counterparts, and gaining extraordinary access to resources and international networks of expertise. Trauma research would thus transform into a reliable source of funding, a relevant and publishable set of research priorities, and a realistic career path.

It is worth noting here that the contemporary psychological discourse around trauma and PTSD in Turkey is deeply indebted to the Marmara Earthquake. This is noteworthy when compared to other contexts, where the study of PTSD gained particular currency in relation to the legacy of war and political violence.[33] As such, an important argument being developed in this book is that, if we are to understand the dynamics and agendas of trauma research in Turkey today, we have to understand its debt to the earthquake. In turn, as I'm arguing in this chapter, this debt is twofold: the enormous therapeutic response that came together in the wake of the earthquake was inseparable from—and at times subordinated to—the epidemiological apparatus that was set in motion concurrently.

Variations and Derivations

The defining epidemiological studies of the Marmara Earthquake—especially the publications based on the SITSES studies—created a baseline against which future studies would evaluate their results and, in the process, established a canon that would stand at the center of the citational practices that constituted it as its own research literature. As with any canon, these studies also called into existence, in their canonicity, a secondary, derivative literature. Amid the frenzy of post-disaster psychiatric intervention and research, other psychiatrists and psychologists—many less well funded, less tapped into global psychiatric institutions and granting agencies, less able to get their results published in prominent English-language journals—struggled to distinguish themselves in a rapidly crowding field. Frequently, they did so by offering variations on the canon's core themes.

The study of the psychological effects of the earthquake in children and adolescents would be one such variation. Combining the ethical figure of the child (as the tragic embodiment of innocence) prominent in humanitarian discourse and the sort of unregulated medical experimentation and experimentality common to social contexts in upheaval,[34] these studies assumed a special place in the psychiatric apparatus that spread through the region. They stand out not only for their quantity, but also for the speed with which they were designed, conducted, and published. I offer but a handful of examples. The first psychiatric study to be published after the earthquake examined the psychological impact of the earthquake on 1,118 children of primary school and high school age living in the region. The study was conducted within the first month after the earthquake and data analysis and write up would be completed in time for publication by year's end—within four months of the earthquake. The study determined that children experienced high rates of anxiety following the earthquake.[35] Several independent studies, all started within weeks of the earthquake and some published within months, determined that children—many as young as two years old—were experiencing severe psychological symptoms, especially acute stress disorder and PTSD.[36] Another study that began psychiatric interviewing as early as two days following the earthquake, this time recruiting students between the ages of ten and sixteen, found that children who were exposed to life-threatening situations demonstrated elevated rates of PTSD, major depression, anxiety symptoms, and widespread impairment, such as hyperarousal and dissociative experiences.[37] This study would, in turn, serve as the basis for several follow-up studies concerned with over-time changes in PTSD and depression and vivid and intrusive memories associated with PTSD.[38]

As with the adult samples, the experimental wheels turned quickly as researchers looked for ways to transform the earthquake into a natural laboratory. Dozens of additional studies with children and adolescents replicated and extended the themes that interested researchers studying the psychological effects of disaster on adults. These studies followed the broad template laid out in the above, with studies examining the prevalence of PTSD among children living in the earthquake region,[39] rates of grief and dissociation among children,[40] the risk and prevalence of psychopathology among childhood survivors (one of which concluded that being trapped under a collapsed building seemed to increase the risk of psychopathology),[41] the relationship between severity of symptoms and proximity to the epicenter,[42] rates of depression and suicidal ideation,[43] and the relationship between parental psychopathology and family functioning on children's post-earthquake psychological problems.[44] Within these studies, we also find a shadow set of instruments (and acronyms) being compiled and administered to create a profile of the earthquake's psychological reality for children, such as the Children's Depression Inventory (CDI), the Child Behavior Checklist (CBCL), the Children's Post-Traumatic Response Reaction Index (CPTSRI), the Fear Survey Schedule, the StateTrait Anxiety Inventory for Children (STAI-C), the Traumatic Dissociation and Grief Scale (TDGS), and the Child PTSD-Reaction Index (CPTSD-RI).

In the years to come, thousands of children would be enrolled into this psychiatric machine. Although my primary interest in this chapter is how this machine came into existence—the sorts of desires and aspirations animating it, the sorts of categories, instruments, and records of publication that underwrote the psychiatric facticity and reality of the earthquake—I don't want to lose sight of the sort of suffering these studies were documenting. Indeed, the tableau of childhood suffering is bleak, even if it only slips out in the grim tabulation of results. To offer but one example: in a study of earthquake fears among 266 students (who completed the Fear Survey Schedule), researchers found that "the ten most frequently reported fears of the exposed group were fear of mother's death, father's death, hell, being trapped in the debris, recurrence of earthquake, death of the family members, earthquake, separation from parents, own death and fire, respectively."[45] I set aside, for the time being, the pressing ethical question of what it means to ask children to list their greatest fears in the immediate aftermath of such a catastrophic event.

As the foregoing indicates, the humanitarian figure of the child was an important domain for the psychiatric rendering of the earthquake. Beyond these studies, a machine of variations and derivations continued along. Struggling for recognition in a field rapidly filling with data and findings, researchers developed a staggering range of projects that capture both the ethical variability of research and the incredible ingenuity and creativity of researchers. To offer but a small selection, studies explored the relationship between post-traumatic stress symptoms and nutritional status ("underweight" and "normal-weight" people had higher rates of paranoid thoughts than "obese" people in the region);[46] rates of PTSD and major depression among elderly residents (those who lived closer to the epicenter had higher rates of both);[47] rates of PTSD, major depression, and anxiety among first responders and frontline medical staff;[48] the effectiveness of the SSRI fluoxetine (Prozac) on the symptoms of PTSD among children and adolescent survivors of the earthquake (participants ranged in age from seven to seventeen years old);[49] the psychological status of relocated earthquake survivors (relocation was a risk factor for increased psychological distress);[50] severity of psychological reactions of women to the earthquake and their use of psychiatric services (elevated in both cases);[51] the relationship between alcohol use disorders and anxiety, social phobia, and other post-traumatic stress symptoms;[52] and a number of studies using hospital records to examine rates of use of mental health services.[53] To this selective list could be added an entire metaliterature that explores everything from the technical minutiae of instrument translation,[54] to generic descriptions of the psychological disorders common after disasters,[55] to a series of essays and commentaries written by psychiatrists and psychologists offering broad reflections on the earthquake.[56] Taken together, this enormous body of research and writing provided a vast reservoir of data, publications, and anecdotes that not only reinforced the canonicity of the canon but also began, with the help of journalists and news hosts, to quickly circulate far beyond scientific journals.

It is easy to grow numb in this rush of instruments, checklists, researchers, diagnostic categories, techniques of data analysis, and acronyms. As one digs through the psychiatric literature born of the earthquake—as an archive—one finds hastily constructed studies giving way to more carefully designed projects, generating more complex data, and further questions. Research agendas expand, refine, and multiply. Disorders gain subcategories, instruments subdivide by different populations, and new populations come into being. Machines link and combine, begetting new machines. Acronyms spill out and pile up. Hierarchies of results and researchers form (with those at the top publishing in prominent English-language international journals). Findings amass and professional capital accumulates, to be parlayed into more grants and funded projects. Review articles in English and Turkish appear, giving the disaster its first professional guides.[57] Across this dramatic and rapid expansion, a web of citational ties thickens and a world starts to gain depth and texture.

At the heart of these distributed operations, as I have been describing in this chapter, was the twinned psychiatric desire to simultaneously treat and measure the psychological effects of the earthquake. The therapeutic and the epidemiological were conjoined and fed one another from the outset. Epidemiological studies would make the earthquake legible. They offered the comforts of order and control. With a "scientific eye," researchers groped through a world in upheaval, continually designing and redesigning therapeutic interventions. In this, the problem of scale discussed in the previous chapter would appear again in altered form. As with the interventions, the urge to measure was always an urge to scale up their findings, to determine the prevalence of psychopathology at the level of populations. Studies and categories relentlessly reified and rose above the reality of people's lives, seeking a kind of transcendent quantitative clarity offered by scaled questionnaires, prevalence rates, and p-values.

The orderliness of findings obscured not only the messiness of the lives of their subjects but also basic questions about the instruments themselves. Indeed, what does one learn from asking a person who recently survived a devastating earthquake (someone who, weeks earlier, lost loved ones, homes, and jobs; whose daily life had come to revolve around trudging through muddy tent encampments in the middle of the winter to get water and food, to argue with government officials about their deservingness for compensation, to prove to banks that, if they were lucky, they owned the home that was destroyed in the earthquake) to fill out a twenty-question survey in which they rank on a scale from 0 to 3 their sleeping difficulties, feelings of depression, or feelings of being upset when something reminds them of the earthquake. Despite their questionable validity, these instruments were, nonetheless, highly productive. The administration of these sorts of questionnaires—repeated tens of thousands of times over the following two years—proved decisive in giving the Marmara Earthquake its distinctive psychiatric form, one organized around a shared set of specific diagnostic categories, themselves articulating a set of assumptions about the psychological experience and subject of disaster.

To be clear, my aim here is not to vilify these researchers. Every psychiatrist and psychologist I met had been moved to action out of a deep sense of concern for others. They devoted countless hours and made significant personal and professional sacrifices over the span of several years to help survivors of the earthquake deal with its emotional fallout. This was difficult and distressing work. Indeed, in time, I would come to recognize how this urge to measure also assumed a protective and even therapeutic function for many of these researchers. For several researchers I interviewed, it seemed as if the process of designing studies, gathering data, analyzing findings, and publishing results was also a means for them to process their own struggle with the forms of loss and suffering they were witnessing. I also don't categorically fault those who saw in this an additional possibility for professional advancement; I certainly don't subscribe to an ethics of purity in which authentic acts of care must be offered, in order to be authentic, without any anticipation of personal gain. The faults that I see are elsewhere, which I return to later.

For now, I want to conclude by simply noting that the labor that constituted the earthquake as a psychiatric event was tremendous. By the formal end of these studies and interventions, hundreds of mental health professionals and thousands upon thousands of research subjects would be conscripted into this psychiatric world making. And this labor would bear fruit. The psychiatric machine would not only produce data but also offer lessons. With it, psychiatrists such as Dr. Mercan could write in their blogs and speak authoritatively on talk shows about the "natural" responses to disasters. Public-facing experts like Dr. Mercan—among many, many others—became translators and relays. The epidemiological becomes pedagogical; instruments become teaching machines. In so doing, a technical, psychiatric rendering of the earthquake begins moving far beyond the earthquake zone, a movement that would prove critical to facilitating the entrance of psychiatric and psychological discourses, psychiatric practices, and psychopharmaceuticals into the everyday life of communities far beyond and long after the earthquake.

SIX

Mediterranean Assemblages

I want to return in this chapter to that moment when Drs. Yavuz and Kaya reached out to a group of Israeli colleagues for advice about how to develop a post-earthquake intervention. Recall that Dr. Yavuz had met one of the Israeli psychiatrists years before the earthquake, while a research fellow in a psychiatric program in the United States. In the aftermath of the earthquake, desperate for ideas about what to do, Dr. Yavuz would get back in touch with this old professional acquaintance, and soon after, they'd be relying on the technical expertise and know-how of these Israeli colleagues to develop their own intervention in a temporary housing settlement near the earthquake's epicenter. In this chapter, I take this instance of informal, transnational collaboration in a moment of large-scale disaster as an opportunity to step back from the immediacy of the Marmara Earthquake to consider how the psychiatric response it attracted fit within broader, transregional networks of medical and psychiatric expertise.

This discussion also offers an opportunity to explore in more depth the distinctively "psychosocial" form that their intervention took. Although a novel approach at the time, psychosocial approaches to post-disaster care would soon become a regular component of humanitarian interventions on a global scale.[1] Indeed, over the past decades, therapeutically inspired psychosocial approaches have come to play a central role in the dramatic expansion of settings for psychological care on a global scale, moving far beyond contexts marked by large-scale crises and, along the way, supplanting long-term investments in clinical and institutional forms of psychiatric care.

From art therapy to assertiveness training, vocational rehabilitation to family counseling, psychosocial approaches have emerged as a dominant idiom for conceptualizing in therapeutic terms an array of social, familial, labor, and interpersonal "problems."[2]

Conventional accounts of these developments typically frame psychosocial interventions as more holistic and contextualized approaches to psychological well-being that emerged in reaction to treatment regimens that medicalized and pathologized experiences of emotional and psychological distress. In this chapter, I suggest that tracing how Dr. Yavuz and his team struggled to develop an intervention in the aftermath of the Marmara Earthquake actually brings into view a different genealogy of the psychosocial. As we will see, their embrace of a psychosocial approach grew not out of a recognition of the social embeddedness of psychological distress, but out of the tension between their therapeutic desires and local resistance to psychiatric care. It was in their efforts to overcome this resistance—in order to scale up the effects of their psychiatric expertise—that a psychosocial intervention took form.

By tracking how their intervention formed both in response to local resistance and in dialogue with transnational networks of psychiatric expertise, the following discussion, first, explores the striking adaptability and mobility of these forms of psychiatric expertise and, second, argues that closely following their movement brings into view a series of novel arrangements of psychiatry, disaster, and security that were forming in the region over this period. In our case, I am particularly interested in how this account of the travel of psychiatric knowledge and practice in a context of large-scale disaster is also a story about the broader, regional conditions of possibility for the circulation of medical expertise—a story that offers an important lesson about the unique capacity of these forms of expertise to draw together two divergent contexts (one characterized by the effects of a destructive seismic event, the other by a lasting politics of colonial occupation) into a common technical, psychiatrically constituted frame. In charting this psycho-political convergence, this discussion highlights how the psychiatric response to the Marmara Earthquake reproduced long-standing dynamics through which Europe's relationship with its colonial peripheries was psychiatrically mediated as it also embodied emergent configurations and routes of psychiatry and sovereignty in the region.

Activating Community, Going Viral

The response of Dr. Kaya and her colleagues to the challenges of providing post-disaster care would take a substantially different form than other groups of psychiatrists and psychologists responding to the earthquake. As discussed earlier, whereas many others held on to the doctor-patient therapeutic dyad as the ideal form of psychological care, and thus struggled to rework a clinic-based model in extreme conditions, Drs. Kaya and Yavuz were among those who more radically reimagined their expertise. Rather than envisioning an intervention that focused on individuals and aimed to multiply points of contact between psychiatric experts and psychologically injured earthquake survivors, they would develop an intervention that envisioned the "community" as the privileged site and setting of therapeutic intervention.

In the blur of despair and therapeutic improvisation that characterized the first months following the earthquake, as they began developing an intervention in a temporary housing settlement near the earthquake's epicenter, Drs. Kaya and Yavuz quickly noticed that the nearby "therapeutic tents"—which offered free mental health care to those in need—were attracting few visitors from the surrounding community. Indeed, as they had anticipated, residents largely avoided these tents. Despite their experiences—of sleeplessness, panic, nightmares, debilitating fear and grief—traditional psychiatry was still looked at with suspicion. Psychiatrists were for the "mad" (*deliler*), and they weren't "mad." They were just struggling.

This observation would turn into a method as the group began exploring other options for psychiatrically engaging survivors. "We started to think about ways to integrate our work into everyday social gatherings," recalled Dr. Yavuz. "We began organizing areas for children to play, or women to gather, that would also create opportunities to treat people." It was here where their attention began to shift to the "community" as a potentially useful site of care. As Dr. Kaya discussed, reflecting the urgency of the moment: "We had to do something. We had a lot of brainstorming sessions, we developed a lot of ideas. And then the idea came to work in the community.... What we took advantage of was looking at the community as a whole, as a unit. Not as individuals. We wanted to make an impact on the community . . . like 'community activation' programs. Something that would move the whole community in a particular direction. Like creating joy, or experiencing grief, or 'mourning the ruined city,' *collectively*."

With the help of their Israeli colleagues, they began developing a community-focused intervention. At its center was a teacher-mediated protocol that aimed to empower participants and mitigate the acute and long-term traumatic effects of the earthquake among school-aged children. With Dr. Kaya working as the field coordinator, they recruited and trained local teachers as "clinical mediators" to lead the classroom component of the intervention. Training sessions sought to develop the capacity of teachers to communicate their emotions so that they and their students would have a shared language to express and manage their trauma-related affects. In the classroom phase of the intervention, which lasted four weeks, teachers led eight two-hour sessions with their students. The sessions were a combination of cognitive behavioral techniques, psychoeducational modules (to teach children about their symptoms, the typical course of trauma-related conditions, and coping strategies), narrative exercises and writing activities (for "reprocessing" traumatic experiences), and a number of play activities.[3] As Drs. Yavuz and Kaya would later recall, the aims of the intervention were ambitious: "Restructuring traumatic experiences, dealing with intrusive thoughts, establishing a safe place, learning about the earthquake and preparing for future earthquakes, mourning the ruined city, controlling bodily sensations, confronting post-traumatic dreams, understanding reactions in the family, coping with loss, guilt, and death, dealing with anger, extracting life lessons, and planning for the future."

Beyond addressing individual psychopathologies, the intervention sought to "reactivate schools" and, in so doing, to "activate community." In contrast to other interventions being developed in the earthquake region that sought to remake and multiply the clinical encounter in the field, Drs. Yavuz and Kaya and their group focused their attention on the interpersonal. Their goal was to weave therapeutic objectives and techniques into everyday, familiar social settings and activities, especially the techniques of emotional self-awareness and communication at the heart of the intervention. As opposed to interventions that required continual expert oversight, they imagined their intervention as holding the capacity to self-replicate and propagate within communities as it transformed both psychological and interpersonal processes. A clinical psychologist on the team described this process in viral terms: "It was just spontaneous. In one of the supervising meetings, the teachers told us that 'We are now doing the same sort of group settings with the parents. You taught us how to communicate, how to behave with the children, so, we're gathering all the parents who have questions about it, and we're teaching them.'" "Maybe, within Turkey," she added, "it will become a sort of virus." In terms of their specific intervention, however, their goal was modest; the intervention would ultimately enroll 320 families.

Although this section of the book has focused on the perspectives of psy experts in the fashioning of a psychiatric response to the earthquake, accounts from those who experienced these sorts of interventions—to which we will shortly turn—show that efforts to conceal psychiatric techniques and aspirations within "the community" were not always able to avoid local resistance. On the one hand, an obvious implication of embedding psychiatric care within the everyday was that the line between social life and psychiatric intervention was being continuously blurred. For people living in the tent settlements, it wasn't always clear when this line was being crossed and they were being unwittingly conscripted into an intervention. "We were having a normal conversation, becoming friendly," complained one former resident, "and I realized that they were conducting a study. 'What kind of study is this, why are you doing a study?' I asked. 'While we're visiting, why are you conducting a study on me? If you're trying to gather information, you know I'm not your patient. I'm not your thing.'" Rumors also often spread that the teams of psychiatrists and psychologists working in the region were using survivors as experimental subjects for pharmaceutical trials (a suspicion that was commonly dismissed by those developing the interventions as a sign of trauma). On the other hand, the model of emotional self-awareness, emotional vulnerability, and affective communication promoted by the intervention was not only unconventional for the largely working-class residents of the settlement, but it also challenged conventional social hierarchies—especially between teachers and students, as well as parents and children. These social hierarchies were points of regular struggle for those implementing the intervention.

As this begins to suggest, Drs. Kaya and Yavuz's psychosocial intervention took shape in a dynamic play between their therapeutic aspirations and the local resistance to psychiatric care they encountered. While the psychiatrists and psychologists I met spoke about this resistance in terms of people's lack of familiarity with the expertise they offered, interviews with residents indicated otherwise. In fact, residents were all too accustomed to hearing stories about the institutional violence of psychiatry. In these tellings, psychiatric institutions were sites of inhumane neglect where those with no families or "bad" families were abandoned. In the face of this deeply rooted suspicion of psychiatry, Dr. Kaya and her colleagues thus worked to ease the concerns of residents by embedding therapeutic techniques within social settings and activities that were not associated with psychiatric expertise—such as play sessions, art and writing activities, women's knitting groups, and other community activities in the settlement.

In other words, they sought to overcome local resistance to psychiatric care—a resistance that they understood to be grounded in older institutional arrangements of psychiatric power—by reworking and integrating their expertise within everyday domains of social engagement. In the process, they hoped that their therapeutic techniques would dissolve into the background of familiar and familial social interactions, imparting new psychiatric horizons onto mundane activities and everyday tasks. Taken together, we begin to see in these efforts to socially integrate psychiatric expertise a defining duality of psychosocial approaches, in the form of a therapeutic compromise that seeks to both mimic and transform the psychological and social dimensions of life.[4]

INTERLUDE
Psychiatry, Disaster, Politics

> The very condition of a deconstruction may be at work in the work, within the system to be deconstructed.
> —JACQUES DERRIDA, *Memoires for Paul de Man*, 1986

Dr. Kaya and her colleagues hoped that the benefits of their intervention would extend far beyond this particular setting, and even beyond the immediate aftermath of the earthquake. By relying on the skills of emotional self-awareness and communication being introduced, they hoped that their intervention would help community members develop communicative skills to better express their feelings with one another, to more effectively (and nonviolently) resolve conflicts, and serve as the basis for creating more open and equitable relationships within families and, in turn, the broader community. Despite its modest therapeutic aspirations—to help children be better able to talk about their emotions—the intervention thus harbored a larger vision: that these techniques of emotional self-awareness and affective communication would have lasting beneficial effects as they fostered the conditions not just for individual recovery but also for a "healthy" community.[5] Put differently, the intervention carried within itself an extrapolated psychiatric future in which a successful intervention would weave therapeutic techniques into the tissue of interpersonal and communal life as it simultaneously transformed both psychological and interpersonal processes.

I want to pause briefly here to note the political entanglements of the therapeutic horizon that animated the improvisations of Dr. Kaya and her colleagues, for they are important for understanding the transnational matrixes of disaster, psychiatry, and sovereignty that interest me in this chapter. It is not difficult to discern the political implications of this communal vision of therapeutic recovery. While they may not have mobilized a defined model of community life, their intervention nonetheless sought to reform participants' capacity to speak about inner emotional worlds as a means of transforming them and, in so doing, create the conditions for an indeterminate but "healthy" future community. Yet, despite the intervention's implicit political aspirations, every person interviewed from this group categorically rejected any suggestion that their work was political. Dr. Kaya talked explicitly about this: "No, no we would like to stay away from politics. . . . There are some groups that are working with a political viewpoint–empowering women, such as human rights associations and foundations. If we were like them, maybe [our findings] . . . would be getting published more easily. We're trying to be as objective as possible." For Dr. Kaya and others in the group, medical and scientific neutrality were imperative to their work. Placing an explicit political agenda ahead of their medical expertise—as they understood other physician-activists doing, especially in the name of human rights[6]—ran the risk of undermining their professional authority, which they understood as contingent on their medical and scientific neutrality.

The discrepancy between the political aspirations of their work and their disavowal of political motives in the name of medical neutrality is a familiar ethical tension within humanitarian interventions.[7] While this disavowal can be understood as a pragmatic reaction to the political and professional realities they were negotiating (as a means of avoiding reprisal from municipal and state authorities, as well as resistance among community members), it can also be understood as a means for them to evade the ethical responsibilities and political implications of their own clinical work. Dr. Kaya suggested as much when she later described her ambivalent feelings about their work. She worried that their intervention was, as she described, "psychologizing the disaster." "I worried that we were reducing the disaster to a pathology of individuals . . . and that we would lose sight of," as she put it, "the economic infrastructure of the trauma." "There were other trauma-related issues for these people—who were poor and uneducated, who had witnessed lots of atrocities, and had lots of bad things happen to them. So, if we were going to focus on earthquake trauma, it was only a superficial part of the whole picture. We wanted to do something more effective, in terms of communication, and understanding, and emotional growth."

Acutely aware of the structural conditions within which they were working, she would go on to describe her apprehension about how their intervention was focusing exclusively on individual symptoms, rather than the larger conditions of people's lives, which she saw as the deeper source of survivors' problems. Indeed, Dr. Kaya was sensitive to the fact that the earthquake belonged to a long history of "atrocities" and was thus continuous with an everyday already filled with crisis, violence, and chronic insecurity. In turn, she worried that their work was in some way abetting the state's efforts to evade culpability, diverting attention away from the ways that the state's relentless promotion of economic development and, with it, inadequate oversight in housing construction contributed in significant ways to the forms of personal suffering and psychological distress they were trying to address.

It is noteworthy that Dr. Kaya's concerns anticipated a set of critiques of trauma-based humanitarian interventions, and global mental health more broadly, that would become increasingly influential in the years to come. At the center of these critiques was an argument that echoed Dr. Kaya's misgivings, that trauma-based interventions framed crises in terms of individual psychopathologies and, in so doing, drew attention away from the structural or political-economic conditions of people's suffering.[8] Beyond merely anticipating these critiques, Dr. Kaya's concerns are particularly noteworthy in that they emerged from her practical and improvised efforts to reimagine her psychiatric expertise in the midst of disaster, as a member of a group of novice practitioners working at the margins of "global psychiatry."[9]

Despite their concerns, Dr. Kaya and her colleagues forged on. They felt that the urgency of people's needs outweighed these political and ethical concerns. Addressing the deeper problems would have to wait. They also recognized that psychiatry, especially during this period, was not a field of expertise being mobilized by the state to deflect its responsibility for the death and destruction occasioned by the Marmara Earthquake. Instead, a geological-political discourse that centered the destructive capriciousness of "nature" would dominate the state's efforts to obscure its complicity in the structural conditions of the disaster. Nevertheless, as we will see, the nascent entanglements of psychiatry, disaster, and sovereignty taking shape here will prove important to our understanding of the ways that these forms of psychiatric expertise traveled through the region at the time.

A Psychiatry of Occupation

The broad dynamics being described here will be recognizable to those familiar with the critical literature on humanitarian psychiatry. In this respect, we can understand the intervention of Drs. Kaya and Yavuz as yet another instance of psy expertise and experts facilitating the entrance of psychiatric and psychological discourses, globalized forms of psy governance, and psychopharmaceuticals into the everyday lives of communities.[10] While indebted to these arguments, I would also come to feel that they were missing something important. That is, I came to share Henrik Ronsbo's concern that these lines of analysis ran the risk of "conjur[ing] up notions of centralized governance and singular logics, which on the one hand overemphasizes the efficacy of discourse while on the other hand blinds us to the complex networks through which knowledge is generated and shared."[11]

With this in mind, I turn in this section to some of the "complex networks" within which Drs. Kaya and Yavuz's intervention took shape. As such, I want to broaden our focus to consider how their improvisational effort to develop a social conception of psychiatric care in the wake of disaster formed within a wider field of transnational collaborations. In tracking closely these collaborations, we'll see that the techniques by which Drs. Kaya and Yavuz sought to animate their therapeutic-political aspirations amid the ruins of the earthquake were themselves indebted to a different sort of political project and its own accompanying formations of disaster. Briefly exploring this transnational entanglement will help us further highlight the conditions of possibility for the circulation of medical expertise in the region and, with it, emerging transregional arrangements of psychiatry, disaster, and security.

I return again to the moment when Drs. Kaya and Yavuz's group was just beginning their work, those exhausting and exhilarating months when, in the midst of massive loss and social chaos, they worked tirelessly to improvise a psychiatric response to the earthquake's destruction. Frustrated with the state's disaster response efforts, and working outside of the formal institutional structures of existing associations and humanitarian organizations, they began to cobble together a "spontaneous" and "unique" intervention. There was no blueprint to realize, no model to implement: "We weren't an association, or a foundation," explained Dr. Kaya, "We were just a lot of colleagues, professional people. We were not a joint effort of any institute or foundation." With a mounting sense of desperation about how they would do something useful, they searched for guidance. It was at this point that Dr. Yavuz reconnected with an Israeli psychiatrist he had met years earlier, a psychiatrist who was part of a team that had developed community-based PTSD prevention programs in Israel. Within weeks, a team of Israeli mental health professionals were on a plane from Israel to Istanbul.

This would be the beginning of a sustained collaboration. As Dr. Yavuz and his Turkish colleagues shuttled back and forth between Istanbul and the earthquake zone, the team of Israeli mental health professionals traveled back and forth from Israel. In the process, a Jewish psychologist from Turkey who had studied psychology in Israel joined the group to help translate and facilitate the collaboration. Throughout the process of developing and implementing the intervention, the team of Turkish psychiatrists and psychologists remained in continual communication with their Israeli colleagues. "After almost every session," recalled one of the psychologists, "we were in some way in contact with one another. If [the Israeli psychiatrists] were here, we would meet and talk, or if they weren't here, we were writing back to them and they were writing us. They were aware of every step. It wasn't like they just gave us the protocol and let us do anything we wanted."

Ideas and techniques moved with striking ease between Turkey and Israel. For Drs. Yavuz and Kaya, the Israelis had the technical expertise to formulate a means of making the disaster psychiatrically knowable and a set of techniques for acting upon the scale of emotional suffering it precipitated. The particular expertise the Israeli experts brought to the earthquake zone was their technical know-how in conceptualizing the social aspect of the psychology of disaster, which would provide the key to scaling up their therapeutic aspirations.

Their expertise in community-based care had been forged, almost a decade earlier, during the first Gulf War (1990–1991), in response to Scud missiles being fired from Iraq into Israel. In a series of influential studies conducted in affected regions of Israel, they developed psychological protocols for measuring the traumatic and psychopathological effects of missile attacks on preschool-age Israeli children. (Blood samples drawn from community members would also render these effects in biological terms.) Over the ensuing years, the group would become specialists in the psychological and psychobiological effects of aerial warfare, as they refined their epidemiological and clinical skills through a series of studies concerned with the retraumatization of Israel civilians with the threat of further missile attacks from Iraq in 1998, the traumatic effects on young Israeli children of missiles fired into Israel from southern Lebanon during the 2006 Lebanon War, and the psychological effects on preschool Israeli children of rockets and mortars fired from the Gaza Strip into southern Israel during the Gaza War of 2008–2009.

To appreciate how the post-earthquake intervention in Turkey was entangled within the logic and technologies of security in Israel, it is important to situate their work in the larger field of trauma research and treatment in Israel during this period. The approach to trauma treatment offered by the Israeli colleagues took form during a period in which a rapidly globalizing discourse of PTSD began to be reworked as it moved into the context of the Israeli-Palestinian conflict. As Keren Friedman-Peleg has argued, studies such as those described here were part of a wider effort to clinically demonstrate the invisible psychic wounds experienced by Israeli citizens—especially children—as well as provide a new language for defining their attachment to the nation.[12] This was a period during which organizations such as the Israel Trauma Center for Victims of Terror and War (NATAL) began promoting a notion of national trauma as a clinical and popular category that wove together experiences of individual psychopathology with conceptions of collective suffering born of the Israeli-Palestinian conflict.[13] Reflecting important professional and societal shifts in how psychiatric discourses and the imperatives of national security aligned, this would prove a critical period during which a "biomedical notion [of PTSD] was naturalized in Israel as an idiom for articulating an ever-expanding panoply of security-relevant distressing experiences."[14]

Psychiatric categories such as PTSD, which had been critiqued as being notoriously indifferent to the political conditions of people's suffering, thus emerged as a medium for negotiating a series of ethno-nationalist power relations in Israel.[15] As the category of PTSD traveled through this environment, it offered a seemingly neutral, clinical vocabulary for conceptualizing a range of psychological and affective experiences emerging from the conditions of Israel's national and regional political project—bearing witness to the suffering of Israeli citizens, reinforcing the militarism of the Israeli state (by positioning the military as the natural protector of the threatened Israeli body and guardian of the psychic vulnerability of its citizens), and further obscuring the forms of everyday violence and dispossession that constituted the conditions of living for Palestinian civilians.[16] Understood in this context, the trauma-based interventions from which Drs. Kaya and Yavuz were drawing inspiration can be understood as features of, or even a setting for, Israel's project of colonial occupation with regard to Palestine.

Indeed, if we follow both Eyal Weizman's and Achille Mbembe's argument that a critical dimension of Israel's occupation consists of its verticality—in which aerial surveillance and policing, infrastructural networks of bridges and tunnels, and the more general management of verticality are central features of Israel's necropolitical regime[17]—we can recognize community-based interventions to address the traumatic effects of aerial bombardment among Israeli children as being deeply entangled within Israel's "politics of verticality."[18] In this instance, they typify the sorts of initiatives and interventions that aim to cultivate what the anthropologist Joe Masco has called "national security affect"—those practices and projects in which the anticipation of mass violence and destruction (e.g., disaster preparedness drills in the United States) are cultivated as a means of recruiting, managing, and calibrating the affective bases of citizenship.[19] In our case, the very way that these community-based PTSD prevention programs in Israel aim to ameliorate the psychological effects of aerial bombardment can be understood as generating the anticipation of such events, thereby, following Masco, cultivating states of affective readiness that, in turn, recruit citizens—willingly or not—into Israel's larger politics of occupation. Put otherwise, the vocabulary and practice of psychiatric intervention as instantiated by these sorts of interventions interweave with discourses, practices, and the spatialization of national security, providing a psychiatric means for formulating the frontiers of a settler-colonial project.

This was the sort of psychiatric and political milieu within which Drs. Yavuz and Kaya's Israeli colleagues worked and the context within which psychiatric ideas of a "healthy" community were being developed and refined. In the months following the earthquake—with the prodding of Dr. Yavuz, a series of visits to Turkey to meet with Drs. Yavuz and Kaya's team, and extended telephone conversations and email exchanges—interventions designed to address the traumatic effects of aerial bombardment in Israel would travel to Turkey to help teachers and students address the traumatic effects of a disastrous earthquake. Following what would become a well-worn path—in which technologies of security developed in the context of Israel's occupation of Palestinian territories are exported globally[20]—expertise (and experts) forged in a settler-colonial context to address the psychological effects of war and occupation moved across transnational networks of psychiatric expertise to be rearticulated amid the post-earthquake destruction of Turkey.[21] In the process, two seemingly disconnected sets of conditions would be psychiatrically reconstituted as interchangeable, if not common, spaces of technical operation.

Psychiatry, Disaster, Security

What does this example—this close account of a group of Turkish psychiatrists and psychologists struggling to patch together a therapeutic intervention in a context of exceptional social, material, and geological upheaval—tell us about the production and circulation of medical knowledge in the region? What does it say, for instance, about the entanglement of medicine and power in the Middle East and the conditions of possibility for the globality of particular forms of medical expertise? While I remain ambivalent about generalizing from Turkey to the broader region—for it runs the risk of enacting older (and recently revitalized) Ottoman imperial fantasies—I do think this example tells us something important about the configurations of crisis, medical expertise, and security that have been forming in the region over the past several decades.

If we are to understand the conditions of possibility for the global movement of particular forms of medical knowledge, it is critical, I argue, that we first take into account the specificity of these sorts of mobility—the ways, in other words, that different forms of medical knowledge and expertise are rendered mobile in different ways. As many have observed, the spread of psychosocial interventions—that heterogeneous assemblage of principles, techniques, and experts that has become the dominant model of psychological treatment in contexts of crisis and disaster—marked a substantial movement of psychiatric discourses and practices beyond clinical spaces.[22] Once outside of the clinic, as the previous example typifies, they have been able to travel with remarkable ease.[23] Psychosocial interventions, as medical technologies, have shown themselves to be striking fluid;[24] they are amorphous gatherings of ideas, people, and materials that are extraordinarily agile and responsive, readily adapting themselves to a range of conditions and capable of quickly and affordably scaling up therapeutic aspirations across communities and populations. As such, the scalability of these sorts of interventions turns not so much on their ability to rise above a context as on their capacity to move through space—those material and social worlds upended by crisis, as well as transnational networks of psychiatric expertise. In this respect, it is striking to juxtapose the mobility of these technologies to the relative immobility of the populations who are their primary recipients.

In turn, the sort of universal psychological subject upon which psychosocial interventions are commonly predicated is essential to this adaptability and mobility. The categories of "trauma" and "PTSD," along with the transnational fields of psychiatric knowledge production and humanitarian intervention that were forming around these categories during this period, are particularly important for understanding the therapeutic mobility at play here.[25] Similarly, the sort of subjects that these interventions presumed—characterized by, among other features, emotional and psychological vulnerability—played a vital role in facilitating relationships within and between different actors and was critical, as a method of commensuration,[26] for diminishing obstacles and freeing these technologies to travel with little apparent resistance. Last, we can't lose sight of the ways that an ethical discourse of medical neutrality similarly facilitated the movement of these technologies from one set of conditions to another. Although there are certainly additional features of this intervention that were important for its mobility, the above ones go a long way to explain how these technologies were able to move with such ease across a devastated material and social terrain.

While these are crucial issues when it comes to making sense of the circulation of psychiatric expertise in the region, I've been concerned in this chapter as much with the fact of their mobility as with the sorts of routes their movements trace. Here, we arrive at a limit of thinking about these interventions in terms of networked assemblages, as discussed in the previous chapter. While such an approach allowed us to appreciate these interventions as heterogeneous and distributed networks of relations, it is also an approach notoriously inadequate for thinking through the structural and historical conditions of these relations.[27]

In my case, on the one hand, I have been struck by the ways that a particular history of psychiatry in the region moves through, if not haunts, the types of psychiatric expertise that formed in the wake of the Marmara Earthquake. In many regards, this is a familiar story. As these Turkish psychiatrists and psychologists struggled to overcome the limits of their own training, as they drew in experts and forms of expertise to address the suffering of their fellow citizens, they found themselves unwitting participants in a much longer history of European psychiatric expertise in the region—a history that stretches back to the circulation of psychiatric knowledge and techniques amid Ottoman military modernization reforms during Europe's First World War as well as to the uses of psychiatry within European colonial projects in the Middle East and North Africa.[28] If we situate our account within this history, what we see happening in the wake of the Marmara Earthquake is a recognizable story about the travel of new forms of psychiatric knowledge and practice through the region in contexts marked by catastrophic disruption and colonial (in)security.

On the other hand, following closely how these technologies actually moved brings into view alternate routes of technoscientific mobility, as well as historically specific arrangements of disaster, psychiatry, and sovereignty. As recent ethnographic and historical research on psychiatry in the Middle East has begun to reveal, the emergence of psychiatric discourses and their social, technical, and political trajectories in the region are more complex than what many (postcolonial) accounts have allowed for, in which psychiatry is positioned as but one of many "tools of empire" used to control and manage local populations. Joelle Abi-Rached, for instance, highlights how the development of psychiatry in Lebanon was not a straightforward expression of Europe's civilizing and expansionary mission—as was the case in North Africa—but took form within a complex and historically shifting convergence of therapeutic desire, transnational expertise, and local pushback.

For Abi-Rached, to understand this history, and the development of psychiatry in the broader Middle East, one must take into account "local (rather than merely colonial) contributions on the development of psychiatric practices and . . . the dynamic flow of local and global exchanges (rather than merely exported forms of knowledges) in shaping institutional practices."[29] In turn, Orkideh Behrouzan, in her ethnography of psychiatry and generational memory in Iran, explores how psychiatric discourses expanded through complex transnational exchanges of psychiatric expertise and shifting semiotic articulations of everyday moods and affects. Rather than an account of how Western forms of psychiatric expertise overrode local realities, Behrouzan offers a rich "bottom-up" understanding of the medicalization of emotional distress in Iran. Taken together, these accounts urge us to complicate and rethink conventional stories about the globalization of psychiatry—which characteristically frame the mobility of psychiatric knowledge and practice in terms of technological diffusion from Europe to its peripheries[30]—as they also draw our attention to the regional specificity of these psychiatric trajectories.

A defining feature of the circuits and assemblages that I have been tracing is that they came into existence outside of formal state, scientific, humanitarian, military, or religious institutions. Although they may have been dependent on the infrastructures and technoscientific vocabularies of these institutions (which made possible Dr. Yavuz's meeting of his Israeli counterpart, the Turkish and Israeli psychiatrists being able to speak a common language of trauma and PTSD, as well as my meeting of Dr. Kaya in Boston), they also point toward a vast network of translocally constituted and enormously flexible formations of psychiatric expertise that are continually being assembled and disassembled at the margins of "global psychiatry." While there are certainly elements of the Marmara Earthquake relief effort that may confirm conventional accounts of the globalization of psychiatry (of experts from western Europe traveling to the region to provide expertise on post-disaster management), and setting aside the important point that psychiatry in Turkey has long been entangled in European forms and institutions of psychiatric expertise,[31] the example of Drs. Kaya and Yavuz's work suggests something different.

In charting this movement through a set of collaborations between a group of psychiatrists and psychologists in Turkey (working, again, outside of formal institutions) and a team of Israeli psychiatrists and psychologists, we see not only tangible examples of these novel routes of mobility but also how, in their movement, they are able to draw seemingly distinct sets of conditions into a common technical frame. With Drs. Kaya and Yavuz's ad hoc and improvisational efforts to develop a therapeutic response to the disaster, forms of expertise forged in a colonial context to manage the affective consequences of occupation travel to a setting of large-scale disaster to mitigate the traumatic effects of an earthquake and, along the way, "activate" a "healthy" community. In the process, dramatic differences in how human agency and political accountability align in these two settings largely disappear within a flow of psychiatric experts and technical know-how. Two divergent settings are thus rendered psychiatrically commensurable.

At the same time that this travel of psychiatric expertise flattens and obscures differences, it also reveals how these settings are animated by overlapping configurations of crisis, disaster, and sovereignty. In Turkey, the science and therapeutics of PTSD would contribute to a sense that the earthquake was an event without history, an exceptional rupturing of inner and outer worlds caused by "nature." In so doing, psychiatry would take part—if only as a minor player—in a wider biopolitical project of concealing the ways that the death and destruction of the earthquake was the realization of a history of economic development that prioritized economic growth over the regulation of home construction and, in the process, generated a population of people who could be killed without political accountability.[32] In Israel, the science and therapeutics of PTSD would convert the necropolitical conditions of occupation into rates of individual pathology and protocols for therapeutic intervention, in which the necessity of a militarized ethno-nationalist project was confirmed and the trauma of a few became scientifically and morally legible while the daily violence and dispossession of others were obscured. Furthermore, in tracing the movement of experts and expertise between these two settings, we also encounter the shared capacity of disaster zones and spaces of coloniality to generate the conditions for medical and technical experimentation.[33]

Due in large part to the continued work of Dr. Kaya, the post-earthquake intervention in Turkey lasted more than two years, which was significantly longer than other interventions in the region. Despite their initial enthusiasm, however, the group's trips became steadily less frequent as the demands of professional lives became increasingly difficult to put off, funding sources less interested, and the long commute more of an obstacle. The assemblage that their intervention represented would not hold together indefinitely, for its conditions had shifted. By the seventh anniversary of the earthquake, when I began regularly visiting the region, little remained of their work.

The intervention would, however, have an afterlife. These psychiatric techniques and technologies were, after all, highly adaptable. Features of it would be integrated into the curriculum of a local school that had been established for children who had lost parents in the earthquake. Meanwhile, Dr. Kaya and a clinical psychologist in the group, having become close friends, grew increasingly interested in community-based research at a point in their careers that allowed for new possibilities. Along with a third psychologist, they established a nonprofit organization that sought to incorporate some of the intervention's approaches to emotional communication and psychosocial well-being into school curricula beyond the earthquake region.

Drs. Kaya and Yavuz's post-earthquake intervention would, in time, also travel back to Israel. Reflecting further psychiatric innovation, their work informed the development of a revised set of interventions to manage the continued psychological effects and negative affects generated by the conditions of occupation. While their Israeli counterparts remained focused on children, the aim was no longer merely to prevent the psychopathologies associated with traumatic experience. The new project sought to also build "resilience" among children, especially in terms of providing them with the skills to cope with possible terrorist attacks. This turn to resilience reflected a wider set of trends, in which the language of "resilience" was supplanting a focus on "vulnerability" within increasingly influential approaches to both humanitarian psychiatry and neoliberal governance.[34]

With its guiding imperative of "bouncing back" and "keeping going" in the face of disasters (including terrorist attacks, pandemics, and a wide range of other calamities), the goal of promoting "resilience" would reposition psychological discourses within the imperatives of national security, thereby shifting the terms of political accountability and animating disaster in new ways. For the Israeli colleagues of Drs. Kaya and Yavuz, the new program sought explicitly to extend their psychological work into the preclinical terrain of anticipation and preparedness. In this expansion from the clinical to the preclinical, these interventions—to borrow Friedman-Peleg and Goodman's characterization of a similar program—sought to "immunize the social body" against potential trauma.[35] Further reflecting the shifting terrains and ties that have come to bind psychiatry and security in the region over the past two decades, these interventions would thus continue their psycho-political labor of constituting communities, calibrating political affects, and managing populations in terms indebted to the psychiatry of disaster.

SEVEN

Remains

This part of the book has followed scores of psychiatrists and psychologists as they left the familiar confines of clinical offices and hospitals and traveled into the social, material, and psychological devastation of the Marmara Earthquake. It has tracked these "novice humanitarians" as they confronted a series of challenges—the limits of their training, a mental health system in disarray, an unimaginable scope of emotional and psychological suffering—and worked to improvise an enormous if dispersed and decentralized post-disaster psychiatric infrastructure. The interventions, protocols, and studies developed here—repeated tens of thousands of times over the ensuing years—would prove critical in giving the Marmara Earthquake its distinctive psychiatric form. Organized around a shared set of diagnostic categories, themselves articulating a set of assumptions about psychological experience and the psychological subject of disaster, the psychiatric response to the Marmara Earthquake thus took shape at a series of overlapping junctures that are by now familiar: at the encounter between long-standing national traditions of psychiatric practice and emergent global regimes of humanitarian intervention, in the tension between compassion for one's fellow citizen and the desire for the production of psychiatric knowledge and professional capital, and at the intersection of a widespread sense that the state had betrayed its promise to protect its citizens and a growing fascination with the promises of neoliberal reform. In the process, the psychiatrists and psychologists responding to the earthquake would draw on and draw in networks of transnational psychiatric expertise, marking out new routes of expertise in the region and revealing novel configurations of psychiatry, disaster, and sovereignty along the way.

If you were to travel through the region today, not much of this past would be readily apparent. That which Drs. Baykal, Eser, Şahin, Kaya, Yavuz, and many more built did not last. Although several of the interventions lasted upward of two years—which is exceptionally long by humanitarian standards—none of the interventions described in the previous chapters was operating by the time I began visiting the region in 2007. The post-disaster psychiatric infrastructure had been largely dismantled. This is not surprising. The vast majority of residents had long since moved out of the post-earthquake settlements and prefabricated housing. They had either migrated from the region altogether or dispersed into the new apartment buildings rapidly expanding around the gulf. Born of disaster, the makeshift post-earthquake psychiatric infrastructure passed on as the conditions changed.

While the interventions were formally over, the remains of this infrastructure could be found scattered throughout the region. In places, there were clear lines of descent. The earthquake, for instance, would leave in its aftermath a psychological trauma research center at a regional medical school and new graduate and certificate programs dedicated to mental health and disaster at other universities. It would also leave behind several professional organizations (e.g., the Psychological Trauma and Disaster Psychiatry Section of the Psychiatric Association of Turkey, the Trauma, Disaster, and Crisis Unit of the Turkish Psychological Association) and inspire a range of conferences, training workshops, and public health and disaster preparedness initiatives.

New professional opportunities would also arise to create new career paths. In step with wider shifts in the field of humanitarian intervention, psychosocial approaches to disaster response attracted particular interest. A group of psychiatrists and psychologists who came together after the Marmara Earthquake would, for example, establish in 2006 the Union of Disaster Psychosocial Services (Afetlerde Psikososyal Hizmetler Birliği, or APHB). Representing the new sorts of collaboration the earthquake fostered—in this case between Turkey's Red Crescent Society (Kızılay), the Turkish Association of Psychologists, the Psychiatry Association of Turkey, the Association of Social Workers, the Psychological Health Association for Children and Youth, and the Turkish Association of Psychological Counseling and

Guidance—they would bring their psychosocial expertise to a widening range of disasters, including floods, traffic and plane accidents, industrial and mining disasters, bombings, and forest fires. In time, APHB became further embedded into the infrastructure of disaster response in Turkey, as well as international psychosocial trauma treatment institutions, with the signing of a formal agreement with Kızılay and UNICEF in 2012. Beyond these sorts of formalized agreements, the number of organizations and associations offering programs based on psychosocial models would proliferate in the decades that followed the earthquake.

The repertoire of instruments and techniques developed in the earthquake proved especially resilient. They would be utilized in one disaster after another over the coming decades to further expand the domestic literature on the psychological effects of disaster. An earthquake in the Van region of eastern Turkey in 2011 proved a particularly important moment in which the instruments, techniques, and networks that emerged out of the Marmara Earthquake were once again mobilized. Unlike in the Marmara Earthquake—which occurred in western Turkey—this context would require additional work from these psychiatric technologies, namely to mediate conditions profoundly disordered by both the earthquake and an interdependent history of Kurdish dispossession and Turkish state violence. Two years later, these same instruments would be used by psychiatrists taking part in the Gezi Park uprising to document the psychological effects of police violence, and from there they would move into the refugee camps forming along Turkey's Syrian border. They would appear once again in the aftermath of another massive earthquake, this time on the border of Turkey and Syria, in 2023—a disaster I return to in the epilogue.

Beyond instances of disaster and crisis, the earthquake would also give rise to a new national priority for mental health services. In fact, the earthquake is widely credited as the catalyst for a series of significant shifts in the distribution of psychiatric services in Turkey, especially with a renewed commitment to expanding community-based forms of mental health care.[1] With this shift to "the community" as a privileged setting for psychiatric care, that which had been a vital, if improvised, means for novice humanitarian psychiatrists to reimagine the scalability of their therapeutic expertise in a moment of crisis thus became institutionalized into the state, reflecting in turn a set of consolidating political agendas and priorities of neoliberal reform in a post-disaster Turkey. By 2017, there were more than 150 community mental health clinics across the country.

As time passed, the remainders of the psychiatric response to the Marmara Earthquake became more difficult to trace. Organizations and groups that formed in the aftermath of the earthquake dissolved as the relief and rebuilding efforts slowed, to reconstitute in new ways later—in a different place, with a new collection of experts and with new acronyms. Those groups that had learned how to track and access funding trends from the European Union were able to last longer, with many shifting their focus away from emergency relief to long-term projects addressing more endemic social problems, such as poverty reduction, domestic violence, women's rights, and educational reform. Further afield, the humanitarian response to the Marmara Earthquake would, in time, facilitate the dramatic expansion of discourses of medical humanitarianism and medical neutrality among human rights advocates and activists in the years to follow.[2]

The earthquake also played a decisive role in creating the sort of psychiatrically minded public that expert commentators, such as Dr. Mercan (whom we met in Chapter 5), were calling into existence in the wake of the Marmara Earthquake. Indeed, for all the mental health professionals I interviewed for this project, one of the positive outcomes of the earthquake was its effect on public discourse about mental health. With the massive psychiatric response to the earthquake, media coverage from the region that conveyed with affective intensity the psychological and emotional turmoil of survivors, the incorporation of psychiatric expert commentators into that coverage, the psychoeducation campaigns occurring in settlements of displaced residents across the region, and the incorporation of mental health themes into disaster preparedness programs and disaster response planning, it became much more common for people to talk openly about their emotional and psychological states. In this regard, the earthquake is widely regarded as a pivotal moment in the ongoing destigmatization of mental illness in Turkey—especially experiences of depression, anxiety, and trauma. This newly public psychiatric discourse, once set in motion, proved appealing. It would increasingly offer a set of terms and frameworks through which people spoke about everyday problems and emotional distress, just as a range of political commentators began formulating Turkey's history through psychiatric idioms (as a sequence of traumas that the nation had to confront and process in order to heal). While there were surely other forces at play here, the earthquake was nonetheless a decisive moment in the consolidation of this new psychiatrically minded public culture.

Although these are important developments to track, to continue to follow the legacy of the psychiatric infrastructure that formed in the wake of the Marmara Earthquake—to continue to map connections and trace scientific and technical genealogies—is to rehearse a tragic operation that was itself at the heart of the psychiatric response to the earthquake, and which proved a defining feature of the earthquake's legacy in the region. That is, to continue in this vein would be to reproduce the very ways that the lives of those who experienced the earthquake were relentlessly obscured within the flood of expertise and expert discourses gathering in the earthquake's wake. With this in mind, I want to turn our attention to those tens of thousands of earthquake survivors who passed through this post-disaster psychiatric infrastructure, whose lives were time and again transformed into diagnostic categories and data points to feed its insatiable appetite for evidence.

At the convergence of geological volatility and psychiatric expertise that characterized the Marmara Earthquake, what forms of life would become possible? Who was able to endure, even thrive, in the long, drawn-out aftermath of the earthquake?

PART III

Living On

EIGHT

"We Have Not Forgotten, We Will Not Forget"

> My eleven-year-old daughter was trapped under a piece of furniture and could not get out. Because the emergency rescue people weren't able to come within the first hour or two, we watched as she lost her life. In front of our eyes. She was talking to us as she died. Her time came slowly, and then she died.
>
> —Fifty-eight-year-old OSMAN, İzmit, 2013

> Perennial suffering has as much right to expression as a tortured man has to scream; hence it may have been wrong to say that after Auschwitz you could no longer write poems. But it is not wrong to raise the less cultural question whether after Auschwitz you can go on living—especially whether one who escaped by accident, one who by rights should have been killed, may go on living. . . . By way of atonement he will be plagued by dreams such as that he is no longer living at all.
>
> —THEODOR ADORNO, *Negative Dialectics*, 1973

> I joined this meeting in Istanbul organized by psychiatrists who had developed a trauma program [after the earthquake]. They were saying, "We did this in Adapazarı, and we did this in Düzce, etc." I told them that it was wonderful that they came at the time of the earthquake, but what have you done for us since the earthquake? Tell me, what did you do for us after the earthquake? We've had to try to overcome [our problems] on our own.
>
> —Fifty-four-year-old ESME, Gölcük, 2013

Unutmadık, unutmayacağız. "We have not forgotten, we will not forget." This phrase dominates the memorial culture that has settled around the earthquake. Every anniversary, television newscasters recount the gruesome

141

death toll of the earthquake: "We have not forgotten, we will not forget." Newspapers—national, regional, and local—recycle images of the earthquake's destruction: "We have not forgotten, we will not forget." Banners for events are printed, social media hashtags trend, Facebook memorial groups reactivate, corporations and government agencies send out their obligatory tweets: "We have not forgotten, we will not forget." This phrase does not, of course, belong alone to the earthquake. It is a stock phrase of collective memorialization in Turkey. Whether it be the assassination of Alevi intellectuals in Sivas on July 2, 1993 ("We have not forgotten July 2, we will not forget July 2!") or the failed coup of July 15, 2016 ("We have not forgotten the martyrs of July 15, we will not forget them!"), it is an insistence to remember that cuts across lines of social, political, and religious difference. As a statement of collective memorialization, it is both a demand and an obligation: do not forget those who suffered and died, because to *not* forget is a collective responsibility that we bear—to the past, for the future.

In contrast to the public, mass-mediated demand to "not forget," this phrase carries different connotations for those who experienced the Marmara Earthquake firsthand, especially those who lost family and friends. One need not promise to remember, because forgetting is impossible. "Oh, darling, we still haven't forgotten," explained a sixty-year-old woman living in the region when asked about what remained of the earthquake ten years later. "Is it something that can be forgotten? We are still alive, but the old areas, where we used to walk around, are of course in all of our memories." Another woman, in her fifties, explained: "I haven't forgotten a moment, a second of that day. They say there is forgetfulness. There is no such thing as forgetfulness." Memory here is not an obligation that one can choose to bear; it cannot but be borne, for forgetting is impossible. The grammar is telling. The common phrase, "We will not forget" (*unutmayacağız*) shifts tense to "We will not be able to forget" (*unutamayacağız*). This impossibility of forgetting, in this altered tense, also signals a future: "I will never forget the screaming of my friend," recounted a resident. "In the end, he couldn't be rescued and I will never forget the sound of his screaming." Another resident described a scene that I, too, cannot forget: "I'll never forget finding a girl in pieces in the rubble. I'll never forget collecting the pieces into a bag."

How could one forget this? How could the earthquake be forgotten? For those who lived the earthquake, there's no escaping the disaster, whether they want to or not. The destruction and its legacy suffuse lives, bodies, and inner worlds. To not forget is a burden, an inheritance, a symptom—one that endures, twenty years later, in the extended aftermath of disaster.

But *they* have been largely forgotten. Despite the annual outpouring of messages insisting that "we have not forgotten," those who lived and survived the earthquake have, in fact, been largely forgotten. The *depremzedeler*, or "earthquake victims," may occasionally pass as nameless specters over people's lips when tremors shake nearby Istanbul—"Remember what happened in 1999, it could happen again"—but public attention has long moved on. They are abstractions of an event that has been eclipsed by a succession of other events, each generating its own commemorative culture of "we will not forget." They are, if discussed at all, object lessons—invoked by faraway teachers urging children to behave during disaster preparedness drills, or by landlords and developers trying to evict stubborn tenants to make way for new, spectacularly profitable developments: "Don't forget what happened to those people in the earthquake. It could be you." What remains today is a harsh juxtaposition: the impossibility of forgetting rubbing up against the fickle attention span of public compassion.

This part of the book is an attempt to push back into awareness the continuing effects of the earthquake in the lives of those who lived it. As such, this is my own insistence, and obligation, to not forget. In returning to the voices and lives of the earthquake's survivors, my discussion thus moves into the towns and cities surrounding the Gulf of İzmit, long after the rubble has been cleared. Although there may be little left that visibly marks this disastrous past, the continuing effects of the earthquake, more than two decades later, are very real. For those who care to look, a vast expanse of lasting grief and pain continues to endure just below the surface of what might appear, to outsiders, as the unremarkable flow of everyday life. This chapter, as an initial entry into this living legacy of disaster, compiles a set of stories, scenes, and encounters to begin sketching some of the recurrent themes that emerged out of conversations and interviews, as it also begins to engage a series of questions about what it means to trace the legacy of the psychiatric response to the earthquake into the disaster's distant future. What remains of the makeshift psychiatric infrastructure that took form in the ruins of the Marmara Earthquake?

And what counts as a remain? As I would quickly discover, tracing the psychiatric legacy of the disaster would require a particular "art of noticing."[1] Given the enormous complexity of the earthquake, as well as the variable ways that the disaster settled into lives and relations over the ensuing two decades, there were few direct lines to follow from a given intervention to the current contours of individual lives. As such, making sense of the legacy of the geological volatility and psychiatric expertise that converged in the aftermath of the Marmara Earthquake necessitated an analysis that moved away from formal histories of psychiatry (typically narrated from within the field, recounting the influence of prominent psychiatrists, the founding of particular institutions and schools, the development of new techniques and categories). Instead, I had to learn how to look and listen for fragments, remains, and resonances of this psychiatric past.[2] At times, these remains were easy to identify and continued to carry with them the sorts of expert categories, techniques, and materials that the humanitarian response to the earthquake had introduced to the region—conversations about changing diagnoses, repeated sessions with psychiatrists, regimens of psychopharmaceuticals that continue to be followed. More commonly, however, this legacy was elusive—a fleeting remark about an encounter with a psychiatrist after the earthquake, a recollection about a news story, a piece of advice gleaned from a neighbor, or a speculation about a friend's hidden motives. It was in these sorts of settings and situations where I'd come to appreciate how the disaster and its psychiatric response endured into the future as a collection of fragments and ruins scattered across the terrain of everyday lives and its corresponding, if less eventful, forms of loss, destruction, and insecurity.[3]

Into the Hills

A resident of the town of Gölcük, returning six months after the earthquake, described a grim scene: "Most of the apartments along the roadside were piles of rubble, there was no one in the streets, and there were no lights on in the houses that remained standing. It was an abandoned and despairing city." The conditions of the city, in this recalling, infused the qualities of its returning residents; moods and materialities flowed into one another. "The exhaustion, pain, and sorrow were in the streets, roads, and buildings. It was lifeless, as if somebody had stopped time just like that, at the moment of the disaster. The color of the trees seemed faded. Green was not green. Yellow was not yellow. The screams of the people we lost are gone but their traces are still everywhere." For the first years after the earthquake, piles of rubble—people's former homes, office buildings, schools, and mosques—remained scattered across the region. What had once been bustling streets and public squares were emptied.

It would take years for infrastructures to be repaired and for new apartment buildings and offices to be built. By 2007, when I first began visiting the region, the earthquake's destruction had been largely cleared. Not only was the rubble gone, but many of the towns had grown significantly. The largest city near the epicenter—İzmit—had nearly doubled in population and, like other cities in the region, was experiencing a housing boom. The financial and technical assistance received from the World Bank and other international donors following the earthquake had dramatically transformed the area. Tightly knit neighborhoods of small homes and modest apartment buildings had been replaced by planned neighborhoods and large apartment towers—many built in the surrounding hills, far from town centers.

Beyond their isolation and noteworthy verticality, these communities were also distinguished by new social arrangements. For many of the residents of these new buildings and neighborhoods, access to post-disaster subsidies was contingent on one's experience of loss and financial hardship due to the earthquake, such that new occupants frequently shared no social connection with neighbors other than the death, suffering, and loss precipitated by the earthquake. As residents would quickly discover as well, many of these new buildings and neighborhoods were not only remotely located but their design was ill suited to familiar forms of community sociability. Then there was their height. For many occupants, simply entering the new building—many more than twelve stories tall—was a daily struggle against debilitating panic and fear.

In the summer of 2013, while on a visit to the region, a local official from the district health directorate offered to give me a ride to a health clinic located in one of these neighborhoods. As the car climbed away from the coast into the foothills of the Samanlı Mountains, it was hard to ignore how the age of the housing abruptly shifted. Just off the major road circling the coast, beyond the narrow streets with tightly clustered five-story apartment buildings that predated the earthquake, the road widened as we began passing one newly constructed apartment building after another. Unlike similar apartment buildings being built in other regions, few businesses occupied their ground floors, which, for a main thoroughfare, was unusual. I assumed this was a lesson learned from the earthquake. The open design of the ground floor had proved a critical vulnerability in buildings that collapsed in the earthquake.

As the car continued climbing, the architecture would transform again. The multistory apartment buildings gave way to an area of villa-style developments—low-rise, multifamily apartment units clustered around grassy courtyards. These developments struck me as particularly curious—what I imagined and later confirmed as the design of foreign consultants who had been, in this case, hired as part of a World Bank project. What proved jarring, however, was less the architecture than the atmosphere. Without commercial spaces, the area lacked the sort of everyday bustle to which I was accustomed. The neighborhood felt deserted. While more than a decade had passed since the earthquake, the neighborhood seemed to offer an unexpected commentary on the earthquake's legacy—a post-disaster interleaving of space, materials, and moods that produced an unsettling public lifelessness.

We continued driving, passing a stretch of empty fields, before arriving at the health clinic. I had been in many of these clinics over the years—for research, for social visits, and for treatment. The small, squat building's interior was typical for these sorts of public neighborhood health clinics—cement walls painted muted colors, posters announcing the latest public health campaign, visitors from the surrounding neighborhood waiting to be seen by one of the clinic's small cadre of nurses and doctors. I later learned that the clinic was the first building built in the area after the earthquake. It was meant—and built—to be temporary. As we waited to meet with the doctor, a stream of residents passed in and out of the clinic—a mother with a child who had injured himself playing soccer, an elderly man asking for medications for his sore throat, a pregnant woman coming for her regular checkup. These sorts of clinics were designed as the front line for the basic health needs of local communities. Although still referred to as *sağlık ocakları*—literally "health hearths"—they had recently been rebranded as *aile sağlığı merkezleri*, or "family health centers," to underscore the pro-family and pro-natalist policies of the ruling political party. Minimalist in their medical technologies, they screened and surveilled, referring those they couldn't help to the local hospital. Like no other medical setting in Turkey, these clinics are deeply embedded within the flow of community life. While the doctors and nurses typically live outside of the neighborhood and regard themselves as outsiders, the location of the clinical spaces makes it impossible for their operations to not be deeply entangled within the surrounding community.

With the backing of a local official in the regional health department, my assistant and I were given a room to interview patients coming into the clinic. The interviews would be truly opportunistic: we would interview adult visitors to the clinic who had the time, willingness, and patience to sit with us. In keeping with the low- and lower-middle-income class profile of the neighborhood, the people we met that day reflected a range of ages, political commitments (typically ranging from lifelong supporters of the social democratic Republican People's Party [CHP] to committed voters of the ruling Justice and Development Party [AKP]), occupations or sources of livelihood (often tied in some way to the region's many factories), educational backgrounds (all with a primary school education, several having completed high school), religious sensibilities (all identified as Sunni, although this varied from nominally to devoutly so), and histories of migration (with many tracing family ties back to the Black Sea coast and central Anatolia). Given the daytime operating hours of the clinic and the gendered nature of caregiving, we would interview many more women (75 percent) than men. The stories that flowed from these encounters brought into view a range of life trajectories, all profoundly altered by the earthquake. Although fourteen years had passed since the earthquake, interviews revealed an enduring psychological and emotional legacy that continued to organize lives.

Trajectories

The earthquake set into motion a vast regional reworking of social and kin ties, and with it the charting of formerly unimaginable life trajectories. To begin exploring the sorts of living legacies of disaster that formed here, I want to focus in this section on a story told to me by Derya. When we met at the local health clinic in 2013, Derya was thirty-two years old and was living with her husband, a laborer at a local workshop, and her two young children. She had come to the clinic to get medicine for her youngest child. Wearing a long skirt and plain white headscarf, Derya was of a generation of young women for whom religious modesty in public spaces had become normative. Despite the hierarchies and formalities of the interview, Derya conveyed a sense of unassuming confidence as she carefully and thoughtfully answered our questions. When asked if she had any lasting injuries from the earthquake, Derya—sitting stiffly in her chair, shifting her attention from the floor to the hands in her lap to us—posed the question to herself, rephrased as, "Is there anything that remains of me?"

As she began answering her own question, a story unraveled of a bright high school student with professional aspirations losing both of her parents as well as thirteen close relatives in the earthquake. With no home to return to after the earthquake, she moved in with an uncle, where she shared a single bedroom with eight other relatives. She was soon sent to Istanbul to live with a maternal uncle who promised to support her in completing her education, despite his fractured relationship with Derya's deceased father. Leaving Gölcük for Istanbul would mean leaving behind her surviving younger brother—who was eight at the time, and with whom she had grown close after the earthquake. Once in her new home, it quickly became apparent that her aunt resented Derya's presence. Derya was not only a drain on a limited budget, but also a reminder of a part of the family that her aunt disliked. The aunt, as Derya recalled, treated her "like a servant."

Eight months after arriving into her uncle's home, Derya would marry her uncle's brother-in-law (the aunt's brother), who had lost his young wife in the earthquake. Derya spoke of the marriage as being at once "free" and "forced." Fourteen years later, the mother of two children, the distinction meant little to her. She was compelled by the circumstances to acquiesce to her aunt and uncle's wishes, a resignation that would get her out of their house and return her to Gölcük. She returned to Gölcük not much more than a year after the earthquake—not as a promising high school student, but as a newlywed. By the year's end, she gave birth to her first child. With her husband struggling to find steady work, their living conditions were difficult: "My first son grew up in the bedroom. The room was the bedroom, the living room, the room where he ate, and his play room. I also fit a television in there. Imagine what it would mean to grow up in such a tiny space?" The cramped space intensified her relationship with her mother-in-law, who made it clear to Derya that she had preferred her son's first wife.

Feelings of social isolation and emotional exhaustion ran through our conversation. Sitting in the doctor's office, recounting her life, Derya spoke of feeling suffocated by life. The pain of all the loss from the earthquake continued to weigh on her: "I continue to live with my pain and the pain of others. Look, I experienced the pain of losing my sibling. I experienced the pain of losing my mother and father. The pain of losing those close to me." Although she was able to find moments of contentment and meaning in raising her two young sons, as she also described finding refuge in God, she felt profoundly isolated. She may have returned to her hometown, but it was no longer the "hometown" of her youth. So many of her close friends had died in the earthquake. To make matters worse, she had settled in one of the new neighborhoods far from the town's center, surrounded by neighbors who were strangers and had, like her, lost many friends and relatives in the earthquake: "I have no one to talk to. I can't even talk with my husband about [the earthquake]." This was not because they had difficulty talking, but because she knew that talking about the earthquake would remind him of the loss of his first wife.

Derya went on to describe how when she is alone—which is often—things get much worse, as she is unable to stop her thoughts from returning to the loss: "I cry a lot. I try not to think about it so much, because I cry when I think. And then I start finding it hard to breathe." Doctors at the clinic, accustomed to such stories and symptoms, prescribed her medication for asthma and recommended that she see a psychiatrist at the large public hospital. "I am thirty-two years old, but I feel like I'm carrying a sixty-two- or seventy-year-old person inside of me. I feel like I'm collapsing . . . It's as if something of me did not come out of the rubble. There's no strength left to endure. I can't stand any longer. I have patience, but I can't endure." With that, Derya quickly broke off the interview, explaining that she needed to hurry home so that she could pick up her children from school.

Derya drew on a vocabulary that was familiar by this point in my research. Early in my fieldwork, I had decided to leave the front pages of my journal blank to collect terms and phrases that I felt captured with clarity what it meant to live the earthquake. Derya would leave her mark on these pages, which slowly grew into a lexicon of disaster and living on:

çökmek: to collapse [as in a building, but also oneself]

çökertmek: to smash, to cause to collapse [as in a building, but also oneself] *mahvetmek*: to ruin, devastate, destroy

yıkılmak: to collapse, be demolished, wrecked, or ruined

sabretmek: to be patient, endure, forbear

dayanmak: to resist, endure, hold on

yıpratmak: to wear out, wear away

mahvolmak: to be ruined, destroyed, obliterated

boğulmak: to choke, suffocate, drown

içine atmak: to gulp down, repress, endure in silence

Looking at these terms now, I'm struck by how so many of them speak simultaneously to the materiality of the earthquake and its affective aftermath, as the terms also slip between outer and inner worlds: to collapse and to bear, to destroy and to wear down. Derya's story also captures how this lexicon is inescapably gendered. So much of Derya's life after the earthquake was determined by men making decisions for her: being sent by one uncle to another uncle and, with that, the abrupt ending of her educational and professional aspirations; her value in her new family turning on her capacity for domestic labor, and then her reproductive capacities; and, subsequently, her social isolation emerging as a byproduct of gendered domestic labor arrangements. Out of this emerged, in Derya's case, a set of gendered affective states characterized by a twinned sense of alienation and exhaustion, of being alone and worn down by life. It is important to keep in mind that Derya reflects but one of thousands of women's lives that were radically reshaped by the earthquake. That is, she indexes but one constellation of relations within an enormous regional and even national rearrangement of social ties and life trajectories that took form in the wake of the earthquake.

Socialities in Ruins

The legacy of the Marmara Earthquake was irreducibly relational. To grasp the significance of this, we must appreciate how social worlds were dramatically transformed by the earthquake in ways that were at once specific and systematic. As we've already discussed, the earthquake was both a singular, world-transforming event and the realization of a series of interconnecting histories that set the stage for the scale and patterning of the earthquake's destruction. With Derya's assistance, I want to extend this point by highlighting the social conditions that played such a decisive role in shaping the earthquake's legacy. That is, I am interested in the specific ways that a range of relationships—within families, among friends, coworkers, and neighbors, as well as the vast terrain of everyday social relations (from daily exchanges with grocers to chance encounters with acquaintances while walking around town)—were transformed by the earthquake and the role this played in charting lives in the decades to follow.

Although there is no systematic data detailing the geographic distribution of death and loss in the region—the state, recall, couldn't even provide an accurate tally of the total number of dead—the stories I've collected over the past decade suggest that death clustered with particular intensity within extended families. As was the case with Derya, social preferences for multigenerational families to live close and economic strategies for financing the construction of apartment buildings created a situation in which it was common for extended families to own several units within a single apartment building. This, together with the financial incentive of contractors to cut corners and the state's failure to adequately regulate housing construction, created a deadly set of conditions in which it was common for multiple generations of the same extended families to die together in the earthquake.

In addition to reflecting this social and familial patterning of death, Derya's experiences also embody the ways that the earthquake would set in motion an enormous reorganization of kin ties in the region. Spouses who lost partners would remarry. New uncles, aunts, and cousins would enter into families. Parents who lost children would, if possible, have more children and a new generation would come to be known collectively as "children of the earthquake." (This phrase was used to describe both the children literally born in the tent cities in the months after the earthquake, as well as the children who would "replace" those lost in the earthquake). Other parents, unable to bear the loss of children, would separate and divorce. Meanwhile, marriage negotiations gained new categories and chronologies. It became relevant whether a prospective spouse was born before or after the earthquake, a query about the potential emotional damage of a prospective partner or the possibility of a previous fiancé or spouse. In short, the earthquake gave rise to an extensive regional remaking of social relations and imaginations.

An important component of the social conditions of the disaster's legacy was the way this reconfiguration of social and kin ties left in its wake a haunted social landscape, as former social arrangements cast a shadow across the present. At times, the earthquake's social legacy was fleeting: hearing an echo of a dead father in the laugh of a child, noticing the posture of a dead aunt in a living cousin, looking around for a deceased parent to share good news. At other times, this legacy was more elaborate and specific. Every time Osman (the fifty-eight-year-old father I quoted at the outset of this chapter) saw his uncle, for instance, he felt the pain of having tried but failed to save his uncle's daughter, his cousin, in the rubble. Namesakes, in turn, cast a long shadow of the disaster across the present, as a generation of children born after the earthquake received the name of a deceased relative.[4] In some instances, newborns were given the names of children who had died in the earthquake, only to have their names changed months or years later, as the new child approached the age of the dead child and the resonances became intolerable. In these sorts of accounts, we can begin to comprehend how the earthquake upended a world thick with social and familial ties and how this would in turn establish one of the earthquake's defining legacies.

This legacy of social and familial loss not only took form through a particular relationship to the past (as a shadow, or a haunting), but also extended into the future in unexpected ways. In his essay "Time Does Not Heal," the film critic Cüneyt Cebenoyan recounts how, days before the earthquake, he and his wife had left their child with their parents in the coastal town of Yalova while they went on a short beach vacation a few hours away. (They didn't want to bring the baby because the car didn't have rear seat belts). When they saw the news of the earthquake, they rushed back to Yalova, only to find the apartment building collapsed. "In a moment, I became a motherless and fatherless child, and a childless father," recalled Cebenoyan. "The earthquake took both my past and my future. My mother, father, and child." Reflecting on his life ten years later—in which the passing of time had *not* healed his wounds—Cebenoyan crystallizes a set of sensibilities, at once geological and emotional, that ran through interviews: "I am still swaying, I am still not myself." Cebenoyan's account captures not only how the earthquake rippled across generations—reaching into the past, extending into the future—but also how the coinciding loss of familial and generational ties generated a sense of not being at home in the world, feelings of alienation that were at once existential and social. Given the ways that death clustered within extended families, and the socially patterned ways that the earthquake severed and remade social and familial ties, Cebenoyan's account narrates an all-too-common set of experiences for those who lived through and were left behind by the earthquake.[5]

Earthquake Psychologies

In describing their experiences of the earthquake, several residents drew a distinction between living (*yaşamak*) and feeling (*hissetmek*) the earthquake. Hasan, who had become a local legend for his heroic rescue efforts following the earthquake, characterized the distinction in these terms:

> "To live" and "to feel," do you know the difference? Chris, you *felt* the earthquake [referring to me having felt tremors from the earthquake in central Turkey, where I was living at the time], but you did not *live* the earthquake . . . We here experienced an earthquake like nothing that has been recorded in the literature. This was not an earthquake, this was a very different event. In other words, for those of us in our homes during the earthquake, during the major shaking, there was this terrifying feeling, this inexplicable feeling. Thousands passed away . . . It was unbelievably bad. The smell. There is not a feeling that can explain these events. As we lived these events, we are grateful that we came out of the rubble, when so many others went to their graves. Everything was out of place and, for this reason, the entire region suffered a great deal.

Hasan's distinction between feeling and living is one that I would hear frequently in conversations and interviews, a phrasing that I later suspected originated with Hasan himself. Regularly interviewed and featured in news reports in and beyond the region following the earthquake, Hasan was regarded by many as a prominent, if unofficial, spokesperson of the earthquake.

I am drawn to Hasan's formulation because of the way it helps us identify a vital legacy of the earthquake. To have "felt" the earthquake—as I did—was to experience it from a phenomenological distance, as the shaking of a world that was external to myself, in which familiar distinctions between subjects and objects remained intact. To have "lived" the earthquake, in contrast, suggests an experience of being engulfed, consumed, and remade by the disaster, as it settles deep into one's body, as an enduring corporeal and affective remainder. For many, a decisive indication that one had *lived* the earthquake was the persistence of a distinctive, residual earthquake psychology (*deprem psikolojisi*), which Hasan also characterized as the region's endemic "August 17 syndrome" (*17 Ağustos sendromu*)—a lasting constellation of unsettling feelings and memories that seemed always ready to surface, especially around the time of the earthquake's yearly anniversary. In the remainder of this section, in an effort to elaborate on the distinction between living and feeling the earthquake, I want to briefly sketch some of the defining qualities of this local "earthquake psychology," especially its characteristic and uniquely debilitating combination of anticipation, insomnia, and grief.

To have lived the earthquake was to be, decades into its future, in a chronic state of nervous anticipation. Interviewee after interviewee described waves of intense panic that swept over them when they felt small vibrations in the ground, frequently from the seismic activity that continued to move through the region. "If there is the smallest tremor, I'm immediately dashing outside," was a regular refrain in interviews. Others described being paralyzed by the fear: "Last year there was this tiny tremor. I suddenly began shaking in panic. I couldn't do anything. I couldn't make myself go outside. I just stayed where I was. My nerves were shot." A former neighborhood official (*muhtar*) who lost several close relatives in the earthquake spoke of this fear as being at once bodily, collective, and inescapable: "You experience this fear. If an ambulance or fire truck passes, for instance, the sound of the siren really affects us. It affects everyone, still. Whether it's a ten-year-old child or a seventy-year-old, it affects them. That is, there is a heart bump [*yürek kabartısı*], how can I describe it to you, this fear that you are experiencing. You live it, you could wait thirty years if you want, but you can't get rid of that fear. You can't get rid of it." And as interviews would reveal, there were no shortage of signs of an earthquake to come—in the lengthening crack on a cement wall, in an ominous dream, in the unusual behavior of an animal.

Many accounts of the earthquake dwelled on the intensity of the darkness that descended on the region after the earthquake, a darkness that would leave its own sort of mark on the disaster's future. Although few beyond one's family witnessed it firsthand, everyone had heard stories of friends and neighbors wearing their street clothes to bed, sleeping with the lights on, and keeping wallets under pillows at night. Just beyond the seeming stillness of the neighborhood at night were lives and worlds in turmoil. More than a decade later, residents recounted regularly waking up in the middle of the night in a state of panic (the earthquake happened at 3:07 a.m.), followed by a sleepless night of emotional upheaval. The account of a woman who lost her eighteen-year-old son in the earthquake is typical: "I'm waking up at 4:00 a.m., 4:30 a.m. many nights. I don't get any sleep. My sleep pattern is still completely exhausted. Even though I have been taking medication for thirteen years, I do not get any sleep. If you come over at 3:00 or 3:30, I'll be up and we can sit and have tea." Similar accounts of disrupted sleep were ever-present in interviews.

Insomnia had seemingly become endemic to the region, even if rarely acknowledged. Although studies of the psychological effects of disasters speak of disordered sleep, nothing prepared me for the corrosive effects that radiated from this nocturnal legacy of the earthquake. As panic and sleeplessness fed off each other, insomnia established a terrible cycle for many: exhausted and emotionally vulnerable from lack of sleep, one would become sensitive to signs of another earthquake, which in turn set off waves of fear and panic that made sleep impossible. Stories of insomnia were also stories that often became pharmaceutical. The vast majority of interviewees talked about using some sort of medication after the earthquake to help with the insomnia and sleep disrupted by nightmares. In the years that followed, medications—for sleep, for anxiety, for depression—were easily accessible and frequently relied on to arrest this cycle, at least until the side effects of the medications became more unbearable than the insomnia. By the time I started visiting these neighborhoods, residents had been cycling through this for nearly a decade.

Then there was the grief. The actual number of people who died in the earthquake will never be known, but stories from those who survived describe death as omnipresent: the witnessing of the death of relatives, friends, and coworkers; the sights of bodies being pulled from the rubble; the identification of dead bodies at the local ice rink; attending funerals in cemeteries overflowing with freshly dug graves; the smell of decomposing flesh enveloping the area. Everyone, in some way, became immersed in death.[6] More than a decade later, together with the nervous anticipation of another disaster and nocturnal upheaval that animated the region's "earthquake psychology," anguish over the loss of family and friends was still powerfully present. Everyday encounters with old acquaintances, or even the turn of the weather, could be enough to draw one back to these scenes of death. Grief was a vital, lasting, and omnipresent feature of the region's earthquake psychology. I explore these experiences of grief in detail in the chapters to come. For now, having introduced the broad contours of this local earthquake psychology, I want to turn to another story that captures the distinctive ways that loss took social and gendered forms in the long aftermath of the Marmara Earthquake.

Neşe

There is a tendency—in the scholarly literature on disaster, as well as among the psychiatrists and psychologists treating the survivors of the Marmara Earthquake, and increasingly among the survivors of the earthquake—to channel discussions of the psychological and emotional aftermath of the earthquake through the language of psychological trauma. Although I regard the clinical discourse of trauma (including "complex trauma") as extraordinarily inadequate when it comes to describing the complexity of lives that formed in the earthquake's aftermath, I did, methodologically, find the psychiatric instruments used to measure the epidemiology of trauma intriguing. Indeed, as I discuss in the following chapter, I would incorporate elements of these instruments into my own interviews. Yet, whereas conventional instruments use close-ended questions to tightly control the range of possible responses (and thereby contain the messy social realities being engaged), I found that they often elicited rich conversations when posed as open-ended questions. They offered, in other words, generative ethnographic openings.

When I asked Neşe—a middle-aged woman who had lost her husband and children, as well as an arm, in the earthquake—if she "felt sad or depressed over the past week" (a standard question of virtually all PTSD screening instruments used after the earthquake, which allowed for four possible choices ranging from "not at all" to "very much"), she sketched a tangled scene of injury and familial loss that echoed across decades:

> I lost my family. At thirty-five years old, my family and my life were demolished. Destroyed. At thirty-five, I no longer had children, nor a marriage. Of course you'd feel sad . . . I am always sad. But I don't show it to anyone. I'm wounded, on the inside. Look, here is my family [showing pictures of her deceased children on her mobile phone]. They are still on my phone. I also have pictures in my bedroom. I talk with them.

Unfortunately, Neşe's account is not unusual. Indeed, after more than a decade of interviewing survivors of the Marmara Earthquake, it has become hard to determine what counts as extreme. In Neşe's case, a sense of still being "wounded on the inside," even a decade later, and the intensity with which she missed the family and friends she lost in the earthquake, reflected a widely felt set of experiences of loss and continuing grief. As with others, the legacy of the earthquake took form in Neşe's life as a shifting relationship with death.

For Neşe, the multiple surgeries that followed the earthquake, the series of psychiatrists and psychologists who met with her, and the regiment of psychopharmaceuticals they prescribed were crucial in helping her "return from the dead." It was, nevertheless, a highly qualified and heavily pharmaceuticalized life. Although she returned to the living, she regarded herself as barely alive—or "not dead"—for long stretches of the past two decades:

> It's five years later, ten years later, fourteen years later, and now we're entering the fifteenth year [after the earthquake]. We're getting worse and worse. Everything is difficult. Both materially and spiritually. Both the pain and the struggle to stay on our feet . . . Our lives are not something that can be explained. Maybe our lives look good from the outside. But you can't see how our children or husbands do not remain. This pain is the pain we feel. This is something I feel.

The pharmaceuticals she was prescribed after the earthquake would become a lifelong strategy for living on, as she moved on and off of them as the years passed: "I've used a lot of medications. I quit using them for a year, for three years, and now I'm using them again. I started again three and a half months ago."

Echoing Derya, Neşe's account indicates some of the particular ways that gender shaped life trajectories following the earthquake. In this instance, Neşe's struggles with life after the disaster were profoundly influenced by the loss not only of family members but also her social position. With the death of her husband and children, Neşe was no longer the wife and mother she was before the earthquake. Given her class background—in which her ability to fulfill heteronormative, patriarchal ideals of the selfless mother and wife were central to her sense of self-worth and social value—the death of her children and husband created a series of challenges to her ability to imagine a meaningful post-disaster life. Moreover, as with other women, the loss of a husband would generate forms of economic vulnerability that conspired with the emotional legacy of the earthquake to undermine efforts to build new lives in the wake of disaster. Neşe's friend, commenting on both of their experiences, described their situation in these terms:

> There is the financial difficulty of people who were left alone. This further destroys people's morale [lit., this "causes people to collapse"]. I lost everything. Materially, there is nothing left. And now I'm going to have to pay rent. If I had a son, he would work. If I had a husband, he would take care of me or do something. But when you are alone you have to pay the rent, you have to make a living.

In Neşe's case, this struggle to support herself financially was further complicated by the physical injuries she sustained in the earthquake, which greatly reduced her ability to enter available labor markets, both formal and informal.

As this begins to demonstrate, experiences of loss such as Neşe's were much more than grief over the loss of a child or a spouse. For Neşe, this loss was also the loss of a social position and, with it, the sense of self-worth it offered and the sorts of futures it made imaginable. As with Cebenoyan, Neşe's experiences formed not only in relationship to past loss but also in the way that this past extended into the future. It was at once the loss of people she loved dearly and the loss of the love she imagined for them in a now-impossible future—the love of an aging husband and wife for their grown children, the love of a grandmother for her grandchildren and great-grandchildren. Along similar lines, we can see here how Neşe's "fall into poverty" was much more than simply a loss of income, as her precarious economic conditions and diminished sense of social value and self-worth continually fed each other. In short, the ways that disaster, loss, and economic precarity converge in Neşe's life—and the lives of many, many other women—gives tangible form to the broader observation that life trajectories in the wake of disasters (and how these trajectories are narrated) are inescapably bound up with one's social position.

Talking Psychiatry

I returned to the same neighborhood clinic where I interviewed Derya, Neşe, Osman, and others in 2019, six years after my first visit. The clinic was still there, continuing to defy its life expectancy by more than a decade. The changes I noticed in the clinic were small and signaled both wider changes in the health care system and shifting political agendas. Reflecting recent efforts to make government sources more efficient, visitors were required to take a ticket from a dispenser and wait for their number to appear on the lighted sign about individual offices. In turn, many of the forms that visitors were to fill out as well as several of the posters on the wall advertising public health campaigns now included Arabic translations, a reminder of the more than three million Syrian refugees being resettled in Turkey. As far as I knew, there had been no refugee resettlement programs in the neighborhood.

On one particularly hot August afternoon, as I wandered the streets of the nearby neighborhoods, I came upon a group of men sitting on a shaded porch of a teahouse, having just come from a funeral in a small mosque across the street. I asked if anyone knew where I could find the local *muhtar*. A young man in the group asked, with characteristic and justified suspicion, why I was looking for the *muhtar*. I explained that I was writing a book about the legacy of the August 17 earthquake and was trying to learn more about the history of the neighborhood. He invited me to join them in the shade. The tea quickly arrived. As we settled into a conversation, I asked the same question I had posed to countless others. What remained today of the earthquake?

Without missing a beat, the person who invited me to sit down—Ümit (who turned out to be the *muhtar*)—began: "It was a big *travma*. People were psychologically broken. Everyone in the city was, from a psychological perspective, broken." He continued on, for several minutes, describing how this trauma had affected people in the neighborhood. A gentleman at a nearby table soon interjected, "For me, it took four to five years for my psychological problems to start. I began obsessively . . ." Before he could finish his thought, Ümit continued on: "This area used to be a village outside the city. Look at it now, thousands of people. But everyone is psychologically broken." With this, they turned their attention to heckling a young man who walked down the street looking at a tablet in his hand ("He's probably from Russia's version of Google, mapping our area"), before continuing on about the lasting "earthquake psychology" that was showing no signs of going away.

Even after more than a decade of research, the ease with which the language of psychiatry surfaced and circulated in these sorts of encounters continues to beguile me. These were not conversations about *delilik*—that rich, polysemous concept of madness—but talk that wove in and out of technical and clinical vocabularies, of *akıl hastalığı* (mental illness), *ruh sağlığı* (mental health), and, more commonly, an assortment of specific diagnostic categories (and their corresponding medications). This was in such sharp contrast to what I encountered while conducting research about religious and ritual forms of healing two decades earlier. While biomedical categories had been ubiquitous, this sort of technically inflected psychiatric talk was exceptionally rare. Now, here, it was pervasive. In turn, *psikoloji* had become an ever-present modifier used to describe subjects, emotional states, and collective responses to the disaster. With this in mind, an overarching aim of this chapter—in addition to recentering the experiences of those who lived the earthquake into our account of the psychiatric legacy of the Marmara Earthquake—has been to take note of the ways that a psychiatric discourse that emerged with the earthquake continues to move through stories, lives, and conversations decades later. In so doing, I'm arguing, we can hear in these sorts of conversations not only the remains of a particular psychiatric past but also the working of a psychiatric subjectivity in the making—what Orkideh Behrouzan has described in writing about psychiatry and generational memory in Iran as "the bottom-up desire for, and the internalization of, psychiatric mindsets as a mode of thinking and a way of understanding, interpreting, and articulating individual and collective experience."[7]

With that said, I want to be careful not to exaggerate the role of the earthquake in these developments. For instance, the dramatically expanded availability of psychopharmaceuticals over the past decade—fed by both increased funding from pharmaceutical companies to support clinical research in Turkey and government interest in the efficiency promised by pharmaceutical care—has assuredly contributed to the ease with which people drew on psychiatric idioms when talking about distress and misfortune, especially those conditions that commonly coincided with the earthquake (such as depression, anxiety, and disordered sleep). Indeed, conversations with local pharmacists suggested that a vibrant psychopharmaceutical ecosystem had settled into the neighborhood (whose residents lacked meaningful access to any form of psychotherapy). Relatedly, over the decades that followed the earthquake, an increasingly visible domestic therapeutic culture would also grow in tandem with this expanding transnational pharmaceutical market, especially within middle- and upper-middle-class households. With this, "therapeutic talk" would enter in new ways into both public culture and state efforts to regulate social life, especially through the family.[8] These developments, taken together, are certainly important to consider when it comes to explaining the frequency with which psychiatric discourses moved through the conversations and interviews that comprised the research for this book. Nevertheless, as I am arguing, the earthquake was a decisive turning point.

But a turning to what? What does it mean to begin relying on psychiatric concepts and categories when discussing personal distress, interpersonal struggles, or nonnormative states? As the foregoing begins to suggest, psychiatric discourses move through social worlds in ambiguous ways. Although their categories and classifications may be indexed to powerful fields and institutions of technical expertise and social regulation, they don't always (if ever?) remain faithful to their origins. In our case, while concepts such as "earthquake psychology" or "August 17 syndrome" certainly bore the traces of the psychiatric history of disaster, neither mapped onto conventional psychiatric categories. Even the vernacular use of *travma* suggested something more or other than the concepts of psychological trauma or PTSD that had been mobilized by researchers in the wake of the Marmara Earthquake.[9] Moreover—and perhaps more importantly—these concepts circulated in these communities not so much to pathologize or categorize but to give the unruly affects of earthquake survivors social and semiotic form.

Appreciating the infidelities of these categories as they circulated through lives and relations thus suggests a different account than one that reads these instances as evidence of the power of psychiatry to override realities or a totalizing psychiatrization of normality. "Although people are indeed interpellated by the categories of classification with which they are confronted," as Veena Das has written about humanitarian psychiatry in a different setting, "they are not entirely remade into the identities imposed by these categories."[10] With this recognition, the sort of analysis developed in Part 2 of this book—in which I traced networks of psychiatric expertise, the design of psychiatric interventions, and the production and circulation of expert knowledge—gives way to a more indeterminate account of the complex ways that the psychiatric infrastructure born of the earthquake lives on, as it continues to move lives, relations, and time more than decades since its disassembling.

NINE

Disaster's Minor Feelings

> People's nervous systems were broken [by the earthquake]. They still are.
>
> —OSMAN, fifty-eight-year-old resident of Gölcük

> From a psychological perspective, we are so frazzled and worn down. Even fourteen years later, we're not able to get rid of this tension, this aggressive irritability.
>
> —PINAR, fifty-year-old resident of Gölcük

> The ordinary hums with the background noise of obstinacies and promises, ruts and disorientations, intensities and resting points. It sediments, rinds up like the skin of an orange, registers invisible airs as public feelings that waver and pulse. It weighs. It demands a tuning in.
>
> —KATHLEEN STEWART, "Atmospheric Attunements," 2010

Living On, Irritably

More than a decade after the Marmara Earthquake, long after the rubble had been cleared and the surrounding towns rebuilt, the remains of the earthquake had become elusive. For most, the earthquake no longer, or only rarely, appeared as a rush of thoughts, images, and feelings that overwhelmed. The moments of intense and debilitating grief, triggered by the unexpected encounter with a reminder of loss, had for most waned over the decades. Instead, the earthquake announced itself quietly—in fleeting moments in the flow of a conversation, the shift in the atmosphere of a room, a subtle but noticeable turn in one's mood. Often it arrived with an inkling of something familiar, a vague sense of a recollection coming forth, only to drift off. These feelings and moods might be vague, but they could be insistent, taking form as a powerful compulsion to flee—a room, a building, a situation. They came, in these moments, with not a clear memory of the disaster but an indefinite but visceral intensity—a body bristling with alertness and a surging wave of panic. For many, in other words, the lasting legacy of the earthquake would be a body on edge—lingering but not quite debilitating feelings of being unnerved, annoyed, and exhausted.

Spending time living and traveling in the region in the decades following the earthquake would attune me to these sorts of bodily and affective legacies of the disaster. In time, and building on the work of the literary critic Sianne Ngai, I came to think of these legacies as representing disaster's "minor feelings"—a loose collection of moods, sensibilities, and affects that lacked hard edges and seemed to allude expert categories and modes of apprehension, yet were chronically unsettling and upsetting.[1] For Ngai, "minor feelings" are those "unprestigious" emotions and ambivalent affects (such as envy, irritation, and anxiety) that are not accorded the stature of the "higher emotions" and "grander passions" (such as anger and fear). Both noncathartic and amoral, they offer neither the charge of righteous anger nor the cathartic promises of the "bigger" emotions. They provide "no satisfaction of virtue, however oblique, nor any therapeutic or purifying release."[2] Quite the opposite, in fact. If anything, they are characterized by their propensity to undermine cathartic and therapeutic processes.

For Ngai, "irritability" holds a special place within this repertoire of minor feelings. Unlike the "grander" emotions of anger and rage, irritability is characterized by its ongoingness and its ambiguous attachment to objects. On the one hand, unlike rage, which cannot be sustained indefinitely, irritability has a "remarkable capacity for duration."[3] Irritability, as a mood, endures. On the other hand, irritability is a mood that "lacks an explicit occasion or object."[4] Being irritable doesn't require a clearly defined object and, as such, irritability is strikingly inclusive. When one is irritable, everything can be annoying. In turn, for Ngai, these qualities of irritability as a minor feeling make it politically ambiguous. Aristotle, she reminds us, warned of the political dangers of irritability. Anger, for Aristotle, is intrinsic to justice; it is the appropriate reaction to an injustice. Irritability, on the other hand, is marked by its excessiveness—of being angry too much, at the wrong thing, or at the wrong time. Irritability, in this respect, is a corrupted form of anger.[5]

In this chapter, I approach pervasive and enduring feelings of irritability and edginess among survivors of the Marmara Earthquake as a distinctive if unexpected affective legacy of disaster.[6] In developing this analysis, I will largely set aside a series of definitional debates over terms such as affect, emotion, and feeling that have characterized scholarly discussions of affect.[7] Instead, I draw inspiration from Yael Navaro's efforts to conceptualize a "different imaginary for affect" that is not unreflexively bound to a set of universalized Western assumptions about affect.[8] For Navaro, importantly, this entails not a search for some sort of romanticized and essentialized radical alterity, but an approach that gives proper analytic weight to the specific historical conjunctures that condition people's affective experience. With this in mind, I am particularly interested in the unique capacity of irritability to trouble boundaries—the ease with which it slides between psychic and bodily registers, as it blurs the emotional and the epidermal.

Irritability, in this regard, denotes experiences of being both or either mildly angry and/or physically sore: that which irritates rubs one (the wrong way); it chafes and leaves one sore. Those who irritate are abrasive, they grate on one's nerves and get under one's skin. Irritability, as such, is about both emotional depth and epidermal surfaces and thus complicates comfortable assumptions about the interiority of feelings.[9] Moreover, in both its pervasiveness and slipperiness, irritability resists signification. Yet—and this is critical for our discussion—it resists signification not because of its exceptionality (as with common formulations of psychological trauma), but because of how, in its ambiguous relationship to objects and occasions, it is diffused through the everyday. It is a "low-intensity" affect that rubs up against social realities, a percolating anger directed at the wrong thing at the wrong time.[10] Irritability, as such, slips between the bodily and affective as it also folds in complex relational entanglements and reaches out to broader arrangements of politics and economy.

While ever-present and regularly remarked on, these sorts of legacies of disaster have attracted little scholarly or clinical attention. This absence is not because experts are unaware. In fact, these sorts of experiences are a common component of clinical profiles of trauma and PTSD. Indeed, the instruments used to generate the sorts of psychiatric profiles of disaster explored in Chapter 6 probed respondents about feeling "on edge," "irritable," or "snappy with others." In turn, studies documenting increased rates of gender-based violence following disasters suggest that this is a recurrent phenomenon.[11] At the same time, experiences of irritability and edginess run through popular and media accounts of traumatic experience in Turkey—where, as with elsewhere, the emotionally volatile and violent masculine subject of trauma (archetypically the war veteran)[12] sits alongside the feminine subject of trauma (who is immobilized by the uncontrolled repetition of traumatic memories and flashbacks) to fill out a collective and deeply gendered public discourse of traumatic experience. Despite these examples, the scholarly and clinical literatures on disaster (in general, and in the specific case of the Marmara Earthquake) remain focused not on the mundane and everyday effects of disaster, but instead on the dramatic, symptomatic, and eventful—especially the role of trauma in shaping experience, identity, and social relations. In so doing, these approaches privilege (and thus render prestigious) a narrow but significant set of human responses to overwhelming and distressing events.

In taking up disaster's "minor feelings," this chapter explores a constellation of palpable and socially relevant sensibilities and moods that have become so intimately enmeshed in everyday lives that they are difficult to isolate from other routine irritations—about the cost of food and fuel, about the traffic and the dust, about work, bureaucracies, and nosy neighbors. Notably, my approach does not entail trying to isolate the earthquake's irritable legacy from these other sources of irritability. Exploring how these traces are embedded within the everyday is, in fact, critical if we are going to understand disasters not as exceptions to but as extensions of the forces and dynamics that constitute the everyday. With this focus on the interleaving of disaster and the everyday, I engage stories not so much on the level of psychological symptom, or even cultural elaboration. Indeed, in the very ways that irritability inhabits the everyday—with its characteristically ambiguous relationships with both occasions and objects—it resists such elaboration, even as it unsettles lives and relations. In this regard, I explore irritability as an affective reality of a post-disaster setting in which the region's geological history lives on as a bodily trace, where bodies and history fold into one another, and where a set of nervous political and economic conditions become inscribed on bodily nervous systems already primed by shared histories of disaster and everyday experiences of chronic insecurity.[13]

Traces of Disaster: On Being Annoyed

The same question posed to four people: What is left of the earthquake today?

Well, whenever there's a [loud] sound, I wince [*irkilirim*]. Whenever I feel the ground vibrating, I am overwhelmed by a desire to flee the room.
—Neşe, 2013

There is of course the uneasiness [*tedirginlik*] that at any moment something will happen. Last night, for instance, I heard a crunching sound in the house. I immediately wondered if the sound was coming from the wall. Is the floor moving? There is always this sort of uneasiness, even when you hear a sound like this.
—Selin, 2013

Yes. I am very much on the alert [*tetikteyim*]. I am ready to explode immediately. When something happens, I feel like it will explode immediately.
—Murat, 2019

Nowadays, I'm more emotional, more sensitive. For instance, with my husband, whenever he says something, I wonder if he has a hidden motive.... Before the earthquake, I didn't care so much. I could laugh and let it pass. But now, "Why did he say that?" "What did I do to make you say that? Did I deserve this?" I'm saying these sorts of things much more. From my perspective, my testiness [*alınganlık*] has greatly increased.
—Pınar, 2007

An epidemic of panic descended on the region after the earthquake. "If one is truthful, psychologically speaking" explained Duygu, a local government official in a small town along the coast, "there is not a person around here who did not have at least one panic attack (*panik atak*) after the earthquake." For Duygu and others, panic attacks established a chronology of post-disaster life, marking out points of crisis in the months and years to follow. In time, in these tellings, this epidemic of panic was slowly eclipsed by a more generalized irritability—an atmosphere of edgy nervousness that shifted in step with the quasi-aftermaths of the disaster's extending future.

By the time I began spending time in the region, more than a decade later, residents regularly turned to the persistence of particular moods and affective states when speaking about the legacy of the earthquake in their lives.

I first met Aslıhan while interviewing visitors to the neighborhood health clinic that I introduced in the previous chapter. It was midsummer and Aslıhan struck me as someone who'd be at home in the coastal towns of western Turkey—capri jeans, flowing cotton blouse, sandals, and short gray hair contrasted against deeply tanned skin. Born in 1942, Aslıhan grew up in a city along Turkey's Aegean coast and moved to the area soon after completing middle school. By the time of the earthquake, she was the mother of four grown daughters, two of whom were still living nearby. The story she told about the earthquake was a familiar one. She and her husband narrowly escaped their apartment building, which collapsed soon after the initial earthquake. They lost all of their belongings in the earthquake, except for the pajamas they were wearing as they fled their home. Although they lost many relatives and friends in the earthquake, Aslıhan was grateful that all of her children survived. (Their twenty-one-year-old daughter was pulled, alive, from the rubble three days after the earthquake.) They would spend the next several years moving from tents to prefabricated homes to, eventually, a hastily (and poorly) constructed apartment in a neighborhood for displaced earthquake survivors located in the hills surrounding the Gulf of İzmit. Financially, they were ruined by the earthquake. The small grocery store run by her husband had been destroyed and the items that survived the earthquake would disappear in the weeks that followed. In turn, they received little assistance from the state beyond the basic supplies distributed in the emergency and temporary housing settlements. As Aslıhan and her family struggled to rebuild their lives, they quickly fell into debt.

When asked what she saw as the lasting traces of the earthquake, she focused on her mood: "Of course I'm trying to live with the medications. But I make everything a problem. This is definitely me. I have some sort of uneasiness. I feel sorry for the neighbors. I get annoyed with the children playing on the road. Even if they are just kicking a ball. Once, there was this boy who was bothering a cat. I wanted to attack him. Again, I have something wrong with me. In the past, I didn't. It started after the earthquake. . . . I get bothered more quickly. I get angry more and the anger explodes more quickly." Osman, one of Aslıhan's neighbors, characterized this mood as endemic to the region: "People's nervous systems were broken [by the earthquake]. They still are. Their psychological states are broken. I tell my wife the same, for instance, that we didn't experience that much death, but our nervous systems are broken. . . . People become angrier. You say something and they immediately get mad. I, for example, get angry. You just get angry. People are just more impatient."

While Aslıhan and Osman understood that this irritability could be traced back to the earthquake, it had long since been woven into the mundane and petty annoyances of the everyday. Osman, for instance, often spoke of the diffused qualities of this general irritability, especially when he struggled to pin down its source. "Is it from them? Or is it from me?" he would ask. "I can't know. . . . I do know that people have become more impatient [*tahammülsüz*], and their lives have also changed a lot." Similarly, as Aslıhan talked about the ease with which she got annoyed at neighbors and the ways that small frustrations quickly became moments of intense anger, the affective legacy of the disaster would come into view as at once dense, palpable, and diffuse. Yet, in those moments when the irritability gathered into an atmosphere and released its charge as an outburst of intense anger, its origins would feel more immediate. This tension between the everydayness (of the irritability) and the immediacy (of its coinciding outbursts of anger) would make it difficult to draw direct lines from small things (such as being annoyed with a kid kicking a ball) to big things (like the Marmara Earthquake). Causes and effects were too opaque and mediated to call this mood a symptom. Instead, as I am suggesting, these sorts of post-earthquake moods and affects of irritability, edginess, and emotional volatility represent a collective and embodied trace of a catastrophic past.

As I became attuned to this terrain of affective unrest, I came to appreciate the rich and expressive vocabulary that existed for describing how feelings of irritability and edginess could quickly transform into anger.[14] With this, my journal's affective lexicon of disaster and living on would expand to include a parallel archive of feelings, moods, and states that belonged as much to the ordinary as to the catastrophic:[15]

sinirli: irritable, edgy

gerginlik: tension, tightness

sıkıntılı: distressed, troubled

tedirginlik: uneasiness, edginess

endişeli: anxious

huzursuz: uneasy, anxious, edgy

alıngan: touchy, sensitive, easily offended

tetikte: on guard, on alert, vigilant

asabi: irritable, nervous, on edge

takılmak: to get stuck on things

tahammülsüz: impatient

Reflecting on these terms now, I am struck how, together, they bring into focus the amorphous and floating qualities of the earthquake's affective legacy. Not only are the boundaries between each term fuzzy—a set of signs and distinctions within a gathering of fluid and overlapping moods and affects—but their objects are similarly elusive. While ambiguous, they also mark out a threshold of intensity, a limit across which lies a more defined anger—a progression from "being annoyed," to "getting mad," to "glowing" with rage (*parlamak*), to "exploding" (*patlamak*).

It is important to underscore how these edgy aftermaths were not, in any straightforward sense, lingering symptoms of a catastrophic event. Osman or Aslıhan "blowing up" was not simply a message in a bottle conveyed from a distant past to the present. Rather, these moods and affects also took form within the shifting conditions of everyday life, to say nothing of other crises and disasters that would unsettle lives in the decades that followed the earthquake. In the long interval between the earthquake and the endemic irritability I was encountering more than a decade later, much had changed—not only in the neighborhood where Aslıhan and Osman were living but also in the country as a whole. There was, in short, much to be irritated by. Although I initially approached this as a knot to untangle—an effort to isolate the specific effects of the earthquake decades into its future—I would, as I began to rethink the earthquake as both an acute event and a chronic condition, come to appreciate how these affective traces of disaster were uniquely able to register the movement of larger operations in this period.

Aslıhan and her husband's struggle to find a home and rebuild their lives over the decade following the earthquake typifies this affective and historical conjuncture. As I'll discuss in more detail in Chapter 11, the single most consistent factor shaping the trajectory of lives following the earthquake was one's housing status at the time of the earthquake. In keeping with dominant approaches to long-term disaster relief, the vast majority of disaster relief programs introduced after the Marmara Earthquake were structured by the conventional logic of "asset replacement."[16] That is, the relief designated for long-term recovery—as compared to the emergency relief distributed immediately after the earthquake (e.g., clothing, food, emergency housing)—aimed to rebuild the region by replacing the distribution of property and wealth in place at the moment of the earthquake.

For individuals and families, this meant that virtually all long-term aid for earthquake survivors was directed toward homeowners, typically in the form of either subsidized loans to purchase new housing or the reconstruction of homes destroyed in the earthquake.[17] In this sort of scheme, the trajectory of Aslıhan's life would give flesh to a truism of disaster studies—that those on the economic margins of society are at once more vulnerable to the effects of disasters and least able to benefit from post-disaster recovery programs and initiatives. As with thousands of others who had been renters before the earthquake, Aslıhan became a long-term resident of the "temporary" housing settlements established in the wake of the earthquake. Making matters worse, beginning in 2000, Turkey's economy entered its worst financial crisis in modern history. With the regional and national economies in tatters, her husband struggled to find work. After repeated efforts to qualify for assistance from the state, they would eventually receive a subsidized apartment in one of the neighborhoods being built in the hills far outside the city.

Spurred by economic reforms introduced in response to the financial crisis, the economy would soon start growing at a frenzied pace. The media—domestic and international—began celebrating the wonders of Turkey's economy and its rapidly growing middle class. With increased access to consumer debt (a product of post-financial crisis economic reforms), middle-class consumption would greatly expand, creating new markers of inclusion within a reimagined social contract of a neoliberalizing Turkey. Aslıhan and her family would be largely left out of this, and the new signs of middle-class success would be experienced by people like Aslıhan as markers of exclusion. The transforming economic conditions did, however, create opportunities for Aslıhan and her family—namely, for more debt. Having lost so many of their relatives in the earthquake—who, together, would have been important economic resources to lean on in times of need—they had few other options. Rebuilding her husband's business would put them in debt. His sudden death in 2004 would lead to more debt. When two of her daughter's husbands died, and one of her other daughters was diagnosed with cancer, she borrowed more money to help support her family.

While the increasing availability of consumer debt offered Aslıhan new opportunities to leverage her limited resources against a future in which she would not be included, her exclusion from the "New Turkey" was never experienced as a verdict. Rather, "bad things" just kept happening to drag her further into debt. Although there might have been moments when these feelings of irritability and edginess began to congeal into a kernel of critical awareness about the forces aligned against her, they usually just annoyed her. In turn, drawing a direct connection from this debt and financial precarity to her temperamental moods and, now, a worsening heart condition, she saw no end in sight: "We still have to pay back our debts. We are still paying. From year to year, we are paying." These comments were followed by what would be a refrain in the interview: "But I'm thankful for the medications. Thank God, I'm doing well, for now. With the medications, I'm on my feet."

Aslıhan's account is indicative of the pervasive sense of irritability, edginess, and emotional volatility that continued to unsettle lives across the region more than a decade after the earthquake. While these everyday sensibilities and intensities rarely rose to the level of a crisis, and largely alluded expert attention, they permeated lives and, together, formed into one of the major legacies of the Marmara Earthquake. And this enduring hum of irritability—the speed with which one became annoyed at everyday mishaps, irritated with family members and neighbors, angry at spouses and relatives—would, in turn, convey to the everyday a sense of immanent threat and an ominous air that a crisis was always on the horizon. In this regard, while these edgy aftermaths of disaster may manifest in everyday annoyances and encounters, they can also be understood as representing, following Ann Cvetkovich,[18] a register of historical experience—as an embodied trace of both the region's geological history and the operations of a nervous political and economic system perpetually generating financial precarity and chronic insecurity in the name of national development.

INTERLUDE

A Question of Questions

This chapter emerged out of a methodological experiment born of curiosity. Early on in the research for this book, I was given access to nearly a thousand completed psychiatric questionnaires that had been filled out by earthquake survivors in the first months following the earthquake. The questionnaires had been developed and administered by a team of psychiatrists and psychologists based at a local medical school. I can vividly recall sitting in a room in the psychiatric unit of the hospital, flipping through the stacks of completed questionnaires. I had long ago read about the results of this study, but the smell that day of the pulpy, decomposing paper would push my attention beyond the data they recorded. I found myself thinking about how the surveys—the actual surveys in my hands—were themselves a set of psychiatric ruins. Their very pages had traveled through the earthquake region more than a decade earlier. The handwritten ink markings dated back to a period when those completing the surveys were coming to terms with the enormity of their loss. And they were being asked to check boxes. "On a scale of 0 to 4, have you been feeling sad lately? Do you have difficulty sleeping? Do you have frightening dreams?"

As I sat in that room in the medical school, more than a decade into the earthquake's future, I recall a certain thrill of having before me the "raw data" that had been used to generate the mass of findings, tables, and graphs so central to the enormous psychiatric literature that the earthquake birthed (see Chapter 5). At the same time, as an anthropologist, I found the surveys frustratingly limited. The cavernous divide between the simplicity of these documents and the claims being made on their behalf was startling, even more so when I paused to think about the chasm between the data points in these surveys and the actual lives of the people who were filling them out. I recall thinking about the simultaneously machinic and magical ways these surveys conjured clarity out of complex and messy realities.

There is, of course, an enormous critical literature that would echo my frustrations. Yet, I had talked to enough people in the region to know that these instruments weren't simply inventing the collection of behaviors and symptoms that comprised them. Although they certainly affected what they were measuring—the psychic state of thousands of people living in makeshift shelters scattered across the earthquake region—they didn't create realities out of nothing. Their magical powers entailed not a conjuring of something out of nothing, but a transforming of that which existed into something both more and else. While these instruments were exceedingly poor at capturing the lived realities of actual lives, they were nonetheless the product of a long scientific history of documenting and categorizing the psychic toll of extreme events. Despite a training that had cultivated in me a deep distrust of such instruments, I recall sitting in that room, breathing in the floating particles of the decaying paper and ink, and thinking more generously about what these instruments were in fact registering. And, more curiously, I wondered whether their operations could be reversed. That is, rather than using them to smooth out and control messy realities, might we use their questions as a sort of guide to illuminating the particular ways that the mess was patterned in the wake of the earthquake? That is, what if we used them as ethnographic questions?

I would end up integrating elements of these instruments into my interviews, raising a series of complicated methodological questions. If I am interested in tracing how the psychiatric response to the earthquake worked to transform people's loss and suffering into symptoms of pathology—how, that is, the earthquake was transformed into a psychiatric event—is it not a self-fulfilling analysis to use the very instruments of this psychiatric world making to examine the affective and experiential legacies of the earthquake? In turn, am I not granting legitimacy to these reifications and their claims to universality? Am I not taking part in their proclivity to render the nonnormative as pathological? While legitimate questions, I would also suggest that they run the risk of exaggerating the power of these categories and instruments in creating the experiences they intend to name and measure. As I have come to appreciate over the course of my research for this book, these surveys were, like the paper they were printed on, fragile in the face of the tremendous forces of life itself. Indeed, the way that this and the following chapters weave in and out of these categories—how they help organize my analysis, yet come into view as thoroughly unstable and malleable social facts—is intended to mirror the ways my interlocutors engaged them. People, in the same breath, would embrace them, judge themselves against them, deploy them strategically, and frequently question and reject them. While I must of course take care to acknowledge their powers, the risk, I feel, is outweighed by the possibility of offering the grounds for a different sort of encounter between anthropology and psychiatry, an encounter other than the current ways in which anthropologists and psychiatrists speak past one another.[19]

Edgy Relations

While the edgy aftermaths of disaster might manifest as individual bodies on edge, they took form, and hold, in relationships—working their way through as they unsettled social fields stretching from the intimacy of domestic ties to everyday encounters with neighbors, friends, coworkers, and strangers. In this section, I want to shift focus to this social legacy of disaster by turning to the neighborhood, or *mahalle*, as a distinctive moral space and affective container of disaster. Neighborliness (*komşuluk*) is an important cultural value that marks the *mahalle* as an ideal and an idealized space for authentic social belonging. The *mahalle*, in this regard, is a quintessential "local moral world,"[20] and neighborliness comprises those qualities that define one's moral actions in such a space—such as providing material and moral support (*maddi ve manevi destek*) to others, sharing resources (from borrowing ingredients to offering small loans), keeping an eye out for one another's children, and watching for and alerting others to the presence of outsiders. Given the ways that gender is domesticated, the *mahalle* also functions as a particularly vital social resource for women—as a space of intimacy, comradery, and shared labor, all of which can go too far. In this sort of social and moral space, watchfulness easily slips into nosiness, feelings of support become feelings of oppressive confinement, and generosity leads to complaints about neighbors becoming excessively dependent (always borrowing, never reciprocating). Neighborliness, in this respect, can also be understood as a social technology of surveillance and normatization. Especially in the sorts of communities where I was working—comprising households financially supported by low-income laborers, civil servants, domestic workers, and small business owners—*komşuluk*, in both idealized and criticized forms, was a tremendously important social and material investment.

The earthquake profoundly disrupted these social, material, and moral worlds. Entire neighborhoods—the material infrastructure of neighborliness—were literally destroyed. The sheer number of deaths of neighbors and relatives would greatly diminish everyday networks of sociality and precipitously shrink local moral worlds. In the months and years to follow—as people were displaced into tents, then resettled into prefabricated homes, and eventually settled into new neighborhoods, among people they didn't know—the precarity of people's living conditions and the psychological fallout of the earthquake would continually undermine efforts to rebuild this sense of neighborliness. When I began visiting these neighborhoods in 2012 and 2013, it was evident that the disruption of neighborliness extended well beyond the urgency of the earthquake's immediate aftermath, and deep into the interstices of social and neighborly worlds decades into the earthquake's future.

Aslıhan talked at length about the social aftermaths of the earthquake. "The earthquake destroyed a lot, unfortunately neighborliness is no more," she explained. "Things are different now. Before the earthquake, there used to be more sharing, affection, and respect. Now, people are selfish. Everyone is in a state of dissatisfaction. There is no respect. No affection remains. Everyone is walking on their own path. People are more selfish. At times, I count myself among them." Seda, a sixty-year-old neighbor of Aslıhan, would echo this sentiment: "How can I say this? I don't trust people very much anymore. I really dislike the way people talk and behave." Aslıhan talked pointedly about how this sense of selfishness born of the earthquake continued to wear on her: "Since my childhood, I have been a person who really loves sharing. But if I look at myself now, I too have become selfish. For instance, if I bought two bottles of water, and I'm living alone, I would give one away. One would stay, the other would go. Now, if a neighbor asked [for a bottle of water], I'd say that I don't have any. I would hide the second bottle. This began after the earthquake. This sort of thing is exhausting me [*beni yoruyor*]." What weighs on Aslıhan here is her culpability in a more generalized failure of reciprocity that is supposed to define the moral ideal of neighborliness. To keep the bottle of water was to remove a vital resource from the world of social interaction, in which the circulation of things was tantamount to the proper ordering of moral relations.

These sorts of conversations frequently became commentaries on how people no longer felt at home in their own neighborhoods. Residents talked about feeling more distant from their neighbors and that neighborhoods were now full of "strangers" and "foreigners," which was contributing to people feeling on edge. Pınar and Osman, for instance, both talked about feeling more distant or estranged (*uzaklaşmış*) from their neighbors. Others talked about feeling alienated (*yabancılaşmış*, literally, becoming foreign or strange) from their neighbors and the neighborhood. While many people had indeed moved out of the region following the earthquake, and there had been a coinciding labor migration of new residents into the area as the industrial sector recovered, the intensity of these conversations suggested that something more than demographic change was at stake. Indeed, these concerns—about alienation and irritation, estrangement and social discord—proved to exert a strong pull in conversations. They reliably drew in other conversations, about other forms of alienation that unsettled residents.

These conversations tended to move in two directions—one reaching outward, one turning inward. In the first, many residents saw in these feelings of alienation the workings of a series of societal shifts and political and economic transformations occurring over this period. Along these lines, Aslıhan's concerns about her own selfishness spoke not only to her economic struggles, which limited her capacity to live up to neighborly ideals of generosity, but it also reflected a prevailing mood of the time—of things feeling different, of people becoming more materialistic and looking out for themselves, and of an intimacy of communal life being lost. These sorts of conversations, as social commentaries, pointed to the flip side of the period's "growing middle class," namely a sense that people were increasingly on their own in navigating the harsh realities of a transforming market economy.

Along with these sorts of structural dislocations, commentaries about social alienation and irritability—especially those that turned on the increased number of "foreigners" in the neighborhood—also pointed toward traces of other disasters. As Murat put it: "The social structure of Gölcük has changed. After the earthquake, many immigrants arrived from different places. When you see them, you become sad. Gölcük was not such a place. It was more elite [*elit*], especially where we lived. It was a more elite, more beautiful area then. Now, things have changed. Society has become more closed, more conservative. Because of those who migrated here, not because of those who stayed." Although few said as much explicitly, it was clear that the "foreigner" entering the region after the earthquake, disrupting the intimacy and solidarity of *komşuluk*, was the specter of the Kurdish migrant. Like others, Murat alluded to how these migrants "came from the east" to take advantage of subsidies being provided by the state for survivors. Feelings of alienation and a sense that "things were different" and "I no longer feel at home" thus converge with an ethno-racialized discourse of Kurdish otherness, such that the actual living signs of other disasters—of people fleeing the state's military siege of the Kurdish region and its corresponding economic deprivation—would be misread as "greedy foreigners" ruining the neighborhood.

At other times, conversations about social alienation and irritability turned inward. They became a pretext not for explaining social discord, but for diagnosing personal ills. In these instances, feelings of irritability and a sense of neighborliness on the decline were interpreted as a reflection of something being wrong within oneself. Given the enormous importance of neighborliness as a moral ideal and the central role it plays in shaping one's sense of social belonging, this wasn't surprising. As such, it is not difficult to discern in these accounts of alterity and alienation a set of commentaries on more generalized feelings of existential alienation, a pervasive sense of not feeling at home in world.[21] Nevertheless, I was struck by the recurrent ways in which people pathologized these feelings of both irritability and alienation. Aslıhan, again, narrated this in terms of something being broken in herself and her relations with others: "Neighborliness is gone. The social life of the town has changed. It has completely changed. Everyone has become more family oriented. . . . There are more differences. Conversations are different. And it feels strange that I am so disturbed by the opinions, speeches, actions, attitudes, and behaviors of others. Why? At those moments, I tell myself that I am sick." Osman, as I understood him, was suggesting something similar when spoke about broken nervous systems. At times, I would find myself entangled in these pathologizing turns inward, with my own expertise being called on to arbitrate. "I have a question for you Chris," asked a woman I interviewed near the earthquake's twentieth anniversary: "You have met all of these people that lived the earthquake. You've heard a lot. Based on this, am I normal?"

Although I have been referring to these feelings of irritability and edginess as *disaster's* minor feelings, it is important to underscore that they are indebted as much to the experience of the earthquake itself as to the disastrous response the earthquake precipitated. For instance, the rebuilding of the region (through state-sponsored development projects, international aid, and private-public partnerships that financed construction) would create a set of spatial and architectural conditions that conspired to intensify feelings of social isolation—such as towering apartment buildings devoid of public spaces and neighborhoods without parks or commercial areas for public gathering. (Echoing my observations on the drive to the health clinic recounted in the previous chapter, Osman complained: "The *mahalle* doesn't have any common social spaces. If you want to sit and have tea with a neighbor, you have to go all the way to the town center.") At the same time, the ways that residents such as Aslıhan repeatedly drew a jagged line from the earthquake, through feelings of irritability, on to individual pathology, speaks to the specific legacy of the earthquake's psychiatric responses. In this respect, we can understand Aslıhan's commentary as an example of how the psychiatric discourse set in motion after the earthquake had, in time, become vernacular— providing her a language to evaluate and comment on both the severity of her negative affects and the disruption of everyday forms of sociality. In turn, and more tangibly, the legacy of the earthquake's psychiatric response—and especially its psychopharmaceutical afterlife—would similarly surface in conversations as speculations about whether feelings of social distance and alienation might be, in fact, an effect of the continued use of the medications that had begun soon after the earthquake.

Return to the Family

> The doctor gave me a small pill [for my sleep problem] and when I came home a wiliness [*hinlik*] occurred to me. If this pill will make me sleep, then. . . . So I began secretly giving the pill to my husband.
> —ZEYNEP, 2013

Feelings of irritability, frustration, and alienation often led to people not wanting to be around others. These instances of social withdrawal, however, rarely led to solitude. Rather, it usually meant spending more time at home and with family members. This is what Aslıhan meant when she observed that, "everyone has become more family oriented." The ways that post-earthquake development strategies worked in tandem with ongoing socioeconomic transformations of the period to encourage households comprised primarily of nuclear families meant that the long aftermath of the disaster often took social form as the intensification of affective attachments within small circles of people. The family, as such, would thus become a conjunction of multiple forces, which would conspire to pattern familial ties and post-earthquake life trajectories in particular ways. I want to touch on one such trajectory in this final section.

At the time of the earthquake, Erol was living in a rented apartment with his wife and two young children on the outskirts of a small town near the earthquake's epicenter. He had spent most of his life in the area, having completed his formal education at a nearby elementary school and, as a young adult, taken a job at the local offices of a major telecommunications company. When the earthquake struck, the five-story building where he and his family were living collapsed immediately. Erol remained trapped under the rubble for five days. Once freed, he would spend eleven days in a hospital in Samsun, nearly seven hundred kilometers away from İzmit. (Because of the strain on the regional health care system, many people injured in the earthquake were transferred to hospitals in their home provinces.) Fortunately, his wife and two children had been visiting relatives on the Black Sea coast at the time of the earthquake, although it took them almost a week to learn that Erol had survived and was in fact in a nearby hospital. It was in the hospital in Samsun where he learned that his parents, siblings, and their children had all died when their nearby apartment buildings collapsed. Once physically able to be discharged, Erol left the hospital, as he put it, "utterly shattered" (*paramparça*): "My entire family was gone. My parents, my brother and sister, they were all gone. Only I remained.... At that point, I was deeply depressed. My psychology was thoroughly broken [*benim psikolojim bozulmuştu iyice*]."

In the year that followed the earthquake, Erol and his surviving family followed a trajectory common among renters, as they moved from a poorly manufactured emergency tent to a slightly better constructed prefabricated house. Unlike the vast majority of survivors, Erol and his remaining family were later offered a unit in an apartment complex that had been built with funds from an international donor. They moved into the apartment in the fall of 2001, more than two years after the earthquake. The stability offered by the new home was short lived. Over the coming years, regional government officials would begin pressuring Erol and his new neighbors to move. They soon began trying to evict the residents. (I turn to the struggle of the residents of this apartment complex in Chapter 11.) When we met in 2013, Erol was still living in the apartment with his family, having recently retired from his job at the telecommunications company where he had worked for most of his adult life.

On the afternoon when I visited him last, he was home with his wife and two daughters. We would end up spending much of the afternoon sitting around, drinking tea, talking, and reviewing the news clippings and court documents Erol had been collecting since they began their antieviction campaign. As Erol walked me through the documents—he had become the resident archivist of their struggle—he talked about the psychiatric care that he continued to intermittently receive and the number of medications (what he described as his "legal drugs") that he had been taking for most of the previous decade. The medications, he explained, helped regulate his most debilitating symptoms, such as his bouts of depression and outbursts of intense anger. As with many others, the use of psychopharmaceuticals had become a vital form of support for Erol, a post-disaster prosthetic that helped him live on. Nevertheless, although the medications took the edge off his nerves, he continued to be easily irritated and socially withdrawn.

Reflecting a familiar retreat to the family, Erol described: "I can deal with my family. I'm able to laugh with them, I'm able to share with them. But I've become antisocial [*antisosyal*] otherwise. Communicating with people is still difficult. I can sit for hours by myself without talking with anyone. Relatives criticize me for this. They say I'm antisocial. Doctors say I should take part in society." This would retrace the themes of another conversation, in which he described: "There is trust in my family. With my family, and my relatives, I'm able to laugh and joke. But, with others, no one has seen me laugh or joke for more than ten years." Erol talked openly about his irritability and his struggle to contain his anger in everyday life. Especially in the years immediately after the earthquake, Erol describes himself as having become a "psychopath" (*psikopat*): "My family and relatives criticized me for this. 'You are very nervous. You answer back. Why are you getting angry? Why are you getting angry and shouting out of the blue?' Before [the earthquake], I wasn't someone to get mad at other people. I was a humanitarian before." While the outbursts had become less common, he continued to struggle with being continually on edge and irritable.

Although Erol showed no signs of a continued "psychological war" in our conversation, its toll on his family—who were present during our conversation—was apparent. As Erol talked about his irritability and anger, his wife, who had been coming and going from the room, paused to join the conversation. She began talking about how, while things were good now, it had been challenging to live with Erol, and his intense and unpredictable outbursts directed at her and the children. His daughters soon joined the conversation, echoing their mother's frustrations. It was clear that they had been through difficult periods, and they openly discussed their struggles to make sense of Erol's irritability and mood swings.

The way they discussed Erol's struggles caught me off guard. The openness with which they described his psychological and emotional states was far from the sorts of silence and sanction one would expect in reading the literature about psychiatric "stigma" in the region or, for that matter, common accounts about working-class masculinity, emotional availability, and family life. Beyond the openness with which they talked about Erol, I was especially struck by the tenderness of their comments. While they were critical of Erol's moods, they weren't resentful. They suggested a kind of solidarity with him in which the irritability and mood swings were something other than Erol, something that had come with the earthquake, which meant that they could go away again at some point.

While Erol and his family are but one example of how post-disaster irritability worked through familial arrangements in the years following the earthquake, domestic dramas like this are to be found across the region, as a lasting relational legacy of the earthquake. Families, like Erol's, have had to develop new ways of being together, as they learned to read the shifting atmospheres of rooms and unspoken cues of family members, to anticipate reactions, and struggle to ease or redirect negative affects. While the dramas were domestic, these familial and affective dynamics of disaster were also a set of structural conditions. Aslıhan's description of earthquake survivors becoming "more family oriented" was not, for instance, simply about residents turning to the family in times of need—as an idealized space of care—but also a patterned response to the ways that post-disaster aid, especially housing assistance, was distributed in the years following the earthquake. That is, the family—normatively constituted by a male head and female and child dependents—would be the principal social unit of resettlement and government relief in the wake of the earthquake.

The family thus became both the primary affective container of disaster and a vital unit of governance, functioning as a central relay between the state and individual citizens.[22] Although Erol's family may have narrated a comforting account of openness, familial love, and collective struggle, this gathering of forces in the family also created a tinder box of grief, irritability, and anger. Pınar, who I interviewed with her husband, a retired naval officer, touched on this when describing how the earthquake had affected their relationship. "Sometimes when we're talking, we just suddenly flare up [*parlıyoruz*]. I flare up, he flares up. Later we ask why we got angry, but, in the moment, we can't understand why." Pınar hints at what others would recount in troubling detail, that these relational manifestations of irritability and anger could easily turn violent. With the widespread loss of family members and friends, together with the resettlement of survivors into neighborhoods where they knew few others, older systems of mutual support and social surveillance had been thoroughly disrupted. As one might expect, these conditions would converge with a post-earthquake "return to the family" to intensify and multiply already too common scenes of domestic and gender-based violence.[23]

Otherwise Than Trauma

By the time I began spending extended periods of time in the region, the Marmara Earthquake had settled deeply into everyday lives as a pervasive and enduring mood, announcing itself quietly in fleeting moments in the flow of conversations, as feelings that unsettled relations, in bodies left on edge. As I worked to understand the contours of this affective legacy of disaster—tracking how the earthquake's effects became domesticated by other social forces and configured by regional post-earthquake rebuilding schemes and national transformations in politics and economy—the earthquake began coming into view less as an acute event or sudden rupture than as a set of chronic conditions and enduring processes. In this regard, I would find in conversations about everyday feelings of edginess, irritability, and alienation a series of unexpected commentaries on both the event itself and the structural dimensions of embodiment, affect, and sociality that define its legacy. Here, the edginess born of a geological event combined with political and economic regimes for a "New Turkey" to deepen the precarity of many earthquake survivors, which in turn intensified already unsettled feelings of edginess, irritability, and alienation. Put otherwise, the disaster's aftermath wove into the quasi-eventfulness of an everyday already filled with innumerable small-scale crises, ruptures, and slow disasters which together animated, following Kathleen Stewart, an "enduring hum" of post-disaster living on. Nervous systems "broken" by the earthquake, as Osman put it, would thus struggle to recover as a political and economic system grew ever more nervous.

It is not altogether surprising that these edgy aftermaths of disaster have been overlooked in the scholarly and clinical literature. In the very ways that this affective legacy weaves into and reconstitutes the everyday, it can be difficult to disentangle the long aftermath of the earthquake from more mundane responses to the conditions of people's lives—of tensions with spouses and neighbors, of ordinary anger about a child's behavior or the pace of traffic, of the seemingly endless frustrations that emerge as one struggles to get by. This sort of legacy is also easy to overlook when it is not something that necessarily concerns everyone. In this regard, the challenge of recognizing this legacy is in part methodological, for these are the remains of disaster that one encounters only by spending extended periods of time in particular places and with actual people as they go about, and as they reflect on, their lives.

The challenge of appreciating these everyday legacies of disaster is also conceptual. Research focused on the experiential and psychological dimensions of disaster continues to maintain an almost-exclusive focus on psychological trauma. Researchers, clinicians, and activists alike seem unable to escape what the anthropologist Erica James has described as the "global political economy of trauma."[24] As I have touched on repeatedly in the previous chapters, reducing our understanding of the psychological and affective legacies of disaster to the discourse of trauma—premised as it is on a universal category of human experience that privileges individual pathological processes over socially and historically embedded forms of (inter)subjective experience[25]—is to close ourselves off from the remarkable variability of lives that formed in the earthquake's aftermath. In this regard, conducting ethnographic research in the region over the decades following the earthquake not only gave me a sense of how the effects of the earthquake persisted long into the disaster's future; it also brought into sharp relief the extent to which the fascination with psychological trauma (and traumatic memory) that dominates North American and European studies of disaster was both limited and limiting.

As became abundantly clear over the course of the research for this book, trauma was but one form among many through which people managed the overwhelming experiences of the earthquake. This is not to suggest that people's response to the earthquake did not take forms that could be characterized as traumatic.[26] My point is that it was not the only way the earthquake's legacy assumed a psychic or affective form. With this recognition, I join others in questioning whether trauma provides the best framework for thinking about the legacies of disaster and political violence.[27] While the study of psychological trauma and traumatic memory has powerfully and productively challenged a wide range of assumptions—especially regarding the bodily entanglements of history, memory, and power—and in so doing, imparted onto academic discourse a renewed sense of moral and political purpose, it has, over time, become an increasingly blunt, all-inclusive, and reified term for talking about the remarkably varied ways that the past can bear on the present.

As talk about the need to "decolonize" trauma studies becomes more insistent,[28] perhaps we have arrived at a point where we should consider abandoning the concept altogether. Or, more modestly, ask what would it mean to look "beyond trauma"?[29] What if, following Veena Das, we were to "train our eyes to look and see what is happening between the crevices of the hard discourses on trauma"?[30] What might we see, for instance, if we refused to frame "irritability" as but another symptom of trauma—to refuse, that is, to subordinate the experiential legacy of the earthquake (yet again) to the overdetermining signifier of trauma? My research—which was, ironically, indebted to the very instruments that have become so central to the psychiatry of trauma—would insist that we think about other approaches and other frameworks for conceptualizing the lived legacy of disaster.

Building on the work of the literary critic Sianne Ngai, I have been arguing that attending to the "minor feelings" of disaster offers just such an alternative approach to thinking through the living legacy of devastating pasts. In contrast to the individualizing and universalizing proclivities of traumatic frameworks, Ngai draws our attention to an enduring constellation of palpable and socially relevant feelings and sensibilities that have come to characterize one of the earthquake's distinctive legacies. As embodied and collective traces of the region's geological history, these minor feelings suffuse everyday lives and gather into lasting moods that take shape within, as they transform, social relationships. And while these affective traces of disaster manifest as bodies and relations on edge, they also register broader operations and speak to the specific historical conjunctures that condition people's everyday lives. Requiring neither explicit occasions nor objects—in their "ongoingness" and "objectlessness," to follow Ngai's formulation—these edgy aftermaths of disaster resist closure and have proved remarkably durable. Both noncathartic and amoral, they also offer neither the charge of righteous anger nor the cathartic promises of the "bigger emotions." In fact, as a pervasive mood and enduring hum, these minor feelings actively work against moments of cathartic or therapeutic release. Uniquely exhausting and socially corrosive, irritability just grinds along.

Yet, this was not an inevitable legacy of the Marmara Earthquake. If, following Ngai, we understand irritability as representing a corrupted form of anger—of being angry too much, at the wrong thing, and/or at the wrong time—what would it mean for there to have been a "right" place and time to express one's anger? What if, put otherwise, there had been a means to hold people accountable for the massive loss of life and property occasioned by the Marmara Earthquake? After all, it wasn't simply an abstract "entrenched logic"[31] manifesting itself in the patterns of loss and destruction, but the deadly product of a series of particular if systemic collusions between state agencies and specific individuals. This was abundantly clear to those who survived the earthquake. Yet the failure of the state to hold its own policies and agents accountable, let alone major actors in the construction industry (with the exception of a handful of contractors), would leave people's desire for justice perpetually unsatisfied. With no place to direct one's anger—with no object or occasion for even catharsis, let alone justice—irritability thrived.

TEN

Loss and the Optimism of Catastrophe

In December 2012, at the urging of psychiatrists and psychologists I had been working with, I attended the International Meeting for Psychological Trauma VII (Uluslararası Ruhsal Travma Toplantıları VII), which, despite its title, attracted a largely domestic audience. It was a remarkable conference. Co-organized by the Psychiatric Association of Turkey (TPD) and the Human Rights Foundation of Turkey (TIHV), the conference gathered several hundred researchers and clinicians specifically interested in social or collective trauma. The conference sought not only to provide clinical training to mental health professionals but also, as the organizers would explain, to demonstrate the value of psychiatric diagnosis as a form of political critique and social witnessing. The conference, hosted at a luxury hotel in Istanbul, featured panels that addressed topics ranging from the epidemiology of PTSD among survivors of police torture to the treatment of "complex trauma" among displaced Kurds in eastern Turkey, from clinical accounts of the persistence of childhood trauma to feminist approaches to treating sexual violence. The origin of the conference, as well as the reason I was there, was the Marmara Earthquake. The careers of the conference organizers, as well as many presenters, had been forged in the earthquake. This annual conference was, in a very tangible sense, a lasting remainder of the disaster, something formerly unimaginable being fashioned from the ruins of the earthquake's psychiatric infrastructure.

On the second day of the conference, I joined a session dedicated to clinical approaches to diagnosing and treating "prolonged grief disorder." Facilitated by a prominent Swiss psychiatrist, the session aimed to introduce techniques for treating lasting and disabling experiences of grief to practitioners in Turkey. The presenter was particularly interested in the work of R. W. Ramsay, who, in the late 1970s, published a series of influential studies on behavioral approaches to what he referred to as "pathological grief." The presenter demonstrated his approach by screening a short film featuring Dr. Ramsay treating a bereaved mother in London, who had lost her son fifteen years prior. The film clip highlighted Dr. Ramsay's distinctively "phobic" approach to "pathological grief"—in which the grieving mother's refusal to confront painful reminders of her son was conceptualized as a phobia, and a valuable treatment option was thus the forced exposure of the mother to reminders of her deceased son. The film showed Dr. Ramsay coercing the mother into staring at pictures of her son, capturing in excruciating visual detail the mother's agitation and anguish.

After the session, feeling exhausted, I started talking with the psychologist who had recommended the session, a prominent senior researcher who had been at the center of some of the more influential work being done in the aftermath of the Marmara Earthquake. In the years since, she had become increasingly involved in trauma research concerned with gender-based violence. She asked me what I thought of the session. I explained that I found the video overwhelming, and that I had a hard time recognizing the "treatment" as therapeutic, and thought, ultimately, that it was violent. It was clear that she didn't share my consternation. Her response, in effect, was, "Well, this is what we're dealing with today, among those who survived the earthquake."

The following summer I returned to Turkey to interview earthquake survivors living in a small town located near the earthquake's epicenter. It was one of the most severely impacted towns in the region. Several thousand residents had died and more than half of its buildings had been either destroyed or severely damaged in the earthquake. The stories of loss and lasting grief that I encountered that summer would underscore how the affective legacy of the earthquake was inescapably the legacy of a relationship with death. It was during this trip that I first met Esra, who I mentioned briefly in the introduction. Esra had lost her son in the earthquake, and the force of her despair and continuing grief seemed unrelenting. It was as if her feelings of loss, and the intensity of her attachment to her lost son, had not diminished in fourteen years.

As we talked that first time, I found my thoughts returning to the conference. Esra's account, along with the other stories of lasting suffering that I was hearing, seemed to reflect precisely the scene of pathological grief staged in the film about Dr. R. W. Ramsay. Indeed, as the psychologists I talked to after the conference session alluded to, the sorts of intense attachments to past loss that Esra described had become a concern among many of the psychiatrists who had responded to the earthquake more than a decade earlier and who continued to intermittently treat patients in the region. I would also discover in our conversation that several of the psychiatrists who attended the conference had actually treated Esra in the first year following the earthquake—before the psychiatrists stopped coming and, as Esra put it, "we were left to try to overcome on our own."

I begin with these interconnected scenes of loss and grief not only because of what they reveal about the global travel of psychiatric forms of knowledge and practice (see Chapter 6), or what they indicate about how this travel of expertise closely tracks the changing symptom profile of survivors of the Marmara Earthquake—from an initial wave of experts on treating acute stress disorder and PTSD to, more than a decade later, experts on prolonged grief disorder. Rather, I begin here because of the converging and juxtaposing formations of loss appearing in these two settings and how they suggest a set of generative questions about the relationship between loss and the passing of time. With this in mind, this chapter explores the ways that narratives of survivors of the Marmara Earthquake recurrently articulated a distinctive relationship between loss and the building of livable futures. Toward this end, I want to focus closely on Esra's story of lasting grief, as a means of drawing out the interplay of subjectivity and temporality, loss and living on, I see forming in the long aftermath of disaster. Esra's experiences, I argue, not only capture the particular ways that lives in this setting were geologically, socially, and politically reconfigured in the years following the earthquake but also lay bare a convergence of environmental, technical, and subjective realities increasingly determining the course of lives on a global scale.

How does one imagine, let alone build, a future in the wake of an event as destructive as the Marmara Earthquake? What sorts of lives did the earthquake's deadly convergence of geological volatility and psychiatric expertise make possible? With these questions, I return to my interest in the temporality of living on. As noted at the outset of this book, the concept of living on was critical in my efforts to trace the lasting consequences of the Marmara Earthquake. On the one hand, I was drawn to the concept for the ways it captured, among earthquake survivors, a nearly ubiquitous rendering of the seeming obstinacy of life in the wake of disaster, an orientation to life and time that was typically glossed with the phrase *hayat devam ediyor* (life goes on). On the other hand, approaching the legacy of the Marmara Earthquake through the temporality of "living on" would help me recognize the specific ways in which geological events, psychiatric expertise, and the shifting political-economic conditions of Turkey converged to chart people's lives in the years that followed the earthquake. In this regard, living on as a concept challenges us to approach the Marmara Earthquake as simultaneously an acute event and a chronic condition, as both a sudden rupture and an enduring process in which the disaster's aftermath weaves into the quasi-eventfulness of the everyday and extends into the future.

In this chapter, I want to further develop my thinking about the temporality of living on by approaching this relationship between disaster and the passing of time as a form of optimism. Although I am not the first to consider the relationship between disaster and optimism,[1] my analysis does not turn on the recent theoretical interest in optimism's cognate, hope.[2] It turns, instead, to the writings of the medieval Muslim theologian Abû Hâmid al-Ghazâlî (c. 1058/450–1111/505). I'm drawn to al-Ghazâlî's work because of the ways it not only reflects an investment in the potentialities of the commonplace and familiar but also embodies a distinctive orientation to the future. Al-Ghazâlî's writings additionally interest me in the ways they push us outside of modern European philosophical genealogies for theoretical inspiration and, in so doing, invite us to think about experiences of loss and disaster beyond the dominant pathological frameworks so common to their analysis. This turn to al-Ghazâlî will help us appreciate both the formative ways Esra builds a future out of the present, but also how this relationship to the future—her optimism—forms through a particular affective history of disaster and political reform in post-earthquake Turkey, one that grows in the interleaving of subjective experience, geological processes, and the period's shifting political and economic realities.

Esra

My initial interest in meeting Esra had been to gain a better understanding of the new sorts of civil society organizations that emerged after the earthquake, especially those addressing the dramatic surge in the number of persons with disabilities in the region. Esra had become well known locally for her work advocating for disability rights following the earthquake. Our conversation, however, would be largely about her son. Esra was forty-one years old at the time of the earthquake. Born and raised in a working-class neighborhood in Istanbul, Esra completed high school in the early 1970s and, soon after, began working in a series of factories, until she married in 1978. In 1985, after the birth of her second child, she and her family left Istanbul to resettle in the area. Not long after moving, her husband would be killed in a traffic accident, leaving Esra to raise her young children. At the time of the earthquake fourteen years later, Esra was living alone with her young son. Her daughter, recently married, had moved to Istanbul to be closer to her husband's family.

Asleep when the earthquake struck, Esra recalled waking up to the building swaying. She rushed out of her room to check on her son, just as the building collapsed under her feet. She would regain consciousness later to find herself trapped under the rubble. "I tried to listen for sounds from my son," she recalled. "It was so dark and I wasn't able to hear anything for the first hour. Then an hour later, I heard his voice." Over the next fourteen hours, she would talk continuously to her son—in turn encouraging, in turn comforting him—until he was rescued and rushed to the hospital. It would take another two hours for Esra to be freed from the rubble.

Esra spent the next eight months in the hospital, undergoing fourteen surgeries on her foot. Unable to leave the hospital, she initially relied on others to locate her son, but no records could be found confirming that he had been admitted into any of the local hospitals. Once out of the hospital and settled, alone, into one of the prefabricated housing settlements that had become ubiquitous in the area, she continued the search for her son, struggling to navigate the settlement's rocky and frequently muddy paths with her injured foot. After a year of searching, she lost hope that her son would be found alive and turned her attention first to morgues in the region and then to the area cemeteries. "At that point," Esra explained, "I was determined that I was going to find my son's body . . . I walked through all of the cemeteries, and eventually came to the cemetery for unidentified bodies, and found a grave that I thought held my son's body." After a costly legal battle and a series of bureaucratic delays—which together lasted nearly four years and left her further in debt—the grave was opened. The DNA test confirmed that it was her son.

Although the identification of her son's body would allow Esra to avoid the terrible fate of so many others, who were never able to find the bodies of loved ones, she described her life as being utterly shattered with the death of her son. The years of frantic searching gave way, with the discovery of his body, to despair. Although all of the interviews I conducted in the region were difficult—particularly those that involved the loss of a child—Esra's account of her life during this period was especially difficult to experience. Fourteen years after the death of her son, when we first met, Esra remained consumed by grief.

The Labor of Living On

"While everyone else thinks about the earthquake once a year, on August 17, we live it. We live it every day." For Esra, like others, the everydayness of the earthquake's legacy was twofold. Not only did she struggle with the loss of her son, as she put it, every day, but she also described "the everyday" as being where and when her most vigilant work of living on was required. These were themes she returned to again and again across the years that spanned our conversations. When I asked her what helped her deal with the continuing feelings of intense grief and loss, she explained: "Keeping myself busy. I keep myself busy. I don't let myself stop." "I spend the day here at the association . . . running around, doing work for the association." She went on to enumerate the varied tasks of maintaining the association—completing reports, arranging assistance for disabled residents, drafting pamphlets, filling out budgets, and so on. "I keep running [around] as much as I can, because I don't want to go home, because . . . I'd be face-to-face with my own pain."

The labor of the everyday, which was at once a struggle with the everyday, was constituted by a set of practices and orientations whose aim was to contain her pain. While work kept her occupied during the weekdays, the evenings and weekends were difficult. "I just can't return home," Esra explained.

"It's so empty, and quiet, and I'm alone." It was at times like this, when she would stop, that she worried that the grief would become unbearable. Not surprisingly, Esra spent a great deal of time at work. When not at work, she worked hard to keep herself busy. A large amount of her time outside of work was taken up running the various errands necessary to keep her life going—to the grocery store, the pharmacy, to pay bills, and so on. Afternoons and evenings were occupied by long walks around town and along the shore. At other times, she passed evenings drinking tea with friends at the café.

When I returned six years later, for the events commemorating the twentieth anniversary of the earthquake, we would meet again. Now retired and struggling to make ends meet on a meager fixed income, Esra described her struggle with the everyday as ongoing. She would repeat, nearly verbatim, what she had told me six years earlier: "As I said, during the day, you keep running as much as you can run and, in the evening, well, you don't want to go home. We are still living this." As I walked around town during this period of fieldwork—tracking down old acquaintances, attending events dedicated to the earthquake, and, at times, like Esra, keeping busy—I would run into her now and again, typically sitting at a café with a friend or neighbor talking for hours on end.

When asked what her and her friends talked about, she explained that they did not talk about their troubles: "Why upset one another with our own sorrows? We all have our problems, we all suffer. After all, everyone in town is in the same condition, everyone living here is the same." This sentiment echoed across interviews in the earthquake region, as both an acknowledgment of shared lives (i.e., there was no need to dwell on experiences of the earthquake that were common knowledge) and an act of consideration (i.e., to talk about one's own struggles threatened to awaken in others their own painful memories of the disaster). While she had close friends who offered to listen to her difficulties—and she knew that this was what the psychiatrists who she saw after the earthquake would recommend that she do—she refused. Instead, her conversations with friends mirrored her everyday strategies of keeping busy—long, rambling discussions about the price of produce or rent, the cost of various items at the store, and the assorted minutiae of the everyday. In hearing Esra talk about her daily life, one gains an appreciation for how much labor keeping busy actually requires.

It is important to recognize that Esra's grief and her efforts to keep busy took shape through a common set of gendered norms and expectations. Beyond the specificity of the intensity of her attachment to her son—which was not uncharacteristic for a setting marked by a strong preference for sons, as well as a preference for patrilocality[3]—Esra was working within a narrow set of possibilities for building a new life following, first, the death of her husband and, subsequently, the death of her son. Reflecting a common constellation of gender- and class-based dynamics in Turkey, Esra's social position (as well as her access to social assistance from the state) was closely bound to her dependence on male family members.[4] In turn, the social spaces, discourses, and forms of moral personhood available to her were tightly bound to her status as a widow and mother, and the particular shape this takes for a mother who has lost a young son. In this regard, being a "good" mother entails remaining in a state of lasting grief, and to indicate otherwise, or that one has built a life that is not defined by this loss, is to risk moral judgment.[5] In contrast to other genres of post-disaster stories I heard—stories, mostly from men, of self-transformation following disaster—Esra was consigned socially to a space and temporality of perpetual mourning.[6] As such, Esra's experiences are in many regards unexceptional in this context, though no less particular or painful.

As I listened to stories from people like Esra over the course of my research, I was struck by how both the clinical language circulating in the region at the time (e.g., prolonged grief disorder) and the social discourse of mourning that was normative in this context (which was highly gendered and foreclosed the possibility of imagining a future not defined by grief) were both formulated on a temporality singularly fixated on past loss. In what follows, I want to make a case for conceptualizing Esra's effort at "keeping busy" as something other than the product of a pathological or paralyzing attachment to the past. Rather, I want to argue that, in these efforts, she is in fact actively fashioning a livable relationship to the future—a relationship between subjectivity and temporality that I regard as *optimistic*.

Optimism: The Perfectness of the Actual

To draw out the futurity of Esra's work of living on, I want to turn to the concept of optimism, especially as it is articulated in the writings of the medieval Islamic theologian Abû Hâmid al-Ghazâlî. In drawing on al-Ghazâlî, there is, of course, complex translational work to acknowledge.[7] What are the limits, for instance, of mobilizing a set of theological arguments from the eleventh and twelfth centuries within the context of contemporary critical anthropological discourse—of moving between two discursive traditions with dramatically different and historically contingent cosmologies and configurations of power and knowledge? In thinking through these questions, it is critical to recognize, following Achille Mbembe and others,[8] the provincialness of all concepts, such that the question of the limits of al-Ghazâlî for analyzing the present is also necessarily a question of the limits of contemporary "theory" for analyzing al-Ghazâlî. At the same time, while I embrace the insistent call to decolonize epistemologies,[9] and while al-Ghazâlî pushes us outside of modern European philosophical traditions, we cannot lose sight of the fact that my engagement with his ideas nevertheless emerges out of my own disciplining within these philosophical traditions. I also want to note that Esra does not look explicitly to al-Ghazâlî for models for building a livable future; she would certainly recognize his name, but not know much about his writings. I'm interested in al-Ghazâlî's writings, however, because, as I will argue, they offer a productive approach to understanding Esra's efforts to build a livable future within the remains of post-earthquake Turkey.

Al-Ghazâlî's writings about suffering and divine justice were at the center of his efforts to resolve the problem of theodicy—namely, how to account for the presence of evil in a world created by a just and omnipotent God? Al-Ghazâlî's response to this problem is typically condensed into the formulation: "There is not in possibility anything more wonderful than what is" (*laysa fi'l-imkān abdaỳ mimmā kān*).[10] That is, the world as it is, is the "best of all possible worlds." Although al-Ghazâlî does not use the term *optimism* in his writings, I use it here because his ideas about theodicy (and the lasting theological debates he inspired on this topic) are commonly framed in terms of the philosophical principle of optimism.[11] Additionally, I am drawn to the term *optimism* because of the way it articulates with, as a generative counterpoint, contemporary writings about the political utility of hope.[12]

To appreciate the implications of what I am calling al-Ghazâlî's optimism, let us begin with his critics. Al-Ghazâlî's argument that "there is not in possibility anything more wonderful than what is" would set in motion intense theological debates that stretched from the twelfth through the nineteenth centuries. Alongside technical, theological commentaries, there formed a series of "commonsense" critiques of al-Ghazâlî: in the face of innumerable examples of wickedness in the world or the massive death, destruction, and suffering wrought by disasters, how could one possibly suggest that we exist in the "best of all possible worlds"? Simply put, for these critics of al-Ghazâlî, there is too much suffering in the world to justify optimism.[13] The concept of optimism attracts similar skepticism among critical thinkers today. At its most dangerous, optimism is ideological and hegemonic—a pacifying fantasy for the marginalized and a luxury for those with means. At its most generous, optimism is a symptom of childlike ignorance born of insufficient knowledge ("If one only knew what was really happening, one wouldn't be optimistic").

Given these critiques, how might al-Ghazâlî's optimism help us understand Esra's project of living on? Within al-Ghazâlî's suggestion that we live in the "best of all possible worlds" moves, I argue, a subtle but radical contention that implicates something quite different from the banal platitudes of conventional ideas of optimism. When al-Ghazâlî suggests that things in this realm "are as they are, only because God has made them so," the implication is that the world is as it is, and if anything is going to make it better, it is not going to come from some sort of outside, future addition to the world. In other words, and following on Eric Ormbsy's exhaustive treatment of al-Ghazâlî's theodicy, "there is not in the realm of contingency, i.e., the realm of things that equally can be and not be, and that require for their existence or non-existence something outside themselves, anything more wonderful than what is."[14] While al-Ghazâlî's unwillingness to grant primacy to the role of human agency (or social inequality) as the origin of suffering, illness, and disaster would likely strike the contemporary reader as critically and morally dubious (as it does me), I want to bracket this for now so as to consider how al-Ghazâlî's ideas posit a distinctive relationship to the future.

Appreciating the radical contingency of the world as imagined by al-Ghazâlî is critical for understanding how futures are figured in this optimism. When al-Ghazâlî argues that "there is not in possibility anything more wonderful than what is," he is making an argument for the "perfect rightness of the actual." As Ormsby characterizes this argument, "The world as it is and not otherwise, the actual state-of-affairs, is superior to any merely hypothetical alternative order."[15] Thus, the optimism of al-Ghazâlî is not about imagining a better or anticipating an optimal future that is made possible by an addition to the present that comes from beyond the world as it is. Put differently, a defining feature of al-Ghazâlî's optimism is that it is *not* predicated on a detachment or divestment from the present so as to imagine an ideal future. It is not, in other words, what Michael Snediker has characterized in his writings on queer optimism as a "futural optimism"—an optimism that "anticipates a relationship to what might be, where the future is the site of optimal possibility."[16] (The Turkish term *iyimserlik*, which is conventionally translated as "optimism," carries the same connotations as this "futural optimism"—a cheery optimism that things will be better in the future.) Whereas a futural optimism is founded on a divestment from the conditions of the present so as to dream of a better or redeemed future, the optimism of al-Ghazâlî does not permit such a disengagement or escape from the present. Yet, to reject a futural optimism does not require one to abandon the future. Rather, to be optimistic is to dwell in a world defined by its contingency (where things could always be otherwise) and, with that, to recognize that a future will necessarily emerge out of the contingency of the present.

While my reading of al-Ghazâlî's optimism shares with others an interest in the "ordinary," "everyday," or "mundane" as important settings and temporalities of subject making, my argument diverges from recent efforts to formulate "hope" as an analytic concept.[17] Although these efforts are important work, they are premised on a future-oriented notion of hope, or a futural optimism, that differs in substantial ways from the optimism of the present suggested by al-Ghazâlî. It is also important to underscore that the optimism that I'm trying to imagine with the help of al-Ghazâlî is not a mode of future making that either expresses or strives for particular subjective states (e.g., happiness). As we will see, this is an optimism that can exist alongside intense pain and grief. At the same time, and relatedly, this optimism opens us to thinking about the subtleties and variabilities of living on in the wake of disaster that may not fit well within such dichotomies as mourning and melancholia (the latter of which Freud famously characterized as a failed, pathological version of the former) or, again, common conceptualizations of psychological trauma and PTSD.[18] In fact, my thinking moves in quite different directions.

The Optimism of Catastrophe

How might the optimism of al-Ghazâlî allow us to approach differently Esra's experiences of loss and living on, the relationship between her intense attachments to the past and the building of a livable future in the prolonged wake of disaster? In responding to this question, I want to consider how her efforts at "keeping busy" and her understanding of the relationship between these everyday practices and the passing of time reflect an investment in the present that is neither simply a symptom of a pathological attachment to the past nor a pathological refusal of the future. In approaching Esra's efforts to live on in this way, my aim is to shift attention beyond a set of themes commonly encountered in the scholarly literature concerning death and grief in Turkey, which—like much of the wider anthropological literature—has tended to focus on meaning-making practices and ritualized activities for culturally managing loss and death.[19] In contrast, I am interested in how Esra's optimism points toward something at once more active than those approaches that center (pathological) attachment and more prosaic than those emphasizing ritualized practices of meaning making surrounding death. Esra, I argue, embodies a struggle with life that suggests a different configuration of loss and living on, of subjectivity and temporality. Optimism, in this respect, operates less as a principle of life or state of mind than as a methodology for living on.

Approaching optimism in these terms casts Esra's efforts to "keep busy" in a different light. Esra, like other survivors of the earthquake, cobbled together a repertoire of strategies to occupy time—running errands, passing evenings with friends, taking long walks around town. While taking a range of gendered forms, such strategies for keeping busy were a recurrent topic of conversation across interviews. In this regard, Esra, like others, worked hard to keep busy, a struggle waged in and with the everyday. Instead of regarding these strategies as symptomatic—as, say, an obsessive and paralyzing attachment to the past—the approach to optimism suggested by al-Ghazâlî invites us to recast seemingly mundane, conventional tasks as creating a space and time for an optimistic form of living on. Esra keeps herself going by keeping herself busy, by being continually engaged in the task at hand. Importantly, these are practices aimed not at "self-fashioning" or the making of a new self. Rather than an escape into an imagined future, or surrender to a devastated past, Esra's everyday practices of "keeping busy" can be understood as fostering an inattention to both future and past attachments, as a means of cultivating an investment in the contingency of the world that clears an opening within which she can grow the present—or, better yet, *allow* a present to grow.[20]

In thinking about Esra's investment in the present as a future-oriented project of living on—as a form, that is, of optimism—I find myself returning to the phrase *hayat devam ediyor*, "life goes on." This phrase ran through our conversations, as well as the interviews I conducted with others who lost friends and relatives in the earthquake. It was a phrase that punctuated conversations, a refrain that marked the end of a reflection on the depth of one's loss and pain: "I lost everything in the earthquake. My family, my home. I had nothing left. But I didn't die. Of course, I had no choice but to continue. Life goes on." Another woman I interviewed, who was Esra's age and had also lost close family members in the earthquake, elaborated on this theme: "People still cling to life. One cannot die with the deceased. One has to live. Life goes on." This phrase captures as it also crystallizes how Esra's investment in the contingency of the present can be understood as a form of optimism.

To say that "life goes on" is not to resign oneself to fate. Rather, it expresses an investment in the present that is at once open, active, and future-oriented. As Esra's comments suggest, the movement of life, which I take to also mean the world, is inexorable. There is no stopping it, because "life goes on." And to live, as one must, necessarily means that one is carried along with it. Drawing on al-Ghazâlî, we can understand this investment in the present as an active investment in the future, for out of the contingency of the present will grow a future, which will be something other than a (traumatic) repetition of the past or a continuation of the present as it is. Another earthquake survivor—someone who had been trapped under the rubble for several days and lost several family members (see Chapter 11)—captured well the dynamic at play here. Recoiling at my question concerning his hope for the future, he explained: "I do not have hope. I live in the daily [*günlük*], the present. I am not a hopeful person. To be hopeful is to be waiting. It's passive, lazy. I am not hopeful, I am obstinate [*inatçı*]." Esra would also reject this sort of hope. Yet, in putting Esra's experiences in conversation with al-Ghazâlî, we can see forming not a hopelessness about the future but rather an optimism (of the present) that is at once a tacit investment in the future. That is, Esra invests in the contingency of the present with a sense of trust or anticipation that a future that is otherwise than the present will take shape out of this contingency. A future will come because the future is obstinate; life goes on, *hayat devam ediyor*.[21]

This approach to optimism also helps us think differently about the sociality at work in Esra's grief. Esra's project of living on is not, after all, a solitary endeavor. She often kept herself busy with others. In this regard, I'm interested in how this investment in the present through mundane practices of keeping busy also articulates a distinctive yet highly gendered mode of social and affective exchange. To spend time with Esra and her friends was to enter a familiar, largely (but not exclusively) women's space of sociality, as one would expect in this setting. Once there, a substantial part of her keeping busy with others consisted of an interpersonal play of silence and shared avoidances. Again, as Esra explained, "Why upset one another with our own sorrows? We all have our problems, we all suffer. After all, everyone in town is in the same condition, everyone living here is the same."[22] With the help of al-Ghazâlî's optimism, I want to resist interpreting this shared silence about shared loss as some sort of collective amnesia or pathological avoidance, or attribute it to some sort of fatalism to which women like Esra are uniquely susceptible (a persistent Orientalist trope). Being with Esra and her friends was to witness a discrete choreography of refusal and silent care, as she and her friends abided by a tacit agreement to not talk about their mutual suffering.[23] Where one may hear silence and call it amnesia, or attribute it to the unspeakability of traumatic experience, or disaster, the sort of optimism suggested by al-Ghazâlî allows us to reframe this silence as an active gesture of recognition and acknowledgment through which an inattention to both future and past attachment is maintained and the conditions for livable futures are being collectively fostered.[24] In this respect, I'd argue that these social relationships were not only instrumental in Esra's efforts at keeping busy but also vital in animating the inexorable movement of life and worlds condensed in the phrase "life goes on," in which the future is obstinate and life goes on because that is what life does.

The final aspect of Esra's optimism I want to address highlights what happens when this investment in the present fails. At several points during our interview, I was struck by a sense of regret that seemed to surface during her discussion of the years she spent looking for her son. Although she never put it into words, and I can thus put this only tentatively, there was a sense that the intense hope animating the search for her son had not allowed her to be in the present, and for this she felt regret. She came closest to articulating this sense of regret when she described her relationship with her grandson: "By the time I had found my son's remains, my grandson was almost five years old. I had missed so much of his life." As I understood her here, Esra came to recognize that her intense investment in the future coincided with a divestment from the present, and with this a period during which she was largely unavailable to others.

My effort to identify Esra's optimism should not be read in normative terms. While I want to depathologize her negative feelings, I also want to be careful not to romanticize her grief. After all, this is not an optimism that has any sort of intrinsic relationship to happiness. Esra is still frequently consumed by negative feelings and speaks of long periods of profound unhappiness. I am also not suggesting that she never imagined a future detached from the present, of a better life free of her current conditions, or that "keeping busy" was her only strategy for living on. In looking over the course of Esra's life since the earthquake, one can identify multiple strategies, each with their distinctive temporalities and relationships between past loss and livable futures. At different points, for instance, she felt that she had benefited from talking with psychiatrists who struggled against the intensity of her attachment to the past. Yet, in the decades since, her efforts of living on have been defined by a refusal of the sort of speech desired by psychiatrists—of talking about her problems as a means of mastery over loss. As such, these efforts rarely find their expression in a narrative poetics of loss and grief. They tend to dwell, instead, in the mundane repetitiveness of her efforts to keep busy.[25] In this regard, we can understand her strategies for living on as being characterized not so much by a distinctive relationship to language as by their relationship to time.

I want to underscore that my interest in al-Ghazâlî is not Esra's interest. Esra did not consider herself religious. She characterized herself as adamantly secular, although she shared with others a broad set of religious ideals, sensibilities, and practices common to Sunni Islam. In this regard, al-Ghazâlî's theodicy does not invite an analysis concerned with how Esra gives meaning to her suffering, nor does it suggest an approach that regards one's relationship with the present as something more than what it is (in which one's engagement with everyday tasks is understood as a symbolic displacement of one's caring for oneself). Instead, such an optimism of the present directs our attention to how Esra's everyday efforts of keeping busy are what they are and as such constitute a project of living on—an investment in the present, because it is out of the present that a livable future will grow.

The Conditions for the Future

Al-Ghazâlî's optimism, as I have characterized it, shares with others a commitment to the indeterminate worldliness of future making. Muñoz's "queer futurity," Biehl and Locke's "anthropology of becoming," and Haraway's "Terrapolis," to take a range of examples, each elaborate on the contingency and always incomplete coming-into-being of the world.[26] In different ways, they also underscore a limit to Al-Ghazâlî's writings, especially when we consider one of the central aspects of Esra's struggle to live on—her desire for accountability and justice. Al-Ghazâlî's formulation of divine justice turns us not toward what angered Esra—a state that failed to manage the disaster, corrupt inspectors, propheteering contractors, indifferent bureaucracies—but toward a conception of divine unity. In this final section, I want to expand from Al-Ghazâlî to address how Esra's project of living on took shape within, as it also reflected, a set of shifting political, economic, and affective realities in Turkey. To understand how and why she inhabits the present as she does, I argue here, we need to situate Esra's experiences within the structural dynamics of her affective responses to disaster and thus recognize the specificity of the present within which her optimism grows. There is, put differently, a politics to Esra's optimism.

Esra's investment in the present did not blind her to the conditions of her suffering. Esra's life after the earthquake was, like so many others, profoundly shaped by a desire for accountability and justice. This desire would both keep her going, especially in the early years after the earthquake, and prolong her suffering. Together with thousands of other earthquake survivors, her struggle to hold people and institutions accountable for the earthquake's destruction yielded few tangible results. The earthquake, as an enormously destructive and complex event, resisted accountability. Beyond predictable political denial and evasion, the disaster did not, for instance, slip easily into the grammar of the law, with its demand for clear evidentiary lines of culpability and frameworks of compensatory damage. One could certainly blame the contractors who built the buildings, but this blame quickly dissipates across multiple contractors, subcontractors, sub-subcontractors, and inspectors. Here, the law's inability to identify culpability and assign blame within the context of large-scale disaster would leave people's desire for justice perpetually unfulfilled. Blame was everywhere and nowhere, free-floating and relentlessly thwarting people's desire for closure.

In seeking accountability, Esra, like others, turned to the state. The state's response to the earthquake, however, was its own sort of disaster. Beyond being astonishingly unprepared for such an event (recall that the state's "emergency relief fund" contained the equivalent of US$4.45 at the time of the earthquake), the national agencies dedicated to emergency response were rife with corruption, actual relief efforts were slow and uncoordinated, and long-term relief efforts and recovery programs—as limited as they were—did little more than set in motion a series of secondary disasters. Esra was not alone in her frustration with the state's response to the earthquake. The 1999 Marmara Earthquake would mark a critical shift in popular conceptions of the Turkish state, a disaster that challenged if not ruptured the idea of the powerful, protective, and paternalistic state. There was a widespread sense that the state had betrayed its fundamental (bio)political obligation; to return to its own metaphors, the promises of *devlet baba* (literally, "father state") to protect its own children were revealed, on a spectacular scale, to be empty.

Over the decades that followed, the urgent temporality of disaster and crisis would settle into the cruddy tempos and slow disasters of the period's dominant political and economic arrangements. Esra, like so many other earthquake survivors, struggled through the financial crisis that the earthquake precipitated. The electoral victory of the pro-Islamist Justice and Development Party (AKP) in 2003, in turn, gave way to a decade of dramatically accelerating integration into the global economy, a rapidly expanding middle class, and a further intensification of neoliberal reforms. Esra experienced these transformations in both tangible and intangible ways. With a fixed income and no savings to speak of, Esra was, like so many others, largely left behind by the economic development of the period. People in Esra's position—like Neşe (Chapter 8) and Aslıhan (Chapter 9)—were not part of the celebrated story of Turkey's economic growth, an exclusion that was only intensified by the rising cost of living. Meanwhile, Esra struggled to maintain her limited income as she navigated a deeply gendered Turkish welfare system, in which women's access to social assistance was organized around their status as a dependent to male family members (i.e., husbands or fathers). Women like Esra, who had neither, experienced new sorts of vulnerability as the drive for economic growth and the weakening of labor protections accelerated over the 2000s.[27] In turn, a push for increased efficiency in a reorganizing health care system created more work for Esra, as she struggled to receive adequate care for her lasting injuries.

Esra's struggles during this period were not only material. The failure of the state to adequately respond to the earthquake would have a continuing effect as she negotiated the shifting political and economic conditions of the ensuing years. For the survivors who remained in the region, distrust in the state's capacity to protect its citizens heightened their sense of vulnerability to another disaster, intensifying the waves of panic that followed the tremors that continued to shake the region. This sense of distrust and vulnerability, together with the state's increasing withdrawal from providing social services, would also leave its mark on the future. Echoing David Scott's characterization of the decline of state-driven modernization projects as the closing of temporal horizons defined by ideas of progress and anticipation,[28] the sort of futures underwritten by the state no longer attracted the same enthusiasm. Broadly speaking, these were the political and economic conditions within which Esra's grief grew over the years that followed the earthquake, and the conditions in which she fashioned her strategies of living on. As such, the nonfutural qualities of her optimism—the cultivation of an inattentiveness to past and future attachments—can be understood as not only a response to the emotional pain of losing a son, but also an effort to build a livable future in the face of closing political and economic horizons.

While we of course have to recognize the varied ways that the earthquake impacted different people's lives (in terms of regional, ethnic, and religious identities; political and party commitments; gender and class; as well as personal histories of disaster), these broader conditions of disaster nonetheless point toward a common ground of Esra's optimism. The cultural models of moral personhood and gender normativity that shaped her experiences of grief and the strategies for keeping busy that she fashioned over the years were drawn from a specific social world and thus reflect the (symbolic, social, and economic) resources available to her as well as the limits of what she regards as possible. As such, Esra's experiences and responses to disaster are not exceptional. There is a long social tradition of living on in this way. In this regard, we can understand this optimism as capturing both, on the one hand, the contingent, interpersonal, and experiential dimensions of living on in the wake of disaster, as well as, on the other hand, the collective, structural, and governed aspects of these experiences. In other words, Esra's optimism—her investment in the contingency of the present, her pragmatic efforts to cobble together strategies for building a livable relationship with the future—can be understood as both a setting and a temporality within which affective experience (of, in this case, loss and grief) meets the structural realities of a historical present.

Livable Futures: Reading al-Ghazâlî in the Present

This chapter has posed a series of questions about the relationship between past loss and future possibility taking shape in the extended aftermath of the Marmara Earthquake. Rather than listening to Esra for signs of pathological attachments to the past, I have instead focused on her efforts of building a livable future in the long wake of disaster, a relationship to the future that I've characterized in terms of optimism. But why call it optimism? Given the depth of Esra's continued suffering, and the ways that her work of living on bears no pretense of aspiring for a "happy" future, why hold onto a term that carries connotations so strongly associated with a cheery enthusiasm for a better and brighter future? These are fair questions. In my case, I have been drawn to the concept of optimism for the way it's able to register—with the help of Abû Hâmid al-Ghazâlî—a distinctive futurity of the present that I heard forming in the long aftermath of the Marmara Earthquake. In this regard, I have found the concept particularly helpful in my efforts to formulate the affective and temporal dimensions of living on after catastrophic loss outside of frameworks of either hope, melancholy, or pathological grief.

Again, this is not an optimism that strives for particular subjective and affective states. While oriented to the future, it is decidedly nonfutural. That is, it is an optimism that does not depend on divesting or escaping from the present to imagine a better future but an optimism predicated on a relationship to the future that turns on an investment in the contingency of the present—that things could always be otherwise. I am thus arguing that there is something worth recuperating in al-Ghazâlî's theodicy and that it offers a productive way to approach the forms of life that can flourish in the wake of catastrophe. In our case, Esra's experiences of disaster, loss, and lasting grief come into view not as pathological attachments to the past—a formulation that Esra expressly refused—but as a cultivated inattention to both future and past attachments. It is through this work, which is premised on a tacit understanding of the world as radically contingent and intrinsically on the move, that an opening in the present is cleared for a different future.

At the same time, Esra's experiences also capture the distinctive and common ways that lives in this setting were geologically, socially, and politically charted in the years following the earthquake. While Esra's life, like all, are singular, the models of moral personhood, the gendered norms of grieving, and the strategies for living on that came together to forge Esra's life over the years following the earthquake emerged from a shared social world. These would, in turn, interleave with the period's shifting political and economic rationales of governance, to foster a distrust in both the state and the sorts of futures it promised. It is with these converging experiential and structural realities in mind that I have come to listen to the stories of lasting loss and grief emerging out of the Marmara Earthquake as providing insights for theorizing the sorts of subjectivities and affective lives multiplying in what Rob Nixon has described as the "slow violence" of environmental crises and climate change.[29] As such, al-Ghazâlî may well be timely reading for the present.

I want to end this chapter by suggesting that we might be able to recognize in Esra's struggle to live on in the long wake of disaster the outlines of a model—the concepts of a plan—for human flourishing within worlds increasingly ravaged by planetary ecological crisis. In this regard, I've been interested in how Esra's optimism speaks toward a more general configuration of conditions and forces that characterize the "attritional lethality" of environmental degradation and climatic transformation.[30] That is, Esra's practical efforts of living on in the aftermath of disaster can be approached as a means for thinking about the sorts of lives forged—and forgeable—in a context profoundly shaped by the combined influences of environmental and geological precarity (with its vast scales and complex convergences of material and social forces that hint at, yet continually escape culpability), medical and technical forms of expertise (which continue to proliferate in contexts of disaster, as a means of predicting, mitigating, and responding to disaster), and shifting rationales and realities of governance (where the idea of the protective state along with its narrative of historical progress—even if they were nothing more than fantasies of futurity for the vast majority of people—both endures and gives way to new forms of market generated vulnerabilities). Put otherwise: in the face of geological and environmental precarity that alludes accountability; the multiplication of medical and technical models of futurity as the dominant idiom of disaster; the eclipse of the idea of the protective state as guarantor of justice and, with it, narratives of futurity built on ideas of progress; and a growing sense of personal vulnerability and exposure, women like Esra cobble together a set of strategies for living on, optimistically. They tend to the present, not as an escape from the past or an excuse to give up on the future, but as an investment in the potentialities of the present from which a future will grow.

ELEVEN

Disability, Gender, Thriving

> Life belongs to the brave people who know how to live it.
> —BÜLENT, thirty-four-year-old resident of Değirmendere

What might it mean to not merely survive a disaster but perhaps even thrive because of it? I am certainly not the first to ask such a question. In writing about possible responses to adversity, the psychologists Virginia O'Leary and Jeanette Ickovics have argued that it's time we begin expanding our clinical attention beyond the detrimental and impairing effects of adverse events. What, they ask, might it mean for someone to actually become a better person through experiences of adversity? To "thrive," as they call this, an individual does not merely "return to a previous state, but rather grows vigorously beyond it, and in that process adds value to life."[1] Thriving is thus a "value-added" concept, one that gets at something more than "survival," "coping," or even "recovery." It offers, they argue, the promise of shedding light on how profound challenges "can provide an opportunity for change and growth."[2] O'Leary and Ickovics's research would provide an influential formulation for a generation of psychologists working to conceptualize "positive" human responses to adversity.

In the decades following the Marmara Earthquake, researchers in Turkey began raising similar questions. In 2013, a year after attending the International Meeting for Psychological Trauma in Istanbul, I found myself back in the earthquake region, talking with a group of psychology graduate students about the psychological legacy of the earthquake. While their knowledge of the literature on post-earthquake trauma was comprehensive, their interest in it was more dutiful than curious. Instead, they talked excitedly about new work being done on "post-traumatic growth" and how the earthquake region might be an ideal setting for this sort of research.[3] This conversation signaled broader shifts. Reflecting both the changing symptom profiles of earthquake survivors and the shifting priorities and fads in global networks of psy expertise (dominated, again, by North American and European concepts and interests), the afterlife of the earthquake's psychiatric infrastructure would undergo a series of transformations over this period. Together with "prolonged grief disorder," the "natural experiment" offered by the earthquake would be drawn further into the disaster's future by a nascent interest in such concepts as thriving and post-traumatic growth among a new generation of psychologists and psychiatrists.

In keeping with my interest in working with the expert concepts that emerged from the earthquake, rather than categorically rejecting them,[4] this chapter takes up a set of overlapping concerns. That is, I want to follow this incipient psychiatric legacy of the earthquake into a set of narratives that were premised on the productive possibility of catastrophic experience—stories, that is, of earthquake survivors being born anew out of catastrophic loss. In the previous chapters, I dwelled in the small moments and everydayness of living on, as a way of thinking about the living remains of the earthquake otherwise than through frameworks indebted to the pathological. In attending to the mundane as both a setting and a temporality for imagining a future in the wake of disaster, I intentionally resisted characterizing these sorts of projects of living on as instances of "thriving." To regard Esra's story as an account of "thriving," for instance, would require us to think capaciously about normative aspirations of living on. Her optimism is not "the happy life," if even "the good life." In this chapter, I want to explore other trajectories of living on that formed in the long aftermath of the earthquake, ones that more comfortably fit conventional and increasingly expert formulations of human flourishing in the wake of catastrophic loss and injury. In other words, this is a chapter about those who both lost and gained much in the earthquake.

When I first started hearing these accounts, it was hard not to be cynical. Given the critical theoretical frameworks that were so readily at hand, and through which I had been formed as a thinker, I found myself suspicious about the "positive" and "hopeful" qualities of these stories. In my initial conceptualization of this chapter, the argument oscillated, like a metronome, between *yes* and *but*. *Yes*, someone has figured out a way to thrive in the wake of catastrophe, *but*, see, are they not reinforcing the norms and aspirations of destructive (and ableist) hegemonic orders in doing so? Aren't such instances of thriving being fashioned with the affective ties and passionate attachments of worlds that are, ultimately, injurious? Should we not avoid making the self-actualized liberal subject of late capitalism—from which the vast majority of survivors were systematically excluded—into some sort of hero or role model? (Yes, they are. Yes, we should.) With these questions and doubts in mind, I want to clear a place in this book for such affirmative stories of living on—not merely to challenge my own critical-cynical scholarly disposition, but also because, in these accounts, we find important lessons about how geological events, psychiatric expertise, and the shifting political-economic conditions of Turkey would converge in the long aftermath of disaster to occasion formerly unimaginable life trajectories. As with the previous chapter, I explore these trajectories of post-disaster life by attending closely to the experiences of an individual, who I'm calling Bülent.

"If Life Goes on Despite Everything, You Will Still Live"

Bülent was twenty-two years old at the time of the earthquake. Like many other young men his age—having completed his mandatory military service, and before that his studies at a vocational high school—Bülent was living at home with his family. The day before the earthquake, overtaken by a restless desire to wander, he spent the day walking the streets of the city. As night began to fall, he walked up into the surrounding hills and looked out over Gölcük, a small town where he had migrated with his family from the east when he was a young child. As it was when he arrived, Gölcük was a dusty coastal town on the shore of one of the most polluted bodies of water in Turkey. It was still an arresting view. He looked out over the navy shipyard, Turkey's second largest, and took in the sky: "The stars in the sky seemed so close that you could touch them." He wouldn't forget the stars.

He returned home late, exhausted from the day's wanderings. Hours later, he was startled awake by what felt like a bulldozer crashing into the building's foundation. He jumped out of bed and looked out the window of their fourth-floor apartment to see a surreal scene, as the buildings swayed and the street below heaved into the frame of the window. The kitchen wall crumbled, sending a cloud of dust into the room. In a panic, with a vague memory of a lesson he had received as a child, he ran into a doorway for safety. He would later learn that this was not a good lesson. The frame held for a few seconds, before collapsing. He regained consciousness under the rubble, with enormous cement columns across his chest and feet. His cousin was pinned on top of him.

More than the pain, Bülent talked in our conversations about the intense darkness and silence of the space. As time passed—he couldn't tell how much—the sound of people moaning began to break the silence. Indistinct sounds of pain became the voices of people he knew calling out for help. For Bülent, this was the "second trauma" of the earthquake: "I heard the voice of Uncle Muzaffer the grocer, the voice of our neighbor Aunt Ayşe, and that voice, and this voice." As morning broke, and as many of the calls for help faded, he heard the voices of relatives outside the rubble calling his name. He returned their calls. Unable to free Bülent, they began supplying him with water and food through a small hole they had cleared. Three days passed before the cement columns could be lifted. His cousin, pinned to his chest, died on the second day. Bülent, once freed, was taken to a hospital where both of his legs, gangrenous, were amputated above the knee.

Bülent characterized his life leading up to the earthquake through an idiom of youthful masculinity familiar to his class background and small-town life in Turkey. Bülent was born in the town of Kars in eastern Turkey in 1976 ("in a house with a dirt floor," as he liked to remind others). In the 1980s, when he was seven years old, his family joined the massive wave of migration toward the western part of the country. Bülent was left with an aunt in Gölcük, as his parents and younger sister continued on to Istanbul, where his father would eventually find work. Recalling the years that led up to the earthquake, he described growing from your typical neighborhood kid (with "my number three shaved head and my patched pants and rubber shoes") to "your typical, young single guy"—passing days and nights hanging out with other male friends, drinking tea and talking in local cafés, watching television, playing soccer, and, when he had some extra money, going to movies.

Bülent's sense of carefree youthful indifference ended with the earthquake. The Gölcük of his youth had been destroyed. His apartment was gone, the streets he wandered were gone, much of the coast had sunk into the sea. Bülent, as with nearly everyone I interviewed in the region, lost many of his closest friends in the earthquake, as well as a large segment of his extended family. He would spend upward of six months in three hospitals recovering from his injuries and many more months in Germany, where, with the help of a family friend, he was able to get rehabilitation. This is where he'd learn to walk with his new prosthetic legs. A year later, he returned to Gölcük—to a new apartment, a dramatically reduced group of family and friends, and an uncertain future.

With his new prostheses, and with the encouragement of friends, Bülent began exploring old hobbies. His long rambling walks around the city became extended hikes and camping trips into the mountains. Bülent would soon become an enthusiast for outdoor adventure, an unexpected passion that embodied wider economic and cultural shifts of the period. As middle-class consumption expanded dramatically during the 2000s, "outdoor adventure"—among other new leisure activities—emerged as an identifiable feature of the tastes and aspirations of a growing middle class. With these shifting tastes and expanding markets, Bülent would be able to take advantage of the increased availability of outdoor "gear"—such as lightweight tents made of synthetic fabric, hiking backpacks, specialized footwear—to push the limits of his transformed body. He began going on regular camping trips with friends. With the help of specialized prostheses, he became an avid rock climber. His phone slowly filled with pictures of him atop mountain peaks, looking out over the surrounding hills, his dark silhouette—including his prosthetic legs—cast against a setting sun. These trips would become vital elements in his efforts of living on—moments of escape that offered him a distance from everyday concerns to reflect on his life: "I would look at the stars and start thinking. . . . Why do people try to complete themselves with money? Is it not just paper? For this, we fight wars." As he would later write, "The longest journey is the journey into oneself, and I had begun that journey."

Although the mountains provided him a space to reflect on life, it was the sea that "freed" him. Learning how to scuba dive proved a turning point in his post-earthquake life. It was where he discovered the "freedom of diving," a point to which he returned many times in our conversations:

Had I tried diving in the past, when I wasn't disabled [*engelli*], perhaps I wouldn't have enjoyed it so much. Because there is no such thing as "disabled" under the water. Everything only comes as far as the edge of the pier. When we were in our mother's womb, we were in water. You are grasping that under the water, the peace of being in your mother's womb. What is it to be disabled underwater? Let's say you are going to climb a set of stairs, for example. It's such a simple thing underwater. But when I'm on land, an extraordinary expenditure of effort and strength is required to climb those stairs. Had I done something like this before [the earthquake], I don't think it would have been this enjoyable. That is, because I did it after the earthquake, it was very enjoyable.

Submerged in the water, returned to the womb, a buoyant Bülent found freedom. Diving freed his "spirit" from the struggles of everyday life: "No matter how much stress, how many problems you have, they ease when you get in the water." Diving would similarly and dramatically shift his thinking about the boundary between the limits of his new body and the limits that the (landed) world imposed on him.

The sea was an oblique yet recurring theme across the research for this book. Stories would time and again return to the sea acting "weirdly" just before the earthquake (with fish jumping out of the water, strange lights appearing in the water at night), the startling imagery of the coast breaking off and sliding into the sea, and how an unknowable number of residents, trapped in the rubble of submerged buildings, had drowned in the earthquake. Bülent would add another variation to these accounts. The sea, in his telling, was neither a menacing sign of danger nor a site of mass death. It was, instead, a place of recovery and possibility. It was an environment where he felt free.

Rather than an escape, this freedom would allow him to literally reenter the scenes of devastation that had so profoundly altered the course of his life. As his diving skills developed, Bülent found himself drawn back to the undersea ruins of the earthquake. In 2014, together with a well-known underwater photographer, Bülent organized a series of dives within the submerged rubble of the earthquake: "They were saying I was crazy. They were saying, 'You're a maniac, you spent three days trapped in the rubble and now you want to enter the same rubble underwater.'" The photographs together with Bülent's narration recount the uncanniness of the scene—of everyday objects strewn across the sea bed, of murky surroundings slowly morphing into familiar streets, restaurants, and parks:

> At first, I couldn't make sense of it. Then I found the signs of several familiar stores. And then the sign for an appliance dealer. [I remembered] that we had a youth club on the top floor of the same building. We hung out there together continuously. I then went into the back of the appliance store and I looked at a refrigerator and washing machine that I found there. They had started to disintegrate. Slowly, I started to see the street. The collapsed hotel that was turning into ruins. On the other side was the Koruk Restaurant, with its patio area, turning into ruins. A [public] telephone. We were looking from above. The sycamore trees still seemed as imposing and beautiful as before. I hugged one of them.

The photographs from the dive are striking. In one, Bülent, with his prosthetic scuba legs, sits in a corroded wheelchair that had been scavenged from the submerged rubble.[5]

In time, Bülent became an avid participant in all sorts of water sports. He continued to push the limits of his new body, and the prosthetic technologies he was continually tinkering with, as he learned how to sail, kayak, windsurf, kneeboard, and jet ski. A decade after the earthquake, he would channel his love of water sports into an organization that aimed to introduce persons with disabilities to the sea. In the meantime, he got married and his wife had their first child. Throughout this period, his outdoor activities gave way to a series of spectacular accomplishments. In 2015, he hiked the grueling 508-kilometer Lycian Way trail. A year later, he gained national notoriety for breaking a world record in free diving. He would break the record again in 2017, on the day of the earthquake's eighteenth anniversary.

Bülent's is a remarkable story. I don't want to lose sight of this. His enthusiasm, creativity, and tenacity are astonishing. Although his experiences might not be as unambiguous as his account of these experiences suggests—Bülent, for instance, spoke of his ongoing struggle against a debilitating "earthquake psychology" and a parallel "psychology of ruins" that left him mentally exhausted and frazzled—he has, nevertheless, been able to develop a decidedly positive relationship to the earthquake. Indeed, he would repeatedly express a sense of gratitude toward the earthquake: "Had it not been for the earthquake, I never would have understood what it meant to be free. I had to lose my legs and learn to scuba dive to understand what it meant to be free." Reflecting more generally on the impact of the earthquakes in his life, Bülent described how he had gained a new sense of purpose and resolve. No longer did he take life, or relationships, for granted. Similarly, he discovered a strength in himself that he didn't know was there. He came to consider his injury as an opportunity rather than an obstacle—an opportunity for imagining a new future for himself.

Alignments

I first heard Bülent's story in the office of a small disability support and advocacy organization. The office was on the ground floor of an aging cement building located deep within Gölcük's commercial district. Other than the newspaper clippings posted on the walls, the space was unexceptional. It was basic and comfortable. I had gone there at the recommendation of a psychiatrist who had been active in the region following the earthquake. This is where I first met Esra. On a subsequent meeting, Esra was joined by another woman and Bülent. We would talk for hours. When the focus of the conversation turned to Bülent, he tethered his phone to a computer in the office and began narrating his experiences as he flipped through the slides of a PowerPoint presentation. This would be the first time I conducted an interview that was accompanied by its own slideshow. It was a good presentation—gripping progression of events, with accompanying images, that marked out a compelling narrative arc in which the protagonist confronts and overcomes a series of challenges.

By the time I met Bülent in 2013, he had given the talk dozens of times (at local schools, factories, government agencies, corporate retreats, and nonprofit organizations) and was slowly building a career as a motivational speaker. His website listed several seminars about "personal development, awareness, and motivation" that he was prepared to lead, each offering different lessons based on variations of his life story. He was also being represented by an agency that handled event bookings. On a return trip in 2019, I would find Bülent seaside—outside of the space where he ran the organization that introduced water sports to persons with disabilities. With a deep tan and wearing long swim trunks and sunglasses, he was sitting and talking with friends. His shaved head and collection of leather necklaces were all familiar from previous visits. The scene was what I imagined of surf schools. Bülent's work had expanded significantly since our last meeting. By this point, he was being invited to major corporate retreats, appearing on talk shows with a national audience (as well as Turkey's edition of *Who Wants to Be a Millionaire?*), and had given several TEDx talks in cities across Turkey. He had also received "behavioral training" from a psychologist, and his work had come to include consulting and life coaching. His first book had recently been released. In short, Bülent was becoming an inspiring role model for a growing audience.

With this section, I want to begin exploring why Bülent's story of perseverance, overcoming, and resilience would prove such an appealing lesson for so many audiences—from school children to civil servants, from factory workers to high-end real estate agents. The line of thinking I pursue here makes the argument that to understand both Bülent's life trajectory, as well as the appeal of his story for a range of audiences, we have to appreciate the subjective, social, and structural conditions of possibility within which they formed. In other words, this chapter considers how the relationship between Bülent's life and its appeal to others takes form as a contingent alignment of personal histories, subjective capacities, available social forms, and structural conditions for life and living on in a post-disaster Turkey.

While his account surely reflects an enduring cultural fascination with stories of masculinist heroic struggle and overcoming, it also gestures, I argue, toward a set of more subtle and emergent social processes taking shape across this period. In particular, I want to consider in what follows how the appeal of Bülent's story speaks in revealing ways about shifting sensibilities regarding life, labor, and self-fulfillment taking shape at this time. That is, I want to explore the ways in which Bülent embodied for his audiences many of the ideals of the expanding markets for middle-class leisure and new desires for expert advice about life that were attracting interest and consumers during this period, which will in turn reveal one of the distinctive ways that the earthquake's psychiatric legacy extended far into the future of disaster. Bülent, in other words, was a man of and for the times.

This is where my discussion begins diverging from the clinical discourses of "thriving" and "post-traumatic growth." First, however, I want to acknowledge that there is much to appreciate in these concepts. Their capacity for providing a set of orientations for exploring the legacies of disaster otherwise than through an approach focused on impairment is important. Similarly, concepts such as thriving and post-traumatic growth are appealing for the ways they maintain an opening within which one can consider the role of social and historical dynamics in shaping psychological processes. Given the seeming fixation on cognitive or neurological determinism within the psy disciplines more broadly, this is certainly refreshing.

Despite their promise, however, these concepts nonetheless inherit a disciplinary bias that grants primacy to individual psychological traits or capacities, such as "openness to experience" or "extraversion," in accounting for one's ability to endure hardship and adapt positively despite adversity. In other words, while these concepts allow room to consider the social and historical dimensions of psychological experience, these dimensions enter as heavily circumscribed "variables," such as social or environmental conditions or social determinants of resilience, and in the end privilege the sovereign (and liberal) psychological subject as the decisive site and setting of thriving. In this chapter, I work to decenter this sort of psychological subject of thriving (who is, coincidentally, a close cousin to the psychological subject of disaster) in order to explore the sorts of social and structural conditions that make it tenable.

This analysis emerges out of a long-term engagement with Bülent and Bülent's narrative across multiple iterations, venues, and platforms. In addition to in-person conversations and interviews, several of his talks were available online—including TEDx talks delivered at different cities in Turkey, several TED-style presentations, and a number of lectures and interviews delivered in multiple venues. I also attended a series of events coinciding with the publication of his memoire in 2019. As such, this chapter takes shape across a wide range of encounters and settings. In what follows, in order to introduce you to the sort of moral world Bülent builds in his talks, I focus on a presentation he gave at a corporate retreat for real estate brokers in 2016. The talk is similar to his other talks, although it is longer (fifty-seven minutes, as compared to twenty or thirty minutes) and set on a more opulent stage. While I won't elaborate on this point, I do want to acknowledge the ironies and returns at play here—as Bülent works to inspire the agents of an industry that was directly responsible for his injuries, and that was at this very moment feeding a construction frenzy that would soon enough (especially with the earthquakes of 2023) become another graveyard for tens of thousands of people.

"Life Belongs to the Brave People Who Know How to Live It"

The many presentations that Bülent has given over the years are typically organized around the same chronology of events as described in the previous section, with different presentations incorporating variations on a limited set of moral lessons about perseverance, courage, personal development, and disability. With these in mind, I want to turn to a seminar he offered at the Third International Broker Camp sponsored by Coldwell Banker in 2016. Coldwell Banker, an international real estate franchise, had entered Turkey in 2013. Taking advantage of the increasing middle-class wealth and growing foreign investment in real estate, Coldwell Banker was trying to establish itself in the luxury home sales market. Its entrance into the real estate market was facilitated by a newly established mortgage finance system in Turkey. Until the 2000s, debt-financed home purchases were rare. Blue Camp, hosted at a luxury hotel along the Mediterranean Sea, was a three-day-long conference for Coldwell Banker brokers in Turkey that featured prominent speakers, workshops, and a range of recreational activities. The conference advertised Bülent's talk as "The Difficult Path to a World Record," although it was in fact a variation of a story he commonly referred to as "The Ant's Eyes."

The recording of the talk opens with Bülent standing up from a table placed on a glossy white stage. He greets the audience, which is for the moment present only as disembodied clapping, and ambles to the center of the stage on his prosthetic legs. A massive screen against which is projected Coldwell Banker logos fills the background. Clicker in hand and headset microphone extending down the side of his face, Bülent welcomes the audience. He is short of breath, perhaps unnerved by the scale of the production. Everything—the stage, the screen, the hotel, the table settings, the dress of the audience—is far more opulent than his typical speaking engagement. Over the next hour, the camera will occasionally pan the room, to capture fifty tables, evenly spaced, with two people in business attire sitting at each table. The setting would be familiar to conference goers, with branded pads of paper and pens placed at each setting, along with a glass of water. Bülent's presentation was a recognizable format. Much like the TED talks he had already given, it was a mixture of personal narrative and moral reflection set to a multimedia presentation of images and videos. As with his other presentations, its aim was to be accessible, emotionally resonant, and inspiring. This version of his talk would offer three unambiguous moral lessons, making it more ambitious than others.

After a short sketch of his childhood and a description of the day before the earthquake, Bülent turns to his experiences on the night of the earthquake. As he recounts how he became trapped beneath the rubble, the talk steps out of itself, to offer its first lesson:

> Now I want to talk a little bit about self-knowledge and personal development . . . How many of us are aware of ourselves? How much are we aware of ourselves? In what ways am I strong? What am I able to do? How much do we love and know ourselves? [The screen fills with a beautiful image of the mountains.] Look at this photograph. Everything is just fine. The sky is blue, the sea is just so, the mountains, the trees . . . The noise of city life and the stress of work is far away. This is what we're looking for, we say. A minute passes. Did I pay the electric bill? What are those at the office doing? What is my girlfriend doing? . . . We begin to move away from the image. It happens to most of us. You are reading a book, a book you really enjoy, you are reading a book, and suddenly you think, "How did I get here"? So you turn back and start reading the book again. But, in life, you can't do that. You cannot turn the moment back a few pages. Life is not a book where you can go back and start reading again. What happened there? We are the prisoners of our feelings and thoughts. We did not give meaning to the moment [*anı anlamlandırmadık*]. We did not experience the moment. . . . For this reason, we say "Carpe diem." But we have distorted the meaning of this phrase. Everyone says, "live the moment" [*anı yaşa*], but, actually, its real meaning is "give meaning to the moment" [*anı anlamlandır*].

Here, Bülent arrives at the heart of the first lesson—to be successful, you must know yourself:

> Life is a path. Sometimes I compare it to driving. If you don't look in the rearview mirror while going backwards, you are definitely going to hit something. You must be always both looking forward and checking in the mirrors behind you. But how? By making quick glances. Life is just like this. We have to constantly look straight ahead. We only look back with quick glances and we see ahead. A self-aware person, a person who knows their self, a person who has completed their personal development, easily determines their goals and knows that they can achieve them. Because

they know well which areas are lacking and which areas are sufficient. And these people set their goals very accurately and know that they will achieve them. Why? Because they know themselves. Knowing oneself and knowing that one can succeed is 80 percent of what one needs to succeed.

This lesson marks the first of several thresholds in Bülent's talk, in which his life (and the story) is propelled forward by moments of self-realization and moral insight.

Bülent reenters the story as he is being freed from the rubble and transported to the hospital, where his legs will be amputated and he'll spend months in recovery. His hospital room becomes another crucible, a threshold through which Bülent will pass and become a different person. Sitting in his hospital bed, with the remaining part of his legs in bandages and the wounds on his back still healing, he asks himself, "Bülent, you are twenty-two years old, what are you going to do?" He turns inward and finds a resolute response. "Bülent, if life goes on despite everything, you will still live."

At this point, Bülent begins introducing the audience to his love of outdoor sports through a video montage of him at a campsite building a fire. "If it took fifteen minutes in the past, it now took a half an hour. Walking on my two hands, I'm able to do it." The video quickly transitions to footage of him rock climbing. Camera positioned above him, it pans out to show how far up the rock face he had scaled. And here we arrive at the kernel of the second lesson, about perseverance and courage:

> I'm a person who is very afraid of heights. Whenever you talk about heights, oh man. But I never gave up on rock climbing. I avoid two things in my life: first is hope, the second is fear. Hope is something that blinds people, in my opinion. It is something that narrows one's effort, reduces one's exertion. You hope and you wait. No. In place of hope, I always prefer obstinance. I am obstinate. But I'm not talking about the type of stubbornness that has become widespread in our society. I'm really talking about wanting something. I'm talking about trying again. And trying again. This goes for all of the things I'm going to be explaining: to try, again and again. Until you succeed, keep trying. The second thing I avoid is fear. Fear captures people. If you are afraid of the dark, you cannot know the brightness of the stars. If you are afraid of water, if you are afraid of the sea, you cannot know the beauty of the underwater world. The boundaries around you shrink, shrink, shrink and you're left with a

tiny homeland. Tiny. You can't go anywhere. No one is saying that you can just get rid of fear. But, there is something else you can put in fear's place. The only thing in the world that cannot be faked: courage.

Extending this lesson on tenacity and courage, Bülent takes the audience through a sequence of images and videos of him engaged in various outdoor and water sports.

One accomplishment after another fills the screen: windsurfing, tennis, sailing, water skiing, off-roading, kneeboarding, free diving. Each exemplifies his tenacity and perseverance. In one video, Bülent is getting thrown from a kneeboard over and over: "Keep trying until you succeed." In another video, he is sailing a boat—GoPro camera in one hand, using his other hand and mouth to pull a rope. He falls out of the boat: "You don't have to be successful at everything you do. There is also falling." But you have to try: "Life belongs to the brave people who know how to live it." A corollary story of technological ingenuity unfolds here as well, as the videos introduce the audience to an assortment of specialized prostheses, many that he and a local craftsman have designed and built themselves. Again, Bülent's perseverance.

As his list of accomplishments extends, the presentation takes up its third lesson. Here, the talk turns to the setting itself, as Bülent describes how difficult it has been for him to navigate the stage. "If there had been a ramp here, or if the stage were a little softer, I could have gotten up here like my speaker friends who came out before me. I'm not speaking strictly critically. I say this to put a problem before your eyes. Now, do you think the obstacle here is the steps, or my two prosthetic legs?" The concept of obstacle (*engel*) becomes the crux of the talk's third lesson. Public buses, sidewalks, and governmental buildings all present obstacles. He describes how he does not care much for the terms commonly used to describe him and his friends—*sakat* (crippled), *özürlü* (defective), or even *engelli* (handicapped). Each misses the critical point: it is the environment that is disabling. "For this reason, I prefer *engellenen* (lit., "those who are blocked or obstructed"). If he can't get on a bus, or enter a building, he is being blocked. Seemingly sensing that his critiques are becoming too direct, he then turns to a video that is a staple of his lessons on disability—showing him and friend with impaired vision riding a tandem bike. He steers, his friend pedals: the two of them complete (*tamamlamak*) each other.

After briefly discussing his work with the Engelsiz Deniz Projesi (Unimpeded Sea Project)—which introduces people who experience obstacles to water sports (and the sense of freedom he discovered in the water)—he ends his talk with the story of an ant. He sketches a scene—with him, having hiked onto a ridge overlooking a valley, reflecting on the meaning of life and the size of the universe. He's drifting into abstractions—as the screen displays a planet receding into the darkness of space. Suddenly, he feels something pulling at his arm: "An ant is trying to take me. Five minutes earlier I was approaching Nirvana, and the ant pulled me back. I stood up and tossed the ant." But he can't let go of the ant. "After I tossed it, I thought about that ant. What kind of spirit does it have? The ant had one goal, to take me. He had an obstacle, that I was much, much bigger than it. It tried to take me, and I threw it. I'm sure that the ant will try again, again, again, to get something bigger than itself again. And in the end, it will surely take something bigger than itself." With that, he returns to the central lesson of the talk: "Never give up, keep trying." The presentation then concludes with a series of brief stories of persons with disabilities overcoming obstacles through perseverance and ingenuity.

A New Man for the Times

At the center of Bülent's philosophy of living on is a clear lesson about tenacity, perseverance, and courage. In the face of challenges and obstacles, one must keep trying: "And trying again, and again and again. Until you succeed, keep trying." And to thrive, one must have the courage to be active in the face of these challenges: "Life belongs to the brave people who know how to live it." Unlike Esra, whose approach to living on was premised on dwelling in the presentness of the everyday, Bülent's is a story of rising above the everyday, through spectacular feats of physical accomplishment. Rather than being dragged along by life as it "goes on," Bülent counsels his audience to seize the day, and "seizing the day" entails giving it meaning. In this respect, Bülent's courage is not a thoughtless race into the future. Rather, it is guided by purposeful self-reflection. To succeed—to become free—one must know oneself, and to know oneself, one must look inward. With the knowledge gleaned through this self-reflection, goals can be set and paths to success charted. At the heart of Bülent's philosophy of living on is thus a twinned struggle—one oriented outward (to the world and its obstacles) and another turned inward (to the obstacles within oneself).

What is it about Bülent's story that makes it appealing to so many audiences? Why would school administrators, corporate retreat organizers, and the directors of nonprofit organizations alike seek him out? There are undoubtedly some broad features and dynamics at play that make his story appealing. Its mythic structure—a protagonist confronting death, gaining knowledge and insight from an ordeal, overcoming one obstacle after another through heroic struggle—surely resonates across many audiences, as does its celebration of a range of publicly compelling gendered norms (e.g., the value of masculine productivity and the heteronormative nuclear family). This is also a setting in which stories of heroic individualism draw force from a powerful nationalist mythos that celebrates masculine strength and resolve in the face of adversity. In turn, Bülent's story is attracting audiences across a period marked by shifts in public discourses about disability, especially as the ruling Justice and Development Party (AKP) worked to promote the state's benevolence and care through increasingly visible public attention to disability politics.[6] It is also surely important that, for many audiences, he is a local hero.

While a familiar story with deep roots, it also spoke to the moment in new ways. By exploring how a set of subjective capacities, social forms, and structural conditions would align in the years following the earthquake to inspire formerly unimaginable life trajectories, and the way it formed into a story to motivate and inspire others, I am interested in how Bülent's story spoke so eloquently to the needs of the moment. On the one hand, Bülent embodied the kind of person needed for the new world taking shape, one increasingly defined by talk of looming disasters, "terrorist" threats, and multiplying insecurities. As discussed already, the state, in the period coming out of the earthquake, had latched onto the earthquake survivor as the embodiment of a new sort of citizen. In the wake of an "unprecedented" disaster, survivors had turned to one another for support, proving themselves resilient in the face of disaster. They helped themselves and were not, crucially, dependent on the state. For those promoting neoliberal reform in the state, the earthquake, despite its tragedies, had revealed the untapped productive potential of citizens, which had for too long been stifled by a paternalistic state. Although the state would hold onto the rhetoric of care and protection, the message was clear that people needed to learn to take care of themselves. In this sort of context,

Bülent offered a story appealing to reformers preaching the virtues of resilience and self-reliance.

On the other hand, Bülent's story about overcoming adversity was also a lesson in the value of having a philosophy. As Bülent put it, playing on the root of a common term for "disabled" (*engelli*), "We overcome obstacles [*engeller*] with the right philosophy and lifestyle." Bülent's is a story about forging, from the ruins of disaster, a new philosophy and a lifestyle that would be a key to not only being resilient but succeeding in the New Turkey. In this regard, the sort of subject being modeled in Bülent's presentations closely tracks the ideals of self-actualization that were becoming widespread within expanding middle-class sensibilities during the period.[7] In turn, for those promoting the virtues and political utility of cultivating resilient citizens capable of "bouncing back" from adversity without the assistance of the state,[8] Bülent's story was certainly appealing. Marking out an ideological convergence that has become common, Bülent's story was appealing to both those who were critical of the state's incompetence and wanted the state to do more to protect its citizens and those who criticized the state for doing too much and creating an overly dependent population.

At the same time, his message of resilience drew audiences within a setting where market forces were increasingly shaping social worlds. Indeed, there would be a particular appetite for Bülent's story of overcoming adversity through the 2000s and into the 2010s, a period during which the earthquake's disaster gave way to a series of economic crises, which were followed by a selective economic boom and rapidly reconfiguring political and economic conditions. In this milieu, having the right mindset and aspirations would become relevant in new ways to one's ability to succeed in the emerging economic and political order. This would be a period, for example, when corporate management more actively sought to motivate workers by fusing goals of personal fulfillment into new regimes of corporate labor. Bülent's story, in this setting, would thus offer inspiration for the "New Man" of a New Turkey. This was not, however, the New Man of an earlier generation of Turkish nationalists,[9] which celebrated the stoicism of the new Republican citizen who was willing to sacrifice self-interest for the sake of the nation. Rather, Bülent's story of tenacity coupled with self-actualization was a symptom and signal of the new entrepreneurial spirit taking form.

In the ways that Bülent's story refracted a set of consolidating middle-class sensibilities regarding life, leisure, and labor, we also encounter again traces of the psychiatric legacy of the earthquake. Bülent's career as a motivational speaker took off at a time when the affective lives and subjective capacities being publicly valued were undergoing a significant shift. Across the 2010s, there was a growing interest among middle-class audiences for new sorts of "experts" to offer guidance about life. This took many forms—in the proliferation of "life coaches" and professional "mentors," as well as in a renewed interest in spiritual guidance from figures ranging from "fortune-tellers" to New Age healers, living saints, and self-described mystics.[10] Public fascination with these new "life" experts was in turn closely bound up with the period's expanding psychologization of the everyday. This was a time, for instance, when a therapeutic culture settled within middle-class markets, feeding new forms of public intimacy (e.g., Oprah-inspired talk shows, match-making programs, home-makeover shows in which Islamic charities invited viewers into the homes of the deserving poor), as well as the increasing psychologization of life problems and family tensions.[11]

This would be the context in which Bülent pursued training in the "behavioral sciences" in order to expand his professional skill set to include life coach (*yaşam koçu*). While life coaching, as a profession, assumed many forms—there was no certification process—its appeal tended to turn on the ability of coaches to offer psychologically inflected advice about managing the stresses of everyday life and finding meaning in an increasingly hostile and materialistic world. Figuring this out, by developing the right life philosophy, offered the promise not only of happiness but also of success and social mobility. In this new market of public intimacy and professional advice, the folksy wisdom that Bülent offered as a disabled earthquake survivor became increasingly peppered with psychological concepts and frameworks. In turn, his "will to struggle" would become the basis for new professional aspirations, as well as a resource to be leveraged to counsel others with a mixture of personal inspiration, psychological advice, and moral education.

It is no accident that one can hear in the advice that Bülent offers the distant echo of the sorts of subjective capacities being cultivated in the post-earthquake psychiatric response. The intervention developed by Drs. Kaya and Yavuz (see Chapters 4 and 6), for instance, was formulated around a similar set of aspirations regarding self-reflection, emotional regulation, and what would later be characterized as "resilience." While it is, of course, impossible to draw a direct line from Dr. Kaya to Bülent (although, as I would discover, there was only one degree of separation between them), there is a clear, if complex, relationship between the psychiatrization of the earthquake and, decades later, the increasing psychologization of public life.

Importantly, Bülent's story is not universally celebrated. Other advocates for disability rights I met worried that his story set unrealistic goals for other persons living with disabilities, as it also reinforced a set of normative bodily ideals that they were trying to challenge. As one such advocate would explain: "Not everyone is like Bülent. He was young at the time, and was able to move forward. He was an exception." For older women (like Esra, Aslıhan, Neşe, and countless others), Bülent's life trajectory and philosophy of living on was assuredly not an option. Although Bülent knew he wasn't a role model for everyone and was sensitive to how his message could be critiqued from the perspective of disability rights—as seen in his demand to his audiences to think about the terms they use to discuss "disabled people" and the important questions he raises about the disabling qualities of the built environment—the overwhelming lesson of his presentation was, nonetheless, about how, through incredible effort and perseverance, he was able to do what others (without obstacles) did, and even more so. In this respect, despite Bülent's awareness of the limits of his own story, we should not lose sight of how it reinforces a set of ableist social and economic norms regarding masculine strength and productivity.[12]

With this in mind, I want to step back momentarily from Bülent's story, to the trajectory of the life it narrates. The broad contours of Bülent's early life are not uncommon. Like thousands of others, Bülent migrated from the eastern provinces with his parents in search of a better life. Years later, fresh out of the military, with limited professional opportunities but a strong work ethic, he experienced unimaginable loss in the Marmara Earthquake. In the face of diminished prospects for work and marriage—and thus his entrance into normative ideals of masculine social belonging—he was able to find new purpose and value through outdoor adventure and heroic feats of physical and mental accomplishment. Along the way, he would get married and start a family. Unlike so many other people who survived the earthquake, Bülent was able to navigate the economic shifts (and crises) of the era without being driven deeper into poverty. Weaving together the lessons he found in the ruins of the earthquake and the emerging economic opportunities of the time, he was able to fashion strategies for living on that were at once personally meaningful, financially viable, and inspiring to others. In other words, Bülent was not merely able to survive the disaster, but thrive because of it.

In appreciating the trajectory of Bülent's life and career, I also found myself repeatedly in awe of both his investment in others and his remarkable savvy. Bülent dedicated a tremendous amount of time to supporting others who were confronting physical and mental obstacles. He offered his life-coaching and mentoring services freely to children with disabilities. He regularly went out of his way to meet persons with disabilities while he was traveling for his speaking engagements. That these were meaningful engagements was made clear to me on one visit to the region, during which I was able to attend an event celebrating the publication of his memoir at a local bookstore. I was struck by how audience members—made up largely of young persons with a wide range of disabilities, along with many caretakers—were enraptured by Bülent. In talking with audience members afterward, many described feeling seen and acknowledged for the first time as something other than an object of pity.

Suspending my own cynical-critical inclinations would allow me to appreciate his extraordinary ability to carve out a life in the wake of a life-altering catastrophe, especially the way he was able to do so beyond the oppressive confines of dominant labor regimes. Whereas residents such as Aslıhan, Neşe, or Esra were not able to take advantage of the new economic arrangements of a new Turkey, Bülent was. He was able to mobilize his love of outdoor sports and adventure and his talent for giving advice into a livelihood. His love of water sports and outdoor adventure in particular fostered a culture within which capitalist conformity was an object of disdain, even if it was an alternative lifestyle that was constitutive of rather than oppositional to emerging markets formations. There is also a story here of Bülent's restless tinkering with his prosthetics to be able to participate in different outdoor activities. Not able to afford the newest prosthetic technologies available in western Europe, he and a local craftsman would fashion their own. Bülent, in other words, was able to forge, through tremendous material and immaterial labor (in his tireless networking and self-promotion, in curating multiple social media platforms, in his ability to combine his entrepreneurial spirit with his commitment to helping others) alternate pathways of social inclusion and economic mobility that spoke in revealing ways about the times.

With this, I return to one of the book's overarching questions. What would it mean to not only survive in a world overturned by catastrophe but perhaps even thrive? Put differently, why are some people able to thrive in the wake of disaster while others are not? It could be argued that my tight focus on Bülent's story does not allow me to generalize much beyond what the anthropologist and psychiatrist Laurence Kirmayer and colleagues have already observed regarding the relationship between disaster and mental health: "The psychological impact of a disaster on any given individual depends on both the personal and collective significance of and response to the catastrophic event."[13] While I find this framing instructive, I would argue that attending closely to the specificities of Bülent's story also offers a series of important insights about what it would look like to operationalize such generic formulations.

That is, rather than looking for answers to questions about resilience and thriving following adversity in the traits and capacities of individuals—which is, again, characteristic of the broader psychological literature on resilience and thriving—my discussion of Bülent is intended to encourage us to look instead at the dynamic and historically contingent relationships between subjective capacities, available social formations, and the structural conditions of living on through which Bülent's life, and its narration, took form. Although the conventions of storytelling that dominate here (especially the sorts one finds in TED talks, and in heroic myths more generally) may privilege accounts of heroic individualism, talking to Bülent brought into view a vast social world that supported him as well as a set of structural realities that were in turn obstacles and opportunities in his endeavors to rebuild his life. Pursuing this line of thought further, however, should not end in merely an acknowledgment of the value of "social support" or the impact of "structural ableism," but rather, it should be a provisional step in a more ambitious exploration of the interpersonal conditions of meaning making and living on.

TWELVE

Urban Renewal and Psychiatric Protest

Renting Disaster

The Red Crescent Society of Iraq was one of the few organizations to recognize the plight of renters in the wake of the Marmara Earthquake. The vast majority of disaster relief initiatives, which focused on re-creating the property arrangements that were in place at the time of the earthquake (e.g., "asset replacement"),[1] directed long-term aid to homeowners, typically in the form of either subsidized loans to purchase new housing or the reconstruction of homes destroyed in the earthquake. Iraq's Red Crescent Society seemed to anticipate the distinctive challenge that renters would face in rebuilding their lives and pledged ten million dollars to support low-income earthquake survivors who had been renters at the time of the earthquake.[2] The bulk of the aid would be used to fund the construction of an apartment complex in the hills surrounding İzmit. The apartments, completed in 2001, would become known by their first residents as "Saddam's Homes."[3]

Unlike much of the post-earthquake development in the region—which consisted of tracts of densely clustered apartment buildings, typically nine to ten stories tall[4]—Saddam's Homes was an expansive complex of two-story buildings spread across a large parcel of land. By the time of my first visit in 2013, although the property was no longer being regularly maintained, one could see the grassy remains of well-manicured grounds, an abundance of shade and fruit trees, breezy courtyards, and park benches scattered along a paved path that took you around the property and out to a scenic overlook that offered a striking view of the city of İzmit, far below, and outward to the Gulf of İzmit. In addition to the attractive surroundings, the apartments were appreciated by residents for being spacious, comfortable, and well constructed. Saddam's Homes was a far cry from the rapidly constructed and imposing cement verticality of the typical post-earthquake construction, where common green space was effectively nonexistent.

Those who gained access to Saddam's Homes were able to escape the fate of many other renters. The state's reconstruction efforts in the region directed enormous funds to the construction of prefabricated homes—funds that would, ultimately, total half the cost of simply rebuilding permanent homes for residents displaced by the earthquake. These prefabricated homes—designed and constructed for short-term use—would become long-term arrangements for many renters. Especially with the severe economic crisis that would begin in 2001, which further slowed the region's recovery, the prospects for those who were not homeowners before the earthquake grew even more uncertain. As reports issued across the first four years after the earthquake would show, there was little annual change in the total number of residents living in prefabricated homes in the region.[5] In time, a secondary housing market would begin to emerge, as occupants began renting their prefabricated homes to labor migrants (commonly from eastern Turkey) looking for affordable housing. Many of these prefabricated homes would also be absorbed structurally into the region, as residents began modifying them to hold growing families. Although they seemed to have become permanent components of the region's housing market, the majority of prefabricated homes would be, by the earthquake's tenth anniversary, removed by the state—placed in storage, transferred to other regions, or sold in block to foreign investors. The only traces left by this history of post-disaster housing would be fields of cement foundations that continued to dot the region, a puzzle left for future generations to solve.

Saddam's Homes, in keeping with the donor's wishes, was to be for those who experienced the most significant loss in the earthquake. To be considered for one of the apartments, survivors were required to submit an application to the provincial government confirming that they had lost a mother, father, or children in the earthquake, that they owned no property in Turkey, that they were renting their home at the time of the earthquake, and that it was either destroyed or rendered uninhabitable. Within months of announcing the program, 7,000 applications were submitted, out of which the 237 most severe cases (and those with some *torpil*, or "influence") were promised apartments. Following the logic of other charity organizations, the selection process was designed to identify the "deserving poor" (or "deserving survivor")[6] and, in so doing, to constitute a community bound both by its economic precarity and experiences of extensive personal loss, in a setting isolated far from the city.

The first residents, all strangers to one another, moved into the newly constructed apartments in November 2001. For many, it was the first time they had lived in permanent housing since the night of August 17, 1999. Although the residents had moved in with the understanding that the apartments were "grants" (*hibe*) from the Iraqi government, the provincial government—who oversaw the apartments—soon began demanding that tenants pay rent for their apartments. Officials would pressure residents to sign a five-year agreement that, among other things, gave the provincial government the authority to evict tenants who failed to pay rent for more than two consecutive months. Not long after signing the agreement, the government began raising rents, pushing many residents further into debt. By the end of the first five-year period, approximately eighty families had been forcibly evicted from their apartments for failure to pay rent. According to residents, the provincial government—typically personified as simply "the *vali*," or provincial governor—wanted to clear out Saddam's Homes to give the apartments to high-ranking civil servants and police officials. With the assistance of a lawyer, the residents of Saddam's Homes took the provincial governor to court, which ultimately ruled that the government could not charge rent for the apartments. In response, the government began charging residents a monthly "fee" (*aidat*), ostensibly for the upkeep of the apartments and property.

In 2006, the remaining residents were presented with a new five-year agreement, one that raised the monthly fees from 60 TL to 200 TL (approximately US$140, an exorbitantly high amount for the region). A large group of residents refused to sign the new agreement—many unable to borrow more money to meet the increased costs—and organized a demonstration in the parking lot of Saddam's Homes. The provincial government responded by sending in antiriot police to break up the protest. During the same period, the provincial government would begin filling the empty apartments with civil servants and police officials. In the months that followed, many of the very people that residents were in open conflict with at regular demonstrations would become neighbors. As one resident explained the dynamic at this time: "These men would beat us at protests and then come back and interact with us as neighbors. Such was the shape of our relationship."

Although there was no shortage of everyday resistances to government pressure and police presence in the period to follow—especially in the form of children vandalizing the apartments given to government officials—the struggle entered a new phase in 2009. In response to mounting police pressure, a group of residents set up a tent at the entrance to the apartment complex, where they took rotating shifts guarding the entrance to alert residents if police or government officials arrived unannounced. In time, the tent became a site of community gathering and a setting for strategizing about possible courses of action. In August 2009—two days before the tenth anniversary of the earthquake—the government sent in dozens of antiriot police officers in response to the effort of residents to prevent a government official from entering the apartment complex, which led to a ten-hour standoff between residents and police. This was the first of several events to generate a minor outpouring of media images showing Saddam's Homes engulfed in tear gas and police officers in antiriot gear beating residents.

This confrontation set the stage for a series of actions that unfolded largely without pause through 2011. During this period, groups of residents organized multiple demonstrations in the center of İzmit, staged protests at the visit of several national political leaders to the city, and marched 350 kilometers to the capital city, Ankara, to present their grievances to the parliament. Regular confrontations with police and government officials at Saddam's Homes also continued with little interruption. As word spread about their struggle, the regular community meetings—hosted in tents that were repeatedly torn down by police, only to be replaced soon after—began to grow. Meetings that began with sixty or seventy people swelled, in time, to several hundred. As one of the main organizers—a middle-aged woman I'll call Emine, who had been one of the original occupants—explained: "When we saw the size of the support from the public for our just struggle, it became apparent that, from then on, we needed a more organized operation. We held several house meetings where we formed into task groups.

While one group worked on legal matters, another group, in order to educate the public, worked on establishing relationships with political parties, civil society organizations, and the press."

As they became more organized, an unanticipated political space began to take shape, a space constituted not through familial or regional ties, nor shared religious, ethnic, or class identities. Although most residents had little more than a grade school education and identified broadly as conservative (having supported the ruling political party in recent elections), they nonetheless spoke of themselves and their neighbors as representing a spectrum of ideological convictions and religious sensibilities. They in fact resisted efforts to pin their activism to a particular ideology or political party, a sensibility that emerged out of their frustration with a number of leftist political parties that attempted to assume leadership over their struggle against the provincial government. Instead, they were bound together by their shared struggle against the state to keep their housing, a struggle that was in turn born of the similarly destructive effects of the earthquake in their lives. As such, this was a political space defined as much by its opposition to the state as by the affective and psychological terrain that had precipitated out of the earthquake's ruins.

By 2011, after scores of events and actions, the remaining residents of Saddam's Homes had settled into a sort of routine with the police—with residents erecting tents in the courtyard, police raiding the complex and tearing down the tents, residents rebuilding the tents, and so on. The residents had also established close relationships with several reporters, who helped keep media attention focused on their struggle. Despite the mounting sense of solidarity, the continued conflicts with the provincial government and recurrent confrontations with the police took its toll. During this period, for instance, a number of residents grew doubtful of the prospects of keeping their apartments and accepted the *vali*'s offer of government-constructed apartments at below-market prices. The remaining residents, in turn, opened a second court case against the *vali* in the European Court of Human Rights (Avrupa İnsan Hakları Mahkemesi, or AİHM, in Turkish), which seemed to invite a further intensification of police action at Saddam's Homes. It was during this time that roadblocks were set up on the roads leading to Saddam's Homes and hundreds of antiriot police would be stationed outside of the entrance, on the ready for regular incursions into the complex. The police presence and repeated confrontations continued until April 2011, when a resident set himself on fire in the parking lot of Saddam's Homes—at which point the provincial government suspended its efforts to evict the residents, thereby beginning a two-year lull in the conflict.

In this final chapter, I want to extend my exploration of the efforts of survivors of the Marmara Earthquake to rebuild their lives by considering the sorts of unanticipated community that would form in the disaster's long aftermath. In particular, I'm interested in the ways that a field of post-earthquake psychiatry—as both an idiom of psychopathology and a form of psychiatric care—converged with systems of post-disaster relief and charity to precipitate novel experiments in collective political life. In tracing the struggle of the residents of Saddam's Homes—a group of earthquake survivors who found themselves living together in an apartment complex in the hills surrounding İzmit, a short distance from the earthquake's epicenter, and just across the gulf from where Esra and Bülent lived—we will encounter additional ways that the earthquake would facilitate psychiatry's movement beyond the clinic, as a form of expertise granted new value to speak about the affective, behavioral, and political vicissitudes of the everyday. With this in mind, this chapter is organized around three critical moments in the efforts of the residents of Saddam's Homes to resist their eviction, moments that highlight the particular convergence of property, protest, and psychiatry at work in their collective project of post-disaster living on.

Cursing the State, and Other Psychopathologies

I want to return here to expand the story of Erol. In Chapter 9, I described Erol's enduring struggle with irritability, erratic moods, and explosive anger—a struggle that had profoundly affected his family. For Erol, the years following the earthquake were a blur of psychiatrists and medications, all of which began in the stretch of time he spent in the hospital following the earthquake. As Erol described this period, "[Hospital officials] were afraid that I might go mad [*deli*], that I might lose my mind [*keçileri kaçırmak*] and become aggressive. They were frightened that I might commit suicide. Because of this, they kept watch over me, expecting that I might do something at any minute." They had good reason to be concerned, for it was in the hospital where he learned that his parents, siblings, and their children had all died when their nearby apartment buildings collapsed: "There was an Egyptian doctor in the hospital who, when he learned that I lost all of my family, said that I had a real problem. So he gave me an injection. What a beautiful moment, when I received that injection. And I would receive an injection the next morning and evening." This would begin what Erol referred to as his two-year psychological "war," a period during which his condition was at its worst. Once physically able to be discharged, Erol left the hospital, mentally "shattered" (*paramparça*) and deeply depressed.

Erol and his family were at the top of the list of loss and suffering that qualified them for an apartment in Saddam's Homes. When we met in 2013, Erol was still living there. He continued to receive intermittent psychiatric care and remained on a number of medications. Despite his social anxieties, Erol was at the center of the residents' struggle to stay in Saddam's Homes. He was active at the meetings in the tents and took the lead in organizing several actions, including the march to Ankara. He was described by others as one of the lead activists of Saddam's Homes. I also came to know him as the resident archivist, maintaining carefully organized binders that collected newspapers reporting about the Saddam's Homes struggle against the government, volumes of legal documents from their trials, as well as a number of documents about the earthquake relief efforts and the history of Saddam's Homes. Although I initially came to him as the community historian, a bigger story opened before me as we talked, a story that captured the ambiguous play between protest, pathology, and psychiatric care that marked the history of Saddam's Homes.

Erol spoke at length about his resentment over how the police were treating him and his neighbors. As people who had experienced so much suffering because of the earthquake, and who had been granted these apartments by Saddam Hussein because of their suffering, Erol felt that the police treatment of residents was reprehensible. Moreover, not only were residents' claims being ignored by the government and the police, but their collective anger was being dismissed as symptomatic of individual pathology. "Do you know how they were seeing us?" Erol asked. "They weren't saying we were 'earthquake victims' [*depremzedeler*]. They saw us as people with mental disorders, as being insane."

On occasion, the dismissal of their anger as pathological turned coercive. Erol offered as an example an event in which a group of residents began swearing at a police commissioner during a live television interview, for which Erol and others were arrested. While in custody, the police would accuse Erol of being "insane" and having lost his "mental faculties" (*akıl melekeleri*). After further interrogation, the police committed Erol to the Erenköy Mental Hospital, one of Istanbul's two large psychiatric hospitals. Once there, he was brought before a group of what he referred to as "professors." As Erol recalled the commitment hearing, the "professors" asked him: "Why are you insulting the state? Why are you cursing the state? You have committed a serious criminal offense against the state . . . This is not rational [*aklı başında*]. It's crazy [*deli*]."

After being briefly assigned to the section of the hospital for severe mental illness, a period that Erol described as terrifying, he fortunately met a sympathetic psychiatrist: "They began doing tests on me on the second day. They attached electrodes to my head and had me go to sleep. Then they talked with me [with the electrodes attached]. They had me say my mother's and father's names to see my reaction. They had me watch television to see what made me angry."[7] Over the coming days, he underwent further testing—answering questionnaires, interpreting images, gauging his response to a range of scenarios, and so forth. On the fourth day, the psychiatrist reassured Erol: "Look, you're healthier than most of us. Honestly, had I lived through what you did [in the earthquake], I would have certainly gone crazy [*tırlatmak*]. After seeing what you saw, that you are still able to remember your own name means you are healthy. . . . You have no signs of madness. [Your problems] are related to the earthquake. I don't know why they sent you to us." With that, the psychiatrist began the process for Erol's release: "You're a person who needs to recover within society, not here."

Erol did not deny that he was easily irritated. He also recognized the connection between the intensity of his anger at demonstrations and his struggle to contain his anger in everyday life. At the same time, however, he took great care in explaining that he had not always been so easily angered. The anger, for Erol, was both a symptom of his experiences of the earthquake and a side effect of the medications he took to treat the effects of the former. That is, he located his anger not in some intrinsic personality trait, but with those series of experiences that had brought him to Saddam's Homes in the first place. Yet this anger was being coded by police as a threatening sign of pathological aggression. As Erol described this dynamic:

> After the earthquake, I was suddenly a "bad person." When I was being questioned by the police, they criticized me for being irritable and rebuffing their questions. "Why are you getting so angry and shouting?" Before, I was never one to make people angry. I was someone who came to agreements with others through talking. This was the type of person I was. I was a humanitarian. But after the earthquake, I was suddenly a "psychopath" [*psikopat*]. It was as if they thought I was sick and were waiting for me to snap. The medications, of course, do have effects. How many years have I been taking them? Medicine, medicine, medicine.

This exchange exemplifies the unstable and insidious play between symptoms of emotional distress, idioms of psychopathology, and the pathologization of political protest that runs through the residents' struggle. In particular, Erol's account highlights the ambiguous relationship between a set of psychological and emotional experiences born of a catastrophic past (e.g., irritability, outbursts of anger) and the affective register of their resistance to the government's efforts to evict them from their homes—with the former shadowing the latter, and the latter channeling the former, in such a way that the two are impossible to disentangle. Yet, for the police, this ambiguity collapses and the politically charged affects animating the residents' protests become signs of a threatening pathology, which in turn validate police aggression and justify Erol's involuntary confinement.

In broad outline, Erol's experiences are familiar. His account of familial loss, psychiatric and pharmaceutical care, political activism, and involuntary hospitalization retraces a story—about the use of psychiatry to pathologize political dissent and protest—that is as old as psychiatry itself. At the same time, Erol's story also brings into view the sorts of novel political communities and subjectivities that were enabled by the field of post-earthquake psychiatry. On the one hand, Erol's struggle to keep his apartment exacerbated his suffering and symptoms, as it repeatedly resulted in violent and humiliating encounters with police. Yet, on the other hand, Erol's struggle with his neighbors to keep their apartments was at the same time a vital project for cultivating his will to endure; it was a project in which he found a social purpose and sense of belonging, a pretext for being with others (despite his anxieties), and a desire to live on that was materialized in his archival efforts to document their collective struggle. And through each weave Erol's personal history of psychiatric care and a more general freeing of a psychiatric idiom in the context of everyday social lives, a development I return to momentarily.

The Limits of Protest

During our conversation in a makeshift social space in the courtyard of Saddam's Homes, İbrahim described the events that led up to his attempted self-immolation. I first learned about the struggle of the residents of Saddam's Homes through a YouTube video documenting İbrahim setting himself on fire. The video captures İbrahim holding a press conference for a small group of reporters gathered in the main parking lot of the complex. After reading aloud a brief statement, he quickly picks up a container of fuel, pours it over his head, and sets himself on fire. In a matter of seconds, an otherwise unremarkable press conference turns into a scene of chaos and despair—as İbrahim, on fire, runs through the crowd and bystanders frantically scream and wail. I found the video deeply unsettling. Moreover, the series of events it documents were in dramatic contrast to the mild-mannered retiree talking with me, two years later, in the courtyard of Saddam's Homes.[8]

İbrahim described, with clinical detachment, the years of organizing and struggle that led up to the event. He narrated his attempted self-immolation as the natural outgrowth of their activism and the escalating police violence. As the government's efforts became more and more violent, İbrahim saw his self-immolation as a reasonable tactic to draw public attention to the injustices they were confronting. He had no intention of dying, nor was the event spontaneous. Over the course of several meetings with a small group of residents—İbrahim had not wanted to include the larger group, for fear that they would either prevent him or warn the media in advance—they carefully planned the action. And it appeared to have the desired effect. When I met İbrahim in 2013, there had been a two-year lull in the government's effort to evict the residents of Saddam's Homes. As some argued, İbrahim had taken the struggle to a level that frightened government officials.

Over the course of interviews with other residents, a more complex picture would begin to take shape. While there was no doubt about his commitment to the residents' struggle against the government, İbrahim was repeatedly described by his neighbors as someone who was attracted to "extremes." They described a person who had been a passionate leftist and labor activist, someone who spoke at length and with intensity about his struggles against capitalism and imperialism. They also described a person attracted by the forms of religious conservatism that had become a more visible component of public life in the years since the earthquake, someone who spoke about his efforts to lead an ethically purposeful life through regular prayer and fasting. Indeed, in our conversation, the ways that he mobilized a familiar leftist vocabulary of class struggle as he also embodied the styles of bodily care and comportment associated with male piety (e.g., neatly trimmed facial hair, modest clothing) spoke toward these shifting commitments. I would come away from these conversations thinking that, locally, İbrahim's self-immolation was regarded by his neighbors as a complex political and psychological drama being played out on a public stage, one put in place by the media attention their struggle had attracted.

Although İbrahim's attempted self-immolation would succeed in pushing the state back, it fractured the residents. The event would bring into the open much of the ambivalence and discord in the group that had been kept in check by their common struggle. As some of his neighbors argued, his self-immolation raised the stakes too high, crossing a limit of protest they had not wanted to cross. They were frightened by the intensity of the event, a fear that was captured in the video footage showing the terror of bystanders as they chased İbrahim through the parking lot in an effort to put out the fire. More seriously, they felt that his actions only fulfilled the government's sense that residents were mentally unstable, if not mentally ill, and dangerous. As such, for these residents, İbrahim's tactics threatened to further justify the use of excessive force by police.

Protest Psychiatry

At one of the nightly community meetings held in the tents in the courtyard of Saddam's Homes in 2009, a resident suggested, as Mustafa recalled the meeting, "Let's go to the hospital, let's go to the psychiatric clinic, and have them give us a certificate confirming that this police repression is causing us psychological damage, that it is making us go crazy [*delirmek*]." Mustafa, who was a teenager at the time, went on to describe how a group of children and their mothers gathered a month later outside of a hospital in downtown İzmit to announce that they were visiting the clinic to seek help for a range of psychological symptoms that had come to plague their children. The cause of these symptoms, according to the gathered residents, was the multiyear police siege of Saddam's Homes. As one resident—a woman in her late sixties—described the three-year period leading up to their visit to the hospital: "Over the past thousand days, we have seen police eight hundred days. We've experienced a number of psychological assaults—tear gas, police batons, security cameras—about which we can do nothing. It's been an environment of conflict." Another resident continued: "This has a negative effect on people. It opens the door to sickness. It makes it difficult for people to communicate. One minute you are talking, and the next you are arguing, and that turns into a fight. This social movement [*toplumsal hareket*] is all a product of this repression." Most worrisome for residents, this environment was having a detrimental impact on the well-being of the young children growing up in Saddam's Homes.

The group of mothers and children gathered at the hospital were seeking an official certificate—what they referred to as a *deli raporu*—that documented the psychological toll of the police violence at Saddam's Homes, a report that would confirm the extent to which they were suffering from a "mental disorder." (The term *deli raporu*, which translates literally as "crazy report," refers both to the general process of certifying that something meets a certain standard, as well as the determination that one is "legally insane.") Although this was a period during which the use of medical reports became an increasingly popular legal and media tool among activists protesting the state,[9] there was dissent within the group about such a psychiatric mode of politics. On the one hand, critics of this tactic were concerned that it would confirm the state's image of them as "crazy." As already mentioned, this concern grew out of their repeatedly violent encounters with police, who would justify their use of violence through claims of self-defense and personal safety. On the other hand, many residents were ambivalent about how this tactic would require them to assume the status of victim in order to be taken seriously.

To be able to understand the debates that emerged here, it's important to appreciate how this ambivalence grew out of a set of specific experiences with a group of organizations established after the earthquake in the name of the *depremzede*, or "earthquake victim." In the wake of the Turkish state's largely failed efforts to manage the disaster, groups of survivors in the region began organizing associations (*dernekler*) of "earthquake victims" to concentrate collective demands for post-disaster aid and coordinate rebuilding efforts in the region. The emergence of these associations—typically referred to as *Dep-Der* (an abbreviation of *depremzedeler derneği*, or "association of earthquake victims") and associated with particular towns (e.g., *Düzce Dep-Der*)—is commonly regarded as a critical moment in the birth of Turkey's "civil society" and, therefore, an important milestone in Turkey's democratic development.[10] The residents of Saddam's Homes whom I interviewed were roundly critical of these associations. They argued that local *Dep-Der*s, as they became more established in the years following the earthquake, grew less willing to challenge the state and ultimately, like the numerous NGOs that had formed following the earthquake, functioned as little more than extensions of the state. Moreover, they argued that this relationship between *Dep-Der*s and the state grew directly out of the willingness of *Dep-Der*s to exploit their status as "victims" of the earthquake in order to gain political influence. For many residents of Saddam's Homes, such a status placed them in a position of dependence (to the state or to charities) that potentially undermined the willingness of the public or the state to take their political demands seriously. In short, they were struggling with the same sorts of questions that scholars studying the politics of humanitarianism and human rights would later identify as decisive: what does it mean to seek political recognition on the basis of one's bodily or psychological damage?

Despite these reservations, the group agreed that seeking a *deli raporu*, if done in combination with other strategies, would bring awareness to their situation and therefore outweigh its potentially undesirable consequences. As Mustafa explained: "That was the goal of our going there. In the six-month period leading up to our going [to the hospital], approximately 100–150 police stood guard in front of the apartments. And in the apartment complex, police were continually walking around in the name of keeping things under control. This situation really affected us, and more than us it affected the small children." As an example, he turned to the subject of play: "If there was a group of ten children, there would be one group of five that would be police and another group of five who would be activists, and the groups would be clashing with one another. They would be hitting one another." This environment, he continued, "was having a bad effect on the mental health [*ruh sağlığı*] of the children. Whenever they would see police, they would become frightened. Without doing anything, they would grow frightened whenever police came." As this begins to suggest, if the initial residents of Saddam's Homes came together through their shared experiences of "earthquake trauma" (*deprem travması*), their children were coming of age through an epidemic of pathological fear and anxiety precipitated by police violence.

The group of residents seeking the *deli raporu* encountered resistance from the moment they arrived at the hospital for their appointment. As Mustafa recalled the events: "We went to the front of the hospital for everyone to read a statement to the press, but we were assaulted by the hospital security guards almost immediately. They forced us to the hospital garden, although a handful of people were able to enter the hospital." Once inside, this smaller group would continue demanding to see a doctor and receive a certification validating their psychological suffering. "One of us made it into an examination room," Mustafa continued. "Again the police forced their way in. They told the doctors that this was an activist and that he should not do anything. Because of this, the doctor became frightened and avoided us. Even though we weren't able to get in, we had achieved our goal." As another resident explained their objectives: "Our goal in this situation was to spread the word to the media. That is, to spread the word about our psychological suffering and the psychological state of our children to the media." Although they were ultimately unable to get the *deli raporu*, the clinical protest offered its own lessons. As one of the mothers present at the hospital explained: "Many of us weren't able to enter the hospital. We weren't able to get a *deli raporu*. What can we do? Where there is no justice, you must get crazy [*adaletin olmadığı yerde deli olacaksın*]."

Experiments

This chapter has traced how a series of devastating experiences of personal and material loss born of a destructive seismic event came together with a nascent field of humanitarian psychiatry and post-disaster regimes of property and charity to constitute a community of strangers and precipitate a novel experiment in collective political life. With this in mind, the three intersecting moments sketched above were intended to capture a series of specific examples of how the psychiatrization of the Marmara Earthquake would extend in particular ways into the disaster's future. They highlight both the ways that experiences of "psychopathology" are inescapably entangled within large-scale political-economic processes,[11] and how, in the decade following the earthquake, psychiatric discourses would reconfigure everyday community lives and, along the way, animate new tactics for and visions of collective action.

For Erol, a set of lasting psychological and affective remains of the earthquake—especially his feelings of edginess and irritability—would weave into and catalyze his angry demands for justice and the collective struggle of his fellow residents against eviction. Erol's anger, however, would be seen as excessive and out of place by the state, coded as a "symptom," and used to justify further police violence and his psychiatric incarceration. İbrahim's story, in turn, charts a similarly ambiguous play between the pathological and psycho-political. In his case, a demand for justice took the form of his attempted self-immolation, a tactic that would push their protests across a threshold of intensity and frighten both other residents and local government officials. Although temporarily successful, his willingness to self-destruct would lead to questions about his sanity and speculation again about the psychological legacy of the earthquake. If this self-immolation was a symptom, what was it a symptom of? A traumatic effect of disaster? A response to a set of political and economic arrangements that made life unbearable and futures unimaginable? Or did it have something to do with his tendency toward political and religious "extremes"? The ambiguity would never be resolved, but the intensity of his protest did undermine people's trust in him and led to a schism in the group.

An alternate configuration of the pathological and psycho-political comes into view in the account of the efforts of residents to acquire medical-legal confirmation of the negative psychological and emotional effects of police repression, in which the sorts of psychiatric idiom that led to Erol's hospitalization are mobilized to assert collective claims for property rights. But what would it mean, residents asked as they deliberated on the right course of action, to seek political recognition on the basis of one's psychological damage? Might this sort of psychological certification have the opposite effect—of justifying further police violence and accelerating their eviction? It was a gamble, one that they decided to take. Erol, as he thought through these questions, would turn the tables, which he had a gift for doing, by soberly observing, "In fact, I think we're being governed by maniacs [*manyaklar*].... They may be saying that I am the one who is mentally ill, but I think they're actually [mentally] ill."

I want to pause briefly to consider further some of the conditions that gave rise to this collective experiment in post-disaster living on. What made claims of and to psychopathology an appealing and potentially effective idiom of protest in this setting—rather than a demand to be dismissed as irrational if not altogether "crazy"? That is, what accounts for the social and political currency of psychiatry in this particular context at this particular moment? For a start, it is important to recognize the familiar lineages of protest at play in the struggle of the residents of Saddam's Homes against the provincial government. Erol's account, for instance, is a story of involuntary hospitalization that is, again, as old as the psychiatric hospital itself, where political dissent is pathologized and hospitalization operates as a form of intimidation and carceral silencing. İbrahim's self-immolation, as well, expresses a familiar genre of protest in Turkey and beyond—a threat of bodily self-destruction intended to bear witness to the state's unjust and unbearable repression. In the case of their visit to the psychiatric clinic, the mobilization of children and women, especially mothers, in political protest is, likewise, a familiar form of political dissent in Turkey.[12] As in previous instances, residents of Saddam's Homes sought to rely on a symbolic economy of innocence and victimhood associated with children and mothers to marshal public sentiment against government repression. The same could be said about their efforts to mobilize medical diagnoses in their critique of the state. Despite these precedents, however, I want to argue that their struggle represents a novel arrangement of psychiatry and protest in post-disaster Turkey.

There are two aspects of this that require elaboration. First, there is the distinctive way that their political demands were founded on claims of psychological and emotional rather than bodily damage. While the use of illness and affliction toward political ends has a long history in Turkey—a confluence of illness and law that has grown significantly with the expansion of human rights-based politics[13]—this has largely been a discourse of bodily damage. Noteworthy in our case, then, is the shift toward a specifically psychiatric idiom, a shift that is in fact staged in the very human rights literature that grew out of the confrontation between the residents of Saddam's Homes and the provincial government. In the following excerpt from a report produced by a prominent human rights association (İnsan Hakları Derneği) about the events at Saddam's Homes, note the shift from bodily to psychological injury:

> Despite having lost more than one close relative, themselves being injured in the earthquake, and having spent long periods of time in the hospital receiving treatment, these earthquake victims [*depremzedeler*] continue to bear the permanent disability and lasting traces of the earthquake on their bodies. These people who lost close relatives—wives, children, mothers, fathers, and siblings—have yet to be freed from the effects of the psychological trauma [*psikolojik travma*] they experienced. Especially with the events of the past two years, these traumas have been triggered [*tetiklemek*], putting them in a state of mind as if they had just recently come out of the earthquake.

I am not suggesting that political dissent has never relied on a psychiatric idiom in Turkey. Indeed, as mentioned earlier, there are prominent examples of psychiatrists mobilizing clinical evidence as a form of political critique.[14] Yet, it is critical to note that this discourse was being mobilized by psychiatrists who were speaking *as* psychiatrists and medical experts. As such, and second, what is distinctive in the case of the residents of Saddam's Homes is the way that we can hear in their protests the resonances of a technical psychiatric vocabulary, here being mobilized by nonexperts to assert a set of legal rights. We thus encounter yet another instance of how psychiatry, in the years following the earthquake, would leave the clinic and enter in new ways into the flow of everyday social exchanges, here as a technical idiom to be mobilized and recognized as a form of moral witnessing and political protest.[15]

As this begins to indicate, the legacy of the psychiatric infrastructure born of the earthquake would extend in complex and ambiguous ways into the future. In the present context, my efforts to track the struggle of the residents of Saddam's Homes to rebuild their lives in the long aftermath of catastrophic loss have not been concerned with identifying some sort of straightforward causal chain of events that links past and present. Rather, my aim has been to remain open to the indeterminacies and specificities of social existences as they form and transform in their movement through an emerging political, psychiatric, and affective terrain of post-disaster Turkey. While the experiences of the residents of Saddam's Homes necessarily reflect a set of dynamics and forces specific to this context, they are also familiar. Indeed, they reflect an all-too-common set of experiences—of an enormously destructive event giving way to a series of secondary catastrophes as survivors try to rebuild lives in conditions marked by both worsening economic precarity and government indifference (if not active repression). In this regard, the broad outline of the story of Saddam's Homes is a local manifestation of a set of political and economic dynamics typical to post-disaster settings—in which the capacity of survivors to rebuild lives turns in large measure on their ability to gain access to long-term aid, which is in turn determined by the sorts of property and wealth arrangements in place at the time of the disaster.

Saddam's Homes no longer exists. In 2013, the government announced its plans to convert the apartments into dormitories. The remaining forty-eight families were to be relocated into a single section of the apartment complex, with the other apartments designated for students. In explaining the continued presence of these families at Saddam's Homes, media reports (which were largely unedited versions of the government's statement) made no reference to the decade-long struggle of the residents to keep their homes. Rather, their presence was reduced to a psychological sequela of disaster: "Because of their fear of heights, [these families] did not want to move into nine-story buildings."[16] Despite claims that these families would eventually be relocated, they were instead evicted. The last news report I was able to find explains, in passing, that the remaining families "having been evicted from [their homes], were resettled in other homes sometime later."[17] Having lost their homes a second time—first by the earthquake, second at the hand of the state—residents thus left Saddam's Homes, much as they had entered, to spread out across the region in search of new housing. In the decade between, a group of strangers that had come together in the aftermath of a massive disaster—expressly because of the severity of their loss and suffering, and lacking claims to property that could survive the earthquake—would cultivate an ethics of neighborliness and solidarity as they moved through (and struggled with) a shifting terrain of post-disaster charity, government corruption, and police repression.

Although the experiment of Saddam's Homes would not last, the forces that gave rise to it—and which also conspired to bring it to an end—would continue to shape the region's redevelopment, and extend in consequential ways throughout the country over the ensuing decade. In terms of housing, the earthquake would inaugurate an era of extraordinary redevelopment of urban landscapes across Turkey through a set of legislative initiatives, policy reforms, and novel financial arrangements that are commonly referred to as *kentsel dönüşüm*, or "urban transformation." Using the destruction caused by the Marmara Earthquake and the threat of another earthquake as a pretext, the state would introduce a sweeping set of urban regeneration schemes and large-scale public infrastructure projects, which resulted in a dramatic remaking of urban neighborhoods and commercial districts, an unprecedented concentration of power and wealth among developers, and a coinciding surge in land seizures and forced evictions with minimal legal oversight or means of legal redress.[18]

While the psychiatric forms of protest mobilized by the residents of Saddam's Homes did not achieve their ultimate objective, the political entanglements of psychiatry and crisis that they represent would have a discernible afterlife. In the years to follow, the language of psychopathology, especially trauma, would gain currency in a range of (oppositional) political discourses concerned with competing conceptions of Turkey's national historical memory, and especially as a means to conceptualize the historical legacy of the often violent exclusion of difference from mainstream Turkish nationalism.[19] More tangibly, as mentioned earlier, the development of psychiatric instruments used to measure rates of PTSD among earthquake survivors (including, of course, the residents of Saddam's Homes) would appear again in psychiatric forensic reports being completed among protestors in the Gezi Park uprising to document the psychological effects of police violence. From there, again, they soon moved into the refugee camps forming along Turkey's Syrian border. In these movements, the Marmara Earthquake comes into view not only as a defining moment in Turkey's history of psychiatric expertise around psychological trauma and the social permissibility of psychiatric discourses for describing personal distress, but also as a critical domestic moment for a set of global developments wherein the language of psychopathology, especially PTSD, began circulating in new ways as idioms of political critique.

EPILOGUE

New Century, Different Disaster

Yüzyılın felaketi. The disaster of the century. On February 6, 2023, Turkey experienced another series of massive earthquakes, this time along its southern border with Syria. The scale of death and destruction was staggering. More than 50,000 residents died and millions more were displaced. Entire city blocks were reduced to piles of concrete and rebar. The earthquakes and subsequent aftershocks all but leveled the city of Antakya, the site of ancient Antioch and home to one of the few remnants of interreligious coexistence in the region. Much of Gaziantep, where nearly a half million Syrian refugees were living, was left in ruins. The video footage streaming from the region would capture in agonizing detail desperate residents, covered in dust and debris, as they scrambled through the rubble searching for survivors. Others, wrapped in thin blankets against the freezing winter weather, gathered in open fields awaiting food, shelter, and warmth. Death was everywhere. A new century, a different disaster.

I am watching the news coverage from the region as I begin drafting this epilogue. The scenes are excruciating to watch. After spending years immersed in the lives and stories of those who lived the Marmara Earthquake, I know that the images and videos I am seeing capture only a sliver of the destruction and suffering. I can fill in the muted video footage with the screams of those trapped in the rubble and the deafening sound of construction equipment. I can smell and taste the cement dust, and imagine the stench of decomposing flesh that is soon to come. Every now and again, an image from the Marmara Earthquake slips into the stream of news coming from the region—an image of a crying child covered in gray dust, an elderly man clutching a loaf of bread. The suffering captured in these images seems so elemental that the clues of their being anachronistic are easily overlooked for the casual observer. For those who recognize their origins, the images are jarring. They blur time and events. They redouble and intensify the suffering streaming across my screen, as they carry me—and thousands of others—to a different time, to a different disaster, to the final months of the previous century.

These images of a former disaster appearing amid the ruins of a present disaster signal a series of deeper resonances. There is so much that is similar. In many regards, this new disaster tells a familiar story: of systemic corruption within a profit-driven housing industry, of the rationalization and politicization of disaster management, of nationalist ideologies that frame the state as the protector of it dependent subjects, and of economic policy that generates a population of people who can be killed without political accountability. And once again, the state would prove itself thoroughly unprepared for the disaster. Although politicians had been invoking the threat of another major earthquake since the Marmara Earthquake—as a justification for their efforts to reform state and society, and as an alibi for the obscene profits being amassed by developers—they had clearly not followed their own advice. Once again, an angry public would learn about widespread corruption and incompetence in the national agencies dedicated to emergency response, and the state would yet again try to distract and deflect blame. Always enamored of a good brand campaign, the ruling Justice and Development Party (AKP) actively promoted the earthquake as "The Disaster of the Century" to shift attention away from its own culpability. Turkey's president—Recep Tayyip Erdoğan—would argue, "It's not possible to be ready for a disaster like this," dismissing those who criticized the government's response as "dishonorable."

Once again, residents who survived the earthquake refused the role of helpless victim. With limited help from the government, survivors quickly established networks of mutual aid. They scoured the ruins—with commandeered machinery, small tools, and bare hands—searching for friends, neighbors, and relatives. International search-and-rescue teams would soon join them in the region. Once again, government incompetence was met with a massive outpouring of public compassion within Turkey. Groups from across the country—feminist collectives, soccer fan clubs, secondary schools, neighborhood and village associations—organized fund drives and the region's ruined roads became clogged with truckloads of donations. Volunteer convoys of bulldozers, excavators, and earthmovers headed to the region. As with the Marmara Earthquake, vast tent settlements quickly filled cleared fields and emptied stadiums, and a massive internal migration was set in motion as survivors left the region looking for safety.

The differences between the two disasters are also revealing. Some reflect the particularities of the earthquake's location. Unlike the Marmara Earthquake, a national border bifurcated the earthquakes zone, adding another gradient of difference that would shape the apportionment of aid (with survivors in Turkey receiving much more government and foreign aid). The effects of the 2023 earthquakes also refracted through a series of ethnic and racial tensions specific to the provinces in Turkey that were most severely affected. The earthquake occurred in a region that had resettled millions of Syrians fleeing the civil war across the border, as part of Turkey's agreement with EU states to help them "cope" with the "Syrian refugee crisis" (a policy, and substantial amount of funds, that aimed, in effect, to create a proxy border for the European Union). In turn, and unlike the Marmara Earthquake, the epicenters of the 2023 earthquakes were in a region with a large Kurdish Alevi population. In both instances, existing anti-Syrian and anti-Kurdish racism would be exacerbated by the disaster, taking material (and lethal) form in the differential distribution of post-disaster aid.

Other differences between the two disasters reflected broader societal shifts that had been occurring far beyond the earthquake region. Since the Marmara Earthquake, the state doubled down on its policy of promoting housing development and construction as a vital engine of employment and national economic growth. By the time of the earthquakes in 2023, the construction industry had doubled its share of the national economy. (The global average, in contrast, declined across the same period.)[1] In the earthquake region, as elsewhere, these trends took the form of a construction boom in the decade leading up to the earthquakes, as the AKP systematically weakened expert oversight of construction safety, sold or granted "zoning amnesties" to owners of existing buildings deemed "substandard," and, with the privatization of building inspections, left the regulation of construction to the free market. Predictably, the region's construction boom was riddled with entrenched corruption, and the contradictions were everywhere to be seen.

At the same moment that the state was using policies justified by seismic risk (and the Marmara Earthquake in particular) to evict residents and redevelop entire neighborhoods in cities across the country, Erdoğan was addressing rallies of supporters in cities throughout the region to boast about how he and his party had "forgiven" hundreds of thousands of property owners for widespread construction violations. These cities would soon become graveyards of collapsed buildings.

The state's disaster response similarly reflected shifts that had been occurring since the Marmara Earthquake, both internationally and domestically. Internationally, the 2023 earthquakes occurred during a period marked by a growing political recognition, if only rhetorically, that we had already entered a planetary ecological crisis. This was also a period when the language of disaster had established itself as a defining idiom for imagining life and survival in the contemporary world and, with this, disaster preparedness and management had become increasingly important components of statecraft and global governance. In this sort of milieu, a global infrastructure of disaster preparedness and response would expand—with more specialized, disaster-specific equipment (rather than just repurposed construction and demolition equipment), more formalized and certified skill sets (each with corresponding brands and acronyms), and multiplying domestic and transregional protocols and agreements. For those who experienced the 2023 earthquakes, this meant that scores of search-and-rescue teams and humanitarian organizations were ready to respond quickly to the unfolding disaster in Turkey and Syria.

Within Turkey, there had been noteworthy improvements in the state's disaster management infrastructure since the Marmara Earthquake, especially in the work of AFAD, the national disaster management agency that had been formed in 2009 to coordinate post-disaster responses. Yet, political trends that marked the period preceding the 2023 earthquakes played out toward disastrous ends. The military, which the AKP regarded with suspicion and had spent the previous decades working to weaken its influence on domestic politics, was blocked from taking part in the initial rescue efforts. Reflecting the AKP's consolidation of state power and Erdoğan's increasing authoritarianism over this period, it would be revealed that the state agencies involved in disaster management, including Kızılay, had been taken over by AKP loyalists, many with no experience in disaster management. In turn, many of these agencies—especially AFAD—seemed more interested in projecting Turkey's humanitarian brand abroad than actually preparing for a disaster at home.

As for responding to an actual disaster, the state, following a familiar political script, actively obstructed the work of other organizations in an effort to monopolize the response efforts. Soon after the earthquakes, the state announced that all rescue efforts and humanitarian aid would have to be approved by AFAD. The state similarly informed the public that donations should be directed to the state and that NGOs active in the region should transfer their funds to the state disaster response efforts. It's important to note that the state's desire to monopolize the disaster response was not a novel political development, even if the specific ways it tried to do so reflected the dynamics of the current regime. In the wake of the Marmara Earthquake, the state showed a similar distrust of nonstate actors and also tried to monopolize relief efforts. The targets, however, were different. Whereas the targets in 1999 were Islamic charities and associations—who were perceived as a political threat to the ruling secular regime—the target of AKP ire in 2023 had shifted to the domestic networks of NGOs that quickly descended on the region (many of which could trace their origins back to the Marmara Earthquake). As much as they tried, regulating these organizations proved difficult. In contrast to the Marmara Earthquake, the state was working within a much more complex financial and media environment. With money transfer capacities integrated into a wide range of social media platforms, organizations were able to reach many more people and collect monetary donations at a scale that was unimaginable after the Marmara Earthquake.

As with the Marmara Earthquake, geological volatility and psychiatric expertise converged quickly in the disaster's aftermath. The outpouring of public compassion that followed the earthquakes would take a decidedly psychological form and, once again, the psychological well-being of survivors assumed center stage. Unlike the Marmara Earthquake, however, this psychological compassion was no longer novel. There was also no need to build from scratch a post-disaster psychiatric infrastructure. While much of what was cobbled together in the wake of the Marmara Earthquake had, in the ensuing decades, disappeared or reassembled elsewhere with a different focus, aspects of it had continued to develop—within university certificate programs dedicated to mental health and disaster, within subunits of national psychiatric and psychological associations, within the research and curricula of psychological trauma research centers, and within the proliferating number of NGOs dedicated to emergency mental health. Even mainstream psychiatric training programs offered opportunities to gain expertise in treating the psychological effects of disaster. Within weeks of the 2023 earthquakes, thousands of psychological counselors across Turkey would receive training in psychological first aid, using an online platform that had been refined during the COVID-19 pandemic.

Meanwhile, the global growth in interest in post-disaster mental health care—a facet of the multiplying ways that disaster preparedness consumed increasing amounts of political attention and national budgets—would provide a rich environment for further domestic growth. In this convergence of local legacies of disaster and shifting priorities of global humanitarian psychiatry, groups and techniques dedicated to post-disaster mental health care had become increasingly formalized, institutionalized, and standardized. More and more practitioners shared vocabularies and techniques, if not fellowships, appointments, and titles. Given these developments, and not surprisingly, the 2023 earthquakes were a psychiatric event from the outset. The scales were ready to slide, psychological subjects of disaster were easily conjured, and a psychiatric machine soon began generating fresh outputs—with new interventions, new teams of experts, more publications, and, of course, more acronyms.

The inventiveness and experimentation that marked the psychiatric improvisations after the Marmara Earthquake had, by this point, given way to a seeming consensus around the advantages of psychosocial approaches. Accordingly, the mental health responses to the 2023 earthquakes would overwhelmingly focus on psychosocial care, especially for children. The paradigmatic materialization of this shift to the psychosocial was the seeming ubiquity, across the earthquake region, of the "psychosocial tent." Within weeks of the earthquakes, Twitter, Instagram, and Facebook feeds filled with pictures of young children sitting in festively decorated tents playing games, crafting, and painting pictures. As the weather warmed, psychosocial interventions would expand outdoors, with children gathering in open areas to sing songs, dance, and play games. Reflecting the diversity of actors responding to the disaster, these interventions were being sponsored and assembled by an array of groups from across the ideological spectrum—from all major political parties to individual universities (public and private), from newspapers and news websites to international and multilateral aid agencies, from prominent corporations to a wide range of humanitarian organizations (both secular and religious). Each tent would have its own corresponding logo. As with the Marmara Earthquake, this focus on the psychosocial was a pragmatic solution. It was uniquely able to wrap up familiar social activities in a package of medical professionalism that was cost effective and required little technical training. In contrast to the Marmara Earthquake interventions, however, they took form within a public ethos less suspicious of psychological discourses and increasingly comfortable with a psychologically imbued therapeutic culture.

Together with international humanitarian organizations offering similar post-disaster psychosocial interventions, the psychiatric response to the 2023 earthquakes represented a further consolidation of a relationship between disaster, medical expertise, and governance that had begun forming in the wake of the Marmara Earthquake, and since expanded apace amid the multiplying disasters that have come to characterize an era of global ecological crisis. With that said, the psychiatric response to the 2023 earthquakes was not simply a straightforward story about the ascendance of the psychosocial. There's also a story to be told about what did *not* happen. Missing from this new scene of disaster, for instance, were the large number of foreign humanitarian NGOs and trauma specialists that had settled in the same region during the Syrian civil war to help treat displaced refugees. In 2016, Erdoğan would seize an opportunity presented by an attempted coup to initiate a sweeping purge of government bureaucracies and crackdown on political opposition. In this, NGOs were a popular target. What would have been a vital potential resource in the aftermath of the 2023 earthquakes was, by this point, largely gone—having been expelled from the country, along with a large number of foreign NGOs, in the years following the coup. Those that remained would be effectively shut down by layers of new bureaucratic obstacles put in place by the government. In this respect, many aspects of the kind of mass psychiatric humanitarian response described in this book would be impossible in this new post-disaster Turkey.

As I began tracking the work of a new generation of psychiatrists and psychologists responding to 2023 earthquakes, I would, again, marvel at their determination and compassion. It was humbling to watch as small groups of people—some mental health professionals, others simply there to help in whatever way they could—developed and realized ambitious interventions amid unimaginable destruction and suffering. While the government likely saw in this, as they had after the Marmara Earthquake, the untapped productive potential of citizens being set free, I found my attention being drawn elsewhere. In some of these impromptu responses (but certainly not all), the forms of organizing and mutual aid that made them possible gestured toward a vision of collective political life at odds with the indifference, hostility, and cynicism that marked the political atmosphere of the time. What they were trying to build was inspiring, even if I often felt that they were using the wrong tools and techniques.

With these tools in mind, familiar questions began gathering. Weren't these technical responses to social and political problems being built around a temporality of disaster that obscured as much as it motivated? What will survivors need in a month, a year, a decade from now—as "life goes on"? Are there other things that could be done at this moment that would be more helpful further down the road? Do they really need *more* psychosocial support, *more* coping strategies, *more* ways to optimize cognitive processes? Obviously, as everyone involved was aware, those who survived the earthquakes would need new homes and livelihoods. Everyone also knew that more humane priorities for economic development, to say nothing of the actual enforcement of existing building codes, would go a long way to preventing similar fates in future disasters. While the material needs were, in many regards, straightforward, what about the immaterial needs of those left behind? While a complex question, I find myself thinking about how so much of the lasting suffering of those I interviewed for this book had emerged not merely from the losses they experienced, but from the ways in which their desire for accountability for those losses was systematically foreclosed. The failure of the state to hold its own policies and agents accountable, let alone major actors in the construction industry, would make it impossible for many to find closure or even meaning, which in turn created a set of conditions within which the Marmara Earthquake's distinctively corrosive and debilitating affective legacy would grow. Nothing thus far suggests a different future for this disaster, although it is reassuring to know that there are colleagues, friends, and interlocutors in the disaster zone already thinking about these questions.

I hesitate to continue in this vein because, once again, I find myself being drawn away from the focus of this book. I find my attention shifting away from the thousands and thousands of individuals who were left behind by the Marmara Earthquake, and who have been largely forgotten in the decades since. While they may have been repeatedly invoked in the days and weeks after the 2023 earthquakes, they were, once again, abstractions of an event that was being eclipsed, if not overwritten, by another disaster. Few paused to consider what this new disaster might mean for those who lived through the Marmara Earthquake. As I reached out to friends and colleagues I'd met during the research for this book, stories—from psychiatrists, psychologists, and residents alike—conveyed a profound sense of disorientation and dislocation. They were thrown off and devastated by the new destruction. In these hasty correspondences, I came to understand not only the distinctive ways that they were experiencing the earthquakes but also how, in these experiences, the legacy of the Marmara Earthquake was being drawn further into the future. As one psychologist friend wrote days after the first earthquake in 2023: "We are safe, thank you . . . but we are not OK. Nothing will be the same from now on. As you can imagine, all the difficult memories are coming to mind. There will be lots of things to be done for sure. We will see. With love."

Acknowledgments

Of the many debts this project has accrued over the past decade, I want to thank, first and foremost, all the people who welcomed me into their homes and shared their stories of the Marmara Earthquake.

I'm indebted to many brilliant and generous colleagues in Turkey who entertained my consistently naïve questions. I want to particularly thank Meltem Kora and Deniz Yücelen for their support and friendship over many years. I benefited tremendously from Fatih Artvinli's curiosity and enthusiasm for this project, as well as his comments on early drafts of chapters. I want to thank Tamer Aker for generously sharing with me his time and extensive professional experiences. The development of this project similarly benefited from many stimulating conversations with Kemal Sayar. A meeting with the writer Müge İplikçi, who had written a book documenting the stories of women who lived through the Marmara Earthquake, would open my mind and push this project in new directions. I would also like to thank a long list of wonderful scholars and clinicians in Turkey, including in no particular order: Bahattin Akşit, Nuray Karancı, Şahika Yüksel, Ufuk Sezgin, Yankı Yazgan, Tuncay Ergene, Verda Tunalıgil, Metin Başoğlu, Ebru Şalcıoğlu, Cengiz Kılıç, Ali Köse, Sanem Güvenç, Gizem Şentürk, and Nazire Üzer.

In the earthquake region, Bülent Coşkun offered crucial support at pivotal moments of this project. As generations of psychiatrists whom he has taught know, his curiosity, generosity, and wisdom are inspiring. I also want to thank Emine Cebeci, Ufuk Koçak, Ekrem Aktuğ, Oktay Tuna, and Erkan Karataş for their assistance and many thought-provoking conversations. In Istanbul, I want to thank Mustafa Kubilay Atlıhan for welcoming my family into his home and Akile Gürsoy for her sustained support of my research, which has been there since I showed up at her doorstep as a young graduate student many, many years ago. Similarly, Mark Soileau has been a vital interlocutor and fellow traveler since the beginning. Thank you.

So much of this project can be traced back to the remarkable community of scholars that make up the "Culture, Psychiatry, and Global Mental Health Seminar" at Harvard University (otherwise known as the "Friday Morning Seminar"). It has been a defining intellectual home for me since this project's inception. Mary-Jo DelVecchio Good set me off to Turkey decades ago and has been a tireless supporter of my work ever since. This project owes much to Byron Good's remarkable openness and generosity as a thinker. Similarly, Michael Fischer has, on multiple occasions, offered generative and challenging feedback that greatly refined my thinking. In turn, this project could not have been possible without the assistance of Kerim Munir, to whom I owe my deepest gratitude. Other members of the Friday Seminar community—especially Sarah Pinto, Sadeq Rahimi, Aslıhan Sanal, and Orkideh Behrouzan—have each left important marks on this book. I also want to thank Arthur Kleinman for the kindness and support he has offered over the years.

There were many critical junctures at which this project took unexpected turns, each time facilitated by the encouragement of others. An early draft of Chapter 10 was presented at Stanford University's "Culture, Mind, and Medicine Seminar," and I thank Angela Garcia for the invitation and her encouraging feedback. Tanya Luhrmann's incisive questions also helped crystallize important aspects of this book. A version of Chapter 6 was presented at the "The Power in Medicine in the Middle East" workshop at the Max Plank Institute for the History of Science. I thank Lamia Moghnieh, Edna Bonhomme, and Shehab Ismail for their work organizing the event, as well as a series of generous and productive comments from Sherene Seikaly, Aslı Zengin, and Omnia El Shakry. At a very early stage, I had the pleasure of convening with a group of remarkable anthropologists who work in Turkey. Thank you Elif Babül for organizing the workshop, and the other participants—Brian Silverstein, Can Açıksöz, Hayal Akarsu, Hikmet Kocamaner, Fırat Bozcalı, and Başak Can—for their collegiality and feedback. An earlier draft of Chapter 12 was presented at the conference "Comparative and Interdisciplinary Approaches in the Field of Turkish Studies," held at Northwestern University. I would like to thank Kent Schull, Sinan Ciddi, and Rita Koryan for their work organizing the conference, and the other presenters for their valuable feedback. In turn, I want to thank Nedim Karakayalı for inviting me to present at the Bilkent University's "Seminar Series on Polity, Society and the World" at a point when I was just beginning to work through some of this book's major arguments.

I want to express particular gratitude to my colleagues in the Department of Anthropology and Sociology at Amherst College. Nusrat Chowdhury and Felicity Aulino provided tremendously valuable feedback on several chapters. Deborah Gewertz, Vanessa Fong, Victoria Nguyen, Caterina Scaramelli, and Utku Balaban offered invaluable comments as well. I'm particularly indebted to the help of Utku Balaban, from whom I have learned a tremendous amount and whom I regard as a role model of intellectual and political integrity. The project benefited in countless ways from conversations with colleagues in the Five College community, including, among many others, Lynn Morgan, Debbora Battaglia, and Bill Girard. I am similarly indebted to colleagues in the Five College Middle East Studies seminar, including but not limited to Elif Babül, Hiba Bou Akar, Monica Ringer, Sahar Sadjadi, and Tariq Jaffer. This project germinated within an interdisciplinary group of faculty and students at Amherst College, and I want to offer particular thanks to Austin Sarat, Tom Dumm, Andrew Poe, Boris Wolfson, Lawrence Douglas, and, especially, Pooja Rangan. Amherst is also where I had the good fortune to meet Oyman Başaran, Seda Saluk, Boran Kuzhan, and Çağla Ay—each of whom contributed in important ways to this project. I'd like to thank Çağla in particular for her last-minute assistance with the manuscript. Thanks as well to Rocio Stejskal for her expert editorial skills. Judy Frank and Ashwin Ravikumar, probably unbeknownst to them, sustained me during the final stages of the writing. Research for this book was supported by grants from the Amherst College Faculty Research Award Program.

There are many more people I would like to thank for the manifold contributions they made to the realization of this project, including Yael Navaro,

Kim Fortun, Peter Redfield, Sa'ed Atshan, Tom Csordas, Atwood Gaines, Carolyn Sufrin, Vivian Choi, Katie Kilroy-Marac, Tomas Matza, Lenore Manderson, Omar Dewachi, Maple Razsa, Yücel Yanıkdağ, and Lara Deeb. I want to express particular gratitude to Can Açıksöz and Zeynep Korkman. I feel like our respective projects have been in a complex dialogue for a long time, for which I have been the most underserving beneficiary. Special thanks as well to John Drabinski. Despite our geographic distance, it always brings me joy to see how often our thinking crosses paths, for which I have again been the most underserving beneficiary. The remarkably talented Jan Šabach designed the cover for this book. It's a true "tour de force," and I can't thank him enough for the care with which he translated the ideas of this book into images. Kate Wahl at Stanford University Press has been an ideal editor. I remain humbled by her enthusiasm for this project. Thank you.

Since this project began more than a decade ago, I have lost several family members. Each of these deaths has, in its own way, deepened my thinking for this book and I would like to acknowledge them. With the passing of my father, I came close, I think, to understanding what my interlocutors meant when they talked about generational loss. To the extent that our lives, and his death, are entangled with the legacies of the petrochemical industry of southern Louisiana, so to have I come to appreciate the ways that feelings of generational loss can take shape through legacies of disaster. With the unexpected passing of my brother, for whom the trajectory of my life is so profoundly indebted, I've come to understand what many of my interlocutors described as the distinctive ways that loss can present itself in moments of accomplishment. I wish he were here to call as I prepare to send off this manuscript. During the writing of this book, I'd also lose my sister-in-law. Watching my surviving brother deal with this loss would deepen my understanding of grief's complexity. Each of you have left important marks on this book.

In a very literal sense, none of this would have been possible without my family. Mom, your courage and adventurousness are inheritances I aspire to live up to. Thank you for everything you've done. Andiyah, Inez, and Zadie—the next generation—I am so lucky to have you in my corner. Your love, humor, and hugs have kept me going through so much of this "study." Finally, there's not a thought in this book that doesn't bear the trace of Joy, the love of my life. Your brilliance, passion, and encouragement have not only sustained me but also made me a better person. Thank you.

Notes

Introduction: Psychiatry in Ruins

1. For conceptualizing the unfinishedness of this model, see Biehl and Locke 2017.

2. Munir et al. 2004.

3. Kim Fortun's work—both as a scholar and assembler of collaborations—has been foundational to my thinking here. For an overview of "disaster STS," see Fortun et al. 2016. See also Tironi, Rodriguez-Giralt, and Michael Guggenheim 2014; Knowles 2014. For an introduction to the range of innovative collaborative work being facilitated by the Disaster-STS network, see https://disaster-sts-network .org/. Among many things I like about this collaborative project is how it understands itself as part of an STS tradition that grew out of a defining body of postcolonial and feminist theory rather than the (later) functionalist abstractions common to Latourian approaches to STS (Fortun 2014, 315).

4. See, among many others, Ong and Collier 2005; Callon and Law 1995; Latour 2005; Law 2009; Tsing 2015.

5. See Fortun and Frickel 2012; Fortun et al. 2016.

6. See esp. the important work of Summerfield 1999; Bracken and Petty 1998; Pupavac 2001.

7. See Fischer 2009.

8. Watters 2010.

9. Artvinli 2014; Kılıç 2014; Yanıkdağ 2013; Bilir and Artvinli 2021.

10. To put this in different theoretical terms, I hesitated to regard the forms of psychiatric knowledge and practice at work here as being hybrid, or the dynamic between European and Turkish psychiatrists as mimetic, any more so than all forms of psychiatric knowledge and practice are multiple, hybrid, and mimetic. I'm thinking here specifically about the lasting influence of Homi Bhabha's (1994) notion of

colonial mimicry within postcolonial science studies. Perhaps I'm being naïve, but I think there's something to be said about how the psychiatrists and psychologists responding to the earthquake understood the arrival of their European counterparts not as supplanting their approaches but as an opportunity to expand and refine their existing psychiatric training.

11. See Seth 2009; Pigg and Adams 2005. A number of psychological and psychiatric anthropologists have similarly worked to disrupt an understanding of the globalization of psychiatric discourses in the model of external imposition, focusing instead on the dynamic ways these discourses are locally mediated. See Anderson-Fye 2003; Lester 2005; Chua 2013; Moore 2016; Behrouzan 2016; Zhang 2020.

12. The always-insightful Stacy Pigg has argued that "we now need to find out more about how science and technology travel, not whether they belong to one culture or another" (quoted in Anderson 2002, 644). This point builds on conversations in postcolonial technoscience that focus on the ways science and technology "travel." See Pigg 2001; Anderson 2002, 2009; Crane 2013; de Laet and Mol 2000; Fullwiley 2011.

13. See Neria, Galea, and Norris 2009; Ursano et al. 2017; Stoddard, Pandya, and Katz 2011; Başoğlu and Şalcıoğlu 2011; Halpern and Tramontin 2007; Ritchie, Watson, and Friedman 2006; Myers and Wee 2005; Kirmayer et al. 2010.

14. Rose 1996, 3–4.

15. Lunbeck 1994.

16. See also Foucault 1977.

17. Estroff 1985; Good et al. 1985; Luhrmann 2001; Rhodes 1995, 2004. The trajectory of my argument also mirrors wider developments in the anthropology of psychiatry in the way that it tracks the movement of psychiatric expertise from clinical to extraclinical sites. See, for examples, the work of Elizabeth Davis (2012, 2018) and Paul Brodwin (2013).

18. See Stoler 2013; Schäfers 2016; Littlejohn 2021.

19. Conceptually speaking, bringing (patching?) together the distinct theoretical genealogies (and sensibilities) represented by an STS-inspired analysis of technoscientific expertise and a critical phenomenological approach to lived experience proved much easier said than done. On the one hand, you have the deterritorializing and methodical (some say tedious) work of mapping seemingly limitless sets of relations that constitute scientific objects and facts. This approach has become synonymous with the work of Bruno Latour (2005; see also many other works). On the other hand, you have the rich, literariness of phenomenological traditions in anthropology, where the case is made that to understand people's experiences, one must make sense of how experience emerges out of bodily, intersubjective, semiotic, and historical relations that are both intensely local and refract broader structural forces (Desjarlais 1997; Garcia 2010; Han 2012; Stevenson 2014; Aulino 2019; Willen 2007). As this indicates, these approaches conceptualize and prioritize subjectivity (among other phenomena) in divergent, at times even oppositional, ways. In many regards, *Living On* mirrors these conceptual differences, such that my discussion of the psychiatric

response to the earthquake privileges the assembling of expert networks, and my exploration of "living on" in the long aftermath of disaster privileges the subjective experience of those who lived through the earthquake.

20. Here, I am deeply indebted to anthropology's abiding concern with experiences of loss in contexts of large-scale destruction, especially instances of political and communal violence, as a means for theorizing subjectivity. See Daniel 1996; Das 2007; Aretxaga 2008; Good, Subandi, and DelVecchio 2007; Crapanzano 2011; Segal 2016.

21. For a critical discussion of the temporalities of disaster, see Roitman 2013; Dole et al. 2015.

22. This formulation of the "obstinacy of life" is indebted to a series of poignant reflections offered by the philosopher John Drabinski (2016) on the occasion of the death of the Iranian filmmaker Abbas Kiarostami. Among Kiarostami's many accomplishments, he directed a semifictional account of a filmmaker traveling through the ruins of an earthquake in Iran in search of survivors, a film that was, for a time, translated as "And Life Goes On."

23. Berlant 2011; Povinelli 2011.

24. See Das (2015) for a nuanced critique of Povinelli's concept of "quasi-events," and especially what Das sees as the reductive ease with which Povinelli's analysis moves between broad structural forces and the specificity of individual lives.

25. See Dumm 1999; Das 2007; Cavell 1994.

26. Good 2020; Rahimi 2021.

27. I am also reminded of Liisa Malkki's (1997) point that the ethnographic imperative to focus on the everyday runs the risk of missing what matters most to some people, namely extraordinary and exceptional events.

28. See Badiou 2005.

29. Nixon 2011; Knowles 2020; Calhoun 2010.

30. See Kauanui 2008; A. Simpson 2014; Coulthard 2014; Rifkin 2014; Estes 2019. There's so much more to say here. For instance, this work also pushes us to think systematically about how theoretical frameworks and language at our disposal are indebted to a specific European history of disaster, and about how we might think about a different theory of disaster that better reflects the historical and social specificity of this setting.

31. See Bullard 1990; Dyson 2006; Taylor 2014. "Disaster studies" also shares this interest in those social determinants that render people and communities vulnerable to disasters. See Oliver-Smith 1996; Hewitt 1997; Wisner et al. 2003; Bankoff 2001.

32. Das (2007, 149), in her incisive writings about communal violence in India, puts it this way: "the everyday provided the grounds from which the event could be grown." For further readings on related themes, see Povinelli 2011; Berlant 2011; Nixon 2011; A. Simpson 2014; Dole et al. 2015.

33. Pupavac 2001, 358.

34. Berlant 2011, 9–10.

35. See Stewart 2010.

36. Behrouzan 2015.

37. Michael Fischer, commenting on a provisional draft of these arguments, captures this point with characteristic insight: "Involved in this response is what Derrida, and I following him, have been calling su-vive, living on—not just survival but creating life relationally through care for others, through attention to the face of the other, as Levinas would put it, or extending life lines as resistance to entropy."

38. Unless otherwise noted, I follow popular and scholarly convention by using *earthquake* to refer to both seismic events.

39. Özbay et al. 2016.

40. As scholars working in settings marked by large-scale disaster would have predicted, see Petryna 2003; Klein 2008; Adams 2013; Simpson 2014.

41. See Kubicek 2002, 767. This surge in civic engagement would also draw in and amplify a number of rights-based discourses and organizations that soon became central to sweeping political reforms introduced as part of Turkey's formal candidacy for EU membership, which had been announced months after the earthquake. Babül 2017; Arat 2007.

42. For scholars of disaster, instances of post-disaster solidarity have been characterized as alternately a "postdisaster utopia" (Wolfenstein 1957) or "paradise" (Solnit 2009), a "democracy of distress" (Kutak 1938), an "altruistic community" (Barton 1969), and a "city of comrades" (Prince 1920)

43. Shafak 2010.

44. Ak 2003, 68.

45. Walton 2017.

46. To finish Shafak's (2010) thought: "We all became one, *even if for a few hours.*"

47. Açıksöz 2015, 271–72.

48. Karacimen 2014; Öniş 2003.

49. Kuyucu 2017.

50. Ewing 2020.

51. Dole 2012.

52. Dole 2012; Gordon Wexler and Dole 2022.

53. Biehl 2005; Das 2007; Fortun 2012; Lepselter 2016.

54. Stevenson 2014. For further reflections on this mode of ethnographic listening, see Good 2012; Pandolfo 2018; Das 2007.

55. See Garcia 2010; Han 2012; Stevenson 2014; Biehl 2005; Kleinman 2006; Pandolfo 2018; Desjarlais 2016.

56. On mobile and multisited, see Marcus 1995; Faubion and Marcus 2009. On the patchwork, see Günel, Varma, and Watanabe 2020. See also D'Amico-Samuels 1991.

57. Blanchot 1986, 7.

58. Kant (1790) 2001; Blanchot 1986.

59. Roitman 2013, 9.

60. See, e.g., Erikson 1976; Oliver-Smith 1996; Hoffman and Oliver-Smith 1999, 2002; Quarantelli 1998; Klinenberg 1995; Dyson 2006; Button 2010.

61. Fortun 2001; Petryna 2002; Masco 2013; Lakoff and Collier 2008; Collier and Lakoff 2021; Adams 2013; Barrios 2017; Choi 2015.

62. Bode 1990; E. Simpson 2014; Seale-Feldman 2020. See also Poniatowska 1995.

Chapter 1: The End of the World

1. See Dole et al. 2015.
2. See Blanchot 1986.
3. The sources used for the information contained in this paragraph included Turkish Red Crescent Society 2006; Scawthorn 2000; Kaya 2000; Erdik 2001; Yüksel et al. 2005; Munir et al. 2004.
4. Koçak 2019, 29.
5. I am certainly not the first person to struggle with this challenge. For a selection of readings that address different implications and facets of this issue, see Boltanski 1999; Fassin 2011; Kleinman and Kleinman 1997; Kleinman, Das, and Lock 1997; James 2010. See also Robbins's (2013) popular if unconvincing critique of anthropology's fascination with suffering.
6. For a further discussion of the term *depremzede*, see Akşit, Serdar, and Tabakoğlu 2004.
7. Ito et al. 2002.
8. Ersoy 2002; Aksoz-Efe, Erdur-Baker, and Servaty-Seib 2018.
9. For a remarkable account of the experiences of religious personnel working in the earthquake region, see Köse and Küçükcan 2006.
10. "We Were Victims of the State" (Devletin Kurbanı Olduk), *Yeni Şafak*, August 20, 1999, 1.
11. For a discussion of the distinctive role of media in the televisual mediation of disaster, see Doane 1990; Rangan 2017.
12. For a broad review of the concept of post-disaster housing in Turkey, with significant attention to ideas of post-disaster housing following the 1999 earthquake, see Baradan 2008.
13. For a discussion of the distinctions between "emergency shelter" and "temporary housing," see Quarantelli 1995.
14. See Kasapoğlu and Ecevit 2001; Ekinci 2000.
15. See Akıncı 2004; Baş 2011.
16. Yıldız 2019.

Chapter 2: A Disaster in the Making

1. Scholars of disaster frequently turn to John-Jacques Rousseau's letter to Voltaire regarding the Lisbon earthquake of 1755 to make this point, in which Rousseau (1756) wrote: "It was hardly nature who assembled there twenty-thousand houses of six or seven stories. If the residents of this large city had been more evenly dispersed and less densely housed, the losses would have been fewer or perhaps none at all."
2. See Klinenberg 1995; Oliver-Smith 1999; Dyson 2006; Taylor 2014; Washington 2020; Steinberg 2006.

3. For reference, neither the Marmara Earthquake (at a magnitude of 7.6) nor the nearby Düzce earthquake (7.2) rank near the top of the world's most powerful earthquakes, measured by magnitude. That honor goes to a 1960 earthquake in Chile that measured 9.5 on the Richter scale. For contemporary comparison, the earthquake in Pakistan in 2005 measured 7.6; the 2008 earthquake in China, 7.9; the earthquake that struck Haiti in 2010, 7.0; and the earthquake in 2004 that set off the tsunami in the Indian Ocean, 9.1.

4. Ambraseys 2002, 2009.

5. Kotil, Konur, and Özgür 2007.

6. The waves of labor migration that populated the region added an important and frequently unrecognized dimension to the coming landscape of disaster, in that many of these migrants were fleeing the state's protracted military campaigns against Kurds in southeastern Turkey. The earthquake, for these migrants, would not be their first disaster. As Penny Green (2005, 540–41) has written, "The cheap, illegal and shabbily built mass housing available to those forced migrants was, in one sense, a symbol of a new freedom and security. In reality, however, it was to provide a graveyard for people twice victimized by a willfully negligent state."

7. Okay et al. 2001.

8. TÜPRAŞ Yıllık Rapor 2000, cited in Aker 2006.

9. For a discussion of the ways that humanitarian action is premised on a notion of distant suffering, see Boltanski 1999.

10. For a discussion of timber framed housing in the Marmara Earthquake, see Lagenbach 2002. For a discussion of the vulnerability of concrete-framed apartment buildings, see Bruneau 2002; Wallace 1999.

11. Green 2005.

12. See Bruneau and Saatçıoğlu 1993.

13. For discussions detailing this entrenched corruption, see Green 2005; Hürol 2009; Sengezer and Koç 2005.

14. Coburn 1995.

15. Green 2005.

16. For a broader discussion of the Turkish state as an object of fantasy and affective attachment, see Navaro-Yashin 2002.

17. Huet 2012, 6.

18. Kafescioğlu 2009.

19. Bein 2008, 909.

20. Ayalon 2015.

21. Ayalon 2015, 71.

22. See Öztin 1994; Ürekli 1995; Sezer 1996; Alkan 1999.

23. Ürekli 1995.

24. Bein 2008, 910.

25. Karancı and Akşit 2000.

26. Kubicek 2002.

27. In 1995, the pro-Islamist Welfare Party (Refah Partisi) won the general elec-

tion and, the following year, formed a coalition government. This would be arguably the first time since the Republic's founding that a religious party controlled the state apparatus. In 1997, the military, charged with defending Turkey's secularist political system, stepped in and forced the coalition out of power. The Welfare Party was subsequently banned based on accusations that it violated the state's founding secularist principles.

28. Quoted in Kinzer 2008, 192.
29. Kinzer 2008, 201.
30. This is not a new sentiment. Indeed, the rise of modern humanitarianism is closely linked to the region where Turkey is today located. See Watenpaugh 2015.
31. Based on research conducted by the World Bank and a survey of 436 randomly selected tents and prefabricated housing units administered within months of the earthquake, Rita Jalali and her colleagues found that "34 per cent [of respondents] said that immediately after the earthquake they received most of the help they did get from relatives, neighbors and through their own efforts. Only 10.3 per cent mention state authorities as providing any help soon after the disaster (this includes the military, locally elected administrator and the state government). Kızılay was mentioned by only 3.4 per cent of those surveyed" (Jalali 2002, 125).
32. Kubicek 2002, 767.

Chapter 3: Novice Humanitarians

1. Coşkun 2004.
2. According to a study conducted by the psychiatrist Cengiz Kılıç (2008), nearly half (42 percent) of a randomly selected sample of 2,000 earthquake survivors sought help from mental health professionals following the earthquake. These are astonishing findings. Despite a historically underfunded mental health infrastructure, an entire region in disarray, and a long history of resistance to psychiatric care, tens of thousands of people would make contact with the mental health system, many for the first time. Moreover, this study does not account for the even larger number of residents who encountered psychiatric expertise in other forms—in "psychoeducation" workshops in tent settlements, among expert commentators on television and radio programs, or through everyday conversation with neighbors, friends, and family.
3. For anthropological reflections on this sort of humanitarian impulse, see Bornstein 2009; Malkki 2015.
4. As with other countries that embraced the promises of a biomedically mediated modernity, Turkey long ago rejected the value of "nonmedical" forms of therapeutic care already embedded within communities (Dole 2012) and invested instead in the hospital and the clinic as ideal sites of mental and emotional health care.
5. Ministry of Health 2006.
6. Munir et al. 2004.
7. Coşkun 2004.
8. See Bilir and Artvinli 2021. Artvinli's illuminating examination of the history of psychiatry in Turkey demonstrates the specific influence of Emile Kraepelin and

his followers on early psychiatry in Turkey, a trend that continues into the present (Artvinli 2014). See also Narter 2006; Öncüler 2013; Soyubol 2022. For a broader anthropological engagement with the assumptions of biological psychiatry, see Kleinman 1988; Gaines 1992; Good 1992; Luhrmann 2001.

9. See Rahimi 2006; Sağduyu et al. 2003; Taskin et al. 2003.

10. The World Health Organization would release its first report on the subject—"Mental Health in Emergencies"—in 2003. In 2007, the Inter-Agency Standing Committee (IASC) released its "Guidelines on Mental Health and Psychosocial Support in Emergency Settings."

11. Fassin and Rechtman 2009, 175.

12. See Livingston 2012; Wendland 2010.

13. See Schlar 2001; Aker 2006.

14. Just to be clear about the "global" nature of this network of psychiatric expertise: while heterogenous in terms of therapeutic orientations, it is nonetheless dominated by DSM-oriented psychiatric categories, its experts and venues of publication are primarily based in research and medical institutions in Europe and North America, and the production and circulation of knowledge and experts in this network are underwritten to a large extent by pharmaceutical markets whose headquarters are similarly based in Europe and North America.

Chapter 4: Experiments in Scale

This chapter is derived in part from the article "Experiments in Scale: Humanitarian Psychiatry in Post-Disaster Turkey" published in *Medical Anthropology* (2020), available at https://www.tandfonline.com/doi/10.1080/01459740.2020.1755284.

1. See Summerfield 1999; Bracken and Petty 1998; Breslau 2000; Watters 2010; Atshan 2013; Pupavac 2001, 2002; Moon 2009.

2. See Fassin and Rechtman 2009; James 2010; DelVecchio Good, Good, and Grayman 2010.

3. See Pandolfi 2003; Bornstein and Redfield 2011; Redfield 2013; DelVecchio Good, Good, and Grayman 2010; Fassin 2007, 2011; Schuller 2012; Ticktin 2011, 2014; Abramowitz and Panter-Brick 2015.

4. Biehl 2016. See also Fischer 2009.

5. Delaney and Leitner 1997; Howitt 1998; Marston 2000; Sheppard and McMaster 2008; Smith 1992; Swyngedouw 1997.

6. Carr and Lempert 2016; Choy 2011; Helmreich 2009; Rajan and Leonelli 2013; Strathern 2004; Tsing 2012, 2015.

7. Tsing 2012, 507–8.

8. Tsing 2012, 507.

9. In addition to changing the names of the psychiatrists and psychologists I interviewed, I have also avoided in this chapter using citations that would easily reveal their identity. I do this not only for purposes of confidentiality, which I recognize has limits. Indeed, readers familiar with the work of mental health professionals in this area may be able to identify some of the people being discussed here simply by the

therapeutic modality they use or a description of their intervention. At the same time, I use pseudonyms, even in these cases, to draw attention away from the idiosyncrasies of individual personalities and toward how they reveal and embody a set of wider processes—which are, ultimately, the focus of my analysis.

10. It is worth mentioning that Dr. Baykal developed a parallel set of interventions during the same period that involved the design and manufacturing of prototype mobile earthquake simulator machines that aimed to intensify the exposure aspect of his trauma treatment. While it sought to similarly minimize the necessity of a psychiatric expert (replacing it, in this case, with a technician), the size and cost of the simulator presented challenges to its scalability.

11. See Rose 1990, 1996.

12. Tsing 2012, 505.

13. Tsing 2012.

14. In the years to come, this would also help facilitate the possibility of collaboration between groups, as well as the mobility of personnel. Indeed, several psychiatrists who had been trained under Dr. Baykal would later become important figures in organizations dedicated to post-disaster psychosocial interventions, and EMDR experts trained in the Marmara Earthquake would later collaborate with psychosocial experts following a major earthquake in the city of Van in 2011.

15. As an aside, if they had looked to the history of psychiatry in Turkey for examples, one could argue that the only guidance about scaling psychiatry to the level of populations would have been eugenic. See Yanıkdağ 2013, 4–5.

16. See, e.g., Young 1995; Leys 2000; Breslau 2000; Fassin and Rechtman 2009.

17. Fassin 2007, 501.

18. See Carr and Lempert 2016.

19. Swyngedouw 1997, 169.

Chapter 5: A Geo-Psychology of Disaster

1. Emphasis in original. See Mercan 1999.

2. Konuk 2006.

3. Callon and Law 1995; Latour 2005; Ong and Collier 2005.

4. Emphasis in original. See Law 2009, 240.

5. See Hacking 1986; Mol 2002.

6. Vision was not always doubled. At times, there was only a scientific eye—in that there were many projects that had no therapeutic aspirations and sought only to measure the prevalence of psychological pathology among earthquake survivors.

7. An extended note about my citational practices is in order here. I want to acknowledge the tension between scientific authorship as public discourse and the ethical obligation of confidentiality to my interviewees when it comes to describing a world constituted in large measure through scholarly citation. How do I chart this network of citations without breaching the confidentiality of my interviewees? While a case can be made that, insofar as I'm exploring their research and publications, I am engaging them as public figures and can therefore use their actual names. At

the same time, I also recognize that in their adding details and commentary to their research during our interviews, we are entering into a more ambiguous discursive space—where something new or beyond the published material is being offered. Although all interviewees were willing to have their names published, I am nonetheless sensitive—based on my past research with Arab immigrant communities in the United States (Dole 2009)—to the fact that no one can anticipate how their statements will be used in the future. As such, confidentiality is a blanket aspiration in my research. At the same time, I recognize that describing their research even in the most generic terms will allow some readers to identify speakers. This is impossible to avoid. In an effort to find a balance between evidentiary obligations and ethical aspiration, I have relegated citations of their published work to the endnotes of the book.

8. Başoğlu et al. 2001.

9. T. Aker et al. 1999.

10. For discussions of the ways that "culture" is conceptualized in such psychiatric frameworks, see Kleinman and Good 1986; Kleinman 1988; Mezzich et al. 1999; Hopper 2008.

11. In particular, see Deleuze and Guattari 1987.

12. Başoğlu, Şalcıoğlu, and Livanou 2002.

13. Livanou et al. 2002.

14. Başoğlu et al. 2004; Kılıç 2003.

15. Şalcıoğlu, Başoğlu, and Livanou 2003, 2007.

16. See Başoğlu, Livanou, Şalcıoğlu, and Kalender 2003; Başoğlu, Şalcıoğlu, Livanou, Kalender, and Acar 2005; Başoğlu, Livanou, and Şalcıoğlu 2003; Başoğlu, Şalcıoğlu, and Livanou 2007.

17. Kılıç and Ulusoy 2003; Kılıç 2008.

18. Başoğlu and Şalcıoğlu 2011.

19. Tural, Aker, and Önder 2004, 451.

20. Tural et al. 2001.

21. Tural et al. 2004, described in Aker, Önen, and Karakılıç 2007.

22. See Kleinman 1988; Taussig 1980; Rose 2019.

23. For a wonderful reflection on the ethnographic possibilities of archival research, see Cox Hall 2018.

24. See Karancı and Rüstemli 1995; Rüstemli and Karancı 1996; Akşit, Karancı, and Balta 1997; Uğuz et al. 2000; Uğuz, Levent, and Soylu 2000; Şener et al. 1997; Miral et al. 1998; Turan and Sayıl 1996. As Tamer Aker et al. (2012, 55) notes in his review of the history of psychiatric and psychological responses to disaster in Turkey, these studies mostly focused on prevalence and risk factors for the development of mental disorders. For an overview of the psychiatric history of the study of earthquakes in Turkey, see Yüksel et al. 2005.

25. See Neria et al. 2007; Wang et al. 2013; Dai et al. 2016; Farooqui et al. 2017.

26. Tural et al. 2004, 451. The Armenian study referred to is Goenjian et al. 1994.

27. Yanıkdağ 2013.

28. Aker et al. 2012, 54.

29. There was a parallel group of studies emerging during this period focused on veterans returning from conflict zone in eastern Turkey. These studies were generally review articles and few empirical studies had been conducted on active-duty soldiers. See Aker et al. 2007; Açıksöz 2015.

30. Dindar 2005, cited in Öncüler 2013, 39–40.

31. Aker et al. 2007; Aker et al. 2012.

32. Fassin and Rechtman 2009.

33. See Young 1995; Leys 2000; Fassin and Rechtman 2009.

34. See Malkki 2015; Babül 2015. See also Petryna 2009.

35. Alparslan et al. 1999.

36. Yorbık et al. 1999, 2004; Abalı et al. 2000; Alyanak et al. 2000.

37. Ekşi and Braun 2009.

38. On over-time changes, see Ekşi and Braun 2009. On memories, see Ekşi et al. 2008.

39. Karakaya 2004; Bal and Jensen 2007; Kılıç, Kılıç, and Yılmaz 2008; Kılıç, Kılıç, and Aydın 2011; Wolmer, Laor, and Yazgan 2003; Wolmer et al. 2005; Bulut, Bulut, and Taylı 2005; Bulut 2013; Dogan 2011.

40. Laor et al. 2002; Wolmer, Laor, and Yazgan 2003; Wolmer et al. 2005.

41. Berkem and Bildik 2001; Demir et al. 2010; Sayıl et al. 2001; Laor et al. 2002.

42. Sabuncuoğlu, Çevikaslan, and Berkem 2003.

43. Vehid, Alyanak, and Ekşi 2006.

44. Kılıç, Özgüven, and Sayıl 2003; Kılıç, Kılıç, and Aydın 2011.

45. Karaırmak and Aydın 2004.

46. Yesilyaprak, Kisac, and Sanlier 2007.

47. Yazgan, Dedeoglu, and Yazgan 2006; Özgüler et al. 2004.

48. Cetin et al. 2005; Çakmak, Aydın, and Can 2004; Acicbe, Aker, and Özten 2003.

49. Yorbık et al. 2001.

50. Edinsel and Elçi 2015.

51. Aksaray et al. 2006; Özmenler et al. 2001; Yargıç et al. 2004.

52. Bozkurt et al. 2003.

53. Özçetin et al. 2002; Meral and Bildik 2001; Kılıç 2008.

54. Başoğlu et al. 2001; Başoğlu and Şalcıoğlu 2001; Geyran et al. 2005; Kocabaşoğlu et al. 2005; Karagüven 2009.

55. Ağaoğlu and Coşkun 2000; Balcıoğlu and Kocabaşoğlu 2000.

56. Gökalp 2002; Coşkun and Coşkun 2000; Karakılıç 2000; Gökler and Yılmaz 2005; Gökalp and Hacıoğlu 2004; Ataklı 2000; Kılıç 2001.

57. See Aker 2006; Aker, Önen, and Karakılıç 2007; Aker et al. 2012.

Chapter 6: Mediterranean Assemblages

This chapter is based on material from an article originally published as "Psychiatry, Disaster, Security: Mediterranean Assemblages" in *Culture, Medicine and Psychiatry* 47 (1): 62–81, 2023, https://link.springer.com/article/10.1007/s11013-022-09799-w.

NOTES TO CHAPTER 6

1. Pupavac 2001, 2002; Fassin and Rechtman 2009; Abramowitz 2014; Seale-Feldman 2020.

2. For a history of the concept of psychosocial, see Abramowitz 2014; Pupavac 2001.

3. The intervention also included a more explicitly psychotherapeutic component. At the completion of the four-week session, and following the administration of another round of screening instruments, individual children who were most severely impacted (based on instrument scores) were recruited into a smaller group psychotherapy component of the intervention.

4. I've come to think of these psychosocial interventions as an embodiment of the dual meaning of the Latin phrase modus vivendi, which connotes both a "way of life" and a "compromise." That is, these psychosocial interventions—as a means to both intervene on social life and evade resistance to conventional psychiatric treatment—can be understood as articulating both a "manner of living" or "way of life" and "a feasible arrangement or practical compromise especially one that bypasses difficulties."

5. It is worth acknowledging how their work diverged from previous generations of community-based interventions in Turkey, in which government representatives or their proxies (frequently trained as doctors or nurses) sought to remake and modernize (rural) communities through a combination of didactic education, social engineering, and coercion. Although Drs. Yavuz and Kaya may have similarly envisioned the community as lacking something that their expertise was uniquely able to provide (e.g., skills of emotional communication), they certainly understood the goals of their intervention in terms that were both less paternalistic and more modest—to help community members identify and develop communicative skills to address the acute and long-term effects of trauma and loss.

6. See Can 2016.

7. See Redfield 2013; Fassin 2011.

8. Summerfield 1999; Bracken and Petty 1998; Pupavac 2001, 2002.

9. Along similar lines, they were critical of groups conducting "fast" interventions in the region after the earthquake. As with others working with psychosocial models, they were critical of the decontextualized nature of these interventions, as well as the logic of efficiency that seemed to come with them. As one psychiatrist who was a prominent figure in the earthquake response critiqued Dr. Baykal's intervention in particular (see Chapter 4): "Of course, the state loves it. All the economic ministers love it. You say if you treat for one session, you spend little money for them." Members of Dr. Baykal's group would in turn critique Dr. Şahin's work on similar grounds.

10. See, again, Summerfield 1999; Pupavac 2001, 2002; Watters 2010. For discussions of these dynamics in the context of the Middle East and North Africa, see Atshan 2013; Moghnieh 2021; Fassin and Rechtman 2009; Howell 2011.

11. Ronsbo 2015.

12. Friedman-Peleg 2014.

13. Friedman-Peleg 2014; Friedman-Peleg and Bilu 2011.

14. Friedman-Peleg and Bilu 2011, 418.

15. Friedman-Peleg 2014; Friedman-Peleg and Bilu 2011.

16. On the military as protector of the Israeli body, see Weiss 2002. On how PTSD has circulated to validate the suffering of Palestinians and bear witness to the brutality of Israeli occupation, see Fassin and Rechtman 2009; Jabr and Berger 2017.

17. See especially Weizman 2012; Mbembe 2003.

18. Weizman 2012. Relatedly, Nikolas Rose (2019) has argued that psychiatry is and has always been a biopolitical science, given its historical role in the eugenics and mental hygiene movements of the nineteenth and twentieth century and its more recent prominence in discourses of risk management and social protection.

19. Masco 2014. For further discussion of the relationship between citizenship, security, and disaster preparedness, see Lakoff 2008; Aradau and van Munster 2012.

20. See Li 2006; Zureik, Lyon, and Abu-Laban 2010.

21. I want to be careful not to exaggerate Israel's exceptionalism in developing these forms of psychiatric expertise. Building on Machold's (2018) effort to complicate critical discourses about technologies of security and surveillance in Israel, it is important to acknowledge that the sorts of psychiatric research and practice being developed in Israel during this period were themselves the products of a long, transnational history of scientific exchange.

22. See Pupavac 2001, 2002; Summerfield 1999.

23. For examples of the study of postcolonial technoscience through idioms of mobility, see de Laet and Mol 2000; Pigg 2001; Anderson 2002; Crane 2013.

24. De Laet and Mol 2000.

25. There is a rich anthropological literature working to denaturalize the sort the psychiatric categories and techniques described here, especially those organized around PTSD. See Young 1995; Breslau 2000, 2004; Fassin and Rechtman 2009; James 2010; Hinton and Good 2016.

26. See Pigg 2001.

27. For a discussion of how such approaches in STS tend toward a functionalist sociology of relations, see Fortun 2014.

28. On the First World War, see Yanıkdağ 2013. On European colonial projects, see Fanon 1963; Keller 2007; Gibson and Beneduce 2017.

29. Abi-Rached 2020, 18. For similar works, see Moghnieh 2023 and Sandal-Wilson 2023. Similar dynamics can be seen in other ethnographically informed historical accounts of the relationship between colonial medicine and societal rupture in the region. See especially Omar Dewachi's *Ungovernable Life* (2017).

30. Among many possible examples, see Watters 2010. For postcolonial critiques of such assumptions, see Anderson 2002.

31. Artvinli 2014; Kılıç 2014; Yanıkdağ 2013; Bilir and Artvinli 2021.

32. Notably, the ways that the state deflected accountability and apportioned blame here was largely distinct from the ethnonationalist discourse of disposability underwriting the ongoing Kurdish conflict at the time. Açıksöz 2019. The location of the earthquake (in western Turkey, which is imagined, within this discourse, as far

removed from the conflict) is decisive in understanding these dynamics. A little more than a decade later, however, several of the psychiatrists and psychologists involved in responding to the Marmara Earthquake would mobilize a discourse of PTSD following an earthquake in Turkey's Kurdish region as a means of critiquing the violence of the Turkish state, not unlike how Palestinian mental health professionals have used the discourse of PTSD to critique the Israeli state (see Jabr and Berger 2017; Fassin and Rechtman 2009), thus offering further examples of the mobility of psychiatry forms of expertise in mediating relations between crisis, disaster, and sovereignty.

33. Klein 2008; Petryna 2003; Li 2006; Khalili 2012.
34. Bracke 2016.
35. Friedman-Peleg and Goodman 2010.

Chapter 7: Remains

1. See Munir et al. 2004.
2. See Açıksöz 2016; Can 2016.

Chapter 8: "We Have Not Forgotten, We Will Not Forget"

1. Tsing 2015.
2. See Lepselter 2016.
3. My approach here is indebted to the work of a range of scholars who have developed a rich theoretical vocabulary for conceptualizing the complex, nonlinear ways that the past works on and in the present. See, in particular, such concepts as afterlives (Benjamin 1996; Zengin 2019; Schäfers 2020; Watson 2020), haunting (Derrida 1994; Gordon 2008; Good 2020; Rahimi 2021), and debris (Stoler 2013). For a regionally relevant discussion of disaster—in this case famine in Lebanon—that is similarly concerned with the nonlinear legacies of disaster, see Brand 2023.
4. Müge İplikçi (2011) movingly explores this phenomenon in her remarkable collection of women's accounts of the earthquake, *Yıkık Kentli Kadınlar*. Relatedly, for a discussion of the capacity of naming to mediate social and familial ties across generations of Canadian Inuit, see Stevenson 2014.
5. Cebenoyan and his wife would die tragically in a traffic accident in 2020.
6. See Lifton 1968.
7. Behrouzan 2016, 119.
8. Korkman 2023; Kocamaner 2019.
9. For a related discussion of the Persian vernacular term *toromā* in relation to a "universal," clinical concept of trauma, see Behrouzan 2018.
10. Das 2015, 108.

Chapter 9: Disaster's Minor Feelings

1. The title of this chapter is indebted to Cathy Park Hong's (2020) extraordinary collection of essays, *Minor Feelings: An Asian American Reckoning*. It is also through Hong that I first encountered Sianne Ngai's (2007) *Ugly Feelings*.

2. Ngai 2007, 6.

3. Ngai 2007, 6–7.

4. Ngai 2007, 179.

5. To extend Aristotle's insights, the defining characteristics of irritability also make it especially unreliable as a political affect. While capitalist political-economic orders may have endless capacities to annoy and generate edginess, irritability is not something that can be easily harnessed to bind, regulate, or optimize subjects. Nor is it particularly effective when it comes to mobilizing movements.

6. My interest in the affective legacy of disaster differs from Barrios's (2017) discussion of affect and disaster reconstruction, which focuses on the role of affect and emotion in assessing the relevance and effectiveness of post-disaster interventions.

7. I follow Ann Cvetkovich (2003, 5) in approaching these terms "more like keywords, points of departure for discussion rather than definition." For an incisive commentary on the implications and stakes for anthropology of these definitional debates within "affect theory," see Parla 2019.

8. See Navaro 2012, 211. For Navaro (2012, 211), importantly, "this is not about finding a culturally distinct, local term for affect. . . . Nor is it similar to the ontological project of finding the truth in the radically *alter* existence of non-Western societies." With this, Navaro also joins other critics who see in affect theory a problematic de-emphasizing of subjectivity, in which presubjective, nonsignifying forces and intensities are granted privileged status and conceptualized as fundamentally autonomous from meaning, intentionality, and cognition. See Martin 2013; Leys 2011; Parla 2019. Incidentally, Navaro points toward the analytic possibilities of "irritability" for registering such a "different imaginary of affect."

9. See Ngai 2007, 208.

10. See Yıldırım 2021.

11. Enarson 1999; Anastario, Shehab, and Lawry 2009; Parkinson and Zara 2013.

12. Relatedly, for a history of the institutionalization of PTSD in Turkey that insightfully situates it within the context of the state's decades-long Kurdish conflict, see Açıksöz 2015.

13. For further reflections on the bodily, social, and political entanglement of "nervous systems," see Taussig 1992.

14. For many, the quality of being quick-tempered (e.g., *çabuk sinirlenen*) was both celebrated and disavowed as one of Turkey's distinctive national traditions. The less euphemistic dimension of this quality points toward a societal normalization of violence (especially gender-based violence), which Deniz Kandiyoti (2016) has argued is intrinsic rather than incidental to Turkey's ruling ideology.

15. This lexicon of disaster and living on draws specific inspiration from Ann Cvetkovich's (2003) *An Archive of Feeling*, in which she similarly works to develop an analysis of the affective legacy of traumatic events that is attuned as much to the ordinary as to the catastrophic.

16. Turkey is not unique in its focus on homeownership as the preferred target of post-disaster relief. See Oxfam 2006.

17. The relationship between property and disaster being played out here was not new. Indeed, it had already long been a component of legal property regimes in Turkey. Disaster Law No. 7269, which was passed in 1959, required the state to finance the reconstruction of housing destroyed by disasters. In the context of the Marmara Earthquake, this resulted in the distribution of 107.9 trillion TL to 59,533 property owners who applied for loans from the government. The legal frameworks represented by this law would be radically transformed—and expanded—following the Marmara Earthquake. See Turkish Red Crescent Society 2006.

18. Cvetkovich 2012, 11.

19. See Singh 2017.

20. See Kleinman and Kleinman 1991.

21. Following Thomas Csordas's (1994) conceptualization of the body as the existential ground of culture and self, we can understand the earthquake as profoundly destabilizing both the material foundation of life and the bodily grounds of one's being in the world.

22. See Kocamaner 2019. In their important introduction to the special issue "Post-Fordist Affect," Andrea Muehlebach and Nitzan Shoshan (2012) similarly discuss both home and nation-state as affective containers and relays.

23. See Altınay and Arat 2009; Kandiyoti 2016.

24. See James 2010, 37. James captures a widely felt sentiment among anthropologists working on humanitarian intervention, especially those that focus on humanitarian interventions with a psychiatric or psychological component. See among others Fassin and Rechtman 2009; Abramowitz 2014; Good, DelVecchio Good, and Grayman 2016; Seale-Feldman 2020.

25. Here I'm relying on a range of important work being done by anthropologists who have insistently problematized the concept of "trauma." See especially Das 2007; Behrouzan 2015, 2018.

26. For a nuanced anthropological reflection on the validity and utility of classic formulations of PTSD as compared to "complex trauma" within post-disaster settings, see Good et al. 2016.

27. See, again, Das 2007; Behrouzan 2015, 2018.

28. See Rothberg 2008; Yıldırım 2021.

29. Behrouzan (2015) has been particularly important in formulating an anthropological insistence that we think "beyond" trauma.

30. Das 2015, 108.

31. See Klinenberg 1995.

Chapter 10: Loss and the Optimism of Catastrophe

This chapter is derived in part from the article "The Optimism of Catastrophe: Loss and Liveable Futures in Post-Disaster Turkey" published in *Ethnos* (2022), https://www.tandfonline.com/doi/10.1080/00141844.2022.2042352

1. Many regard Voltaire's fierce rejection of Leibniz's optimism in the wake of the Lisbon earthquake of 1755 as a foundational, inaugurating moment of the Enlight-

enment (see Huet 2012). I thus write with a keen awareness of the irony of my interest in optimism in the aftermath of an earthquake.

2. See Crapanzano 2003; Miyazaki 2004; Lear 2006; Mattingly 2010; Kleist and Jansen 2016; Parla 2019.

3. Whereas it is expected that a daughter will one day marry and leave home, a son (and his children) is expected to remain closer to (if not at) home and thus become a regular part of a multigenerational family life. The loss of an only son is therefore the loss of this sort of anticipated future.

4. This constellation is also embedded within a set of patriarchal discourses intrinsic to Turkey's founding nationalist ideologies and the ongoing reproduction of state power. See Arat 2000; Özyeğin 2000; Dedeoğlu and Elveren 2012; Sirman 2005; Kandiyoti 2016; Babül 2015.

5. Özar and Yakut-Çakar 2013.

6. See Das 2007.

7. I say "of course," but it's worth noting that this translational work isn't typically acknowledged or demanded when it comes to drawing on, say, modern European philosophical traditions. Some readers of earlier drafts of this asked, "Why al-Ghazâlî?" Notably, they didn't ask "Why Deleuze?" or "Why Blanchot?"

8. Mbembe 2021; Chakrabarty 2000.

9. Mignolo and Walsh 2018.

10. For this discussion of al-Ghazâlî, I rely on the translations provided by Ormsby (1984). See also Burrell's (2001) translation of al-Ghazâlî's *The Revival of the Religious Sciences*, specifically the volume *Faith in Divine Unity and Trust in Divine Providence*.

11. See Ormsby 1984.

12. Other anthropologists have drawn on al-Ghazâlî to explore questions of subjectivity, especially from a (Lacanian) psychoanalytic perspective. Ewing 1997; Pandolfo 2018. I am interested in a different facet of al-Ghazâlî's work, one that concerns a distinctive formulation of one's ontological relationship to the world and, from this, a particular relationship to time and temporality.

13. This critique has proved resilient. Voltaire, writing six centuries after al-Ghazâlî, would use this precise argument to fiercely critique Gottfried Wilhelm Leibniz in the wake of the Lisbon earthquake of 1755.

14. Ormsby 1984, 179.

15. Gilles Deleuze's rereading of Leibniz resonates with al-Ghazâlî here. "Miseries are not what was missing [from Leibniz's world]," writes Deleuze (1993, 68), "the best of all possibilities only blossoms amid the ruins of the Platonic Good. If this world exists, it is not because it is the best, but because it is rather the inverse; it is the best because it is, because it is the one that is."

16. Snediker 2009, 15.

17. For discussions of the everyday as a site of subject making, see, among others, Das 2007; Stewart 2007; Han 2012. For examples of the recent interest in "hope," see note 2 in this chapter.

18. Nor, for that matter, is this necessarily the sort of "cruel optimism" that Berlant (2011) has so insightfully explored as an orientation to the future through an attachment to or desire for that which harms us.

19. For scholarly considerations of death and grief in Turkey, see Aksoz-Efe, Erdur-Baker, and Servaty-Seib 2018; Ersoy 2002; Zengin 2019. The major themes of these works are similarly reflected in the wider anthropological literature on death and grief, which is, broadly speaking, organized around the way people draw on culturally authorized forms and institutions to mark, manage, and formulate individual emotional attachments to the deceased and rework relationships between the living and the dead. For useful reviews of this literature, see Robben 2018; Silverman, Baroiller, and Hemer 2021.

20. I am reminded here of Veena Das's (2007, 7) account of survivors of political violence in India, for whom "life was recovered not through some grand gestures in the realm of the transcendent but through a descent into the ordinary." In contrast to my analysis, Das is specifically concerned with the discursive strategies through which these survivors struggle to reinhabit the world.

21. For further reflections on the formulation "obstinacy of life," see again Drabinski 2016.

22. While this silence was never total, the norm among her friends leaned heavily toward not speaking about their experiences of the earthquake. Esra, for example, would periodically tell her story to reporters (much as she told it to me), but it was offered not in the spirit of sharing her troubles as a means of recovery. Rather, she offered her story if she thought it would remind officials and those beyond the region of the lasting effects of the earthquake.

23. Felicity Aulino (2019) observed a similar interpersonal play of silence in her work on caregiving in Thailand. For Aulino, such dynamics of care are embedded within Buddhist formulations of the transient nature of thought and emotion.

24. Blanchot 1986. I am also reminded of Renato Rosaldo's (1988, 176) characterization of the force of grief among his Ilongot interlocutors: "The concept of force calls attention to an enduring intensity in human conduct that can occur with or without the dense elaboration conventionally associated with cultural depth. Although relatively without elaboration in speech, song, or ritual, the rage of older Ilongot men who have suffered devastating losses proves enormously consequential in that, foremost among other things, it leads them to behead their fellow humans. Thus, the notion of force involves both affective intensity and significant consequences that unfold over a long period of time."

25. Here I am particularly indebted to those anthropologists and feminist scholars who have critically engaged, on many grounds, the tendency to grant primacy to narrative and speech as the means and site of healing, recovery, and care. See Csordas 2002; Das 2007; Cvetkovich 2012; Fischer 2007.

26. Muñoz 2009; Biehl and Locke 2017; Haraway 2016.

27. See Buğra and Yakut-Çakar 2010; Dedeoğlu and Elveren 2012; Özar and Yakut-Çakar 2013.

28. Scott 2014.
29. Nixon 2011.
30. Biehl and Locke 2017.

Chapter 11: Disability, Gender, Thriving

1. O'Leary and Ickovics 1995, 128.
2. O'Leary and Ickovics 1995.
3. Like "thriving," post-traumatic growth seeks to capture the "positive psychological change experienced as a result of the struggle with highly challenging life circumstances." See Tedeschi and Calhoun 2004.
4. Relevant to this commitment, it is noteworthy that this technical discourse of resilience and post-traumatic growth mobilizes many of the same core concepts found within works inspired by affect theory, especially notions of thriving and enduring. They also share an affection for Nietzsche's oft-quoted maxim "What doesn't kill me makes me stronger"—albeit with radically different assumptions.
5. The photographs would form the basis of an exhibition at a local cultural center supported by the nearby Ford factory and the Vehbi Koç Foundation.
6. See Dikmen Bezmez's excellent work on this topic, especially Bezmez 2013. For a related discussion of disability politics among veterans in Turkey, see Açıksöz 2019.
7. Özyeğin 2015.
8. See Bracke 2016; Rose and Lentzos 2017.
9. The New Man (*Yeni Adam*) was a defining figure of early Republican nationalist reform. This was not unique to Turkey. Other modernist projects of nation building also turned to the reform, enlightenment, and engineering of a new citizen who would be the basis upon which the new nation was to be built. In Turkey, as elsewhere, this figure was fashioned in the image of the clean, healthy, rational, hardworking, productive, and scientific-minded citizen. Above all, this New Man was the figure of self-sacrifice—capable of subordinating self and difference to the ideal of the transcendent nation.
10. On fortune-tellers, see Korkman 2023. On saints and others, see Dole 2012.
11. See Korkman 2023.
12. At the same time, we can understand his presentation as also reproducing a normative story in which one's social value turns on one's capacity to form a heteronormative nuclear family.
13. Kirmayer et al. 2010, 159.

Chapter 12: Urban Renewal and Psychiatric Protest

This chapter is based on material from an article originally published as "The House That Saddam Built: Protest and Psychiatry in Post-Disaster Turkey," *Journal of the Ottoman and Turkish Studies Association* (2015), https://muse.jhu.edu/article/745097/pdf.

1. As described in Chapter 9, the vast majority of disaster relief programs in Turkey implemented after the 1999 earthquake were structured by the conventional

logic of "asset replacement," which is a common approach to longer-term disaster relief (Oxfam 2006). Given the gender disparity in home and land ownership, this post-disaster financial precarity also tracked sharply along gendered lines.

2. A common variation of this account suggests that the Red Crescent Society of Iraq donated $10 million in oil.

3. Over the course of my research, residents of Saddam's Homes offered many interpretations of the geopolitical significance of the Iraqi government's aid. Trying to discern the political motivations of the donation was made all the more difficult by the time that had elapsed since the earthquake, a period over which the meaning of Saddam Hussein had shifted dramatically—from regional dictator and US gadfly to a global figure around which much of the War on Terror revolved. These varying meanings of Saddam Hussein were readily apparent in the way residents used the name "Saddam's Homes" as a term that expressed an ironic confluence of utopian (American) ideas of suburban development and Saddam Hussein's reputation as a brutal dictator.

4. In İzmit, much of the subsidized housing would be newly constructed on the hills surrounding the city, where it was determined that the land was less vulnerable to the effects of seismic activity. Although a significant amount of the initial post-earthquake construction would be funded by the World Bank, İzmit had by 2005 established an experimental municipal agency, Kent Konut, that built low-income housing and worked closely with private banks to secure below-market interest rates for buyers. An important aim of the agency was to remain more flexible than the national Housing Development Agency (TOKİ), especially by outsourcing the financing of construction to private banks. Kent Konut would come under public scrutiny by 2012, at which point it had begun funding the construction of affordable housing by building and selling luxury apartments, such that affordable housing in the city became a by-product of new development.

5. Baş 2011; Konuk et al. 2006.

6. See Işık 2014.

7. Erol explained that his most intense reaction came when Prime Minister Tayyip Erdoğan appeared on television, a reaction that the psychiatrist administering the test regarded as nonpathological.

8. Death, protest, and disaster would converge again in uncannily similar ways following the Van earthquake of 2011, when a group of residents facing eviction from the shipping containers they had been living in as "temporary housing" for years began a series of hunger strikes. For an outstanding exploration of the history of such forms of "necro-resistance" in Turkey, see Bargu 2014.

9. See Başak Can's (2016) important work on this topic.

10. See Jalali 2002; Akşit, Tabakoğlu, and Serdar 2003; Özerdem and Jacoby 2006.

11. Good et al. 2007.

12. See, e.g., Baydar and İvegen 2006; Göker 2013 for discussions of the ongoing vigils staged by mothers—known, commonly, as "Saturday Mothers"—whose sons or

daughters disappeared after being detained by security forces, especially by military forces in the Kurdish region of southeastern Turkey.

13. See Can 2016.

14. See Başoğlu et al. 1994a; Başoğlu et al. 1994b; Paker, Paker, and Yüksel 1992.

15. One can of course identify precursors to such developments. See, e.g., Nadire Mater's *Mehmedin Kitabı* (Istanbul: Metis Yayınları, 1999), in which one finds examples of a (semi)technical psychiatric discourse being used to critique the traumatic effects of the Kurdish conflict on Turkish soldiers.

16. Milliyet 2014.

17. Özgür Kocaeli 2014.

18. See Kuyucu and Ünsal 2010; Angell 2014; Eren and Özçevik 2015.

19. See Kaya 2015 and Açıksöz 2016

Epilogue: New Century, Different Disaster

1. See Utku Balaban's (2023) "There's Nothing Natural about Turkey's Earthquake Disaster."

References

Abalı, O., Ü. Tüzün, Ü. Göktürk, K. Gürkan, B. Alyanak, and I. Görker. 2000. "Marmara Depremi Sonrasında Çocuk ve Ergenlerde Görülen Akut Psikolojik Reaksiyonlar." *Ulusal Çocuk ve Ergen Ruh Sağlığı ve Hastalıkları Kongresi* 1 (20).

Abi-Rached, Joelle M. 2020. *Asfuriyyeh: A History of Madness, Modernity, and War in the Middle East*. Cambridge, MA: MIT Press.

Abramowitz, Sharon Alane. 2014. *Searching for Normal in the Wake of the Liberian War*. Philadelphia: University of Pennsylvania Press.

Abramowitz, Sharon, and Catherine Panter-Brick. 2015. *Medical Humanitarianism: Ethnographies of Practice*. Philadelphia: University of Pennsylvania Press.

Acicbe, Ö., T. Aker, and E. Özten. 2003. "Kocaeli Üniversitesi Tıp Fakültesi Hastanesi Çalışanlarında Ruhsal Travma ve Etkileri." *39. Ulusal Psikiyatri Kongresi Poster Bildiri*. Antalya, Turkey.

Açıksöz, Can. 2015. "Ghosts Within: A Genealogy of War Trauma in Turkey." *Journal of the Ottoman and Turkish Studies Association* 2 (2): 259–80.

———. 2016. "Medical Humanitarianism Under Atmospheric Violence: Healthcare Workers in the 2013 Gezi Protests in Turkey." *Culture, Medicine and Psychiatry* 40 (2): 198–222.

———. 2019. *Sacrificial Limbs: Masculinity, Disability, and Political Violence in Turkey*. Berkeley: University of California Press.

Adams, Vincanne. 2013. *Markets of Sorrow, Labors of Faith: New Orleans in the Wake of Katrina*. Berkeley: University of California Press.

Adorno, Theodor. 1973. *Negative Dialectics*. London: Routledge.

Ağaoğlu, B., and A. Coşkun. 2000. "Deprem ve Çocuk Ruh Sağlığı." *Psikiyatri Psikoloji Psikofarmakoloji (3P) Dergisi* 8 (1): 53–55.

Ak, Behiç. 2003. *Fay Hattı*. Istanbul: TEM Yapım Yayıncılık.

Aker, Tamer. 2006. "1999 Marmara Depremleri: Epidemiyolojik Bulgular ve Toplum

Ruh Sağlığı Uygulamaları Üzerine Bir Gözden Geçirme." *Türk Psikiyatri Dergisi* 17 (3): 204–12.

Aker, Tamer, Özgür Erdur-Baker, Ilgın Gökler Danişman, and Banu Yılmaz. 2012. "Disaster Experience of Turkey: An Overview from a Psychological Perspective." *Pakistan Journal of Social and Clinical Psychology* 10 (2): 54–59.

Aker, T., P. Önen, and H. Karakılıç. 2007. "Psychological Trauma: Research and Practice in Turkey." *International Journal of Mental Health* 36 (3): 38–57.

Aker, Tamer, Melih Özeren, Metin Başoğlu, Cem Kaptanoğlu, Atilla Erol, and Behice Buran. 1999. "Clinician Administered Post Traumatic Stress Disorder Scale (CAPS) Reliability and Validity Study." *Turkish Journal of Psychiatry* 10 (4): 286–93.

Akıncı, Ferah. 2004. "The Aftermath of Disaster in Urban Areas: An Evaluation of the 1999 Earthquake in Turkey." *Cities* 21 (6): 527–36.

Aksaray, G., G. Kortan, H. Erkaya, Ç. Yenilmez, and C. Kaptanoğlu. 2006. "Gender Differences in Psychological Effect of the August 1999 Earthquake in Turkey." *Nordic Journal of Psychiatry* 60 (5): 387–91.

Akşit, B., N. Karancı, E. Balta. 1997. "Ekim 1995 Dinar Depremi ve Godot Beklentisi." *Psikiyatri, Psikoloji, Psikofarmakoloji (3P) Dergisi* 5 (2): 51–55.

Akşit, B., A. Serdar, and B. Tabakoğlu. 2004. "Earthquake Survivors Associations, Civil Society and State in Urban Marmara Region, Turkey." In *Conference on Comparative Urban Landscapes and Their Subaltern Citizens-Subjects in the Middle East and South East Asia*. Lahore: Lahore University of Management Sciences.

Akşit, B., B. Tabakoğlu, and A. Serdar. 2003. "Deprem Bağlamında Sivil Toplum Kuruluşları ve Devlet İlişkilerinin: Yazılı Medyada Kuruluşu Üzerine Gözlemler." In *Kültür ve Modernite*, edited by G. Pultar, O. İncirlioğlu, and B. Akşit, 157–79. Ankara: Türkiye Kültür Araştırmaları ve Tetragon Yayını.

Aksoz-Efe, Idil, Ozgur Erdur-Baker, and Heather Servaty-Seib. 2018. "Death Rituals, Religious Beliefs, and Grief of Turkish Women." *Death Studies* 42 (9): 579–92.

Al-Ghazâlî, Abu Hamid. 2001. *Faith in Divine Unity and Trust in Divine Providence*. Edited by David Burrell. Louisville, KY: Fons Vitae Publishing.

Alkan, Mehmet. 1999. "Toplumsal ve Siyasal Açıdan 1894 İstanbul Depremi." *Toplumsal Tarih* Ekim: 16.

Alparslan, S., A. Koşkar, S. Şenol, and I. Maral. 1999. "Marmara Depremini Yaşayan Çocuk ve Gençlerde Ruhsal Bozukluk ve Kaygı Düzeyleri." *Çocuk ve Gençlik Ruh Sağlığı Dergisi* 6 (3): 135–42.

Altınay, Ayşe Gül, and Yeşim Arat. 2009. *Violence against Women in Turkey: A Nationwide Survey*. Istanbul: Punto.

Alyanak, B., A. Ekşi, D. Toparlak, G. Peykerli, and R. Saydam. 2000. "Depremden Sonraki 2–6 Aylık Sürede Travma Sonrası Stres Bozukluğunun Ergenlerde Araştırılması." *Çocuk ve Gençlik Ruh Sağlığı Dergisi* 7 (2): 71–80.

Ambraseys, N. 2002. "The Seismic Activity of the Marmara Sea Region over the Last 2000 Years." *Bulletin of the Seismological Society of America* 92 (1): 1–18.

———. 2009. *Earthquakes in the Mediterranean and Middle East: A Multidisciplinary Study of Seismicity up to 1900*. Cambridge: Cambridge University Press.

Anastario, Michael, Nadine Shehab, and Lynn Lawry. 2009. "Increased Gender-Based Violence Among Women Internally Displaced in Mississippi Two Years Post-Hurricane Katrina." *Disaster Medicine and Public Health Preparedness* 3: 18–26.

Anderson, Warwick. 2002. "Postcolonial Technoscience." *Social Studies of Science* 32 (5): 643–58.

———. 2009. "From Subjugated Knowledge to Conjugated Subjects: Science and Globalisation, or Postcolonial Studies of Science?" *Postcolonial Studies* 12 (4): 389–400.

Anderson-Fye, Eileen P. 2003. "Never Leave Yourself: Ethnopsychology as Mediator of Psychological Globalization among Belizean Schoolgirls." *Ethos* 31 (1): 59–94.

Angell, Elizabeth. 2014. "Assembling Disaster: Earthquakes and Urban Politics in Istanbul." *City* 18 (6): 667–78.

Aradau, C., and R. van Munster. 2012. "The Securitization of Catastrophic Events: Trauma, Enactment, and Preparedness Exercises." *Alternatives: Global, Local, Political* 37 (3): 227–39.

Arat, Yeşim. 2000. "Gender and Citizenship in Turkey." In *Gender and Citizenship in the Middle East*, edited by Suad Joseph, 275–86. Syracuse, NY: Syracuse University Press.

Arat, Zehra F. Kabasakal, ed. 2007. *Human Rights in Turkey*. Philadelphia: University of Pennsylvania Press.

Aretxaga, Begoña. 2008. "Madness and the Political Real: Reflections on Violence in Postdictatorial Spain." In *Postcolonial Disorders*, edited by B. Good, S. Hyde, S. Pinto, and M. J. Good, 43–61. Berkeley: University of California Press.

Artvinli, Fatih. 2014. "More Than a Disease: The History of General Paralysis of the Insane in Turkey." *Journal of the History of the Neurosciences* 23: 127–39.

Ataklı, C. 2000. "Bakırköy Ruh ve Sinir Hastalıkları Hastanesi: Deprem Bölgesinden İzlenimler." *Psikiyatri Psikoloji Psikofarmakoloji (3P) Dergisi* 8 (1): 60–62.

Atshan, Sa'ed. 2013. "Prolonged Humanitarianism: The Social Life of Aid in the Palestinian Territories." Ph.D. diss., Harvard University.

Aulino, Felicity. 2019. *Rituals of Care: Karmic Politics in an Aging Thailand*. Ithaca, NY: Cornell University Press.

Ayalon, Yaron. 2015. *Natural Disaster in the Ottoman Empire*. Cambridge: Cambridge University Press.

Babül, Elif. 2015. "The Paradox of Protection: Human Rights, the Masculinist State, and the Moral Economy of Gratitude in Turkey." *American Ethnologist* 42 (1): 116–30.

———. 2017. *Bureaucratic Intimacies: Translating Human Rights in Turkey*. Stanford, CA: Stanford University Press.

Badiou, Alain. 2005. *Being and Event*. London: Bloomsbury.

Bal, A., and B. Jensen. 2007. "Post-Traumatic Stress Disorder Symptom Clusters in Turkish Child and Adolescent Trauma Survivors." *European Child & Adolescent Psychiatry* 16 (7): 449–57.

REFERENCES

Balaban, Utku. 2023. "There's Nothing Natural about Turkey's Earthquake Disaster." *Public Seminar* (blog). February 16, 2023. https://publicseminar.org/essays/theres-nothing-natural-about-turkeys-earthquake-disaster/.

Balcıoğlu, İ., and N. Kocabaşoğlu. 2000. "Depreme Psikososyal Bakış." *Yeni Symposium* 38 (4): 168–70.

Bankoff, Gregory. 2001. "Rendering the World Unsafe: 'Vulnerability' as Western Discourse." *Disasters* 25 (1): 19–35.

Baradan, Berna. 2008. "Review of Literature for the Concept of Post-Disaster Housing in Turkey." *Gazi University Journal of Science* 21 (2): 43–49.

Bargu, Banu. 2014. *Starve and Immolate: The Politics of Human Weapons*. New York: Columbia University Press.

Barrios, Roberto E. 2017. *Governing Affect: Neoliberalism and Disaster Reconstruction*. Lincoln: University of Nebraska Press.

Barton, A. 1969. *Communities in Distress*. Garden City, NY: Doubleday.

Baş, Sibel. 2011. "Post Disaster Temporary Housing: The Production of Place in the Case of 1999 Marmara Earthquakes in Kocaeli." Master's thesis, Middle East Technical University.

Başoğlu, M., C. Kılıç, E. Şalcıoğlu, and M. Livanou. 2004. "Prevalence of Posttraumatic Stress Disorder and Comorbid Depression in Earthquake Survivors in Turkey: An Epidemiological Study." *Journal of Traumatic Stress* 17: 133–41.

Başoğlu, M., M. Livanou, and E. Şalcıoğlu. 2003. "A Single-Session with an Earthquake Simulator for Traumatic Stress in Earthquake Survivors." *American Journal of Psychiatry* 160 (4): 788–90.

Başoğlu, M., M. Livanou, E. Şalcıoğlu, and D. Kalender. 2003. "A Brief Behavioural Treatment of Chronic Post-Traumatic Stress Disorder in Earthquake Survivors." *Psychological Medicine* 33 (4): 647–54.

Başoğlu, M., M. Paker, E. Ozmen, O. Taşdemir, and D. Sahin. 1994. "Factors Related to Long-Term Traumatic Stress Responses in Survivors of Torture in Turkey." *JAMA* 272 (5): 357–63.

Başoğlu, M., M. Paker, O. Paker, E. Ozmen, I. Marks, C. Incesu, D. Sahin, and N. Sarimurat. 1994. "Psychological Effects of Torture: A Comparison of Tortured with Nontortured Political Activists in Turkey." *American Journal of Psychiatry* 151 (1): 76–81.

Başoğlu, M., E. Şalcıoğlu, and M. Livanou. 2001. "A Study of the Validity of a Screening Instrument for Traumatic Stress in Earthquake Survivors." *Journal of Traumatic Stress* 14: 491–509.

———. 2002. "Traumatic Stress Responses in Earthquake Survivors in Turkey." *Journal of Traumatic Stress* 15: 269–76.

———. 2007. "A Randomized Controlled Study of Single-Session Behavioral Treatment of Earthquake-Related Posttraumatic Stress Using an Earthquake Simulator." *Psychological Medicine* 37 (2): 203–14.

Başoğlu, M., E. Şalcıoglu, M. Livanou, M. Özeren, T. Aker, C. Kılıç, and Ö. Mestçioğlu. 2001. "A Study of the Validity of a Screening Instrument for Traumatic Stress in Earthquake Survivors in Turkey." *Journal of Traumatic Stress* 14 (3): 491–509.

Başoğlu, M., E. Şalcıoğlu, M. Livanou, D. Kalender, and G. Acar. 2005. "Single-Session Behavioral Treatment of Earthquake-Related Posttraumatic Stress Disorder." *Journal of Traumatic Stress* 18 (1): 1–11.

Başoğlu, Metin, and Ebru Şalcıoglu. 2011. *A Mental Healthcare Model for Mass Trauma Survivors: Control-Focused Behavioral Treatment of Earthquake, War, and Torture Trauma*. Cambridge: Cambridge University Press.

Baydar, Gülsüm, and Berfin İvegen. 2006. "Territories, Identities, and Thresholds: The Saturday Mothers Phenomenon in İstanbul." *Signs: Journal of Women in Culture and Society* 31 (3): 689–715.

Behrouzan, Orkideh. 2015. "Beyond 'Trauma': Notes on Mental Health in the Middle East." *Medicine Anthropology Theory* 2 (3): 1–6.

———. 2016. *Prozak Diaries: Psychiatry and Generational Memory in Iran*. Stanford, CA: Stanford University Press.

———. 2018. "Ruptures and Their Afterlife: A Cultural Critique of Trauma." *Middle East Topics & Arguments* 11: 131–44.

Bein, Amit. 2008. "The Istanbul Earthquake of 1894 and Science in the Late Ottoman Empire." *Middle Eastern Studies* 44 (6): 909–24.

Benjamin, Walter. 1996. "The Task of the Translator." In *Walter Benjamin: Selected Writings, Volume 1*, 253–63. Cambridge, MA: Harvard University Press.

Berkem, M., and T. Bildik. 2001. "İzmit Depreminde Hospitalize Edilen Depremzede Çocuk ve Ergenlerin Klinik Özellikleri." *Anadolu Psikiyatri Dergisi* 2 (3): 133–40.

Berlant, Lauren. 2011. *Cruel Optimism*. Durham, NC: Duke University Press.

Bezmez, Dikmen. 2013. "Urban Citizenship, the Right to the City and Politics of Disability in Istanbul." *International Journal of Urban and Regional Research* 37 (1): 93–114.

Bhabha, Homi K. 1994. *The Location of Culture*. London: Routledge.

Biehl, João. 2005. *Vita: Life in a Zone of Social Abandonment*. Berkeley: University of California Press.

———. 2016. "Theorizing Global Health." *Medicine Anthropology Theory* 3 (2): 127–42.

Biehl, João, and Peter Locke. 2017. *Unfinished: The Anthropology of Becoming*. Durham, NC: Duke University Press.

Bilir, Merve, and Fatih Artvinli. 2021. "The History of Mental Health Policy in Turkey: Tradition, Transition and Transformation." *History of Psychiatry* 32 (1).

Blanchot, Maurice. 1986. *The Writing of the Disaster*. Lincoln: University of Nebraska Press.

Bode, Barbara. 1990. *No Bells to Toll: Destruction and Creation in the Andes*. New York: Scribner's.

Boltanski, Luc. 1999. *Distant Suffering: Morality, Media and Politics*. Cambridge: Cambridge University Press.

Bornstein, Erica. 2009. "The Impulse of Philanthropy." *Cultural Anthropology* 24 (4): 622–51.

Bornstein, Erica, and Peter Redfield. 2011. "Forces of Compassion: Humanitarianism Between Ethics and Politics." Santa Fe: SAR Press.

Bozkurt, O., Ö. Pektaş, Ö. Kalyoncu, H. Mırsal, and M. Beyazyürek. 2003. "Anksiyete ve Alkol Kullanım Bozukluğu İlişkisi: Bir Olgu Sunumu." *Bağımlılık Dergisi* 4 (3): 123–26.

Bracke, Sarah. 2016. "Bouncing Back: Vulnerability and Resistance in Times of Resilience." In *Vulnerability in Resistance*, edited by Judith Butler, Zeynep Gambetti, and Leticia Sabsay, 52–75. Durham, NC: Duke University Press.

Bracken, Patrick, and Celia Petty. 1998. *Rethinking the Trauma of War*. London: Free Association Books.

Brand, Tylor. 2023. *Famine Worlds: Life at the Edge of Suffering in Lebanon's Great War*. Palo Alto, CA: Stanford University Press.

Breslau, Joshua. 2000. "Globalizing Disaster Trauma: Psychiatry, Science, and Culture after the Kobe Earthquake." *Ethos* 28 (2): 174–97.

———. 2004. "Cultures of Trauma: Anthropological Views of Posttraumatic Stress Disorder in International Health." *Culture, Medicine and Psychiatry* 28 (2): 113–26.

Brodwin, Paul. 2013. *Everyday Ethics: Voices from the Front Line of Community Psychiatry*. Berkeley: University of California Press.

Bruneau, Michel. 2002. "Building Damage from the Marmara, Turkey Earthquake of August 17, 1999." *Journal of Seismology* 6: 357–77.

Bruneau, Michel, and M. Saatçıoğlu. 1993. "Performance of Structures during the 1992 Erzincan Earthquake." *Canadian Journal of Civil Engineering* 20 (2): 305–25.

Buğra, Ayşe, and Burcu Yakut-Çakar. 2010. "Structural Change, Social Policy Environment and Female Employment: The Case of Turkey." *Development and Change* 41 (3): 517–38.

Bullard, Robert D. 1990. *Dumping in Dixie: Race, Class, And Environmental Quality, Third Edition*. New York: Routledge.

Bulut, S. 2013. "Predictors of Posttraumatic Stress Symptoms in Children and Adolescents After an Earthquake Related School Building Collapse in Turkey." *Revista Latinoamericana de Psicología* 45 (1).

Bulut, S., S. Bulut, and A. Taylı. 2005. "The Dose of Exposure and Prevalence Rates of Post-Traumatic Stress Disorder in a Sample of Turkish Children Eleven Months After the 1999 Marmara Earthquakes." *School Psychology International* 26: 55–70.

Button, Gregory. 2010. *Disaster Culture: Knowledge and Uncertainty in the Wake of Human and Environmental Catastrophe*. Walnut Creek, CA: Left Coast Press.

Çakmak, H., R. Aydın, and Y. Can. 2004. "Kocaeli İli 112 Acil Yardım Birimlerinde Çalışan Personelin Geçmiş Afetlerden Etkilenme ve Olası Afetlere Hazırlık Durumlarının Saptanması." *Ruhsal Travma Toplantıları III: Afet Sonrası Ruh Sağlığı: Önleme, Tedavi ve Örgütlenme Sözel Bildiri*. Istanbul.

Calhoun, Craig. 2010. "The Idea of Emergency: Humanitarian Action and Global (Dis)order." In *Contemporary States of Emergency*, edited by D. Fassin and M. Pandolfi, 29–58. New York: Zone Books.

Callon, Michel, and John Law. 1995. "Agency and the Hybrid Collectif." *South Atlantic Quarterly* 94 (2): 481–507.

Can, Başak. 2016. "Human Rights, Humanitarianism, and State Violence: Medical Documentation of Torture in Turkey." *Medical Anthropology Quarterly* 30 (3): 342–58.

Carr, E. Summerson, and Michael Lempert, eds. 2016. *Scale: Discourse and Dimensions of Social Life*. Berkeley: University of California Press.

Cavell, Stanley. 1994. *In Quest of the Ordinary: Lines of Skepticism and Romanticism*. Chicago: University of Chicago Press.

Cetin, M., S. Kose, S. Ebrinc, S. Yigit, J. D. Elhai, and C. Başoğlu. 2005. "Identification and Posttraumatic Stress Disorder Symptoms in Rescue Workers in the Marmara, Turkey, Earthquake." *Journal of Traumatic Stress* 18 (5): 485–89.

Chakrabarty, Dipesh. 2000. *Provincializing Europe: Postcolonial Thought and Historical Difference*. Princeton, NJ: Princeton University Press.

Choi, Vivian. 2015. "Anticipatory States: Tsunami, War, and Insecurity in Sri Lanka." *Cultural Anthropology* 30 (2): 286–309.

Choy, Timothy. 2011. *Ecologies of Comparison: An Ethnography of Endangerment in Hong Kong*. Durham, NC: Duke University Press.

Chua, Jocelyn Lim. 2013. "'Reaching Out to the People': The Cultural Production of Mental Health Professionalism in the South Indian Public Sphere." *Ethos* 41 (4): 341–59.

Coburn, Andrew. 1995. "Disaster Prevention and Mitigation in Metropolitan Areas: Reducing. Urban Vulnerability in Turkey." In *Informal Settlements, Environmental Degradation and Disaster Vulnerability: Turkey Case Study*, edited by R. Parker, A. Kremer, and M. Munasinghe. Washington, DC: IDNDR and World Bank.

Collier, Stephen, and Andrew Lakoff. 2021. *The Government of Emergency: Vital Systems, Expertise, and the Politics of Security*. Princeton, NJ: Princeton University Press.

Coşkun, Bülent. 2004. "Psychiatry in Turkey." *International Psychiatry* 1 (3): 13–15.

Coşkun, B., and A. Coşkun. 2000. "Marmara Depremi Sonrasında Kocaeli Bölgesi İçin Toplum Ruh Sağlığı Hizmetleriyle İlgili Görüşler." *Psikiyatri Psikoloji Psikofarmakoloji (3P) Dergisi* 8 (1): 63–67.

Coulthard, Glen Sean. 2014. *Red Skin, White Masks: Rejecting the Colonial Politics of Recognition*. Minneapolis: University of Minnesota Press.

Cox Hall, Amy. 2018. "Archival Labyrinth: Words, Things and Bodies in Epistemic Formation." *Tapuya: Latin American Science, Technology and Society* 1 (1): 170–85.

Crane, Johanna. 2013. *Scrambling for Africa: AIDS, Expertise, and the Rise of American Global Health Science*. Ithaca, NY: Cornell University Press.

Crapanzano, Vincent. 2003. *Imaginative Horizons: An Essay in Literary-Philosophical Anthropology*. Chicago: University of Chicago Press.

———. 2011. *The Harkis: The Wound That Never Heals*. Chicago: University of Chicago Press.

Csordas, Thomas. 1994. *The Sacred Self: A Cultural Phenomenology of Charismatic Healing*. Berkeley: University of California Press.

———. 2002. *Body/Meaning/Healing*. New York: Palgrave Macmillan.

Cvetkovich, Ann. 2003. *An Archive of Feelings: Trauma, Sexuality, and Lesbian Public Cultures*. Durham, NC: Duke University Press.

———. 2012. *Depression: A Public Feeling.* Durham, NC: Duke University Press.

Dai, Wenjie, Long Chen, Zhiwei Lai, Yan Li, Jieru Wang, and Aizhong Liu. 2016. "The Incidence of Post-Traumatic Stress Disorder Among Survivors After Earthquakes: A Systematic Review and Meta-Analysis." *BMC Psychiatry* 16: 188.

D'Amico-Samuels, Deborah. 1991. "Undoing Fieldwork: Personal, Political, Theoretical and Methodological Implications." In *Decolonizing Anthropology: Moving Further Toward an Anthropology for Liberation,* edited by Faye Harrison, 68–87. Arlington, VA: American Anthropological Association.

Daniel, E. Valentine. 1996. *Charred Lullabies: Chapters in an Anthropography of Violence.* Princeton, NJ: Princeton University Press.

Das, Veena. 2007. *Life and Words.* Berkeley: University of California Press.

———. 2015. *Affliction: Health, Disease, Poverty.* New York: Fordham University Press.

Davis, Elizabeth Anne. 2012. *Bad Souls: Madness and Responsibility in Modern Greece.* Durham, NC: Duke University Press.

———. 2018. "Global Side Effects: Counter-Clinics in Mental Health Care." *Medical Anthropology* 37 (1): 1–16.

Dedeoğlu, Saniye, and Adem Elveren, eds. 2012. *Gender and Society in Turkey.* London: I. B. Tauris.

Delaney, David, and Helga Leitner. 1997. "The Political Construction of Scale." *Political Geography* 16 (2): 93–97.

Deleuze, Gilles. 1993. *The Fold: Leibniz and the Baroque.* Minneapolis: University of Minnesota Press.

Deleuze, Gilles, and Felix Guattari. 1987. *A Thousand Plateaus: Capitalism and Schizophrenia.* Minneapolis: University of Minnesota Press.

DelVecchio Good, Mary-Jo, Byron Good, and Jesse Grayman. 2010. "Complex Engagements: Responding to Violence in Postconflict Aceh." In *Contemporary States of Emergency: The Politics of Military and Humanitarian Interventions,* edited by Didier Fassin, 241–68. Cambridge, MA: MIT Press.

Demir, T., D. Demir, L. Alkas, M. Copur, B. Dogangun, and L. Kayaalp. 2010. "Some Clinical Characteristics of Children Who Survived the Marmara Earthquakes." *European Child & Adolescent Psychiatry* 19 (2): 125–33.

Derrida, Jacques. 1986. *Memoires for Paul de Man.* New York: Columbia University Press.

———. 1994. *Specters of Marx: The State of the Debt, the Work of Mourning, and the New International.* Translated by Peggy Kamuf. New York: Routledge.

Desjarlais, Robert. 1997. *Shelter Blues: Sanity and Selfhood Among the Homeless.* Philadelphia: University of Pennsylvania Press.

———. 2016. *Subject to Death: Life and Loss in a Buddhist World.* Chicago: University of Chicago Press.

Dewachi, Omar. 2017. *Ungovernable Life: Mandatory Medicine and Statecraft in Iraq.* Stanford, CA: Stanford University Press.

Dindar, Cemal. 2005. "Türkiye'de Psikiyatrinin İşleyişi ve İşlevi." In *12. Ulusal Sosyal Psikiyatri Konferansi.* Eskişehir, Turkey.

Doane, Mary Ann. 1990. "Information, Crisis, Catastrophe." In *Logics of Television*, edited by P. Mellencamp, 222–39. Bloomington: Indiana University Press.

Dogan, A. 2011. "Adolescents' Posttraumatic Stress Reactions and Behavior Problems Following Marmara Earthquake." *European Journal of Psychotraumatology* 2: 5825–32.

Dole, Christopher. 2009. "Security and Insecurity on a Global 'War on Terrorism': Arab-Muslim Immigrant Experience in Post-9/11 America." In *International Migration and Human Rights: The Global Repercussions of U.S. Policy*, edited by Samuel Martinez, 117–32. Berkeley: University of California Press.

——. 2012. *Healing Secular Life: Loss and Devotion in Modern Turkey*. Philadelphia: University of Pennsylvania Press.

Dole, Christopher, Andrew Poe, Austin Sarat, and Boris Wolfson. 2015. "When Is Catastrophe? An Introduction." In *The Time of Catastrophe*, edited by Christopher Dole, Andrew Poe, Austin Sarat, and Boris Wolfson. New York: Routledge.

Drabinski, John. 2016. "Abbas Kiarostami, Rest in Peace." Blog post, July 4. http://jdrabinski.com/2016/07/04/abbas-kiarostami-rest-in-peace.

Dumm, Tom. 1999. *A Politics of the Ordinary*. New York: New York University Press.

Dyson, Michael. 2006. *Come Hell or High Water: Hurricane Katrina and the Color of Disaster*. New York: Basic Books.

Edinsel, Kerim, and Özcan Elçi. 2015. "Psychological Distress Among the Non-Relocated and Relocated Survivors After the August 17th 1999 Earthquake in Turkey." *Journal of International Social Research* 8 (38): 573–82.

Ekinci, Oktay. 2000. *Rant Demokrasisi Çöktü: Deprem Yazıları*. Istanbul: Anahtar Kitabevi.

Ekşi, A., and K. Braun. 2009. "Over-Time Changes in PTSD and Depression Among Children Surviving the 1999 Istanbul Earthquake." *European Child and Adolescent Psychiatry* 18 (6): 384–91.

Ekşi, A., G. Peykerli, R. Saydam, D. Toparla, and K. Braun. 2008. "Vivid Intrusive Memories in PTSD: Responses of Child Earthquake Survivors in Turkey." *Journal of Loss and Trauma* 13 (2–3): 123–55.

Enarson, Elaine. 1999. "Violence Against Women in Disasters: A Study of Domestic Violence Programs in the United States and Canada." *Violence Against Women* 5 (7): 742–68.

Erdik, Mustafa. 2001. "Report on 1999 Kocaeli and Düzce (Turkey) Earthquakes." In *Structural Control for Civil and Infrastructure Engineering*, edited by Fabio Casciati and Georges Magonette, 149–86. Singapore: World Scientific.

Eren, Miraç, and Özlem Özçevik. 2015. "Institutionalization of Disaster Risk Discourse in Reproducing Urban Space in Istanbul." *ITU A|Z* 12 (1): 221–41.

Erikson, Kai. 1976. *Everything in Its Path: Destruction of Community in the Buffalo Creek Flood*. New York: Simon and Schuster.

Ersoy, Ruhi. 2002. "Türklerde Ölüm ve Ölü İle İlgili Rit ve Ritüeller." *Milli Folklor* 54: 86–101.

Estes, Nick. 2019. *Our History Is the Future*. New York: Verso.

Estroff, Sue. 1985. *Making It Crazy: An Ethnography of Psychiatric Clients in an American Community*. Berkeley: University of California Press.

Ewing, David. 2020. "Turkey Braces for Yet Another Currency Crisis." *New York Times*, August 27. https://www.nytimes.com/2020/08/27/business/turkey-currency-crisis.html.

Ewing, Katherine Pratt. 1997. *Arguing Sainthood: Modernity, Psychoanalysis, and Islam*. Durham, NC: Duke University Press.

Fanon, Frantz. 1963. *Wretched of the Earth*. New York: Grove Press.

Farooqui, Mudassir, Syed A. Quadri, Sajid S. Suriya, Muhammad Adnan Khan, Muhammad Ovais, Zohaib Sohail, Samra Shoaib, Hassaan Tohid, and Muhammad Hassan. 2017. "Posttraumatic Stress Disorder: A Serious Post-Earthquake Complication." *Trends in Psychiatry and Psychotherapy* 39 (2): 135–43.

Fassin, Didier. 2007. "Humanitarianism as a Politics of Life." *Public Culture* 19 (3): 499–520.

———. 2011. *Humanitarian Reason a Moral History of the Present Times*. Berkeley: University of California Press.

Fassin, Didier, and Richard Rechtman. 2009. *The Empire of Trauma: An Inquiry into the Condition of Victimhood*. Berkeley: University of California Press.

Faubion, James, and George Marcus, eds. 2009. *Fieldwork Is Not What It Used to Be: Learning Anthropology's Method in a Time of Transition*. Ithaca, NY: Cornell University Press.

Fischer, Michael M. J. 2007. "To Live with What Would Otherwise Be Unendurable: Return(s) to Subjectivities." In *Subjectivity*, edited by J. Biehl, A. Kleinman, and B. Good, 423–45. Berkeley: University of California Press.

———. 2009. *Anthropological Futures*. Durham, NC: Duke University Press.

Fortun, Kim. 2001. *Advocacy After Bhopal: Environmentalism, Disaster, New Global Orders*. Chicago: University of Chicago Press.

———. 2012. "Ethnography in Late Industrialism." *Cultural Anthropology* 27 (3): 446–64.

———. 2014. "From Latour to Late Industrialism." *HAU: Journal of Ethnographic Theory* 4 (1): 309–29.

Fortun, Kim, and Scott Frickel. 2012. "Making a Case for Disaster-STS." *An STS Forum on the East Japan Disaster* (blog). https://fukushimaforum.wordpress.com/online-forum-2/online-forum/making-a-case-for-disaster-science-and-technology-studies/.

Fortun, Kim, Scott Gabriel Knowles, Vivian Choi, Paul Jobin, Miwao Matsumoto, Pedro de la Torre III, Max Liboiron, and Luis Felipe R. Murillo. 2016. "Researching Disaster from an STS Perspective." In *The Handbook of Science and Technology Studies*, edited by Ulrike Felt, Rayvon Fouche, Clark Miller, and Laurel Smith-Doerr, 1003–28. Cambridge: MIT Press.

Foucault, Michel. 1977. *Discipline and Punish*. New York: Vintage Books.

Friedman-Peleg, Keren. 2014. "Between Jewish Settlers and Palestinian Citizens of Israel: Negotiating Ethno-National Power Relations Through the Discourse of PTSD." *Culture, Medicine and Psychiatry* 38 (4): 623–641.

Friedman-Peleg, Keren, and Yoram Bilu. 2011. "From PTSD to 'National Trauma': The Case of the Israel Trauma Center for Victims of Terror and War." *Transcultural Psychiatry* 48 (4): 416–436.

Friedman-Peleg, Keren, and Yehuda C. Goodman. 2010. "From Posttrauma Intervention to Immunization of the Social Body: Pragmatics and Politics of a Resilience Program in Israel's Periphery." *Culture, Medicine and Psychiatry* 34 (3): 421–442.

Fullwiley, Duana. 2011. *The Encultured Gene: Sickle Cell Health Politics and Biological Difference in West Africa*. Princeton, NJ: Princeton University Press.

Gaines, Atwood. 1992. "From DSM-I to III-R." *Social Science and Medicine* 35 (1): 3–24.

Garcia, Angela. 2010. *The Pastoral Clinic: Addiction and Dispossession along the Rio Grande*. Berkeley: University of California Press.

Geyran, P., N. Kocabaşoğlu, A. Çorapçioğlu Özdemir, and İ. Yargıç. 2005. "Peritravmatik Dissosiyasyon Ölçeği (PDEQ) Türkçe Versiyonunun Geçerlilik ve Güvenilirliği." *Yeni Symposium* 43 (2): 79–84.

Gibson, Nigel, and Roberto Beneduce. 2017. *Frantz Fanon, Psychiatry and Politics*. London: Rowman and Littlefield.

Goenjian, A., L. Najarian, R. Pynoos, A. Steinberg, G. Manoukian, A. Tavosian, and L. Fairbanks. 1994. "Posttraumatic Stress Disorder in Elderly and Younger Adults After the 1988 Earthquake in Armenia." *American Journal of Psychiatry* 151: 895–901.

Good, Byron. 1992. "Culture, Diagnosis and Comorbidity." *Culture, Medicine and Psychiatry* 16 (4): 427–46.

———. 2012. "Theorizing the 'Subject' of Medical and Psychiatric Anthropology." *Journal of the Royal Anthropological Institute* 18 (3): 515–35.

———. 2020. "Hauntology: Theorizing the Spectral in Psychological Anthropology." *Ethos* 47 (4): 411–26.

Good, Byron, Henry Herrera, Mary-Jo DelVecchio Good, and James Cooper. 1985. "Reflexivity, Countertransference and Clinical Ethnography: A Case from a Psychiatric Cultural Consultation Clinic." In *Physicians of Western Medicine: Anthropological Approaches to Theory and Practice*, edited by Robert A. Hann and Atwood D. Gaines, 193–221. Dordrecht: Springer Netherlands.

Good, Byron, Mary-Jo DelVecchio Good, and Jesse Grayman. 2016. "Is PTSD a 'Good Enough' Concept for Postconflict Mental Health Care?" In *Culture and PTSD*, edited by Devon Hinton and Byron Good, 387–417. Philadelphia: University of Pennsylvania Press.

Good, Byron, Subandi, and Mary-Jo DelVecchio Good. 2007. "The Subject of Mental Illness: Psychosis, Mad Violence, and Subjectivity in Indonesia." In *Subjectivity: Ethnographic Investigations*, edited by João Biehl, Arthur Kleinman, and Byron Good, 243–72. Berkeley: University of California Press.

Gordon, Avery. 2008. *Ghostly Matters: Haunting and the Sociological Imagination*. Minneapolis: University of Minnesota Press.

Gordon Wexler, Mikayla, and Christopher Dole. 2022. "Giving Care a Platform:

The Use of Instagram by Mothers of Children with Chronic Illness." *Medicine Anthropology Theory* 9 (3): 1–20.

Gökalp, Peykan. 2002. "Disaster Mental Health Care: The Experience of Turkey." *World Psychiatry* 1 (3): 159–60.

Gökalp, Peykan, and M. Hacıoğlu. 2004. "The Aftermath of the 1999 Earthquake in Turkey: Questions and Answers." *International Journal of Mental Health* 33 (1): 5–12.

Göker, Zeynep. 2011. "Presence in Silence: Feminist and Democratic Implications of the Saturday Vigils in Turkey." In *Social Movements, Mobilization and Contestation in the Middle East and North Africa*, edited by Joel Beinin and Frédéric Vairel, 107–24. Stanford, CA: Stanford University Press.

Gökler, I., and B. Yılmaz. 2005. "Psikoloji Penceresinden Afetler: Deneyimler, Bakış açısı, Öneriler." *Psikiyatri Psikoloji Psikofarmakoloji (3P) Dergisi* 13 (3): 7–12.

Green, Penny. 2005. "Disaster by Design: Corruption, Construction and Catastrophe." *British Journal of Criminology* 45 (4): 528–46.

Günel, Gökçe, Saiba Varma, and Chika Watanabe. 2020. "A Manifesto for Patchwork Ethnography." *Cultural Anthropology, Fieldsights.* https://culanth.org/fieldsights/a-manifesto-for-patchwork-ethnography.

Hacking, Ian. 1986. "Making Up People." In *Reconstructing Individualism*, edited by Morton Sosna and David Wellbery, 161–171. Stanford, CA: Stanford University Press.

Halpern, James, and Mary Tramontin, eds. 2007. *Disaster Mental Health: Theory and Practice.* Belmont, CA: Brooks/Cole.

Han, Clara. 2012. *Life in Debt: Times of Care and Violence in Neoliberal Chile.* Berkeley: University of California Press.

Haraway, Donna Jeanne. 2016. *Staying with the Trouble: Making Kin in the Chthulucene.* Durham, NC: Duke University Press.

Helmreich, Stefan. 2009. *Alien Ocean: Anthropological Voyages in Microbial Seas.* Berkeley: University of California Press.

Hewitt, Kenneth. 1997. *Regions of Risk: A Geographical Introduction to Disasters.* Harlow, UK: Longman.

Hinton, Devon, and Byron Good, eds. 2016. *Culture and PTSD: Trauma in Global and Historical Perspective.* Philadelphia: University of Pennsylvania Press.

Hoffman, Susannah M., and Anthony. Oliver-Smith. 2002. *Catastrophe and Culture: The Anthropology of Disaster.* Santa Fe, NM: School of American Research Press.

Hong, Cathy Park. 2020. *Minor Feelings: An Asian American Reckoning.* New York: One World.

Hopper, Kim. 2008. "Outcomes Elsewhere: Course of Psychosis in 'Other Cultures.'" In *Society and Psychosis*, edited by Craig Morgan, Kwame McKenzie, and Paul Fearon, 198–216. Cambridge: Cambridge University Press.

Howell, Alison. 2011. *Madness in International Relations: Psychology, Security, and the Global Governance of Mental Health.* London: Routledge.

Howitt, Richard. 1998. "Scale as Relation: Musical Metaphors of Geographical Scale." *Area* 30 (1): 49–58.

Huet, Marie-Hélène. 2012. *The Culture of Disaster*. Chicago: University of Chicago Press.

Hürol, Yonca. 2009. "Can Architecture Be Barbaric?" *Science and Engineering Ethics* 15 (2): 233–58.

İplikçi, Müge. 2011. *Yıkık Kentli Kadınlar*. Istanbul: Everest Yayınları.

Işık, Damla. 20114. "Vakıf as Intent and Practice: Charity and Poor Relief in Turkey." *International Journal of Middle East Studies* 46 (2): 307–27.

Ito, A., Balamir Üçer, Şerif Barış, Ayako Nakamura, Yoshimori Honkura, Toshio Kono, Shuichiro Hori, Akira Hasegawa, Riza Pektaş, and Ahmet Mete Işikara. 2002. "Aftershock Activity of the 1999 Izmit, Turkey, Earthquake Revealed from Microearthquake Observations." *Bulletin of the Seismological Society of America* 92 (1): 418–27.

Jabr, Samah, and Elizabeth Berger. 2017. "The Trauma of Humiliation in the Occupied Palestinian Territory." *Arab Journal of Psychiatry* 28 (2): 154–59.

Jalali, Rita. 2002. "Civil Society and the State: Turkey after the Earthquake." *Disasters* 26 (2): 120–39.

James, Erica Caple. 2010. *Democratic Insecurities: Violence, Trauma, and Intervention in Haiti*. Berkeley: University of California Press.

Kafescioğlu, Çiğdem. 2009. *Constantinopolis/Istanbul: Cultural Encounter, Imperial Vision, and the Construction of the Ottoman Capital*. University Park: Pennsylvania State University Press.

Kandiyoti, Deniz. 2016. "Locating the Politics of Gender: Patriarchy, Neo-Liberal Governance and Violence in Turkey." *Research and Policy on Turkey* 1 (2): 103–18.

Kant, Immanuel. 2001. *Critique of the Power of Judgment*. Translated by Paul Guyer and Eric Matthews. Cambridge: Cambridge University Press.

Karacimen, Elif. 2014. "Financialization in Turkey: The Case of Consumer Debt." *Journal of Balkan and Near Eastern Studies* 16 (2): 161–80.

Karagüven, Ü. 2009. "Reliability and Validity Study of Turkish Form of the Psychological Distress Scale." *Eğitim Araştırmaları-Eurasian Journal of Educational Research* 36: 179–92.

Karaırmak, O., and G. Aydın. 2004. "Depremzede Çocukların Korkuları." *Psikiyatri Psikoloji Psikofarmakoloji (3P) Dergisi* 12 (1): 3–10.

Karakaya, I., B. Ağaoğlu, A. Çoşkun, Ş. Şişmanlar, and Y. Öç. 2004. "Marmara Depreminden Üç Buçuk Yıl Sonra Ergenlerde TSSB, Depresyon ve Anksiyete Belirtileri." *Türk Psikiyatri Dergisi* 15 (4): 257–63.

Karakılıç, H. 2000. "Deprem Sonrası Psikiyatrik Yaklaşım." *Türkiye'de Psikiyatri* 2 (2): 104–11.

Karancı, Nuray A., and Bahattin Akşit. 2000. "Building Disaster-Resistant Communities: Lessons Learned from Past Earthquakes in Turkey and Suggestions for the Future." *International Journal of Mass Emergencies & Disasters* 18 (3): 403–16.

Karancı, Nuray, and A. Rüstemli. 1995. "Psychological Consequences of the 1992 Erzincan (Turkey) Earthquake." *Disasters* 19 (1): 8–18.

Kasapoğlu, Aytül, and Mehmet Ecevit. 2001. *Depremin Sosyolojik Araştırması: Hasarları Azaltma ve Toplumu Depreme Hazırlıklı Kılma*. Ankara: Sosyoloji Derneği.

Kauanui, J. Kēhaulani. 2008. *Hawaiian Blood: Colonialism and the Politics of Sovereignty and Indigeneity*. Durham, NC: Duke University Press.

Kaya, Duygu Gül. 2015. "Coming to Terms with the Past: Rewriting History Through a Therapeutic Public Discourse in Turkey." *International Journal of Middle East Studies* 47 (4): 681–700.

Kaya, Yalçın. 2000. *Depremden Kalanlar: 17 Ağustos'un Ardından Deprem, Devlet ve Toplum*. Istanbul: Otopsi.

Keller, Robert. 2007. *Colonial Madness: Psychiatry in French North Africa*. Chicago: University of Chicago Press.

Khalili, Laleh. 2012. *Time in the Shadows: Confinement in Counterinsurgencies*. Palo Alto, CA: Stanford University Press.

Kılıç, C., E. Kılıç, and İ. Aydın. 2011. "Effect of Relocation and Parental Psychopathology on Earthquake Survivor-Children's Mental Health." *Journal of Nervous and Mental Disease* 199 (5): 335–41.

Kılıç, C., and M. Ulusoy. 2003. "Psychological Effects of the November 1999 Earthquake in Turkey: An Epidemiological Study." *Acta Psychiatrica Scandinavica* 108: 232–38.

Kılıç, Cengiz. 2001. "Treatment Strategies for Post-Traumatic Stress Disorder: Need for Brief and Effective Interventions." *Acta Psychiatrica Scandinavica* 104: 409–11.

———. 2003. "Deprem Sonrası Görülen Ruhsal Sorunların Saptanması ve Tedavisi İçin Geliştirilen Bir Projeyle İlgili Deneyimler." *Kriz Dergisi* 11 (1): 5–12.

———. 2008. "Depremzedelerde Ruh Sağlığı Hizmeti Kullanımı: 1999 Depremlerinin Sonuçları." *Türk Psikiyatri Dergisi* 19 (2): 113–23.

Kılıç, E., H. Özgüven, and I. Sayıl. 2003. "The Psychological Effects of Parental Mental Health on Children Experiencing Disaster: The Experience of Bolu Earthquake in Turkey." *Family Process* 42 (4): 485–95.

Kılıç, Emine Zinnur, Cengiz Kılıç, and Savaş Yılmaz. 2008. "Is Anxiety Sensitivity a Predictor of PTSD in Children and Adolescents?" *Journal of Psychosomatic Research* 65 (1): 81–86.

Kılıç, Rüya. 2014. *Deliler ve Doktorları Osmanlı'dan Cumhuriyet'te Delilik*. Istanbul: Tarih Vakfı Yurt Yayınları.

Kinzer, Stephen. 2008. *Crescent and Star: Turkey Between Two Worlds*. New York: Farrar, Straus & Giroux.

Kirmayer, Laurence J., Hanna Kienzler, Abdel Hamid Afana, and Duncan Pedersen. 2010. "Trauma and Disasters in Social and Cultural Context." In *Principles of Social Psychiatry*, 155–77. Hoboken: John Wiley & Sons.

Klein, Naomi. 2008. *The Shock Doctrine: The Rise of Disaster Capitalism*. New York: Picador.

Kleinman, Arthur. 1988. *Rethinking Psychiatry: From Cultural Category to Personal Experience*. Boston: Free Press.

———. 2006. *What Really Matters: Living a Moral Life Amidst Uncertainty and Danger*. Oxford: Oxford University Press.

Kleinman, Arthur, Veena Das, and Margaret M. Lock, eds. 1997. *Social Suffering*. Berkeley: University of California Press.

Kleinman, Arthur, and Byron Good, eds. 1986. *Culture and Depression*. Berkeley: University of California Press.
Kleinman, Arthur, and Joan Kleinman. 1991. "Suffering and Its Professional Transformation: Toward an Ethnography of Interpersonal Experience." *Culture, Medicine, and Psychiatry*: 15: 275–301.
———. 1997. "The Appeal of Experience; The Dismay of Images: Cultural Appropriations of Suffering in Our Times." In *Social Suffering*, edited by Arthur Kleinman, Veena Das, and Margaret Lock, 1–23. Berkeley: University of California Press.
Kleist, N., and S. Jansen. 2016. "Hope over Time: Crisis, Immobility and Future-Making." *History and Anthropology* 27 (4): 373–392.
Klinenberg, Eric. 1995. *Heat Wave: A Social Autopsy of Disaster in Chicago*. Chicago: University of Chicago Press.
Knowles, Scott. 2014. "Learning from Disaster? The History of Technology and the Future of Disaster Research." *Technology and Culture* 55 (4): 773–84.
Knowles, Scott Gabriel. 2020. "Slow Disaster in the Anthropocene: A Historian Witnesses Climate Change on the Korean Peninsula." *Daedalus* 149 (4): 192–206.
Kocabaşoğlu, N., A. Ç. Özdemir, İ. Yargıç, and P. Geyran. 2005. "Türkçe 'PTSD Checklist—Version' (PCL-C) Ölçeğinin Geçerlilik ve Güvenilirliği." *Yeni Symposium* 43 (3): 126–34.
Kocamaner, Hikmet. 2019. "Regulating the Family Through Religion." *American Ethnologist* 46 (4): 495–508.
Koçak, Ufuk. 2019. *Sınırsız: Enkaz Altında Son, Deniz Altında Sonsuz Nefesin Hikayesi*. Istanbul: İnkılap.
Konuk, Emre, James Knipe, İbrahim Eke, Hakan Yuksek, Asena Yurtsever, and Sinem Ostep. 2006. "The Effects of Eye Movement Desensitization and Reprocessing (EMDR) Therapy on Posttraumatic Stress Disorder in Survivors of the 1999 Marmara, Turkey, Earthquake." *International Journal of Stress Management* 13: 291–308.
Korkman, Zeynep. 2023. *Gendered Fortunes: Divination, Precarity, and Affect in Postsecular Turkey*. Durham, NC: Duke University Press.
Kotil, E., F. Konur, and H. Özgür. 2007. "The Economic Impacts of Gulf Earthquake." In *International Earthquake Symposium*, 737–44. Kocaeli, Turkey.
Köse, Ali, and Talip Küçükcan. 2006. *Deprem ve Din*. Istanbul: Emre Yayınları.
Kubicek, Paul. 2002. "The Earthquake, Civil Society, and Political Change in Turkey: Assessment and Comparison with Eastern Europe." *Political Studies* 50 (4): 761–78.
Kutak, R. I. 1938. "The Sociology of Crises: The Louisville Flood of 1937." *Social Forces* 16: 66–72.
Kuyucu, Tuna. 2017. "Two Crises, Two Trajectories: The Impact of the 2001 and 2008 Economic Crises on Urban Governance in Turkey." In *Neoliberal Turkey and Its Discontents: Economic Policy and the Environment Under Erdoğan*, edited by Fikret Adaman, Bengi Akbulut, and Murat Arsel, 44–74. New York: Bloomsbury.
Kuyucu, Tuna, and Özlem Ünsal. 2010. "'Urban Transformation' as State-Led Property Transfer: An Analysis of Two Cases of Urban Renewal in Istanbul." *Urban Studies* 47 (7): 1479–99.

Laet, M. de, and A. Mol. 2000. "The Zimbabwe Bush Pump: Mechanics of a Fluid Technology." *Social Studies of Science* 30 (2): 225–63.

Lagenbach, Randolph. 2002. "Survivors Among the Ruins: Traditional Houses in Earthquakes in Turkey and India." *APT Bulletin* 33 (2–3): 47–56.

Lakoff, Andrew. 2008. "From Population to Vital System: National Security and the Changing Object of Public Health." In *Biosecurity Interventions*, edited by Andrew Lakoff and Stephen Collier, 33–60. New York: Columbia University Press.

Lakoff, Andrew, and Stephen Collier. 2008. *Biosecurity Interventions*. New York: Columbia University Press.

Laor, N., L. Wolmer, M. Kora, D. Yucel, S. Spirman, and Y. Yazgan. 2002. "Posttraumatic, Dissociative and Grief Symptoms in Turkish Children Exposed to the 1999 Earthquakes." *Journal of Mental and Nervous Disease* 190 (12): 824–32.

Latour, Bruno. 2005. *Reassembling the Social: An Introduction to Actor Network Theory*. Oxford: Oxford University Press.

Law, John. 2009. "Seeing Like a Survey." *Cultural Sociology* 3 (2): 239–56.

Lear, Jonathan. 2006. *Radical Hope: Ethics in the Face of Cultural Devastation*. Cambridge, MA: Harvard University Press.

Lepselter, Susan. 2016. *The Resonance of Unseen Things: Poetics, Power, Captivity, and UFOs in the American Uncanny*. Ann Arbor: University of Michigan Press.

Lester, Rebecca J. 2005. *Jesus in Our Wombs: Embodying Modernity in a Mexican Convent*. Berkeley: University of California Press.

Leys, Ruth. 2000. *Trauma: A Genealogy*. Chicago: University of Chicago Press.

———. 2011. "The Turn to Affect: A Critique." *Critical Inquiry* 37 (3): 434–72.

Li, Darryl. 2006. "The Gaza Strip as Laboratory: Notes in the Wake of Disengagement." *Journal of Palestine Studies* 35 (2): 38–55.

Lifton, Robert Jay. 1968. *Death in Life: Survivors of Hiroshima*. New York: Random House.

Littlejohn, Andrew. 2021. "Ruins for the Future." *American Ethnologist* 48 (1): 7–21.

Livanou, M., M. Başoğlu, E. Şalcıoğlu, and D. Kalendar. 2002. "Traumatic Stress Responses in Treatment-Seeking Earthquake Survivors in Turkey." *Journal of Nervous and Mental Disease* 190 (12): 816–23.

Livingston, Julie. 2012. *Improvising Medicine: An African Oncology Ward in an Emerging Cancer Epidemic*. Durham, NC: Duke University Press.

Luhrmann, Tanya. 2001. *Of Two Minds: An Anthropologist Looks at American Psychiatry*. New York: Vintage Books.

Lunbeck, Elizabeth. 1994. *The Psychiatric Persuasion: Knowledge, Gender, and Power in Modern America*. Princeton, NJ: Princeton University Press.

Machold, Rhys. 2018. "Reconsidering the Laboratory Thesis: Palestine/Israel and the Geopolitics of Representation." *Political Geography* 65: 88–97.

Malkki, Liisa. 1997. "News and Culture: Transitory Phenomena and the Fieldwork Tradition." In *Anthropological Locations*, edited by Akhil Gupta and James Ferguson, 86–101. Berkeley: University of California Press.

———. 2015. *The Need to Help: The Domestic Arts of International Humanitarianism*. Durham, NC: Duke University Press.

Marcus, George. 1995. "Ethnography in/of the World System: The Emergence of Multi-Sited Ethnography." *Annual Review of Anthropology* 24: 95–117.

Marston, Sallie. 2000. "The Social Construction of Scale." *Progress in Human Geography* 24 (2): 219–42.

Martin, Emily. 2013. "The Potentiality of Ethnography and the Limits of Affect Theory." *Current Anthropology* 54 (S7): S149–58.

Masco, Joseph. 2013. *The Nuclear Borderlands: The Manhattan Project in Post–Cold War New Mexico.* Princeton, NJ: Princeton University Press.

———. 2014. *Theater of Operations: National Security Affect from the Cold War to the War on Terror.* Durham, NC: Duke University Press.

Mater, Nadire. 1999. *Mehmedin Kitabı.* Istanbul: Metis Yayınları.

Mattingly, Cheryl. 2010. *The Paradox of Hope: Journeys Through a Clinical Borderland.* Berkeley: University of California Press.

Mbembe, Achille. 2003. "Necropolitics." *Public Culture* 15 (1): 11–40.

———. 2021. *Out of the Dark Night: Essays on Decolonization.* New York: Columbia University Press.

Meral, B., and T. Bildik. 2001. "Depremin Marmara Üniversitesi Tıp Fakültesi Çocuk Psikiyatrisi Polikliniği'ne Başvuru Profili Üzerine Etkisi." *Anadolu Psikiyatri Dergisi* 2 (1): 29–35.

Mercan, Sibel. 1999. "Deprem Sonrası Görülebilecek Psikiyatrik Sorunlar Nelerdir?" *Populer Medikal.* http://www.populermedikal.com/psikiyatri/depremsonrasi.asp.

Mezzich, Juan, Laurence Kirmayer, Arthur Kleinman, Horacio Fabrega, Delores Parron, Byron Good, Keh-Ming Lin, and Spero Manson. 1999. "The Place of Culture in DSM-IV." *Journal of Nervous and Mental Disease* 187 (8): 457–64.

Mignolo, Walter D., and Catherine E. Walsh. 2018. *On Decoloniality: Concepts, Analytics, Praxis.* Durham, NC: Duke University Press.

Milliyet. 2014. "Irak Hükümetin Yardımıyla Depremzedeler İçin Yapılan Konutlar Yurt Oluyor." *Milliyet*, September 7, 2014. http://www.milliyet.com.tr/irak-huku metinin-yardimiyla-depremzeler-kocaeli-yerelhaber-369955.

Ministry of Health of Turkey (Türkiye Cumhuriyeti Sağlık Bakanlığı). 2006. "Republic of Turkey National Mental Health Policy." Ankara: Türkiye Cumhuriyeti Sağlık Bakanlığı.

Miral, S., Ö. Özcan, A. Baykara, and B. Yemez. 1998. "Dinar Depremi Sonrası Çocuklarda Kaygı ve Depresyon." *Çocuk ve Gençlik Ruh Sağlığı Dergisi* 5 (1): 16–22.

Miyazaki, Hirokazu. 2004. *The Method of Hope: Anthropology, Philosophy, and Fijian Knowledge.* Stanford, CA: Stanford University Press.

Moghnieh, Lamia. 2021. "Infrastructures of Suffering: Trauma, Sumud and the Politics of Violence and Aid in Lebanon." *Medicine Anthropology Theory* 8 (1): 1–26.

———. 2023. "The Broken Promise of Institutional Psychiatry: Sexuality, Women and Mental Illness in 1950s Lebanon." *Culture, Medicine, and Psychiatry* 47 (1): 82–98.

Mol, Annemarie. 2002. *The Body Multiple: Ontology in Medical Practice.* Durham, NC: Duke University Press.

Moon, Claire. 2009. "Healing Past Violence: Traumatic Assumptions and Therapeutic Interventions in War and Reconciliation." *Journal of Human Rights* 8 (1): 71–91.

Moore, Erin. 2016. "Postures of Empowerment: Cultivating Aspirant Feminism in a Ugandan NGO." *Ethos* 44 (3): 375–96.

Muehlebach, Andrea, and Nitzan Shoshan. 2012. "Introduction." *Anthropological Quarterly* 85 (2): 317–43.

Munir, Kerim, Tuncay Ergene, Verda Tunaligil, and Nese Erol. 2004. "A Window of Opportunity for the Transformation of National Mental Health Policy in Turkey Following Two Major Earthquakes." *Harvard Review of Psychiatry* 12 (4): 238–51.

Muñoz, Jose Esteban. 2009. *Cruising Utopia: The Then and There of Queer Futurity*. New York: NYU Press.

Myers, Diane, and David Wee. 2005. *Disaster Mental Health Services*. New York: Routledge.

Narter, Meltem. 2006. "The Change in the Daily Knowledge of Madness in Turkey." *Journal of the Theory of Social Behavior* 36 (4): 409–24.

Navaro, Yael. 2012. *The Make-Believe Space: Affective Geography in a Postwar Polity*. Durham, NC: Duke University Press.

Navaro-Yashin, Yael. 2002. *Faces of the State*. Princeton, NJ: Princeton University Press.

Neria, Yuval, Sandro Galea, and Fran Norris. 2009. *Mental Health and Disasters*. Cambridge University Press.

Neria, Y., A. Nandi, and S. Galea. 2008. "Post-Traumatic Stress Disorder Following Disasters: A Systematic Review." *Psychological Medicine* 38 (4): 467–80.

Ngai, Sianne. 2007. *Ugly Feelings*. Cambridge, MA: Harvard University Press.

Nixon, Rob. 2011. *Slow Violence and the Environmentalism of the Poor*. Cambridge, MA: Harvard University Press.

Okay, O. S., L. Tolun, F. Telli-Karakoç, V. Tüfekçi, H. Tüfekçi, and E. Morkoç. 2001. "İzmit Bay (Turkey) Ecosystem After Marmara Earthquake and Subsequent Refinery Fire: The Long-Term Data." *Marine Pollution Bulletin* 42 (5): 361–69.

O'Leary, V. E., and J. R. Ickovics. 1995. "Resilience and Thriving in Response to Challenge." *Women's Health* 1 (2): 121–42.

Oliver-Smith, Anthony. 1996. "Anthropological Research on Hazards and Disasters." *Annual Review of Anthropology* 25 (1): 303–28.

———. 1999. "'What Is a Disaster?' Anthropological Perspectives on a Persistent Question." In *The Angry Earth*, edited by Anthony Oliver-Smith and Susannah M. Hoffman, 18–34. New York: Routledge.

Ong, Aihwa, and Stephen J. Collier, eds. 2005. *Global Assemblages: Technology, Politics, and Ethics as Anthropological Problems*. Malden, MA: Wiley-Blackwell.

Ormsby, Eric. 1984. *Theodicy in Islamic Thought: The Dispute over Al-Ghazali's Best of All Possible Worlds*. Princeton, NJ: Princeton University Press.

Oxfam. 2006. "The Tsunami Two Years On: Land Rights in Aceh." http://oxfam.ca/sites/default/files/file_attachments/the-tsunami-two-years-on-land-rights-in-aceh_2.pdf.

Öncüler, Emine. 2013. "Globalization and the Networks of Expertise in Turkey: The Politics of Autism." PhD diss., Columbia University.

Öniş, Ziya. 2003. "Domestic Politics Versus Global Dynamics: Towards a Political Economy of the 2000 and 2001 Financial Crises in Turkey." *Turkish Studies* 4 (2): 1–30.

Özar, Şemsa, and Burcu Yakut-Çakar. 2013. "Unfolding the Invisibility of Women Without Men in the Case of Turkey." *Women's Studies International Forum* 41: 24–34.

Özbay, Cenk, Maral Erol, Aysecan Terzioğlu, and Z. Umut Türem, eds. 2016. *The Making of Neoliberal Turkey*. New York: Routledge.

Özçetin, A., M. Özkan, A. Ataoğlu, and C. İçmeli. 2002. "Bir Üniversite Hastanesi Psikiyatri Polikliniğine Başvuran Hastaların Sosyo-Demografik Tanılar ve Depremle İlişkileri." *Düşünen Adam* 15 (3): 149–57.

Özerdem, Alpaslan, and Tim Jacoby. 2006. *Disaster Management and Civil Society: Earthquake Relief in Japan, Turkey and India*. London: I. B. Tauris.

Özgüler, N., F. Maner, S. Çobanoğlu, T. Aker, and O. Karamustafalıoğlu. 2004. "Yaşlılarda Travma Sonrası Stres Bozukluğunda Eş Tanı Özellikleri." *Düşünen Adam* 17 (3): 141–45.

Özgür Kocaeli. 2014. "Arızlı'da Kız Yurdu İçin Çalışma Başladı." *Özgür Kocaeli*, January 29, 2014. http://www.ozgurkocaeli.com.tr/haber/arizlida-kiz-yurdu-icin-calisma-basladi-153008.html.

Özmenler, K., T. Karlıdere, and S. Battal. 2001. "Depremzede Ruhsal Danışma Merkezine Başvuranların Sosyodemografik Özellikleri ve Semptom Sıklıkları." *Kriz Dergisi* 9 (1): 13–18.

Öztin, Feriha. 1994. *10 Temmuz 1894 İstanbul Depremi Raporu*. Ankara: T.C. Bayındırlık ve İskan Bakanlığı Afet İşleri Genel Müdürlüğü Deprem Araştırma Dairesi.

Özyeğin, Gül. 2000. *Untidy Gender: Domestic Service in Turkey*. Philadelphia: Temple University Press.

———. 2015. *New Desires, New Selves: Sex, Love, and Piety Among Turkish Youth*. New York: New York University Press.

Paker, M., Ö. Paker, and Ş. Yüksel. 1992. "Psychological Effects of Torture: An Empirical Study of Tortured and Non-Tortured Non-Political Prisoners." In *Torture and Its Consequences*, edited by Metin Başoğlu. Cambridge: Cambridge University Press.

Pandolfi, Mariella. 2003. "Contract of Mutual (In)Difference." *Indiana Journal of Global Legal Studies* 10 (1): 369–81.

Pandolfo, Stefania. 2018. *Knot of the Soul: Madness, Psychoanalysis, Islam*. Chicago: University of Chicago Press.

Parkinson, Debra, and C. Zara. 2013. "The Hidden Disaster: Domestic Violence in the Aftermath of Natural Disaster." *Australian Journal of Emergency Management* 28: 28–35.

Parla, Ayse. 2019. *Precarious Hope: Migration and the Limits of Belonging in Turkey*. Palo Alto, CA: Stanford University Press.

Petryna, Adriana. 2003. *Life Exposed: Biological Citizens after Chernobyl.* Princeton, NJ: Princeton University Press.

———. 2009. *When Experiments Travel: Clinical Trials and the Global Search for Human Subjects.* Princeton, NJ: Princeton University Press.

Pigg, Stacy. 2001. "Languages of Sex and AIDS in Nepal: Notes on the Social Production of Commensurability." *Cultural Anthropology* 16 (4): 481–541.

Pigg, Stacy Leigh, and Vincanne Adams, eds. 2005. *Sex in Development: Science, Sexuality, and Morality in Global Perspective.* Durham, NC: Duke University Press Books.

Poniatowska, Elena. 1995. *Nothing, Nobody: The Voices of the Mexico City Earthquake.* Philadelphia: Temple University Press.

Povinelli, Elizabeth A. 2011. *Economies of Abandonment: Social Belonging and Endurance in Late Liberalism.* Durham, NC: Duke University Press.

Prince, Samuel. 1920. *Catastrophe and Social Change.* New York: Columbia University.

Pupavac, Vanessa. 2001. "Therapeutic Governance: Psycho-Social Intervention and Trauma Risk Management." *Disasters* 25 (4): 358–72.

———. 2002. "Pathologizing Populations and Colonizing Minds: International Psychosocial Programs in Kosovo." *Alternatives: Global, Local, Political* 27: 489–511.

Quarantelli, Enrico. 1995. "Patterns of Shelter and Housing in US Disasters." *Disaster Prevention and Management* 4 (3): 43–53.

———. 1998. *What Is a Disaster?* New York: Routledge.

Rahimi, Sadeq. 2016. *Meaning, Madness and Political Subjectivity: A Study of Schizophrenia and Culture in Turkey.* New York: Routledge.

Rahimi, Sadeq. 2021. *The Hauntology of Everyday Life.* New York: Palgrave Macmillan.

Rajan, Kaushik, and Sabina Leonelli. 2013. "Introduction: Biomedical Trans-Actions, Postgenomics, and Knowledge/Value." *Public Culture* 25 (3 71): 463–75.

Rangan, Pooja. 2017. *Immediations: The Humanitarian Impulse in Documentary.* Durham, NC: Duke University Press.

Redfield, Peter. 2013. *Life in Crisis: The Ethical Journey of Doctors Without Borders.* Berkeley: University of California Press.

Rhodes, Lorna A. 1995. *Emptying Beds: The Work of an Emergency Psychiatric Unit.* Berkeley: University of California Press.

———. 2004. *Total Confinement: Madness and Reason in the Maximum Security Prison.* Berkeley: University of California Press.

Rifkin, Mark. 2014. *Settler Common Sense: Queerness and Everyday Colonialism in the American Renaissance.* Minneapolis: University of Minnesota Press.

Ritchie, Elspeth Cameron, Patricia Watson, and Matthew Friedman, eds. 2006. *Interventions Following Mass Violence and Disasters.* New York: Guilford Press.

Robben, Antonius, ed. 2018. *A Companion to the Anthropology of Death.* Malden, MA: Wiley.

Robbins, Joel. 2013. "Beyond the Suffering Subject: Toward an Anthropology of the Good." *Journal of the Royal Anthropological Institute* 19 (3): 447–62.

Roitman, Janet. 2013. *Anti-Crisis*. Durham, NC: Duke University Press.
Ronsbo, Henrik. 2015. "A Republic of Remedies: Psychosocial Interventions in Post-Conflict Guatemala." In *The Clinic and the Court*, edited by Ian Harper, Tobias Kelly, and Akshay Khanna, 265–95. Cambridge: Cambridge University Press.
Rosaldo, Renato. 1988. "Grief and a Headhunter's Rage." In *Text, Play, and Story*, edited by Edward Bruner, 178–95. Prospect Heights, IL: Waveland Press.
Rose, Nikolas. 1990. *Governing the Soul*. New York: Routledge.
———. 1996. *Inventing Ourselves: Psychology, Power, and Personhood*. New York: Cambridge University Press.
———. 2019. *Our Psychiatric Future*. Cambridge, UK: Polity Press.
Rose, Nikolas, and Filippa Lentzos. 2017. "Making Us Resilient." In *Competing Responsibilities*, edited by Susanna Trnka and Catherine Trundle, 27–48. Durham, NC: Duke University Press.
Rothberg, Michael. 2008. "Decolonizing Trauma Studies: A Response." *Studies in the Novel* 40 (1–2): 224–34.
Rousseau, Jean-Jacques. 1756. "Rousseau to Voltaire, 18 August 1756." In *Correspondence complète de Jean Jacques Rousseau*, edited by J. A. Leigh, 4:37–50. Liverpool, UK: Liverpool University Press.
Rüstemli, A., and N. Karancı. 1996. "Distress Reactions and Earthquake-Related Cognitions of Parents and Their Adolescent Children in a Victimized Population." *Journal of Social Behavior and Personality* 11 (4): 767–80.
Sabuncuoğlu, O., A. Çevikaslan, and M. Berkem. 2003. "Marmara Depreminden Etkilenen İki Ayrı Bölgede Ergenlerde Depresyon, Kaygı ve Davranış." *Klinik Psikiyatri Dergisi* 6 (4): 189–97.
Sağduyu, A., T. Aker, E. Özmen, K. Ögel, and D. Tamar. 2003. "Halkın Şizofreniye Bakışı ve Yaklaşımı Üzerine Bir Epidemiyolojik Araştırma." *Türk Psikiyatri Dergisi* 12: 99–110.
Sandal-Wilson, Chris. 2023. *Mandatory Madness: Colonial Psychiatry and Mental Illness in British Mandate Palestine*. Cambridge: Cambridge University Press.
Sayıl, I., S. Canat, R. Akdur, E. Kılıç, R. Uslu, H. Özgüven, B. Öncü, et al. 2001. "Depremzede Ailelere Yönelik Koruyucu Müdahale Çalışması." *Kriz Dergisi* 9 (1): 1–12.
Scawthorn, Charles. 2000. "The Marmara, Turkey Earthquake of August 17, 1999: Reconnaissance Report." Multidisciplinary Center for Earthquake Engineering Research: University of Buffalo, State University of New York.
Schäfers, Marlene. 2016. "Ruined Futures: Managing Instability in Post-Earthquake Van (Turkey)." *Social Anthropology* 24 (2): 228–42.
———. 2020. "Afterlives: An Introduction." *Allegra Lab* (blog). https://allegralaboratory.net/afterlives-introduction/.
Schlar, Caroline. 2001. "Creators of Their Future: A Psychosocial Programme for the Earthquake Area in Turkey." In *Psychological Support: Best Practices from Red Cross and Red Crescent Programmes*. Geneva: IFRC.
Schuller, Mark. 2012. *Killing with Kindness: Haiti, International Aid, and NGOs*. New Brunswick, NJ: Rutgers University Press.

Scott, David. 2014. *Omens of Adversity: Tragedy, Time, Memory, Justice.* Durham, NC: Duke University Press.

Seale-Feldman, Aidan. 2020. ""The Work of Disaster: Building Back Otherwise in Post-Earthquake Nepal." *Cultural Anthropology* 35 (2): 237–63.

Segal, Lotte Buch. 2016. *No Place for Grief: Martyrs, Prisoners, and Mourning in Contemporary Palestine.* Philadelphia: University of Pennsylvania Press.

Sengezer, Betül, and Ercan Koç. 2005. "A Critical Analysis of Earthquakes and Urban Planning in Turkey." *Disasters* 29 (2): 171–94.

Seth, Suman. 2009. "Putting Knowledge in Its Place: Science, Colonialism, and the Postcolonial." *Postcolonial Studies* 12 (4): 373–88.

Sezer, Hamiyet. 1996. "1894 İstanbul Depremi Hakkında Bir Rapor Üzerinde İnceleme." *Tarih Araştırmaları Dergisi* 18 (29): 174.

Shafak, Elif. 2010. "The Politics of Fiction." *TEDGlobal 2010.* https://www.ted.com/talks/elif_shafak_the_politics_of_fiction.

Sheppard, Eric, and Robert B. McMaster. 2008. "Scale and Geographic Inquiry: Contrasts, Intersections, and Boundaries." In *Scale and Geographic Inquiry: Nature, Society, and Method,* 256–67.

Silverman, Gila S., Aurélien Baroiller, and Susan R. Hemer. 2021. "Culture and Grief: Ethnographic Perspectives on Ritual, Relationships and Remembering." *Death Studies* 45 (1): 1–8.

Simpson, Audra. 2014. *Mohawk Interruptus: Political Life Across the Borders of Settler States.* Durham, NC: Duke University Press.

Simpson, Edward. 2014. *The Political Biography of an Earthquake: Aftermath and Amnesia in Gujarat, India.* New York: Oxford University Press.

Singh, Bhrigupati. 2017. "An Uncritical Encounter Between Anthropology and Psychiatry." *Medicine Anthropology Theory* 4 (3): 153–165.

Sirman, Nükhet. 2005. "The Making of Familial Citizenship in Turkey." In *Challenges to Citizenship in a Globalizing World: European Questions and Turkish Experiences,* edited by F. Keyman and A. İçduygu, 147–72. London: Routledge.

Smith, Neil. 1992. "Geography, Difference and the Politics of Scale." In *Postmodernism and the Social Sciences,* edited by J. Doherty, E. Graham, and M. Mallek, 57–79. London: Macmillan.

Snediker, Michael D. 2009. *Queer Optimism: Lyric Personhood and Other Felicitous Persuasions.* Minneapolis: University of Minnesota Press.

Solnit, Rebecca. 2009. *A Paradise Built in Hell: The Extraordinary Communities That Arise in Disaster.* New York: Penguin Books.

Soyubol, Kutluğhan. 2022. "Finding *Ruh* in the Forebrain: Mazhar Osman and the Emerging Turkish Psychiatric Discourse." *Medical History* 66 (3): 225–41.

Steinberg, Ted. 2006. *Acts of God: The Unnatural History of Natural Disaster in America.* Oxford: Oxford University Press.

Stevenson, Lisa. 2014. *Life Beside Itself: Imagining Care in the Canadian Arctic.* Berkeley: University of California Press.

Stewart, Kathleen. 2007. *Ordinary Affects.* Durham, NC: Duke University Press.

———. 2010. "Atmospheric Attunements." *Rubric* 29 (3): 445–53.

Stoddard, Frederick, Anand Pandya, and Craig Katz, eds. 2011. *Disaster Psychiatry: Readiness, Evaluation, and Treatment.* Washington, DC: American Psychiatric Publishing.

Stoler, Ann Laura. 2013. *Imperial Debris: On Ruins and Ruination.* Durham, NC: Duke University Press.

Strathern, Marilyn. 2004. *Partial Connections.* Walnut Creek, CA: AltaMira Press.

Summerfield, Derek. 1999. "A Critique of Seven Assumptions Behind Psychological Trauma Programmes in War-Affected Areas." *Social Science and Medicine* 48 (10): 1449–1462.

Swyngedouw, Erik. 1997. "Neither Global nor Local: 'Globalization' and the Politics of Scale." In *Spaces of Globalization,* edited by Keven Cox, 137–66. New York: Guilford Press.

Şalcıoğlu, E., M. Başoğlu, and M. Livanou. 2003. "Long-Term Psychological Outcome for Non-Treatment-Seeking Earthquake Survivors in Turkey." *Journal of Nervous and Mental Disease* 191: 154–60.

Şalcıoğlu, E., M. Başoğlu, and M. Livanou. 2007. "Post-Traumatic Stress Disorder and Comorbid Depression Among Survivors of the 1999 Earthquake in Turkey." *Disasters* 31 (2): 115–29.

Şener, Ş., D. Özdemir, S. Şenol, E. Karacan, and S. Kargın. 1997. "Dinar Depreminden Sonra Ankara'da Yatılı Okula Yerleştirilen Ergenlerde Travmanın Psikolojik Etkileri: Bir Ön Çalışma." *Çocuk ve Gençlik Ruh Sağlığı Dergisi* 4 (3): 135–44.

Taskin, E., F. Sen, O. Aydemir, M. Demet, E. Ozmen, and I. Icelli. 2003. "Public Attitudes to Schizophrenia in Rural Turkey." *Social Psychiatry and Psychiatric Epidemiology* 38: 586–92.

Taussig, Michael. 1980. "Reification and the Consciousness of the Patient." *Social Science & Medicine* 14B (1): 3–13.

———. 1992. *The Nervous System.* New York: Routledge.

Taylor, Dorceta. 2014. *Toxic Communities: Environmental Racism, Industrial Pollution, and Residential Mobility.* New York: New York University Press.

Tedeschi, Richard G., and Lawrence G. Calhoun. 2004. "Posttraumatic Growth: Conceptual Foundations and Empirical Evidence." *Psychological Inquiry* 15 (1): 1–18.

Ticktin, Miriam. 2011. *Casualties of Care: Immigration and the Politics of Humanitarianism in France.* Berkeley: University of California Press.

———. 2014. "Transnational Humanitarianism." *Annual Review of Anthropology* 43 (1): 273–89.

Tironi Rodó, Manuel, Israel Rodriguez-Giralt, and Michael Guggenheim, eds. 2014. *Disasters and Politics: Materials, Experiments, Preparedness.* Malden, MA: Wiley-Blackwell.

Tsing, Anna Lowenhaupt. 2012. "On Nonscalability: The Living World Is Not Amenable to Precision-Nested Scales." *Common Knowledge* 18 (3): 505–24.

———. 2015. *The Mushroom at the End of the World: On the Possibility of Life in Capitalist Ruins.* Princeton, NJ: Princeton University Press.

Tural, Ü., T. Aker, and E. Önder. 2004. "Posttraumatic Stress Disorder and Comorbid Depression after Marmara Earthquake: An Epidemiological Study." Paper presented at the Annual Meeting of Disaster Psychiatry Outreach, Miami.

Tural, Ü., H. Aybar Tolun, I. Karakaya, A. Erol, M. Yıldız, and S. Erdoğan. 2001. "Marmara Depremzedelerinde Travma Sonrası Stres Bozukluğuna Eşlik Eden Başka Bir Ruhsal Hastalık Gelişiminin Yordayıcıları." *Türk Psikiyatri Dergisi* 12 (3): 175–83.

Tural, Ü., B. Coşkun, E. Önder, A. Çorapçioğlu, M. Yıldız, C. Kesepara, I. Karakaya, et al. 2004. "Psychological Consequences of the 1999 Earthquake in Turkey." *Journal of Traumatic Stress* 17: 451–59.

Turan, N., and I. Sayıl. 1996. "Dinar Depreminde Can-Mal Kaybına Uğrayanlar Üzerinde Kıyaslamalı Bir Psikososyal Çalışma." *Kriz Dergisi* 4 (1).

Turkish Red Crescent Society. 2006. *1999-Marmara Earthquake Case Study*. Ankara: Turkish Red Crescent Society.

Uğuz, Ş., B. Levent, and L. Soylu. 2000. "Psikiyatrik Yardım Açısından Ceyhan Adana Depreminin Genel Bir Değerlendirilmesi." *Psikiyatri Psikoloji Psikofarmakoloji (3P) Dergisi* 8 (1): 91–92.

Uğuz, Ş., B. Levent, L. Soylu, O. Kocabas, and S. Demirci. 2000. "98 Adana-Ceyhan Depreminden Sonra Ortaya Çıkan Akut Stres Bozukluğunun Araştırılması." *Klinik Psikiyatri Dergisi* 3 (3): 16–20.

Ursano, Robert, Carol Fullerton, Lars Weisaeth, and Beverly Raphael, eds. 2017. *Textbook of Disaster Psychiatry*. Cambridge: Cambridge University Press.

Ürekli, Fatma. 1995. *İstanbul'da 1894 Depremi*. Istanbul: İletişim Yayınları.

Vehid, H., B. Alyanak, and A. Ekşi. 2006. "Suicide Ideation after the 1999 Earthquake in Marmara, Turkey." *The Tohoku Journal of Experimental Medicine* 208 (1): 19–24.

Wallace, John. 1999. "Building Performance in the 17 August 1999 Izmit (Kocaeli), Turkey Earthquake." In *CUREe Open Symposium*, Tokyo.

Walton, Jeremy F. 2017. *Muslim Civil Society and the Politics of Religious Freedom in Turkey*. New York: Oxford University Press.

Wang, Chong-Wen, Cecilia L. W. Chan, and Rainbow T. H. Ho. 2013. "Prevalence and Trajectory of Psychopathology Among Child and Adolescent Survivors of Disasters: A Systematic Review of Epidemiological Studies Across 1987–2011." *Social Psychiatry and Psychiatric Epidemiology* 48 (11): 1697–1720.

Washington, Harriet. 2020. *A Terrible Thing to Waste: Environmental Racism and Its Assault on the American Mind*. New York: Little, Brown.

Watenpaugh, Keith David. 2015. *Bread from Stones: The Middle East and the Making of Modern Humanitarianism*. Berkeley: University of California Press.

Watson, Matthew C. 2020. *Afterlives of Affect: Science, Religion, and an Edgewalker's Spirit*. Durham, NC: Duke University Press.

Watters, Ethan. 2010. *Crazy Like Us: The Globalization of the American Psyche*. New York: Free Press.

Weiss, Meira. 2002. *The Chosen Body: The Politics of the Body in Israeli Society*. Stanford, CA: Stanford University Press.

Weizman, Eyal. 2012. *Hollow Land: Israel's Architecture of Occupation*. New York: Verso.
Wendland, Claire L. 2010. *A Heart for the Work: Journeys Through an African Medical School*. Chicago: University of Chicago Press.
Willen, Sarah. 2007. "Toward a Critical Phenomenology of 'Illegality': State Power, Criminalization, and Abjectivity Among Undocumented Migrant Workers in Tel Aviv, Israel." *International Migration* 45 (3): 8–38.
Wisner, Ben, Piers Blaikie, Terry Cannon, and Ian Davis. 2003. *At Risk: Natural Hazards, People's Vulnerability and Disasters*. 2nd ed. New York: Routledge.
Wolfenstein, M. 1957. *Disaster: A Psychological Essay*. Glencoe: Free Press.
Wolmer, L., N. Laor, C. Dedeoğlu, J. Siev, and Y. Yazgan. 2005. "Teacher-Mediated Intervention After Disaster: A Controlled Three-Year Follow-Up of Children's Functioning." *Journal of Child Psychology and Psychiatry* 46 (11): 1161–68.
Wolmer, L., N. Laor, and Y. Yazgan. 2003. "School Reactivation Programs after Disaster: Could Teachers Serve as Clinical Mediators?" *Child and Adolescent Psychiatric Clinics of North America* 12: 363–81.
Yanıkdağ, Yücel. 2013. *Healing the Nation: Prisoners of War, Medicine and Nationalism in Turkey, 1914–1939*. Cambridge: Cambridge University Press.
Yargıç, İ., P. Geyran, N. Kocabaşoğlu, and A. Çorapçıoğlu. 2004. "Bin Dokuz Yüz Doksan Dokuz Marmara Depremi Sonrası Posttravmatik Stres Belirtilerinin Şeddetini Belirleyen Risk Faktörleri: Kesitsel Saha Çalışması." *Yeni Symposium* 42 (1): 3–8.
Yazgan, I., C. Dedeoglu, and Y. Yazgan. 2006. "Disability and Post-Traumatic Psychopathology in Turkish Elderly After a Major Earthquake." *International Psychogeriatrics* 18 (1): 184–87.
Yesilyaprak, B., I. Kisac, and N. Sanlier. 2007. "Stress Symptoms and Nutritional Status Among Survivors of the Marmara Region Earthquakes in Turkey." *Journal of Loss and Trauma* 12 (1): 3–10.
Yıldırım, Umut. 2021. "Spaced-Out States: Decolonizing Trauma in a War-Torn Middle Eastern City." *Current Anthropology* 62 (6): 717–40.
Yıldız, Kadir. 2019. "Yıkıntılarının Arasından Yeniden Doğan Kent: Gölcük." *Anadolu Ajansi*, 16 August 2019.
Yorbık, Ö., S. Dikkatli, A. Cansever, and T. Söhmen. 2001. "Çocuklarda ve Ergenlerde Travma Sonrası Stres Bozukluğu Belirtilerinin Tedavisinde Fluoksetinin Etkinliği." *Klinik Psikofarmakoloji Bülteni* 11 (4): 251–56.
Yorbık, Ö., D. Akbıyık, P. Kırmızıgül, and T. Söhmen. 2004. "Post-Traumatic Stress Disorder Symptoms in Children After the 1999 Marmara Earthquake in Turkey." *International Journal of Mental Health* 33 (1): 46–58.
Yorbık, Ö., T. Türkbay, M. Erkmen, S. Demirkan, and T. Söhmen. 1999. "Çocuk ve Ergenlerde Depremle İlişkili Travma Sonrası Stres Bozukluğu Belirtilerinin Araştırılması." *Çocuk ve Gençlik Ruh Sağlığı Dergisi* 6 (3): 158–64.
Young, Allan. 1995. *The Harmony of Illusions: Inventing Post-Traumatic Stress Disorder*. Princeton, NJ: Princeton University Press.

Yüksel, Şahika, Ufuk Sezgin, Peykan Gökalp, and Mustafa Sercan. 2005. *Bir Depremden Sonra . . . Bir Depremden Önce . . . ADEPSTEP*. Istanbul: IPS İletişim Vakfı.

Zengin, Aslı. 2019. "The Afterlife of Gender: Sovereignty, Intimacy, and Muslim Funerals of Transgender People in Turkey." *Cultural Anthropology* 34 (1): 78–102.

Zhang, Li. 2020. *Anxious China: Inner Revolution and Politics of Psychotherapy*. Berkeley: University of California Press.

Zureik, Elia, David Lyon, and Yasmeen Abu-Laban, eds. 2010. *Surveillance and Control in Israel/Palestine: Population, Territory and Power*. London: Routledge.

Index

AFAD (Afet ve Acil Durum Yönetimi Başkanlığı), 3, 250, 251
AKP (Justice and Development Party), 21, 147, 202, 222, 248, 249, 250, 251
affect, 17, 31, 163–64, 275n6, 275n8; and gender, 150, 199; and history, 164, 189, 275n8; as legacy of disaster, 163–64, 168, 182–83; as remains, 154, 242; as site of return, 37, 51; and the state, 64, 126, 131, 236
al-Ghazâlî, Abû Hâmid, 189, 193–200, 201, 204–05, 277n10; and anthropology, 277n12
alienation, 150, 152, 176–77, 178, 182–83, 185
anger, 163–64, 167–69, 180–82, 233, 235–36, 242
Antakya, 247
assemblage, networked, 99, 103, 129

Berlant, Lauren, 14–15, 17, 278
biopolitics, 68, 78, 131, 273
Blanchot, Maurice, 29, 278n24
burial, 46

care, 24, 72, 114, 199, 222, 264n37, 278n23
children of the earthquake, 151–52
civil society, 19–20, 67–68, 190, 240
clinical ethnography, 11
community, 86–88, 92, 117–18, 119, 121, 127, 131, 136
community based mental health care, 23, 27, 73, 86, 126, 132, 136–37, 272n5
complex trauma, 156, 186, 276n26
crisis, 14, 29, 54
Csordas, Thomas, 276n21
Cvetkovich, Ann, 71, 168, 275n7, n15

Das, Veena, 161, 184, 263n24, 263n32, 278n20
death, 45–46, 151, 155–56, 157; anthropology of, 197, 279n19
decolonizing: disaster, 16, 263n30; epistemologies, 194; trauma, 184
Değirmendere, 47
Deleuze, Gilles, 102, 277n15
Demirel, Süleyman, 66
dep-der (*depremzedeler derneği*), 240

309

Derrida, Jacques, 120
disability, 31, 222, 225, 279n6
disaster: psychiatrization of, 4, 24, 94, 225, 242; and representation, 29, 35; and smell, 45, 47, 49, 155, 247; and sound, 39–41; and subjectivity, 79, 89, 93, 109, 134; writing the, 29, 68
disaster psychiatry, 10, 79, 82, 106–07
disaster relief, 65–67, 130, 170, 181, 202, 228, 275n16, 279n1
disaster studies, 16–17, 30, 170, 183, 263n31; and anthropology, 29
disaster management, 61–64, 248, 250; and modernity, 61–62
DSM-IV (Diagnostic and Statistical Manual of Mental Disorders-IV), 102, 104, 105, 268n14

earthquake victim (*depremzede*), 3, 42, 143, 240, 265n6
Ecevit, Bülent, 47
economic crisis, 20–21, 170–71, 202, 229,
engelli, 220, 223
Erdoğan, Recep Tayyip, 21, 248, 280n7
Estes, Nick, 12
ethnography, 24; and listening, 24, 26, 144, 264n54
everyday, 6, 15–17, 52, 119–20, 165, 168, 171, 182–83, 191–92, 196, 221, 263n27, 263n32, 277n17; psychologization of, 224; as site of struggle, 191, 200

family, 160, 178, 181–82, 222, 224; as affective container and economic relay, 181, 276n22
Fassin, Didier, 74, 93
fatalism, 90, 199
forgetting, 142–43
Fortun, Kim, 96, 261n3, 273n27
Freud, Sigmund, 196
future (of disaster), 6, 144, 152, 154, 158, 193, 195–200, 203–04, 277n3; livable futures, 14, 18, 188, 194

gender, 150, 157, 165, 174, 193, 197, 199, 202, 207–27; 279n1; and grief, 203, 205
Gezi, 136, 246
global psychiatry, 82, 106–07, 122, 130, 252
Good, Byron, 276n26
Gölcük, 41, 46, 47, 51, 66, 103, 144, 148, 176, 209, 210, 211, 214
grief, 13, 143, 155–56, 278n19, 278n24; gender and, 193, 203, 205; pathological, 97, 186–88, 191–93, 200, 208

hope, 19, 189, 194, 196, 198, 204, 219
human rights, 121, 137, 240, 243–44
Human Rights Foundation of Turkey (TIHV), 186
humanitarianism, 8–10, 67, 93, 121, 137, 240, 251, 266n9; and anthropology, 77, 267n3; and children, 111; humanitarian psychiatry, 74, 77–79, 89, 94–95, 102, 108, 115, 122, 123, 128, 132, 161, 252, 276n24; and race, 58, 75
Human Rights Association (İnsan Halkları Derneği), 244

improvisation, 7–8, 30, 71, 74, 99, 123
irritability, 163–65, 168, 169, 171, 177, 184–85, 275n8; and justice, 163, 275n5
Israel: psychiatry and occupation, 126–27, 273n16, 273n21; trauma and national identity, 125–26; trauma research and treatment in, 125, 126, 132
İzmit (Kocaeli), 26, 47, 55–56, 104, 145, 228–29, 231, 233, 239, 280n4

justice, 163, 185, 201, 241, 242,

Kiarostami, Abbas, 263n22
Kleinman, Arthur, 265n5, 270n10

Latour, Bruno, 261n3, 262n19
Law, John, 99
Leibniz, Gottfried, 176n1, 277n13, 277n15
life coaching, 215, 224, 226
living on, 5, 12–18, 149–50, 168, 188, 191, 196, 196–198, 200, 203–06, 209, 221, 225, 227, 264n37
loss, 13–14, 31, 152, 156, 158, 188–89, 193, 197, 200, 277n3; generational, 260

mahalle (neighborhood), 174–75, 176, 177
masculinity, 165, 181, 215, 222, 225
memorialization, 4, 42, 141–42
methods, 23–28, 156, 172–73; as patchwork, 28
minor feelings, 31, 162–63, 177, 184–85, 274n1
mourning and melancholia, 196
mutual aid, 18–19, 20, 67, 248, 254; and neoliberal reform, 20, 136, 222

Navaro, Yael, 164, 266n16
nechronology, 45–46
necropolitics, 126, 131
neoliberal reform, 19–20, 21, 60, 134, 136, 170, 202
neighborliness (komşuluk), 174–75, 176, 177, 245
nervous system, 165, 168, 171, 182, 275n13
Ngai, Sianne, 163, 184–85, 274n1
nongovernmental organization (NGO), 19–20, 49, 67–68, 251–52, 253
novice humanitarians, 7, 72, 74, 99, 134, 136

obstinacy of life, 14, 189, 198, 199, 219, 263n22
optimism, 189, 193–96, 197–200, 201, 203, 204–05, 276n1, 278n18; futural optimism, 196, 203, 204; of the present, 196, 198, 200

Orientalism, 90, 199
Ottoman Empire: and disaster management, 59, 62–64; and psychiatry 9, 107, 129

psychopharmaceuticals, 107, 114, 119, 123, 155, 157, 160, 178, 236
phenomenology: critical phenomenology, 262–63n19; and experiential approaches to disaster, 30, 36, 51–52, 173, 183–84
post-traumatic growth (PTG), 208, 215–16, 279n3
Povinelli, Elizabeth, 14–15, 263n24
precarity, 158, 171, 182, 245, 279–80n1
prolonged grief disorder, 186, 188, 193
psychiatry: and anthropology, 173; and biopolitics, 131, 273n18; defined, 10–11; and epidemiology, 98, 101–02, 103, 113, 114, 125, 156, 186; and globalization, 77, 116, 130, 262n11; history of in Turkey, 9, 73, 129, 130, 267n8; and liberalism, 82; as machine, 103–105, 111, 112, 114, 252; and subjectivity, 160; as vernacular, 161, 178, 274n9
Psychiatric Association of Turkey (TPD), 74, 135, 186
psychiatric institutions, 74, 120
psychiatric knowledge production, 10, 99–100, 105, 106; and professional capital, 100, 105, 113, 134
psychiatric world making, 8, 99, 114, 173
psychosocial intervention, 88, 91, 94, 115–16, 120, 128, 135–36, 252–254, 272n2, 272n4
public intimacy, 224
post-traumatic stress disorder (PTSD), 6, 9, 83, 92, 101–04, 107–12, 125–26, 130, 131, 161, 196, 246, 273n16, 273n25, 273–74n32, 275n12; and humanitarian intervention, 9, 16–17, 108–09, 128

quasi-aftermaths, 166
quasi-events, 15, 182, 189, 263n24

renters, 170, 179, 228–29
resilience, 132, 215, 216, 223, 224, 279n4
Rose, Nikolas, 10–11, 273n18
ruins, 1, 5, 11–12, 19–20, 23, 26, 55, 106, 144, 150, 172, 213, 223, 248, 263n22

Sakarya, 26
scaling and scalability, 78–79, 88–89; and global health, 78; of psychiatric expertise, 5, 89–94, 109, 128, 136;
science and technology studies (STS), 6, 8, 78, 261n10, 262n11, 262n19; disasters and, 96, 261n3
slow death, 14
slow disaster, 15, 182, 202
sociotechnical infrastructures, 8, 99
sovereignty, 6, 22, 116, 123, 123, 129, 131, 135
state: as authoritarian, 18, 21, 250; as fantasy, 266n16; as paternalistic, 4, 18, 20, 48, 61, 202, 222; as protector, 20, 48, 61, 64, 67
stigma, 74, 87, 137, 181
Stewart, Kathleen, 182

subjectivity, 82, 188–89, 209, 262n19, 263n20, 275n8; psychological subjectivity, 79, 82, 85, 89–92, 93, 128, 216; and psychological vulnerability, 27, 68, 126
Syrian refugees, 159, 246–47, 249, 253

temporality: 15, 16, 45; of disaster, 14, 17, 29 193, 202, 254; of living on, 188–89; and subjectivity, 188, 193, 197
therapeutic culture, 116, 224
thriving, 207–209, 215–16, 227, 279n3; and affect theory, 279n4
torture, 108, 186
trauma: decolonizing trauma, 184; history of trauma studies in Turkey, 96, 108; otherwise than, 17, 182–85, 208; traumatic memory, 17, 85, 110, 163, 165, 183–84; and unspeakability, 29, 164, 199
Tüpraş oil refinery, 1, 39, 56, 57
Turkish Psychological Association, 97, 135

Voltaire, 276n1, 277n13

Yalova, 47, 57, 152

www.ingramcontent.com/pod-product-compliance
Lightning Source LLC
Jackson TN
JSHW082113040225
78413JS00002B/2